THE MECHANICS OF SPRINTING

AND HURDLING

Ralph V. Mann, Ph.D.
Amber Murphy, M.S.
2015 Edition

THE MECHANICS OF SPRINTING AND HURDLING

Ralph V. Mann
Amber Murphy

Dedicated To
Gerald McDonald, Jim Hay, Harmon Brown, and Bert Lyle

This work would not have been possible without the help of the "old guard" group of coaches who have been around since the early days. We have learned more from this group than from all of our number crunching analysis efforts. This group includes Clyde Hart, Curtis Frye, Loren Seagrave, John Smith, Gary Winkler, George Williams, Remi Korchemny, Tony Veney, and Bobby Kersee. We would also like to thank the "new guard" group of coaches who have continued the tradition of imparting their experience to our efforts to understand how our athletes perform their amazing feats. This group includes Darryl Woodson, Dennis Mitchell, Lance Brauman, Rana Reider, Darrell Smith, Amy Deem, and Andreas Behm.

Copyright © 2015
Dr. Ralph V. Mann

This work may <u>not</u> be reproduced or transmitted in whole or in part by any means, without written permission. For information, contact Ralph V. Mann, 10620 Southern Highlands Pkwy, Suite 110-189, Las Vegas, NV 89141

Table of Contents

PART ONE: GENERAL CONCEPTS... 1

1   Identifying the Limiting Factors in Sprinting and Hurdling 2
2   Maximizing the Limiting Factors in Sprinting and Hurdling 18
3   Balanced Training: Intelligent Compromising 21
4   Getting the Most from the Performer Potential... 23

PART TWO: UNDERSTANDING THE SPRINT PERFORMANCE....................... 35

5   Understanding the Sprint Performance... 36

PART THREE: START MECHANICS.. 73

    Introduction: The Start Golden Position... 74
6   Critical General Performance Descriptors for the Start................................ 76
7   Critical Specific Performance Descriptors for the Start................................ 99

PART FOUR: MAXIMUM VELOCITY MECHANICS... 117

    Introduction: The Sprint Golden Position.. 118
8   Critical General Performance Descriptors for the Short Sprints................. 120
9   Critical Specific Performance Descriptors for the Short Sprints................. 128
10   Critical General Performance Descriptors for the Long Sprints................. 149
11   Critical Specific Performance Descriptors for the Long Sprints................. 158

PART FIVE: FRONT SIDE AND BACK SIDE SPRINT MECHANICS................. 167

12   Front Side and Back Side Sprint Mechanics... 168

PART SIX: UNDERSTANDING THE HURDLE PERFORMANCE....................... 176

13   Understanding the Hurdle Performance.. 177

PART SEVEN: HURDLE MECHANICS.. 192

    Introduction: The Hurdle Golden Position... 193
14   Critical General Performance Descriptors for the Short Hurdles............... 195
15   Critical Specific Performance Descriptors for the Short Hurdles............... 213
16   Critical General Performance Descriptors for the Long Hurdles............... 258
17   Critical Specific Performance Descriptors for the Long Hurdles............... 271

PART EIGHT: FRONT SIDE AND BACK SIDE HURDLE MECHANICS............. 288

| 18 | Front Side and Back Side Hurdle Mechanics | 289 |

APPENDIX A: INDIVIDUAL SPRINT ANALYSIS 291
APPENDIX B: INDIVIDUAL HURDLE ANALYSIS 293

PART ONE: GENERAL CONCEPTS

CHAPTER 1

IDENTIFYING THE LIMITING FACTORS IN SPRINTING AND HURDLING

The purpose of a successful Sprint performance is to cover a required distance in as short a time as possible. The purpose of the Hurdle performance is the same, with the added goal of successfully negotiating the required number of barriers. Toward this end, however, there are a number of Limiting Factors that must be taken into consideration. Among these factors include limitations on the biological makeup of the performer, factors induced by the environment, rules that govern the event, and the equipment restrictions that are imposed upon the performance. The degree to which these factors limit an athlete's performance are due to both unalterable physical limitations acquired genetically, as well as those areas that can be altered such as conditioning and environmental management. The simple fact is that the most successful Sprint or Hurdle performance will be produced by the athlete that successfully maximizes the potential of all of these Limiting Factors.

Performer Related Limiting Factors

By a wide margin, the most critical Limiting Factor in both Sprinting and hurdling, as well as any athletic performance, resides in the physical attributes of an athlete. With the exception of a single factor, these characteristics are inherited genetic traits that a successful athlete, through fortune, inherits from his or her ancestors. These Performer Related Limiting Factors include:

1. **Anthropometric Potential**
2. **Strength Potential**
3. **Endurance Potential**
4. **Flexibility Potential**
5. **Mental Potential**
6. **Mechanics Potential**
7. **Conditioning Potential**
8. **Development Level**

With the exception of the Development Level factor, all of these characteristics are given to an athlete through luck of the genetic pool, and represent the potential in each of these areas for the athlete. Few, if any, performers ever maximize the potential in each of these areas, however, the greatest athletes have been blessed with both high potential in each of the critical areas as well as the determination to tap the enormous potential that was bestowed upon them.

Anthropometric Potential

The **Anthropometric Potential** or "body build" that an athlete inherits has long been recognized as a critical determinate in deciding an athlete's level of potential success in sports performance. Obviously, a body height of over 2 meters (seven feet) definitely gives an athlete the

Anthropometric Potential to be a proficient basketball or volleyball player. This body build also, however, eliminates the athlete from performing successfully in such sports as gymnastics, diving, or wrestling. In fact, every sport that is sufficiently advanced will feature, as its most elite performers, those athletes that have similar anthropometric characteristics. As an example, if the Olympic champions in the 100 meters, shot put, and marathon were assembled in one place, there would be little doubt as to which athlete would belong to which event simply by visual observation of their body builds.

This anthropometric factor can not only be directly applied to the Sprint and Hurdle races, but can also further be broken down into the two major events of both races. Currently, for the Short Sprints (100 and 200 meters) and Hurdles (110 meters for Men and 100 meters for Women), the least limiting anthropometric makeup consists of an athlete of slightly greater than average height (6'0" in Men and 5'6" in Women) with excessively long legs and well developed muscular structure. In contrast, in the Long Sprint and Hurdles, the body build with the least limitations tends to be somewhat taller than the Short race Sprinters and Hurdlers (6'3" for Men, and 5'9" for Women), with similar excessive leg length but with a less bulky muscular structure.

The differences between the two types of athletes stem from the differences between the Short and Long races. Since the Short race is greatly dependent upon the Start, as well as the athlete's ability to quickly achieve and maintain Maximum Velocity, a shorter more bulky and powerful human performance model is required. In addition, in the Short Hurdle race, the presence and spacing of the barriers (close together with insufficient room to fit three strides) serves to further demand this type of performer.

In contrast, since the 400 meters adds a further dimension of endurance, certain anthropometric body alterations must be made to account for this demand. In this case it means decreasing the relatively bulky build of a Short Sprinter or Hurdler who can perform with little regard for the fatigue factor, to that of a taller less bulky Long Sprinter or Hurdler who must use a frame that is more conducive to endurance sprinting. In addition, as in the Short Hurdle race, the presence and spacing of the barriers (far apart with the need to stretch to achieve thirteen (Men) or fifteen (Women) strides) serves to further demand this type of performer.

With the advanced development of the Men's Sprints and Hurdles, and the rapid rise in the quality of both Women's events, this trend will become even more distinct in the future.

Strength Potential

The second of the Performer Related Limiting Factors involves the **Strength Potential** of an athlete. Within this potential, there are three major types of strengths that are critical in the successful Sprint/Hurdle performance. An athlete must possess the ability to produce high levels of strength or force in a **static, dynamic,** and **elastic** situation.

Static strength relates to the ability to produce force in those instances when the athlete's segments are stable or moving at a fairly low rate of flexion or extension. As shown in Figure 1-1a, the body is able to produce 100 percent of its maximum force at these low speeds of contraction.

The production of **dynamic strength** involves the ability to produce force when the body limbs are moving at high velocities. As can be seen in Figure 1-1a, as the speed of contraction increases, the body's ability to produce force significantly **decreases**. Thus, the body's ability to recruit muscle force to change the angular Velocity of a segment moving at 350 degrees per second is reduced by 50 percent of the force available when the segment is at rest. Although all athletes must live with this problem, the strength decrement is not the same for all performers. The genetically gifted have the ability to maintain the level of strength to a greater degree as the speed of movement increases.

The relationship between dynamic strength and speed of contraction shown in Figure 1-1a pertains to the classic situation where the muscles involved in the activity contract and produce a shortening in their fibers. This type of contraction is termed **concentric**, and can be seen in actions ranging from the act of standing from a sitting position (quadriceps shortening to extend the lower leg at the knee: gluteals and hamstrings shortening to extend the upper leg at the hip) or performing a bicep curl (biceps shortening to flex the lower arm at the elbow).

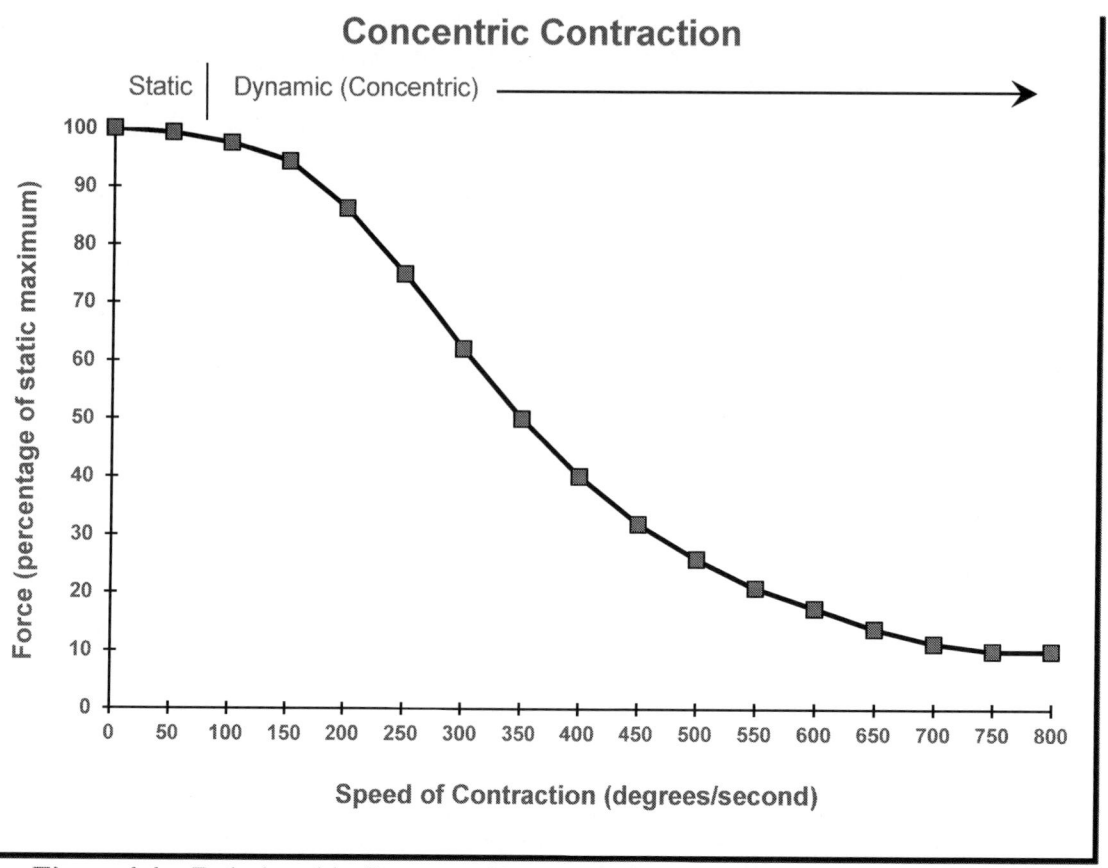

Figure 1-1a: Relationship Between Force and Speed of Concentric Contraction

The production of dynamic strength is further complicated when the concept of **eccentric** contraction is introduced. This type of action occurs when the muscles that are working are actually lengthening. This lengthening may be voluntary or involuntary in nature. If an athlete is handed a curling bar with 225 Kilograms (≈500 Pounds) attached, with the lower arm already fully flexed, it is a safe bet that the bar will force the lower arms to extend regardless of how hard the athlete contracts the biceps muscles. Although this is an extreme example of forced eccentric contraction, the majority of cases of this type of action are controlled in nature. The act of sitting from a standing position (the controlled lengthening of the quadriceps allowing the flexion of the lower leg at the knee: the controlled lengthening of the hamstrings and gluteals allowing the flexion of the upper leg at the hip), as well as the return of the weight to the starting position during a bicep curl (the controlled lengthening of the biceps to allow extension of the lower arms at the elbow) are typical examples.

The complication occurs due to the unique ability of the body to produce higher levels of force during eccentric contractions. As shown in Figure 1-1b, as the speed of eccentric muscular contraction increases, the body's ability to produce force **increases** significantly. As with concentric contraction, the strength increase is not the same for all performers. The genetically gifted have the ability to produce a greater strength increment as the speed of eccentric movement increases.

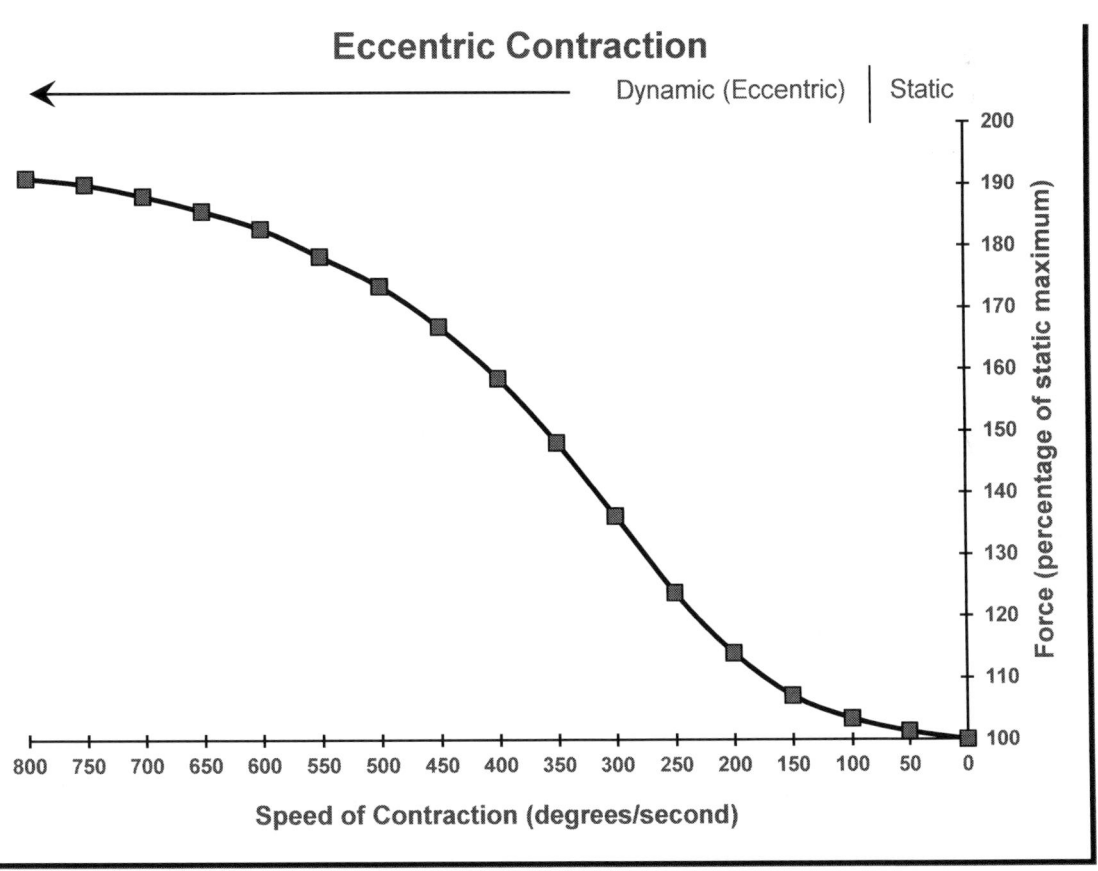

Figure 1-1b: Relationship Between Force and Speed of Eccentric Contraction

Understanding the strength potential differences between concentric and eccentric contraction is critical since any dynamic action can be deemed either difficult or effortless depending upon the type of contraction required to produce the movement. For example, at Touchdown in the sprinting action, the upper leg of an elite athlete is moving at over 600 degrees per second. If the muscles required to produce the required force at this point are contracting concentrically, then this muscle group would be a major Limiting Factor in performance since the muscles would have great difficulty in being productive in this situation (see Figure 1-1a). In contrast, if the muscular action is eccentric in nature, then the body's ability to produce the required forces will be a much easier task (see Figure 1-1b), relegating this action to non-critical.

Concentric and Eccentric strength is typically trained using dynamic overload. For relatively slower movements, training is done in a weight room environment using classic weight exercises. For faster movements, various forms of dynamic (i.e. Olympic) lifts or plyometrics are employed.

Although the ability to produce both static and dynamic force is critical in both sprinting and hurdling, the two are not directly related. It has been shown that an athlete's ability to produce large forces in the static area does not guarantee that the athlete will also have the ability to produce large forces in the dynamic situation.

Finally, every athlete is given a level of ability to use the elastic components of the body (muscles, ligaments, tendons, etc.) to produce a spring-like force in certain situations (**elastic strength**). Much like a spring, when the segments are dynamically loaded during a performance, the springy components are stretched. Depending upon the inbred ability of this system to respond (called the spring constant), the components produce an elastic force. It is not clear whether this force potential can be trained, however, dynamic lifts and plyometrics are currently the training mode of choice.

In summary, for an athlete to maximize the potential of the Limiting Factor imposed by strength limitations, they must be gifted with a large potential in the static, dynamic, and elastic areas.

Endurance Potential

The **Endurance Potential** of a Sprint/Hurdle athlete is related to both physiologically based **strength** endurance and **cardio-pulmonary** endurance, especially in the Long events.

An athlete's ability to produce large forces, both statically and dynamically, over the entire race is critical since, even in the Short races, there is a measurable decrement in performance due to fatigue. As the distance increases to 400 meters, this strength endurance potential becomes a major Limiting Factor. Thus, those performers gifted with great Anthropometric and Strength Potential, but lacking in Endurance Potential, will find success in the Short Sprints or Hurdles but will be unable to compete at the highest levels in the Long events.

Although not a significant factor in the Short Sprint/Hurdle event, the physiological Endurance Potential of an athlete becomes a significant factor in the Long races. As the performer is pushed past the 300 meter distance, the body's ability to maintain the muscular contractions needed to deliver the required forces, perhaps secondary to the increased acidity levels in the muscle that are a product of the extended sprinting or hurdling action, becomes a decisive factor in performance.

Flexibility Potential

Flexibility Potential is yet another genetic gift that affects performance. Although virtually all children demonstrate impressive joint ranges of motion, the true degree of this gift will only be seen after maturity. Thus, anthropometric limitations in the skeletal, muscular, ligament, or tendon structures will come to the forefront as the athlete reaches adulthood.

In addition, a number of outside factors can affect the mature Flexibility level. As the strength of the muscles and tendons are increased, it is inevitable that flexibility will decrease, even in the best designed programs. The biggest non-genetic factor affecting flexibility, however, is neglect. Maintaining flexibility through proper stretching is not an enjoyable task and, therefore, it tends to be one of the most ignored tasks in athletics.

Regardless of an athlete's talents, they can all be rendered useless if the performer cannot physically place their body into the correct mechanical positions. Nothing can limit the ability of an athlete to perform the proper motions more dramatically than a lack of flexibility.

If a sprinter cannot shift their hips forward at Touchdown, or a hurdler cannot properly flex their Lead Leg to their trunk, then they will never be able to achieve their performance potential. This lack of flexibility can result in loss of performance level in two major areas: **Physics** and **Mechanics**.

There is no magic in Physics. There are laws that will always be followed, regardless of the hopes or prayers of either the coach or athlete. Thus, if a 110 Meter hurdler is not flexible enough to easily bring their Lead Leg to their chest when clearing the hurdle, then Physics **dictates** that the athlete will have to go higher over the barrier for proper clearance. This results in more energy expended at both Takeoff (to jump higher) and Touchdown (to stop the fall from a higher height), a longer Air Time, and a disruption of the flow of the Mechanics of hurdle clearance. So, while the better hurdlers are back on the ground and moving to the next hurdle, the less flexible hurdler is wasting both time and energy. Multiply this ten times (for each barrier), and the effect will be significant.

Mechanical advantage is a powerful tool that proficient athletes utilize to their great advantage. Placing the body in the correct position, at the proper time, with the body segments moving in the right direction and speed is the only way to maximize this potential. Thus, if lack of flexibility results in an athlete being physically unable to reach this "correct" position, then the performance will suffer. If a sprinter is not flexible enough in their pelvic area to shift their hips forward at Touchdown, then they are forced to "sit back" at foot strike. This position not only shifts the body center back (insuring more braking forces), but also presents a "soft" (less rigid) body position which leads to time consuming hip flexion, as well requiring the hips to move through a longer range of motion (both time and energy wasteful). Multiply this action anywhere from 45 to 250 times (for each Ground Phase) during a Short or Long Sprint race, and the detrimental effects are evident.

Whether the event is Sprints or Hurdles, Long or Short in length, the number of instances where flexibility becomes a major problem in limiting performance is large. In fact, experience has shown that athletes are, on average, less flexible than the average individual. A major effort needs to be made to ensure that lack of flexibility does not become a Limiting Factor in an athlete's performance.

Mental Potential

The **Mental Potential** of an athlete is probably the most misunderstood, underestimated, and underdeveloped area of all of the limiting performer related factors in sprinting and hurdling. In understanding this statement, some knowledge is required concerning all of the mental challenges and barriers a great athlete must either handle or overcome to achieve an elite level of performance. First and foremost, an athlete must have the mental strength to dedicate large amounts of their time, effort, and energy toward the achievement of a goal that is difficult, if not impossible, to accomplish.

Imagine the mental strength required for an athlete to gamble that their inherited potentials are superior to all their competitors, that they will be able to avoid the potential injuries that are a constant hazard in the Sprint/Hurdle performance, that they can coordinate their conditioning to reach their pinnacle at the proper time, while at the same time avoiding the potential illness or freak accident that would circumvent all of their preparation. All of this so that they may perform at a level that would place them at the top of their profession. Assuming that their goal is to medal in a major championship, the odds of being in the top three in the world at any particular time is not a gamble on which most people would bet a significant portion of their life.

If an athlete indeed has the Mental potential to accept such a challenge, they must then muster their mental forces to withstand the stresses of intensive year-round, daily training sessions that will lead them to their performance goals. Add to this their need to focus their concentration during competition; maintaining their confidence through injury, defeats, and personal setbacks; handling all matter of adversities; as well as handling the successes. There are numerous stories concerning the athlete that met with such continuing success during their rise to elite status that they ignored their difficult areas of Conditioning to the point of eventually losing to a more superiorly conditioned athlete. Similarly common is the example of the brilliant athlete who, after several defeats, eliminated themselves from greatness by relegating themselves to less than elite status within their own mind.

Mechanics Potential

The **Mechanics Potential** of an athlete, or the performer's native ability to place the body segments in certain required positions during the performance, is but another of the Limiting Factors in any event. This ability is related in the greatest degree to the physical makeup of the athlete, including the Anthropometric design as well as the neuro-muscular arrangement, Strength, and Flexibility of the system as a whole.

To a lesser degree, however still significant, are the limitations that the athlete develops either through their formative years or through training practices. Thus, an athlete with extensive ballet training will invariably walk with their toes everted from the center line simply due to the positional and muscular demands of the activity. Likewise, a poorly designed strength program can, in fact, severely restrict both the strength and flexibility of the athlete. Thus, an athlete's ability to mechanically produce the best sprinting or hurdling action is due to both inherited and acquired limitations.

The reason why the Mechanics plays such a critical role in performance is because this is the Factor that determines how the available resources that an athlete possesses are delivered. These resources are made available in the following manner:

1. **Expended Force**: Drawing from all of the Individual Limiting Factors, this is the amount of Force that an athlete can deliver in a given situation. The Mechanics Potential has nothing to do with this, but it can be used to effectively apply it to accomplishing the goals of the event.
2. **Effective Force**: This is the part of the total Expended Force that is directed toward producing a successful performance. Proper Mechanics may not always be able to direct all of the Expended Force into Effective Force, but it always will deliver the greatest amount possible.
3. **Impact Force**: In the Sprints and Hurdles, the greatest level of force the body must contend with occurs at Touchdown. The quality of the Mechanics when this occurs can make the difference between effectively using most of this force, or losing most of the force in an uncontrolled crash.

Conditioning Potential

As every coach knows, athletes differ in their ability to withstand the rigors of training. Some athletes are fragile, while others can train at high levels for long periods of time. When a sport progresses to the point of professionalism, and athletes are spending large amounts of their time developing their talents, a performer's ability to withstand repeated training bouts, or their **Conditioning Potential**, becomes a major factor of success.

As in most athletic potentials, Conditioning ability is genetic. Intelligent training approaches can, however, better exploit this potential. Successful coaches and athletes quickly learn that managing the level of physical stresses during training can lead to better productivity. In addition to this concerted effort to avoid problems in the first place, a constant vigil on an athlete's physical state and aggressive resolution of any potential problem is paramount. Experience indicates that virtually every physical problem that develops could have been avoided or minimized if the warning signs were recognized.

Development Level

As with the Mechanics and Conditioning Potential, the final Performer Related Limiting Factor, **Development Level**, is only partially due to inherited factors. Basically, development can be described as the level at which the Anthropometric, Strength, Endurance, Flexibility, Mental, Mechanics, and Conditioning Potential of the athlete are achieved. Thus, if an athlete has been granted great potential in all areas, their initial development level will be greater than a lesser gifted athlete.

Figure 1-2 shows the **Current Level** and **Remaining Potential** of an athlete that was very gifted in every Limiting Factor. The Current Level is the level of development the athlete now has achieved. The Remaining Potential is the possible improvement that remains in each factor. The total of both determines how close the athlete can come to reaching the maximum known human performance in each factor.

Although the athlete profiled in Figure 1-2 is very gifted, unless a good coach helps in the development of those factors that are currently well short of their potential (Strength, Endurance, Mechanics), the performer will never achieve greatness.

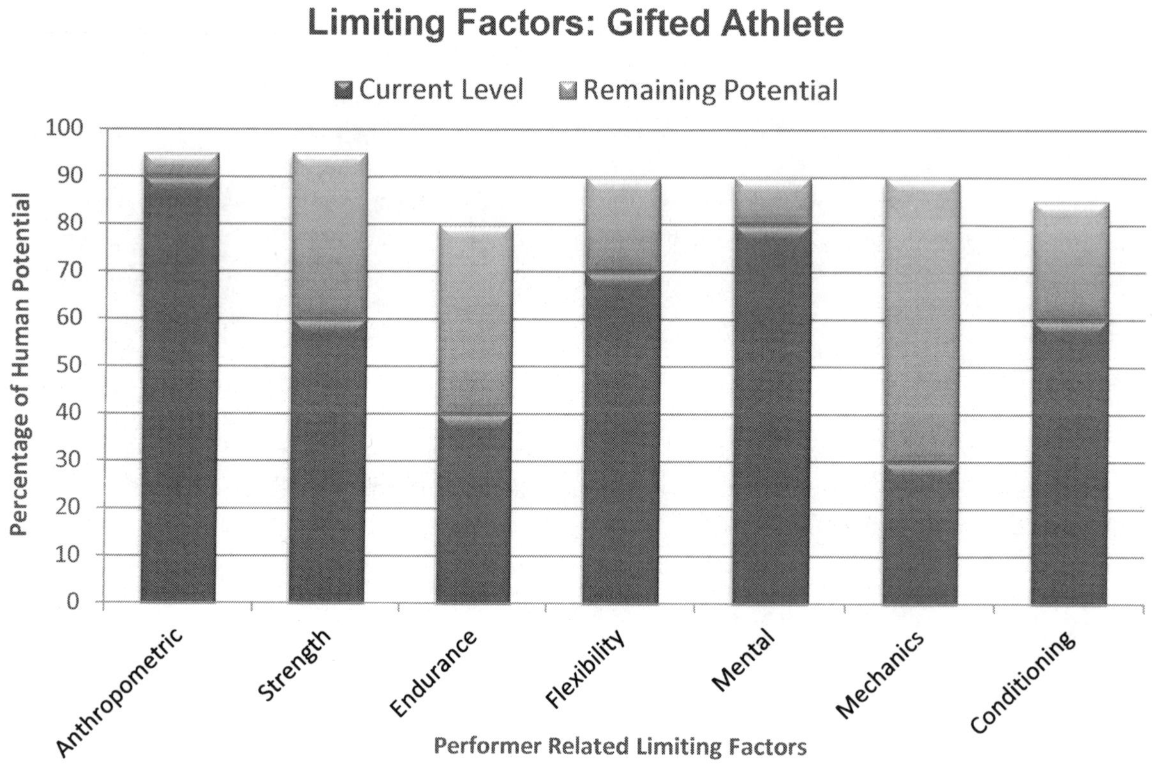

Figure 1-2: Performer Related Limiting Factors of a Gifted Athlete

In contrast, Figure 1-3 shows the Current Level and Remaining Potential of an athlete that was genetically restricted in several Limiting Factors. Since the Current Level is exactly the same as the gifted athlete (Figure 1-2), both of these performers would produce similar results at their present development level. However, since the athlete in Figure 1-3 has limited future development potential in Strength, Endurance, and Mechanics, they will never be able to excel at the elite level regardless of the quality of their coach, their dedication, or their desire.

The frustrating reality to both athletes and coaches is that the total development level for each Limiting Factor (Current Level + Remaining Potential) cannot be determined early in an athlete's career. Only after several years of the athlete in Figure 1-3 attempting to develop their Strength, Endurance, and Mechanics with little progress could the conclusion be made that these areas simply did not have sufficient genetic potential for success.

An often seen problem at the elite level occurs when a superbly gifted athlete is restricted by one Limiting Factor. The level of performance at the elite level of sprints and hurdles means that if an athlete has even one low potential Limiting Factor, they may never reach the pinnacle of their event.

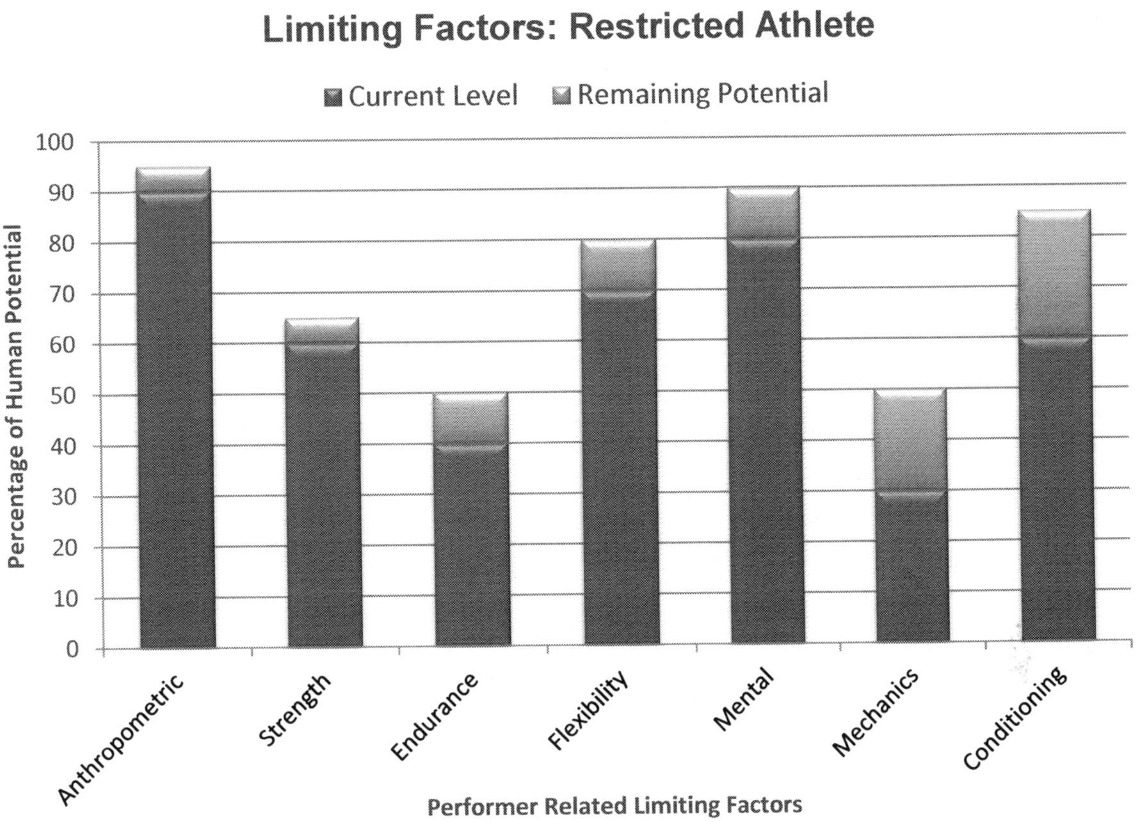

Figure 1-3: Performer Related Limiting Factors of a Restricted Athlete

Assuming that there is sufficient room for improvement, the degree to which improvement is produced is directly related to the effort extended by the athlete to achieve the maximum potential in each of the performer related areas. This factor is commonly termed 'shape', as in 'the athlete is in good shape'. It is evident however, that this term implies more than simply how hard an athlete trains.

The history of the development of every sport points to the ability of a truly gifted athlete to succeed in the sport, during the sport's initial stage, without a major commitment to maximizing the **Development Level**. Due to his personal situation, as well as a lack of training knowledge, Jesse Owens succeeded in spite of the fact that his efforts at development were minimal in both quality and quantity.

As a sport develops, the involved athletes discover that talent alone, however impressive, is no longer sufficient to ensure success. At this point in the development of the sport, the importance of training is discovered.

Finally, as a sport reaches maturity, the athletes discover that there is simply not sufficient time available to properly train all the areas (Strength, Endurance, Flexibility, Mental, Mechanics, Conditioning) required for maximum success. Even if sufficient time can be budgeted, the stresses placed upon the body in an intensive training program will eventually lead to a physical breakdown when taken to extremes. It is at this point that athletes are forced to become **efficient** in their training efforts, in an attempt to gain the most from each of the budgeted efforts. This search for efficiency leads to an interest in scientific research in the areas of Physiology, Biomechanics, Motor Learning, and Psychology. Regardless of the sport, the athletic group that first turns to research has reaped great performance and success benefits. In Track and Field, the Soviets and Germans were the earliest beneficiaries of this foresight.

> In summary, it is evident that the Performer Related Limiting Factors in sprinting and hurdling are overwhelmingly related to those potentials that are genetically bestowed upon an athlete. Thus, the old belief that anyone can be successful in an athletic event if they truly want to succeed, or out-train their opponents, is simply not supported by either research or experience. On the other hand, both the Sprint and Hurdle events have evolved to the point where genetic potential alone is not sufficient to ensure an athlete's success at the elite level.
>
> The increased efforts to turn to scientific research to improve the training process of gifted athletes, and the successes of those nations that have succeeded in this effort, has painfully proven the point to those countries that have ignored the degree to which intelligent training can affect the success of the performance.

Environmental Related Limiting Factors

The second major Limiting Factor with which a Sprint and Hurdle athlete must contend is the **Environment** in which the event takes place. Since all competitions, to date, take place on Earth, the four major environmental factors of gravity, wind resistance, friction, and energy return must be endured. Of these factors, gravity imposes the greatest burden on the athlete.

Gravity: Working in the Vertical (upward and downward) direction, the force of gravity compels the sprinter to expend considerable effort to project the body upwards so that it can remain airborne for sufficient time to move down the track. Likewise, since "whatever goes up must come down", the sprinter must also contend with the gravitational effects created at the end of the Air Phase when the next ground contact occurs.

The hurdler must contend with these same forces during the Sprint strides between the barriers. When negotiating the hurdles, however, all of these forces increase dramatically since the athlete must project the body much higher in order to clear the barriers.

Wind Resistance: Although the Earth's atmosphere is relatively transparent, any athlete will tell you that the wind resistance, or assistance, can play a major role in athletic performance. It should be realized that, as a sprinter or hurdler moves down the track, the athlete must push the air molecules out of the way. At fairly low velocities this resistance is a minor factor, however, at the velocities produced in an elite effort the wind resistance becomes a significant performance factor. This is true due to the fact that wind resistance increases according to the square of the speed in which the air molecules strike the runner. Thus, as an athlete doubles the forward speed, the wind resistance increases four times. This non-linear increase can easily be qualified by asking any athlete to describe the effort required to run **into** a one meter per second wind as opposed to running **with** a one meter per second wind. Although the difference of wind speed striking the body is less than 9 percent of the total Sprint Speed, the athlete will correctly identify the required effort to be much greater.

Friction: Another group of environmental Limiting Factors, again created due to gravitational effects, pertains to ground contact factors that the athlete must endure. The first is the effects of Horizontal (forward and backward) friction between the Earth and that part of the foot that comes in contact with the ground. Although the presence of friction allows the performer to firmly grab the ground and apply the required forces, it also produces forces that hinder the forward progress of the athlete. In contrast, the lack of friction or slipping that occurs between the track, the footwear, and the athlete's foot leads to some loss of productive force as the performer attempts to project the body into the next Air Phase of the Sprint or Hurdle stride.

Energy Return: The second ground contact problem with which the athlete must contend is rebound, or energy return factors. As with any two colliding objects, the runner will have a tendency to rebound from the Earth surface to some degree. Depending on the nature of the objects that collide, this rebound factor can be either beneficial or detrimental. If the track surface is properly "tuned" or springy in nature, and the athlete utilizes the proper footwear and Mechanics, the performer can actually get an assist in performance. Likewise, if the track is poorly tuned (too hard or soft), or the athlete has poor footwear or Mechanics, the effect will be either to deliver a jarring blow during each ground contact (due to hard surface, poor Mechanics, or under-supported footwear) or force the performer to expend greater amounts of energy to complete the ground contact phase (soft surface, poor Mechanics, or over-supported footwear).

In summary, the major environmental related factors that affect the Sprint and Hurdle performance include the effects of gravity, wind resistance, ground contact friction, and rebound forces. Although the limitations imposed by these factors cannot be eliminated, with an understanding of the role of each factor, the resulting effect can either be minimized or even used as a performance enhancer for the athlete.

Rules Related Limiting Factors

The Limiting Factors placed upon the Sprint event by **Rules** are both small in number and straightforward. Those additional **Rules** placed on the Hurdle event have a much greater impact upon the event. For both events, the first and foremost rule is that the performance must be totally human powered. Although some consideration is given to the benefit that four Environmental factors have on the race, this rule is sufficiently straightforward to leave little ambiguity in its application.

The second common Sprint/Hurdle rule requires that the performer begin the race at rest, or zero Velocity in all directions. Although some concessions have been made to assist the athlete in overcoming this situation (as in the acceptance of the use of starting blocks and spikes), this rule has admirably withstood the test of time.

For the Sprints, the distances of the acknowledged Olympic races have been set at 100, 200, and 400 meters. Although this is an unalterable and unexploitable rule, the mandated distances and the physiological makeup of the human body does suffice to divide the races into the two distinct events: the Short Sprints (100 and 200 meters), and the Long Sprints (400 meters).

For the Hurdles, the distances of the acknowledged Olympic Hurdle races have been set at 110/100 and 400 meters, with the hurdle heights higher and the Hurdle distances closer for the Short races. Although this is an unalterable and unexploitable rule, the mandated distances and the physiological makeup of the human body do suffice to divide the Hurdle races into the two distinct events. The Short Hurdles (110/100) are designed to maximize the hurdling effort, while the Long Hurdles (400) are designed to provide a technical challenge at near flat 400 Sprint Velocity.

To better understand the problems that the Hurdle athlete must overcome, a summary of the rule imposed demands of the four races are listed in Table 1-1. Note that the Hurdle height and spacing are unalterable, while the step pattern and step length between are the typical performance results that the elite athlete has adopted to produce the best performance in each event.

	110 M	100 W	400 M	400 W
Hurdle Height	1.07 m (42.0 in)	.84 m (33.0 in)	.91 m (36.0 in)	.76 m (30.0 in)
Hurdle Spacing	9.1 m (30.0 ft)	8.5 m (27.9 ft)	35 m (114.8 ft)	35 m (114.8 ft)
Step Pattern (Preferred)	3 steps	3 steps	13 steps	15 steps
Step Length Between	2.00 m (6.6 ft)	1.93 m (6.3 ft)	2.50 m (8.0 ft)	2.20 m (7.0 ft)

Table 1-1: The Rule Imposed Demands of Hurdling

These demands are going to impede the hurdler according to the size of the typical athlete in the event. The degree that the rules affect the average elite hurdler in each of the events is shown in Table 1-2.

Note that the **Hurdle Height to Performer Leg Length** percentage is presented as an initial indicator of the Vertical effort that the athletes in each event are forced to exert to clear the barriers. It is evident that the Men's 110 Hurdle height exacts the greatest demand, the Women's Short race and the Men's Long race are about the same, while the Women's 400 Hurdles requires the least.

	110 M	100 W	400 M	400 W
Hurdle Height to Leg Length	**122%**	**100%**	**103%**	**91%**
Height Raise to Sprint Rise	**419%**	**292%**	**333%**	**293%**
Required Rise to Sprint Rise	**409%**	**120%**	**232%**	**100%**
Steps Between to Sprint Length	**89%**	**95%**	**109%**	**112%**

Table 1-2: The Relative Demands of Hurdling

The **Height Rise to Sprint Rise** is the percentage increase that the elite hurdlers **actually** elevate the Body COG (Center Of Gravity), in comparison to the elite sprinter, to clear the hurdle. Thus, the male 110 Hurdler raises the body over 400 percent higher than the elite male sprinter, while the female 100 Hurdler raises the body just under 300 percent higher than the elite female sprinter. When this result is compared with the **required** elevation that is needed to clear the barrier (**Required Rise to Sprint Rise**), a good indication of the actual hurdling demands of each event can be estimated. As the Table indicates, the actual result of the Men's 110 Hurdles is closest to the required demands (419% to 409%), with the Men's Long race being the next most difficult (333% to 232%). In contrast, the Women's 400 Hurdles is farthest (293% to 100%) to the required demands with the Women's Short Hurdles not far behind (292% to 120%).

What these hurdle height demand results indicate is that, in the Short Hurdles, the Women's Hurdles are proportionally too low when compared to the Men's event. This conclusion is further supported if the purpose of the Short Hurdle race is to challenge the hurdling abilities of the athlete, since the hurdle effort produced by the Women 100 Hurdlers is much less demanding than the Men. Furthermore, the results also indicate that the height of the Women's Long Hurdles is also too low. This conclusion is supported by the large clearance heights and lack of hurdle form utilized by the Women Long race Hurdlers.

Moving from the demands of Hurdle height to the demands of the hurdle placement, the **Steps Between to Sprint Length** is a comparison of the Stride Length of the steps between the hurdles to the typical Sprint Stride Length at the same Velocity. As can be seen, the Stride Length requirements for the Men's 110 Hurdles are the most restrictive, while the Women's 400 Hurdles are the most expansive. Both the Men's and Women's elite Short race hurdlers must severely shorten the strides between the barriers while both of the Long races demand a much longer Stride Length.

What these between Hurdle Stride Length results indicate is that, in the Short Hurdles, both the Men's and Women's Hurdles are positioned too close together for the elite athlete to take their normal Sprint Stride Length. This conclusion is further supported when it is realized that, as the event improves and athletes run faster, this problem only becomes worse. Thus, a coach must understand that, as their athlete approaches the elite level of Hurdle performance, the limitations imposed due to the current rules of the event must be addressed. The consequences of a number of these limitations will be discussed in the Mechanics section.

In summary, rules are employed in sport to standardize the competition. The critical restraints on both sprinting and hurdling dictate that the athlete must complete the race using only human supplied power, must begin the race from complete rest, and shall cover a standardized distance.

In addition, for the Hurdle events, there are additional rules that dictate the height and distance settings for the barriers. In the Short Hurdles, the rules have become a large, detrimental factor in hindering performance, as well as affecting the Mechanics of the event. In the Long Hurdles, the rules also impose significant, if slightly different problems.

Equipment Related Limiting Factors

The final major Limiting Factor in Sprint/Hurdle performance involves the athlete's use of **Equipment**. Without exception, the selection of equipment is designed to exploit, to the greatest extent possible, those Limiting Factors dictated by the environment or rules of the event. Thus, the selection of clothing can be used to alter the wind resistance factor, the selection of running shoes and spikes (and even the track) can be employed to control the friction and rebound factors, and starting blocks can be used to minimize the detrimental effect of the rule requiring the event to begin from a stationary position.

With the widespread availability of the latest equipment, no elite sprinter should be at a disadvantage in the equipment area.

In summary, the Sprint/Hurdle athlete has been given the potential to utilize equipment to exploit the Limiting Factors of environment and rules.

> **Chapter Summary:**
>
> The first step toward understanding the Sprint/Hurdle performance is recognizing the following Limiting Factors for the event:
>
> 1. **Performer Related Limiting Factors**
> 2. **Environmental Related Limiting Factors**
> 3. **Rules Related Limiting Factors**
> 4. **Equipment Related Limiting Factors**

The next step becomes one of determining which of these factors provides the best avenue toward the development of the athlete.

CHAPTER 2

MAXIMIZING THE LIMITING FACTORS IN SPRINTING AND HURDLING

In reviewing the major Limiting Factors in the Sprint/Hurdle performance, they fall in three categories:

1. **Those that are unalterable**
2. **Those that are slightly alterable**
3. **Those that are definitely alterable**

Unalterable Factors

Those Limiting Factors that fall into the unalterable category include:

1. **Anthropometric Potential**
2. **Strength Potential**
3. **Endurance Potential**
4. **Flexibility Potential**
5. **Mental Potential**
6. **Mechanics Potential**
7. **Conditioning Potential**
8. **Human Powered Criteria**
9. **Start From Rest Criteria**
10. **Specified Distance Criteria**

Note that these unalterable factors are either genetically endowed factors or rules set forth to govern the event. Under the ethical rules of competition, any attempt to alter the performer related potentials through the use of surgical procedures, drugs, or other invasive techniques, or the explicit act of attempting to circumvent the rules of event, would be considered cheating. These options, therefore, will not be discussed.

In summary, the potential for performance inherited by an athlete at birth cannot be legally enhanced. Since this genetic factor is the greatest contributor to success, it lends considerable credence to the conclusion that great athletes are born, and then made.

Likewise, the rules of performance in the Sprints and Hurdles are, by intent, morally unalterable.

Slightly Alterable Factors

Included in the list of slightly altered Limiting Factors are:

1. **Gravity**
2. **Wind Resistance**
3. **Ground Contact Factors**
4. **Equipment**

Of these factors, both gravity and wind resistance are dictated by the site of competition and the type of weather encountered during the day of competition. Thus, a high altitude competition with an aiding wind will assist a Sprint/Hurdle performance while a low altitude and detrimental wind situation will be detrimental to performance. In fact, several long standing world Sprint and Hurdle records were set by athletes who were fortunate enough to encounter beneficial gravity and wind resistance situations.

In the case of the other slightly alterable factors, the detrimental effects of interaction with the ground can be controlled using superior Sprinting or Hurdling Mechanics. In addition, the beneficial potential of ground contact can be enhanced by the use of equipment that elicits the greatest amount of rebound effect from the interacting surfaces.

> In summary, although the factors of gravity, wind resistance, friction, rebound, and equipment design can make a difference in the performance of the Sprint/Hurdle event, overall their contribution is relatively minor in nature. However, since the difference between winning and losing has been reduced to such a small margin, this area should not be overlooked.

Highly Alterable Factors

Included in the list of highly altered Limiting Factors are:

1. **Development Level (Training)**

As previously indicated, the Development Level can be defined as the level of development of the Performer Related Limiting Factors. Of the seven factors, only the Anthropometric and Conditioning areas are considered untrainable. Thus, beginning from a basic, unalterable maximum potential, the training effort is a process of reaching the Strength, Endurance, Flexibility, Mental, and Mechanics potentials of the athlete. Of these factors, the Strength, Endurance, Flexibility, and Mental factors can be developed independently. Thus, static strength can be developed in the weight room with traditional lifts, and dynamic and elastic (?) strength through the use of dynamic lifts and plyometrics without any regard to the development of Endurance or Mental factors. Likewise, the

Endurance, Flexibility, and Mental potentials can be developed independently without requiring any interaction from the other areas.

In contrast, the area of Mechanics is the only factor that both affects and is affected by the other performer related factors. Without the proper Strength and Flexibility levels, several of the critical positions required for superior Sprint/Hurdle performance simply cannot be achieved. Likewise, without proper Endurance and Mental toughness, these beneficial mechanical positions cannot be maintained as fatigue becomes a factor in the performance. On the other hand, proper Mechanics decreases the amount of energy and strength expenditure, which not only makes the performance more effective but delays the onset of fatigue.

> In summary, although the genetically endowed factors are unalterable, they must be considered as undeveloped gifts. Thus, the Training factor becomes the key to the development of an athlete's potential.

Chapter Summary:

Of the factors that affect the Sprint/Hurdle performance, the area that dictates the true potential of an athlete, the genetically endowed physical potential, cannot be altered or affected (legally). Likewise, the rules governing the event cannot be improperly exploited.

In contrast, the environmental effects of gravity, wind, and friction can be manipulated for the benefit of the performer. In many cases this is accomplished by innovative use of equipment. Unfortunately, these factors are only slightly alterable and, at best, represent a minor improvement potential.

The area of Development (Training) provides the greatest amount of potential alteration since it provides the means by which to develop the athlete's endowed physical potential. Thus, it is evident that, to maximize the Sprint or Hurdle potential of an athlete, the focus must be placed on the Development area.

The next concern is how to make the most out of the training effort.

CHAPTER 3

BALANCED TRAINING: INTELLIGENT COMPROMISING

For a number of reasons, it is impossible to maximize the potential of all of the Performer Related Limiting Factors. First, there is simply not enough time during the athlete's day to maximally stress all of the performance factors. More importantly, the body simply cannot withstand the constant stress required to produce such comprehensive changes in all of these areas. The Sprint and Hurdle events have advanced to the point where many athletes are competing on the ragged edge of both injury and overtraining. Finally, although all of the factors have a degree of independence, they are all interrelated to varying degrees, sometimes in a conflicting manner. For instance, the muscle bulk required to maximize the Strength potential serves to decrease the overall Flexibility and Endurance levels of an athlete. Likewise, the stress of high intensity, uncomfortable Sprint Endurance training rapidly decreases the Mental resiliency of an athlete.

Time Management

The successful programs have recognized that a Sprint/Hurdle athlete has an average of about two productive hours a day for performance improvement. Moreover, within this time period, an athlete can be stressed at the highest levels of performance for an average of only about three minutes total. Properly managing these time restrictions is the most critical aspect of the balanced training concept.

If balanced training is ignored then stress levels imposed on an athlete, whether mental or physical, can become debilitating. Once the athlete enters a state of overtraining, the current season has been lost. Virtually every veteran athlete has experienced this overtraining problem. Once the athlete has been pushed "off the cliff", there is no recovery and the remaining portion of that season is, for all practical purposes, over.

The complexity of balanced training is made even more difficult with the realization that every athlete is individual in their training requirements. Some athletes can handle enormous levels of physical and/or mental stress, while others are very fragile in one or both areas. Ignoring this fact will ensure the eventual failure of both the coach and the athlete.

Factor Management

If an athlete cannot hope to develop all of their Performer Related Limiting Factors to their maximum levels, the intelligent compromise is to identify the most critical Factors and place the greatest emphasis in those areas. In the Short Sprint and Hurdle events, the three most critical areas are Strength, Flexibility, and Mechanics. Thus, the successful Short race Sprinter or Hurdler will be the athlete that can produce the greatest amount of beneficial force. This entails developing the required static, dynamic, and elastic strength, and then properly applying it to move the body down the track.

In addition, the strength endurance subphase of Endurance and Mental conditioning are both supportive areas in the Short races. Endurance **is** a factor since there is a measurable decrement in performance in the latter stages of both the Short Sprints and Hurdles. In the Mental area, although race strategy and the stress of dealing with fatigue are not major factors, there are a significant amount of "mind games" that occur between Short Sprint and Hurdle competitors that require a significant degree of mental toughness.

Finally, the cardio-pulmonary factor of Endurance is simply not a critical factor in the Short Sprint/Hurdle race. Thus, unless the training of this factor is done as a stress reliever or basic conditioning tool, it is not necessary.

In the Long Sprint and Hurdle events, since the race is of sufficient length to require serious demands from the strength endurance capabilities of an athlete, this portion of the Endurance area must be elevated into the critical group along with the Strength, Flexibility, and Mechanics factors. In addition, the fatigue factor and the race distance greatly increase the mental stress of the race, which requires the elevation of the Mental area into the critical group as well. Unfortunately, by moving five major areas into the critical group, training compromises will have to be made for this event.

To complicate matters, by extending the race distance, the demands on the cardio-pulmonary factor of the Endurance capabilities of the body do become a moderate factor. Thus, off season endurance based training takes on actual development significance, and should be a part of a Long Sprinter/Hurdler's yearly training regimen.

Chapter Summary:

In the Short Sprint and Hurdles, the three most critical areas are Strength, Flexibility, and Mechanics. The Long races demand the addition of the areas of Endurance (strength) and Mental.

Once these critical training factors have been identified, the manner in which these areas will be applied in the Sprint/Hurdle performance, to get the most out of the development effort, must be identified.

CHAPTER 4

GETTING THE MOST FROM THE PERFORMER POTENTIAL

Throughout this presentation, emphasis has been placed upon the importance of the Mechanics potential and its development using a proper training process. This emphasis was intentional since the development of proper Mechanics will be the focal point through which all of the other Limiting Factors will be related in the discussion of the development of a superior Sprint/Hurdle performance. This approach has evolved over the years since it became evident early on that successful development and implementation of all of the Limiting Factors can be evaluated by observing the Mechanics of a performer.

In developing the Mechanics of the Sprint and Hurdle events, a number of barriers must be successfully crossed. They include a realistic evaluation of potential, a dedication to the training process, and the foresight (or fortune) to locate a proficient coach.

Athlete's Barriers To Success

In an athlete's attempt to maximize the Mechanics Potential, no compromise in the level of performance should be acceptable unless an athlete is willing to concede certain points. First, if a Short Sprint/Hurdle athlete concedes that their Anthropometric, Strength, or Flexibility potential is not up to elite caliber, then less than elite performance is justifiable. In the Long races, the same question must be asked for not only these potentials, but also the Endurance (strength) and Mental potential of the athlete.

The second road block that the athlete must contend with involves the Training aspect. If the athlete is unwilling or unable to develop the Performer Related Limiting Factors to the greatest degree possible, then the elite level of performance should be deemed unreachable.

Practice Verses Competition

There has always been a debate among coaches regarding the difference between the Mechanics of an athlete in practice and in a competition. A large number of coaches believe that, in the heat of competition, their best athletes perform at a higher level because they resolve many of the problems seen in the practice situation.

It is true that all athletes perform better in competition, but **it is not due to any sudden resolution of mechanical flaws** present in practice sessions. The performance improvement is, in fact, simply due to the athlete's ability to produce greater levels of Strength and Endurance under the pressure of competition.

Since longitudinal data has been collected on hundreds of athletes, in both practice and competition, it can be unequivocally stated that, regardless of the quality of the performer, **whatever mechanical errors an athlete displays in practice will also be seen in competition**. In fact, the statistics are so conclusive that this statement can be termed a certainty.

This conclusion is actually a godsend since a coach now knows that the problems observed in practice need to be addressed if the Mechanics produced in competition are to improve. Since it is also true that **whatever mechanical strengths an athlete displays in practice will also be seen in competition**, it makes the practice results even more beneficial.

More importantly to the coaching community, this reality means that the importance of the coach becomes more essential since what is done on the track (both good and bad) translates directly to the competitive environment.

The Coach/Teacher

History has shown that the level of coaching that an athlete receives will significantly affect the final performance result. The only thing more detrimental then a total absence of coaching expertise is the presence of a poor coach. Likewise, a major factor in an athlete's ability to develop all areas of either the Sprint or Hurdle performance is the presence of a proficient coach.

There are two major characteristics of a proficient coach: knowing **how** to teach as well as **what** to teach. Although properly identifying and understanding "what to teach" is a formidable task, the development of the "how to teach" requirement is even more difficult. This is due to the fact that, although there are certain performance factors that will always be critical in sprinting or hurdling, each athlete is different in their ability to learn, the manner in which they learn best, how they must be treated, and how they best respond. For example, one 400 meter sprinter may be an outgoing, confident, fast learner, with a short attention span who learns best with visual feedback. In contrast, another Long Sprinter may be an introverted, hardworking, slow learning, mechanically oriented individual who learns best from written diagrams. Although the proficient coach will be teaching both athletes the same information, the manner in which it is presented must differ considerably if both are to achieve the most from the learning process.

Under the "what to teach" requirement, a good coach must understand how to maximally develop the Limiting Factors in sprinting or hurdling, and combine them in a manner in which allows their athlete to mechanically use these factors to the athlete's best ability. Over the past thirty-plus years, the data that have been collected on the Sprint/Hurdle performance in the USATF High Performance Project has been directed toward identifying what to teach. Toward this end, a large number of elite athletes (Men and Women, Short and Long race Sprinters and Hurdlers) were filmed during competition. These performances were analyzed and statistically compared within each event, as well as with non-elite sprinters and hurdlers, to determine the differences in performances. This information has been both corroborated and expanded upon by several laboratory controlled research efforts using the elite athlete group.

Of the two major areas that a proficient coach must develop, it is not the goal of this presentation to tell the coach "how to teach". It is felt that this area was initially developed during the coach's educational process, and it is an art that they have developed over a number of years of successful application. With that said, whereas most of the older coaches were trained as teachers in an academic setting, many of the young coaches do not have this background.

A caution must be made, therefore, that without knowledge on how people learn, a coach cannot reach their teaching potential. The science of motor learning is well developed, and the information available should be studied by any coach who wants to get the most out of their athletes. **Currently, the inability or unwillingness for a coach to actively teach (change) their athletes is the weakest aspect of the development of US athletes.**

The Elite Sprint/Hurdle Coach

There are thousands of proficient Track coaches in the US, however, there are only a handful of coaches that can consistently attract and **effectively** develop elite athletes. History has shown that talent can spring from anywhere, and many coaches have had one (or several) of these gifted athletes 'walk through the door'. However, it is the rare coach that has what it takes to begin with a talented elite level athlete and bootstrap that opportunity into an environment that attracts a consistent number of elite performers.

In observing the rare Elite Coach, there are several characteristics that separate them from the typical coach:

The Guru

Of all of the Elite Coach characteristics, there is only one that can be found in every one of this group – what has been termed the "Guru Complex". Every successful Elite Coach has the core belief that they alone can get the **best** out of every one of their athletes. Moreover, if an athlete will commit to following their program, they will get better. Finally, and most importantly, they believe that whatever level of performance their athlete has currently achieved is only part of the journey toward a better performance in the future.

All of the other characteristics are important, but without this one a coach will not be successful dealing with elite athletes. Athletes with world class talent have egos that match their level of success, and they are looking for a coach that can convince them that it is in their best interest to put their lives in the hands of a coach that will fully develop their potential.

There have been numerous coaches that have been blessed with a talented individual, but then fail to capitalize on the opportunity to fully develop this athlete (or future athletes) by not instilling confidence in the individual, being afraid to make changes for fear of ruining the athlete, or are content with simply managing the athlete (i.e. 'get them to the meet on time'). In these cases, the athlete rarely achieves their full potential, while the coach squanders their chance to move into the elite coaching ranks. Eventually, the athlete moves on to another coach.

On the other hand, there are several instances where a coach has all of the Elite Coach characteristics that will be discussed herein, but does not have the Guru Complex. This is a truly unfortunate situation because the athletes that they do work with routinely get better, but they simply do not have the ability to attract, inspire, and work with the high end elite performer.

Those coaches that are blessed with this Svengali charisma typically rise to the top of the coaching profession and, since athlete performance is the benchmark of a successful elite coach, they all are considered successful. There **are** a very few of this elite group that rise above the term 'successful', and achieve the status of 'legendary'. The difference does not lie in their level of success on the track, but the success of their athletes off the track. Typically, these coaches have the following credentials:

1. A large number of successful elite athletes, the majority of which speak highly of the them.
2. A large number of former assistant coaches that go on to become successful in their own programs.
3. The majority of their athletes complete their education, and become solid citizens in the real world.
4. Coaches in the profession speak highly of them.

As far as performance success, these characteristics have little value. However, the best of the best, and the ones that will be fondly remembered, have these character strengths.

The Trainer

The second most common characteristic of Elite Sprint/Hurdle Coaches is the ability to successfully train or condition their athletes. For elite athletes under the age of 24, the easiest way to improve performance is to simply increase the level of training. Thus, even if a coach has little or no knowledge of training theory, biomechanics, physiology, or any of the other areas that would make them a more effective coach, simply pouring on more and more training load, year after year, will result in performance improvement.

Around the age of 24, however, the athlete approaches their maximum strength levels, and simply adding more training load becomes less and less effective. Moreover, this is typically when the training levels become so intense that injuries start becoming an issue. For the coach that lacks the knowledge discussed previously (training theory, biomechanics, etc.), and chooses not to invest the time to acquire them, their options become limited. Historically, these are the coaches that have a tendency to turn to the use of semi-legal, or illegal training methods.

The Elite Coach that becomes the most effective Trainer is one who invests the time to understand the science behind what is commonly known as the Training Theory. Understanding how the body reacts to training stress is a complex subject, and one that is constantly evolving. This knowledge allows the coach to develop their athletes more efficiently, as well as understanding how far each athlete can be effectively stressed. Moreover, it is, by nature, affected by all of the remaining characteristics found in Elite Coaches.

The next four characteristics are considered support areas that serve to improve the Elite Coach's knowledge of Training Theory. The first two are at the top of the list because they are dynamically applied on the track in real time, which makes them more complex in their successful execution. The last two are just as important, but since their application is crafted in a static, off the track environment, they are more controllable by the coach.

The Biomechanist

As will be seen in subsequent Chapters, the "Bottom Line" in both sprinting and hurdling comes down to how the athlete produces Horizontal Velocity using the variables **Stride Rate and Stride Length**. Since Biomechanics is the science of understanding how the body moves to produce these types of results, this area of knowledge becomes the third most important characteristic of an Elite Sprint/Hurdle Coach.

Some coaches are gifted with the ability to watch an athlete and intuitively determine the proper (and improper) Mechanics in their performance. Often this skill is present without any training in Mechanics. It is these coaches that, with additional knowledge in the area, become extremely successful in producing successful athletes.

Coaches not blessed with this gift of Mechanics are still able to be just as effective, however, it takes a lot more effort on their part. Instead of just watching a performance, and putting the numbers together with the movement, they have to film, review, and work at understanding each athlete.

Both types of individuals can be an effective coach Biomechanist, it's just more time consuming for the less gifted.

The Teacher

All the knowledge in the world is useless if the coach cannot get it across to their athletes. Along with the genetic gift of being able to naturally see effective movement patterns as discussed above, the ability to teach is another inherent talent. Since Motor Learning is the science of understanding how the body acquires (or alters) movement patterns, this area of knowledge is as important as Mechanics in the process of producing improvement in athletes.

Some coaches are gifted with the ability to evaluate an athlete and intuitively determine how to get across the information needed to make a change in performance. Often this skill is present without any training in motor learning. It is these coaches that, with additional knowledge in the area, become extremely successful in producing successful athletes.

Coaches not blessed with this gift of teaching are still able to be just as effective, however, it takes a lot more effort on their part. Instead of just intuitively knowing how to get their information across, they have to understand each athlete and develop teaching strategies that will work best in each situation.

Both types of individuals can be effective teachers, it's just more time consuming for the less gifted.

The Physiologist

If a coach is truly going to understand how best to train an athlete, they must understand how the body works internally. The key to understanding strength and endurance training; eliciting improvements in the muscles, tendons, and ligaments; maximizing the response of the nervous system; integrating nutrition into the training process; and numerous other body processing tasks all revolves around understanding the science of physiology.

The huge volume of knowledge required to maximize the benefits of training the body is beyond the ability and time available of any coach. Fortunately, all a coach has to do is recognize the importance of this area, and find experts to assist in formulating a program that effectively integrates the best physiological concepts.

The successful coaches realize that the key is to understand the basic physiological concepts, then keep abreast of the improvements and advances as they take place.

The Psychologist

Probably the most difficult, and least rewarding task a coach has is dealing with is the mental aspects of the coaching process. Since the coach must deal with both the athlete's mental stresses of training and competition, AND the stresses of their day to day life, it can become a daunting task. Add to this the fact that each athlete has their own set of on and off track problems, and the task becomes even more difficult.

Most Elite Coaches develop enough knowledge of Sport Psychology from experience and working with psychologists over the years to handle most of the normal on and off track stresses. For those unusual cases where the athlete finds the stress overwhelming, the proficient coach will direct the athlete to a qualified psychologist.

As with the field of physiology, the good thing about mental stress is that problems typically develop over time, and the solution doesn't rely on the coach solving it from one Sprint or Hurdle run to the next. The key for the successful coach in this area is to always have options for their athletes, and not allow them to have no place to turn for help when it is needed. For those athletes that are mentally tough, it may mean help only in extreme crises. For others, it may involve working with a psychologist on a continuing basis.

The successful coaches realize that the key is to understand the basics of mental stress, treat every athlete as an individual, and have professional resources for those that need them.

_____

The last characteristic has little to do with the direct success of the coach's athletes, but everything to do with the success of the coach themselves.

_____

The Businessman

Great coaches have failed because they don't know how to properly run a business. These failures can run the gauntlet of:

1. Failing to secure an agreement with their athletes that ensure success for both parties. This can range from monetary payments, training expectations, lifestyle commitments, and numerous other factors. Regardless of the issues, if both parties do not fully understand what is expected from each other, the relationship can be a time bomb with an unknown (but inevitable) detonation period.
2. Failing to organize critical tasks. This can range from failure to ensure their athletes get the necessary support training (medical, physiotherapy, nutrition, mental, etc.), to their inability to perform the tasks demanded of their job (NCAA regulations, facility management, support people management, etc.).

Business sense is something that is routinely overlooked when a coach does things correctly. If they manage their athletes well, and ensure their program runs smoothly, no one notices because nothing is wrong. Only when something goes wrong, sometimes terribly wrong, do the problems of poor business practices surface. More than one Elite Coach has been fired, been financially compromised, or driven from the sport due to these types of problems.

Over the years, from experience or observing the success and failures of other coaches, the Elite Coach finds a way to resolve these issues.

_____

In understanding what it takes to become an Elite Coach, it should surprise no one that most of these coaches are older. In fact, there are very few under the age of 50, with a large number over

60. Even if they have the innate ability to handle elite athletes, it simply takes a long time for a coach to develop all the skills required to produce successful athletes at this extreme level of performance.

Model Concepts

The statement "every athlete is an individual" is a recognized truth. Unfortunately, some coaches use this idea as an excuse to avoid changing what an athlete does in the process of improving performance. This avoidance allows them to evade having to choose a direction that change has to occur, since doing so would force them to actually recognize that change in one direction is beneficial in the event they are coaching. And once they go down the "slippery slope" of acknowledging that some performance concepts are true for all athletes, they feel that they are no longer treating athletes as individuals. Once this occurs, and they begin recognizing a large number of these concepts exist, they are forced to develop a Model by which to teach toward. But since "everyone knows there is no ONE Model" and "every athlete is an individual", some coaches conclude that this concept of changing something to improve performance needs to be avoided at all costs. So, they reason that perhaps it is best not to begin such a journey, and simply get the athlete fitter and hope the athlete figures out what changes they need to do (if any) on their own.

Ignoring the horrific logic errors that this thinking requires, these coaches fail to realize that every coach (including them), regardless of their level of competence, has a Model that they teach toward. They may disavow it, disown it, or run from it, but the minute they walk on the track and watch their first athlete move down the track, they are teaching toward a Model.

There is no sane coach that would allow their sprinter to compete in the 100 meter dash by hopping down the track on two legs. The very concept of performing in this manner is unacceptable not because the primary purpose of moving from the start to the finish isn't achieved (it is), but because hopping down the track is slower than running down the track. The point here is that, by acknowledging that running, as opposed to hopping, down the track in the 100 meters is the ONLY way to be successful, then you have a Sprint Model that you are teaching toward. You can still believe that "every athlete is an individual", and still skip the part where you have all your sprinters hop (or crawl, or skip, or cartwheel, etc.) down the track in the off chance that their "individual" nature may make them faster using this alternative method.

For the sake of argument (and future reference) let's assume that, for whatever reason, an athlete actually exists that can hop the 100 meters in 16 seconds, while they can only run it in 18. Would a good coach still change the athlete into a runner, or allow them to continue hopping because it "works best" for them? Furthermore, knowing that the limitations in performance that hopping imposes when competing with the rest of the world (as a group), would a good coach still stick with hopping knowing that the athlete would never have a chance to become a great 100 meter performer?

Although this is an extreme example used to stimulate rational thinking, there is a much more relevant example. In 1963 Dick Fosbury "turned his back" on the straddle technique and showed the world that there was a better way to perform the high jump. It wasn't a case of the new technique being better for Dick because it happened to be better for him as an "individual", it was better for him because it was a better way to jump – for everyone. Today, there are exactly **zero** percent of the elite jumpers that don't use some form of the Flop to compete in the high jump.

So, should a good jumps coach have every jumper they work with try the straddle technique in the off chance that they could jump higher than they can with the Flop? And what happens when the very real possibility occurs where an athlete can actually jump better with this old style? Would a good coach still change the athlete into a Flopper, or allow them to continue straddling because it "works best" for them? Furthermore, knowing that the limitations in performance that straddling imposes when competing with the rest of the world (as a group), would a good coach still stick with straddling knowing that the athlete would never have a chance to become a great jumper?

As was discussed in the characteristics of Elite Coaches, these coaches teach their athletes to become better by understanding the event well enough to know which way change must take place. For example, an Elite Sprint Coach would put the following performance choices in the same category of choosing running over hopping:

1. Front Side Mechanics over Back Side Mechanics[1]
2. Short Ground Time over Long Ground Time
3. Average Air Time over Short or Long Air Time

Every one of these concepts apply to every one of their Sprint athletes, regardless of how "individual" they are. In fact, these staples of elite Sprint performance are considered Model Concepts for the same reason that the Flop is better than the straddle – they simply work better. None of the Elite Coaches would waste time having their sprinters try Back Side Mechanics, longer Ground Time, or longer or shorter Air Time. These coaches are in the business of producing elite athletes, and they can't afford to waste time with inferior concepts.

There are two disclaimers that must be made at this point. First, not all great Sprint athletes have excellent (at the elite level) results in Front Side Mechanics, Ground Time, and Air Time. There are simply too many other factors that are involved in athletic performance (mostly talent, but also all the other factors that have and will be discussed) to conclude that excellence in any one factor (except talent) is critical.

Second, the belief that all Elite Coaches teach a rigid Model performance is incorrect. If anyone thinks that the Stride Rate and Stride Length of Carmelita Jeter and Usain Bolt are (or should be) the same are missing the point. Because of their "individual" differences, both of these results will be different for each athlete. What the better coaches do is teach **toward** a Model, which means that both Jeter and Bolt are great because they both emphasize Front Side Mechanics, short Ground Time,

---

[1] As will be presented herein, Front Side Mechanics is the concept of sprinting while trying to keep all body segments in front of the body. Back Side Mechanics is the term used when the body segments are in the back of the body.

and controlled (not too long and not too short) Air Time that produces their "individual" Model Stride Rate and Stride Length.

For a coach, accepting the idea that there are Model concepts in every event they coach leads to two consequences. The first is that their athletes will get better, regardless of their level of performance. The second is that this will lead the coach down the "slippery slope" toward excellence because each of these three Model concepts has multiple components that must be examined if the concept is to be fully understood. It's relatively easy to accept the fact that Front Side Mechanics is the way to go, but understanding how the best sprinters produce this action and, more importantly, how to get the athletes to create it is a much more difficult endeavor.

The journey to become an Elite Coach is long, but herein lies the first step.

The Individual Model

Since the early days of the Modeling efforts for the Sprints and Hurdles, statistical analysis has been employer to identify, as a group, which of the athlete's individual factors affect their performance **regardless of their level of performance**. Some of these differences are not surprising. Taller athletes produce longer Stride Lengths than shorter athletes when sprinting at the same Speed. Likewise, shorter athletes produce higher Stride Rates than taller athletes at the same Speed. These examples are but two in a long list of changes that have been built into each athlete's Model Sprint or Hurdle performance.

Once these changes have been made, the next step is to add all of the characteristics that make a great sprinter/hurdler for each specific event. The result is a Model that fits the individual athlete, and performs at world record levels with the most efficient movement patterns. This Model, and the analysis results it produces to achieve its performance level, are the benchmarks that are used to evaluate the strengths and weaknesses of the elite athlete.

There is an alternative Model approach that has some support in the coaching community. As a response to the belief that "every athlete is an individual", the basis for this idea is to use the athlete themselves as the sole determinate of how their Model performs. Thus, by collecting data on the athlete over several performances, the Model for that athlete will be their movement patterns from their best performance or performances.

For a myriad of reasons, this approach does not work. Since hundreds of elite athletes have been followed throughout their careers, there is sufficient long term data to test this approach. The major reasons this method is flawed are:

1. **The Best Performance Fallacy**: There are so many factors other than Mechanics that affect an athlete's performance that simply using a performance mark as a reason to conclude the athlete's Mechanics are the "best" is simply not valid. External factors like time of year, importance of the meet, wind, altitude, and temperature can drastically alter the final result.

Add to this the Internal factors of the athlete's own fitness level (strength, endurance, mental, etc.) and you have a situation where all of these factors will overwhelm any attempt to relate an individual's best performance to excellence in Mechanics.
2. **The Athlete's Individual Consistency**: As discussed previously, regardless of the situation, practice or meet conditions, an athlete will demonstrate the same mechanical strengths and weaknesses. Thus, looking at the athlete themselves, even in their best performance, will not tell you what needs to change to improve performance.

There are several, complex statistically based reasons that this approach does not work, but these two reasons alone are sufficient to abandon this approach entirely.

It is interesting to note that, if an athlete runs a variety of Sprint events (100, 200, 400) in competition then, by using the same statistical methods that are employed to the entire group of sprinters in a single event, virtually all of the Model concepts of sprinting can be identified. The relationships are much weaker due to the number of performances (a few with a single athlete compared to thousands for the group), but this approach does work. The problem is that few Sprint athletes (and no Hurdle athletes) run more than one event in championship competitions. And even if they do, it takes years to collect enough data for a valid analysis. Moreover, since the same conclusions are going to be reached, it is foolish to wait years before applying the knowledge to the athlete as soon as possible.

Numbers Don't Lie

At this stage of the High Performance Program, it is felt that the "what to teach" area has been comprehensively investigated. It is now known, to a high degree of specificity, what an athlete needs to do on the track to perform at the elite level of sprinting and hurdling.

In simple terms, if an athlete can produce a specific time to the 10 meter mark (an overall measure of success in Starting) and generate a certain combination of Stride Rate and Stride Length (a direct determinate of Maximum Horizontal Velocity), then the result will be a world class performance. Do these two things and nothing else matters, because the **numbers don't lie**. In over thirty years of analyzing elite athletes, there has been no case where a performer generated bad analysis numbers in these areas and produced great results.

Thus, the bottom line is that both athlete and coach need to strive to both understand, and then achieve, these critical performance variables. Unfortunately, it's not as easy as just timing the first 10 meters of the Start and measuring the Stride Rate and Length at Full Speed. Instead, the coach (and if possible the athlete) must understand all of the complex variables that go into producing these two general results.

When USA Track and Field began applying sports science to the Sprints and Hurdles, the number of coaches that were involved with elite athletes was almost on a one-to-one basis. The first

Sprint Seminar was attended by 28 coaches to cover 30 elite athletes. Today, there are typically less than 10 coaches that handle over 90 percent of **both** the Sprint **and** Hurdle athletes.

The coaches that initially embraced these approaches reaped the benefit of gaining a distinct advantage over coaches that continued down the old path of guessing what needed to be improved in their athlete or, even more limiting, were unwilling to make any changes because they were afraid of somehow ruining their athlete. These success stories are the Elite Coaches that are described within this Chapter.

So, over time, these innovative coaches built a record of improving their athletes, and other athletes began seeking them out. This small group of coaches now represents the core of elite athlete development in the US.

Using the Mechanics area of the Sprint/Hurdle performance, the results that the successful coaches now employ as the benchmarks of excellence will be presented in the next Chapters.

Chapter Summary:

If an athlete can justifiably refuse to accept limitations on their individual potential, and they have access to a coach that understands "how to teach", then the only roadblock to success is understanding "what to teach".

The task of working with elite athletes takes a specific type of coach. These Elite Coaches have distinct characteristics, the most important one being the Guru Complex.

All coaches, whether they recognize it or not, teach **toward** a Model. The better coaches have a much more comprehensive and advanced Model.

The remaining presentation that follows is directed toward answering this "what to teach" question.

PART TWO: UNDERSTANDING THE SPRINT PERFORMANCE

CHAPTER 5

UNDERSTANDING THE SPRINT PERFORMANCE

To truly understand the Sprint performance, three topics must be addressed. First, the critical areas of interest for the entire Sprint performance need to be identified. Second, the positions of interest within the areas need to be described. Finally, the basic Mechanics of the critical areas need to be examined. All of these are required if a coordinated understanding is to be accomplished.

Critical Areas of the Sprint

The Horizontal Velocity graph of Figure 5-1 provides the information required to determine the critical areas of the Sprint performance.

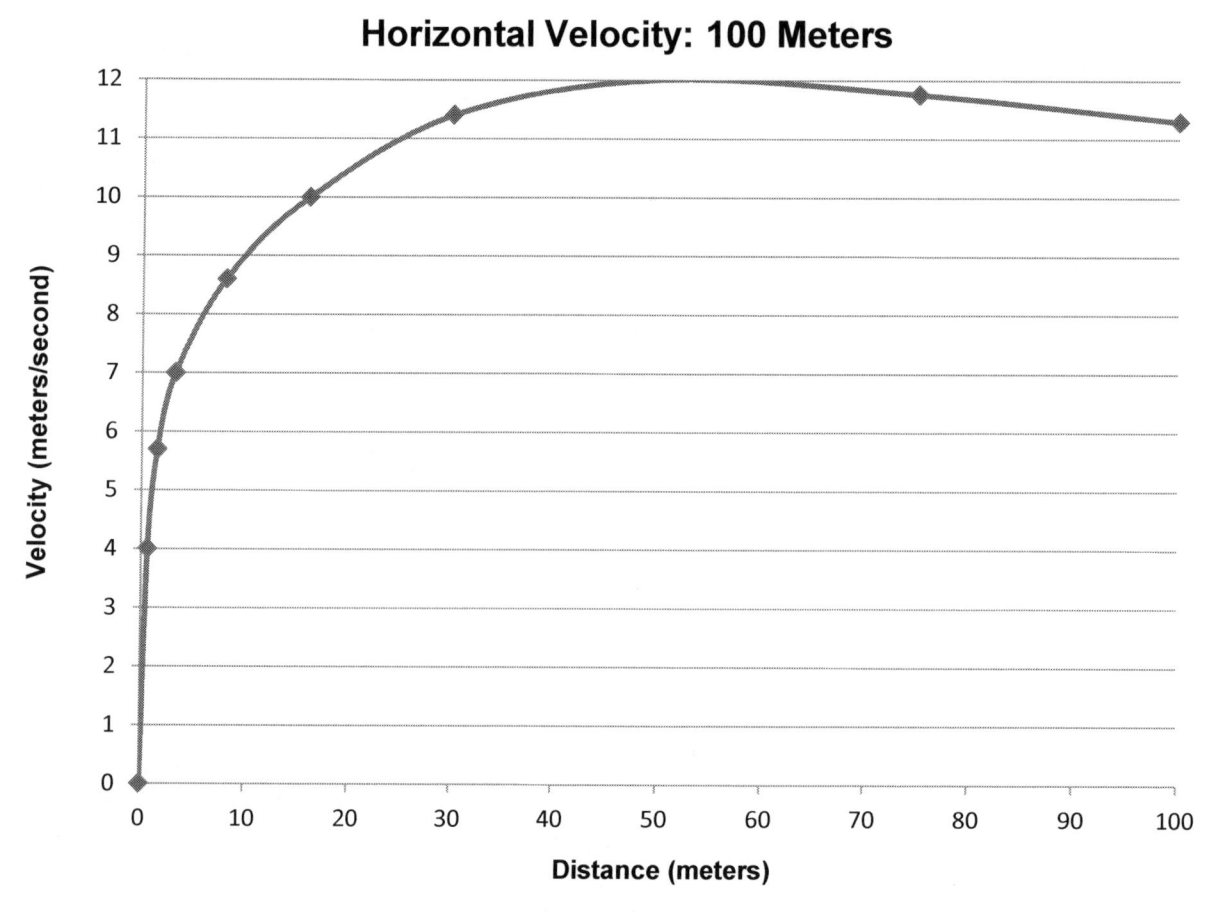

Figure 5-1: Horizontal Velocity in the Men's 100 Meters

Understanding the Sprint Performance

The Figure points to the fact that the Horizontal Velocity in the 100 meters changes constantly throughout the entire race. This contradicts the typical concept of the Sprint being divided into Start and the Maximum Velocity phases. Instead, the race should be divided into the following phases:

1. Reaction Time
2. **Acceleration**
    a. **Start**
        i. Two Leg Drive
        ii. One Leg Drive
        iii. First Step
        iv. Second Step
    b. Transition (Steps 3-10)
3. **Maximum Velocity**
    a. Attaining
    b. Maintaining

Once the specifics of each of these phases are understood, it becomes apparent that the most important components are **Acceleration** and **Maximum Velocity**. Furthermore, the critical portion of the Acceleration phase is the **Start**.

Reaction Time is a contributor to the overall Sprint time, however, since it has been found to be unrelated to Sprint performance, it will not be focused upon. Transition is a critical aspect of Sprint performance, however, as will be seen, if the concepts of the Start and Maximum Velocity are properly understood, this phase will take care of itself.

The Positions of Interest

To properly describe the Sprint action within the Critical Areas, the positions of the athlete at the important points within the areas of the **Start** and **Maximum Velocity** need to be identified.

The Start SubPhases

Little research has been focused on understanding the Sprint Start, and even less on the Hurdle Start. Every experienced coach, however, will agree that the Start is a critical part of every Sprint/Hurdle event.

As stated above, the Start is being described as beginning with the first measurable exertion on the blocks, and ending with the termination of the Air Phase of the second step after block clearance. A review of the Horizontal Velocity results shown in Figure 5-1, focusing on block clearance and the first two steps, demonstrates why this division was made. In reviewing this Figure, note how steeply the Velocity curve rises until the athlete reaches 7 meters per second, which occurs at the end of the second step.

Figure 5-2 shows the Horizontal Velocity results during block clearance and the first two steps of the Start. An elite male 100 meter sprinter can generate over 4 meters per second at ground Touchdown coming out of the blocks (TD 1). Then, during ground contact of the first step, the Velocity is increased to 6 meters per second. Finally, the second step (beginning at TD 2) Velocity is further increased to 7 meters per second. Thus, by the end of the second step (TD 3), the sprinter has generated well over half of his Maximum Velocity. It is apparent, therefore, that the main goal of the Start is to produce maximum Horizontal Velocity coming out of the blocks and during the first two steps. From this explosive beginning, it will take another 20 meters (or more) before the sprinter approaches their Maximum Velocity.

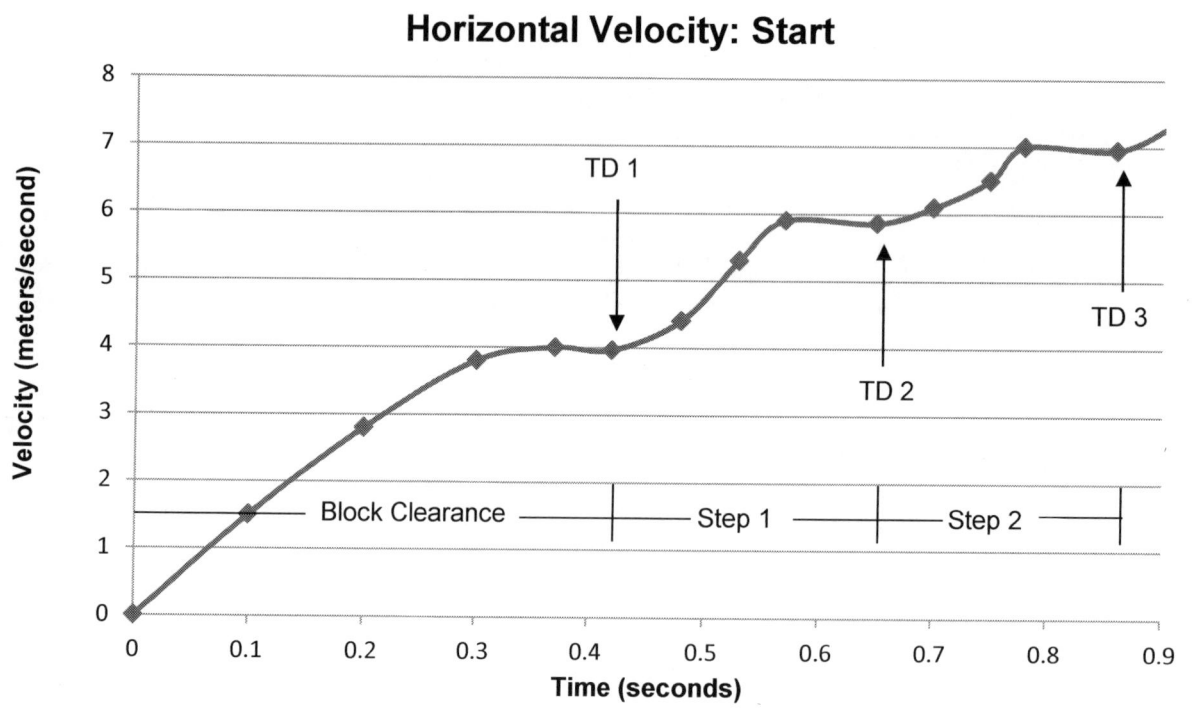

Figure 5-2: Horizontal Velocity During The Start

Since the magnitude of the change in Horizontal Velocity generated during block clearance and the first two steps of the Sprint race is radically different than any other portion of the race, the Start is defined to occur during this period. After the second step, the Mechanics of the Sprint begin a transition from a powerful Horizontally directed drive to a more Vertically directed effort seen in the Maximum Velocity Sprint Mechanics.

Preparation for the Start begins with the Block Position. Block settings are a personal choice, but the best sprinters set their blocks in a similar manner. The front block distance is set so that the lead knee, if placed on the ground, is positioned slightly behind the starting line. As a rule, the front block is typically set at approximately 60 percent of the distance from the rear block to the starting line.

Understanding the Sprint Performance

The components, or subphases of the Start begin at the Set position (Figure 5-3).

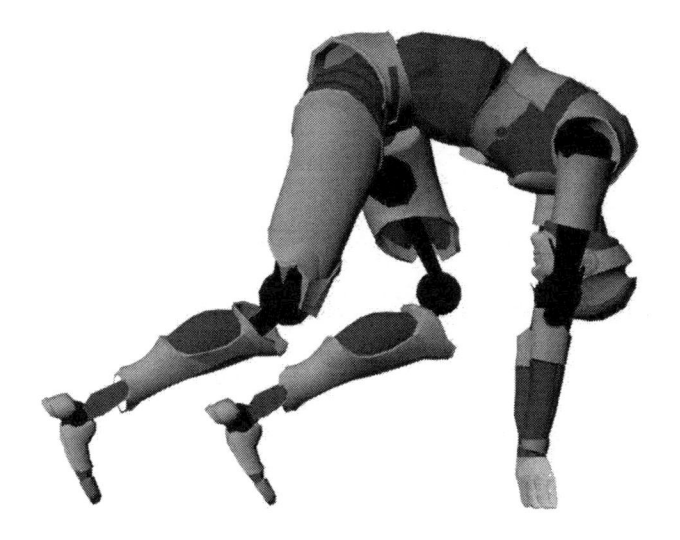

Figure 5-3: The Set Position

After the gun, subphase one of the Start begins with a two leg drive and ends when the rear foot leaves the blocks (Figure 5-4).

Figure 5-4: The End of the Two Leg Drive

Block contact ends with the completion of the one leg drive subphase (Figure 5-5).

Figure 5-5: The End of the One Leg Drive

Block clearance ends with a short Air Phase. The First Step subphase begins with Touchdown of the rear foot coming out of the blocks (Figure 5-6).

Figure 5-6: The First Step Touchdown

Understanding the Sprint Performance

The First Step ground contact ends with Takeoff of the rear foot (Figure 5-7).

Figure 5-7: The First Step Takeoff

The First Step subphase ends with a short Air Phase. The Second Step subphase begins with Touchdown of the front foot coming out of the blocks (Figure 5-8).

Figure 5-8: The Second Step Touchdown

The Second Step ground contact ends with Takeoff of the front foot (Figure 5-9).

Figure 5-9: The Second Step Takeoff

Finally, the Second Step subphase ends (along with the Start phase) with ground contact (Figure 5-10).

Figure 5-10: The Third Step Touchdown (End of Start)

The Maximum Velocity SubPhases

The critical phases of the Maximum Velocity portion of the Sprint performance have been well defined. It focuses around the leg position, and begins with the foot Touchdown subphase (Figure 5-11).

Figure 5-11: Touchdown

The next subphase occurs when the body center of gravity (COG) crosses over the Touchdown position (Figure 5-12).

Body Center (COG)

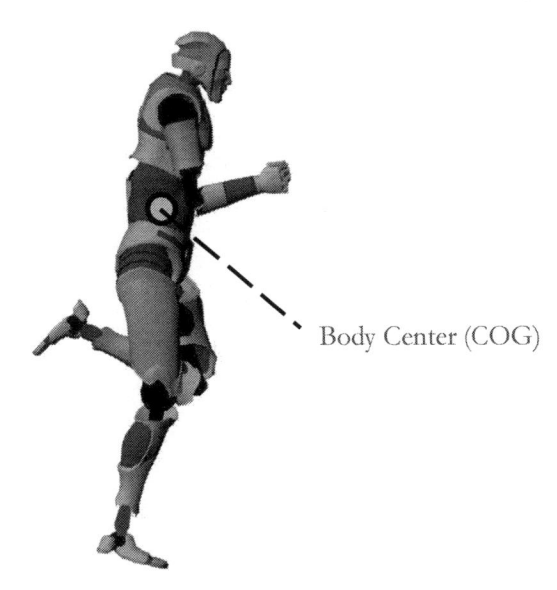

Figure 5-12: Mid Support

The next critical position occurs when foot Takeoff occurs (Figure 5-13).

Figure 5-13: Takeoff

The next subphase occurs when the upper leg completes its maximum backward extension position (Figure 5-14).

Figure 5-14: Full Upper Leg Extension

The next critical position occurs when the recovery lower leg reaches its maximum flexion position (Figure 5-15).

Figure 5-15: Maximum Lower Leg Flexion

The next subphase occurs when the ankle of the recovery leg crosses the knee of the Ground Leg (Figure 5-16).

Figure 5-16: Ankle Cross

The final critical position occurs when the recovery upper leg reaches its maximum recovery position (Figure 5-17).

Figure 5-17: High Knee

With the critical areas and positions identified, the basic Mechanics can be addressed.

The Basic Mechanics

In the attempt to understand the Mechanics of the Sprint performance, and how the critical Limiting Factors are involved, a basic understanding of the physics of the activity is crucial.

Remembering that the purpose of the Sprint run is to cover the required distance in as short a time as possible, it is a reasonable, therefore, to assume that this requires the production of as great a Horizontal (down the track) Velocity as possible. From this conclusion, it then becomes evident that, to produce this Horizontal Velocity, a great amount of Horizontal effort or force must be produced by the sprinter. Thus, it is universally believed that the Mechanics of a successful Sprint performance must be based around this goal of producing large amounts of Horizontal force while in contact with the ground.

Although the production of Horizontal Velocity is the key to Sprint performance, the production of Horizontal force is **not** the critical mechanical factor in achieving this goal. It is true that, during the starting or primary acceleration phase of the Sprint run (covering the first 10 meters of the race), the production of Horizontal ground force is of critical importance. In addition, the Maximum Velocity that the athlete can produce is dependent upon how long productive Horizontal forces can be applied. The question is, what limits the performer's ability to generate greater Horizontal forces in the Start (to get out faster) and at Full Speed (to improve Maximum Velocity)?

As will be seen, the key to successful sprinting is dependent on the ability to properly manage the force capability of the athlete.

1. To maximize the Start performance, the goal must be to produce maximum Horizontal force while minimizing forces in all other directions (primarily Vertical).
2. During the Transition, the goal must be to efficiently move from the end of the Start to the achievement of Maximum Velocity.
3. To produce the greatest Maximum Velocity, the goal must be to minimize forces in all other directions (primarily the Vertical) so that some productive Horizontal force can still be produced. As long as the TOTAL Horizontal force created during ground contact is positive, Horizontal Velocity will increase.
4. Once Maximum Velocity is reached, the goal must be to produce the large level of Vertical force required to maintain proper Mechanics while continuing to produce the small amount of positive Horizontal force needed to maintain Maximum Velocity.

To understand these goals, the concept of force needs to be reviewed. Newton's first and second laws indicate that, to change Velocity, a force must be applied in the direction in which the Velocity is to be altered. In the Sprint performance, this concept can be stated as:

$$\text{Force} = \text{Mass} * \text{Change in Velocity} / \text{Ground Time}$$

where **Force** is the effort the athlete pushes on the ground to drive the body down the track (forward, upward, or sideways), **Mass** is essentially the weight of the sprinter, **Change in Velocity** is the alteration in the Speed moving down the track (forward, upward, or sideways), and **Ground Time** is the time the sprinter is in contact with the ground during the force application.

Using this concept, the force demands for the Sprint can be determined in all possible directions.

Lateral Force

Since Lateral (sideways, across the track) movement is not productive at any time during the Sprint race (Start, Transition, or Maximum Velocity), the Lateral change in Velocity should be kept to zero at all times. Thus:

Lateral Force = Mass*(0)/Ground Time = 0 Newtons (0 Pounds)

Any portion of an athlete's force potential that is wasted in the Lateral direction will detract from the effort required in the other two directions.

Note: Results will always be presented using the Metric system, with English system conversions whenever possible. Force, in the Metric system is measured in Newtons, with One Newton equal to 0.1 Kilograms or 0.22 Pounds.

Horizontal Force

It seems intuitive that, since the primary purpose in the Sprint is to move the body down the track, the ability to produce positive Horizontal (down the track) force is the most important factor in successful sprinting.

The Start: During the starting phase of the Sprint, the athlete must apply large amounts of Horizontal force to change the down-the-track Velocity of the body from a resting position (Velocity=0) to as high a value as possible at the end of the second step.

Realizing that the mass of the typical elite male sprinter is approximately 77.5 Kilograms (170 Pounds), and the Ground Time during the Start (block time plus first two steps) is approximately .50 seconds, the average amount of Horizontal force that the athlete must generate to produce an elite level change of 7.0 meters per second during ground contact can be calculated at:

Horizontal Force = 77.5*(7.0)/0.50 = 1085 Newtons (243 Pounds)

Since the majority of this force must be produced by a single leg (except the brief two legged push while in the blocks), this level of force demand is impressive.

To check the reality of this result, the actual forces exerted during the start can be determined. Using a measurement device embedded in the ground (a force platform), the forces in all directions (Lateral, Horizontal, and Vertical) can be determined. The results shown in Figures 5-18 indicate that the Horizontal force demands during the blocks portion of the Start reaches the predicted levels when averaged over time (Average Force). Combining the Horizontal force of both legs, the average result is well above the 900 Newton (200 pound) level.

The same force levels are found in the next two steps of the Start. Thus, these high levels of exertion (both predicted and actual) confirm the expected importance of high Horizontal force production at the beginning of the Sprint race.

As an interesting side note, the results also indicate that since the arms are in contact with the ground at the beginning of the Start, they can actually produce a small beneficial Horizontal force during the first portion of the movement.

Horizontal Force: Blocks

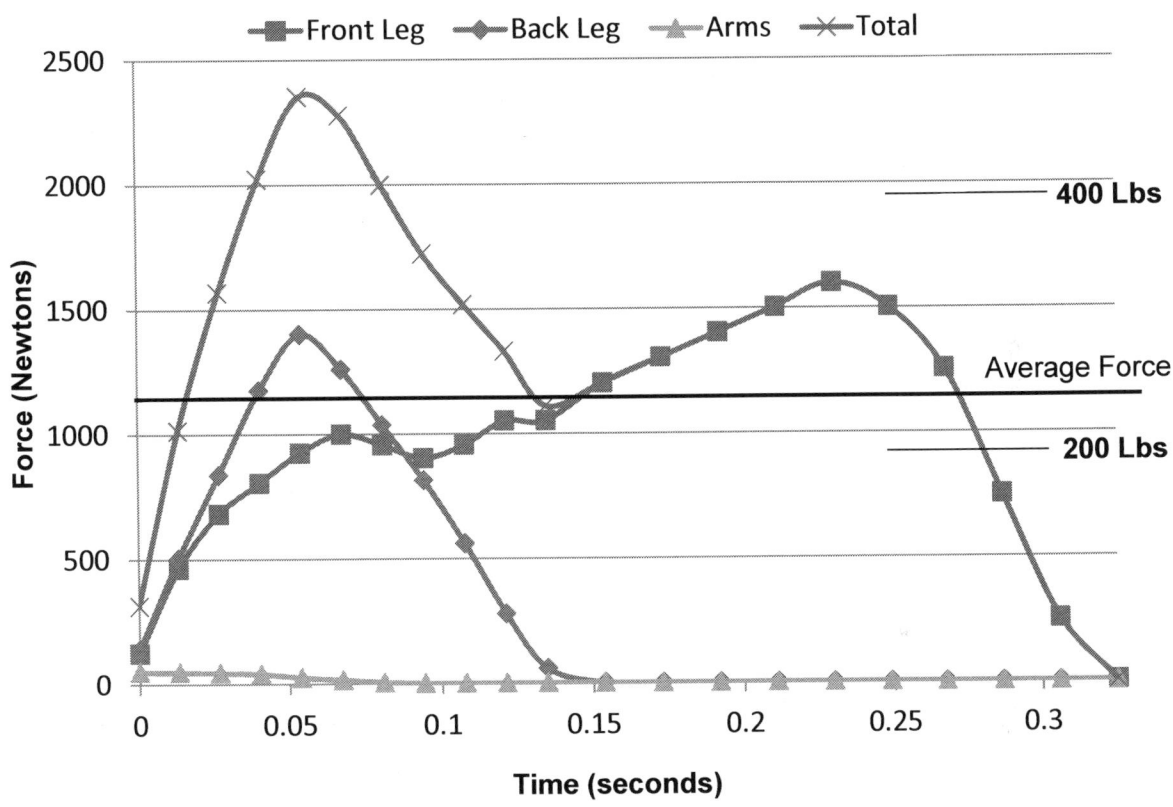

Figure 5-18: Horizontal Block Forces In The Start

Maximum Velocity: As Maximum Velocity is reached, the **change** in Horizontal Velocity is zero since the athlete cannot further increase the Sprint Speed. Thus, as shown in the equation, since the sprinter is no longer changing the Horizontal Velocity, the Horizontal force that the sprinter is producing approaches zero.

$$\text{Horizontal Force} = \text{Mass}*(0)/\text{Ground Time} = 0 \text{ Newtons (0 Pounds)}$$

The question that then must be asked is why the athlete is unable to produce additional Horizontal force and, therefore, increase the Maximum Velocity of the Sprint. The beginning of the answer lies in the actual Horizontal forces generated during ground contact.

In reality, as shown in the force platform trace of Figure 5-19, at Maximum Velocity Horizontal forces actually **are** being created by the athlete.

Horizontal Ground Force: Ground Contact

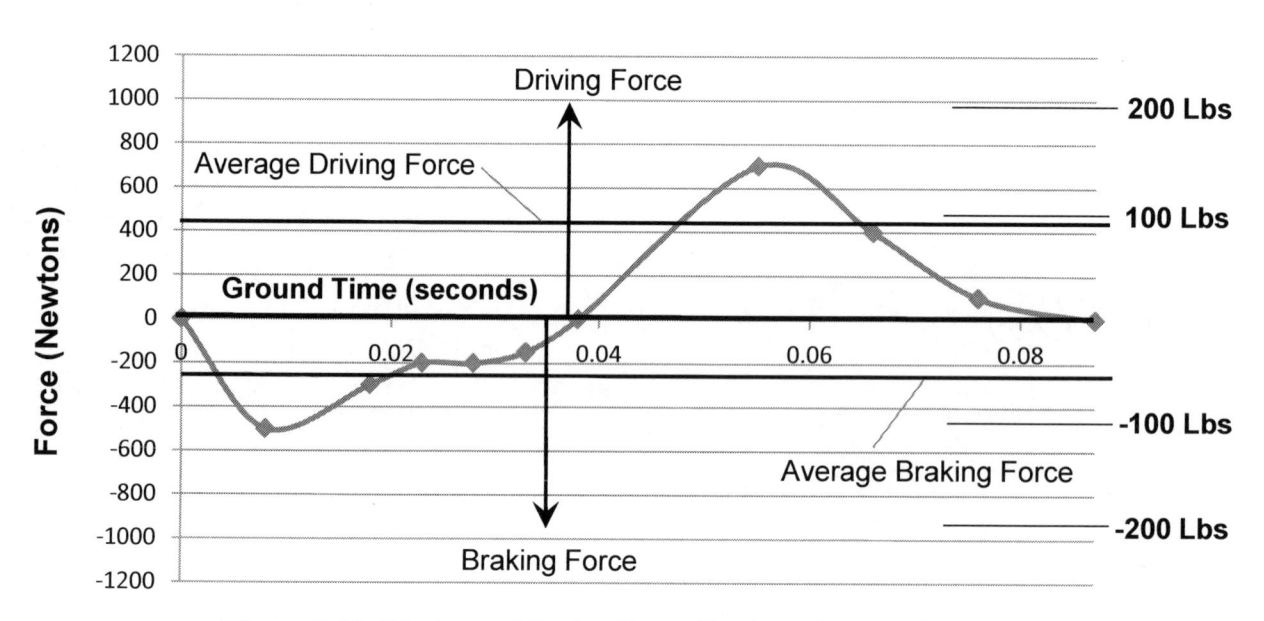

Figure 5-19: Horizontal Sprint Force During Ground Contact

For the first half of ground contact, the Horizontal force is a braking (negative) force that actually slows the sprinter. In the second half of ground contact, the Horizontal force is a driving (positive) force that more than gains back the Velocity lost during the first half. The average braking force is a meager 250 Newtons (50 Pounds), while the average driving force is around 420 Newtons (95 Pounds).

The three questions that this actual Horizontal force information immediately poses are:

1. Since, as discussed above, at Maximum Velocity the total force should be zero, why is the driving force so much higher than the braking force?
2. Why can't a powerful Sprint athlete generate more than a measly 420 Newtons (95 Pounds) of driving force?
3. Why would a sprinter want to slow themselves down by creating braking forces every time they strike the ground?

The explanation as to why the driving force must be higher than the braking force is simply due to the fact that, in addition to balancing the braking force, the athlete must also overcome the forces created due to wind resistance. Even if the Sprint race is run without any wind reading, since the elite Sprint athlete is moving at over 12 meters per second (100 Men), they are crashing into the stationary air molecules at 12 meters per second.

Using the complex equations for drag forces in this situation, the wind resistance creates a constant braking force of about 35 Newtons (8 Pounds) on the typical elite sprinter. Thus, the higher driving force exerted during the second half of ground contact must be greater to counteract the combined braking forces due to wind resistance **and** the braking force produced during the first half of ground contact.

Although the calculations for the wind forces created on the body during the Sprint are not presented herein, it should be noted that the force is increased (or decreased) by the square of the speed that the athlete hits the air molecules. Thus, if the wind resistance increases from 12 to 24 meters per second (running into a 12 meter per second wind), the braking force would increase from 35 Newtons (8 Pounds) to 130 Newtons (30 Pounds). This is why all sprinters hate to run into a headwind (and love to run with the wind).

Finally, the reason why an athlete cannot produce more driving force (and run faster when at Maximum Velocity), as well as why there is an apparent waste of Horizontal force (braking at Touchdown) is discussed in the next section.

Vertical Force

In the Sprint race, since the Vertical movement of the body is measured in a few centimeters, it makes sense that this direction would play a minor part in performance. In reality, the exact opposite is the case.

The Start: Although the body center (COG) is only raised about 0.6 meters (≈2 feet) during the .50 seconds of ground contact, to accomplish this Vertical Velocity change must average 2.0 meters/second during the three Start Ground Phases. Thus, the average Vertical Force is:

$$\text{Vertical Force} = 77.5*(2.0)/.50 = 310 \text{ Newtons (70 Pounds)}$$

Although this force is not the same magnitude of the Horizontal Start force, the tally is not complete. As shown in Figure 5-20, the actual Vertical force generated during the block phase is much greater than 310 Newtons. In fact, as can be seen, the average force is over 1000 Newtons.

This higher than expected result is necessary because the Earth's gravitational attraction requires that, while simply standing on the Earth, a person must exert a Vertical force equal to their body weight simply to support themselves. Thus, the total Vertical force that the sprinter must exert during the Start must include the effort required to support the sprinter's own body weight. Thus, assuming the sprinter weighs 760 Newtons (170 Pounds), the average Vertical force during **each** ground contact during the Start would be:

Total Vertical Force = 310+760 Newtons = 1070 Newtons (240 Pounds)

Thus, in reality, the actual Vertical demands of the Start are virtually the same as the Horizontal, which is a startling revision of conventional coaching belief. And, as will be seen, as Maximum Velocity is achieved the Vertical emphasis shift becomes even greater.

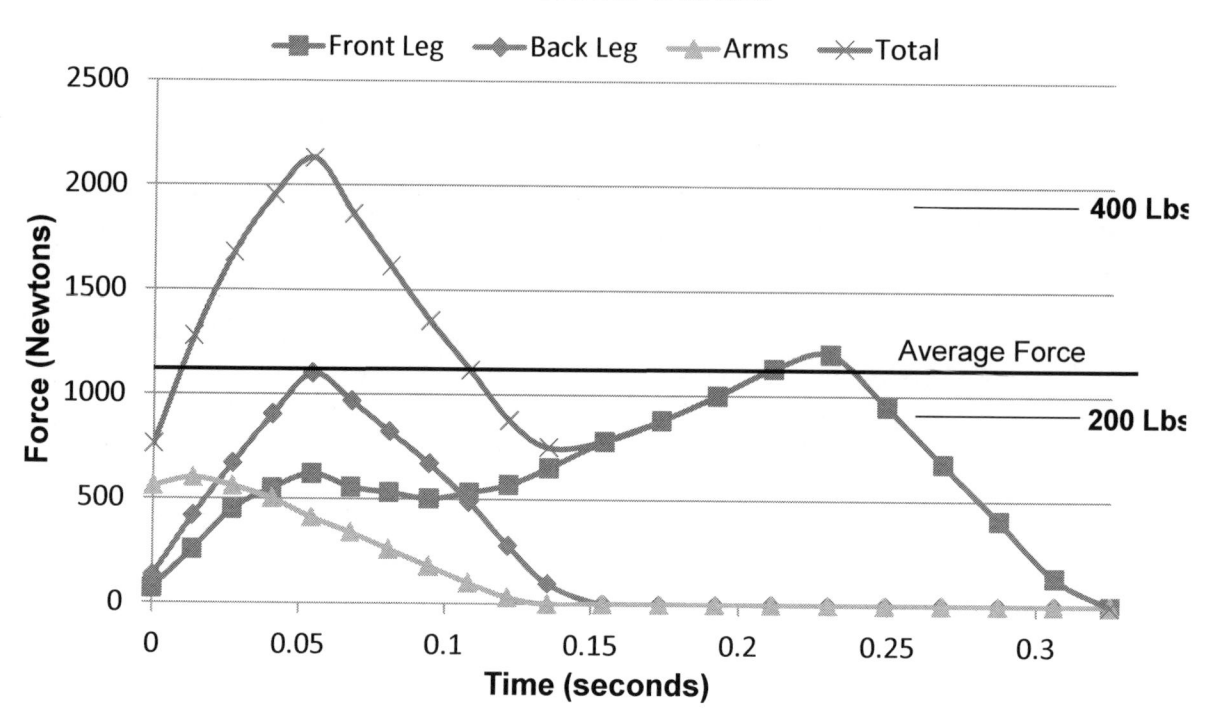

Figure 5-20: Vertical Block Force

As in the Horizontal direction, since the arms are in contact with the ground at the beginning of the Start, they also produce a beneficial force during the first portion of the movement. In contrast, however, the magnitude of this force is large enough to make a significant contribution.

Maximum Velocity: Although the force demands in the Horizontal direction decrease as Maximum Velocity is attained, there are no similar decrements in the force requirements in the Vertical direction.

Due to the presence of gravity, the Sprint action must consist of a series of alternating Ground and Air Phases. To accomplish this, the sprinter must increase the Vertical Velocity of the body to a value of approximately 0.5 meters per second (≈1.6 feet per second) upward at the point where the foot leaves the ground. Then, during the Air Phase, gravitational pull rapidly reverses the sprinter's upward Velocity and, as Touchdown once again occurs, the performer's Vertical Velocity has been altered to approximately 0.5 meters per second downward. During the ensuing Ground Phase, the sprinter must reverse this downward Velocity to again produce the 0.5 meters per second upward Velocity as the next Takeoff position is achieved. Thus, at maximum Sprint Velocity, although the Horizontal Velocity is not changing, the Vertical Velocity is changing at the rate of 1.0 meter per second (from 0.5 meters per second downward to 0.5 meters per second upward) during each ground contact phase.

Realizing that the Ground Time at Maximum Velocity is approximately .087 seconds for an elite sprinter, the amount of Vertical force that the athlete must produce to make a change of 1.0 meter per second during ground contact can be calculated at:

Vertical Force = 77.5*(1.0)/.087 = 890 Newtons (200 Pounds)

Thus, throughout the **entire** Maximum Velocity portion of the Sprint race, a large Vertical effort must be produced to project the body into the air. Now, if this were the only demand that gravity extracted from the sprinter, the world record would be under eight seconds. Unfortunately, as with the Start, gravitational attraction requires that the sprinter must also support their body weight.

Thus, the total Vertical force that the sprinter must exert to stop the downward Velocity and produce the upward Velocity to project the body into the next Air Phase must include the effort required to support the sprinter's own body weight. Thus, assuming the sprinter weighs 760 Newtons (170 Pounds), the total Vertical force during **each** ground contact would be:

Total Vertical Force = 890+760 Newtons = 1650 Newtons (370 Pounds)

As can be seen, the Vertical force demands upon the sprinter are impressive. In fact, when compared with the Horizontal forces created at Maximum Velocity, the Vertical force is about ten times greater. Upon closer inspection, it becomes evident why this demand is the major limiting element in Sprint performance.

To understand the unique problems presented to the sprinter in their attempt to produce this Vertical force, the limitations of the body's force production capabilities must be examined. As can be seen in the results measured by a force platform (Figure 5-21), due to mechanical efficiency and body position, an athlete is unable to produce a level, steady Vertical force during ground contact. Thus, if an average Vertical force of 1650 Newtons is required (as in the example), the force must be achieved by producing large values during certain phases of the Ground Phase to compensate for other portions where the Vertical force potential is lower. Thus, this situation actually demands that the athlete be able to produce a maximum Vertical force that is significantly greater than the average force required.

The Vertical demand becomes more apparent when it is realized that, during the 100 meter Sprint, the athlete must complete approximately 50 strides; each demanding a Vertical force that is at the limit of the athlete's capability. It is evident that, with these repetitive demands, fatigue will play a factor in even the shortest of the Sprint races. If this conclusion can be made for the shortest Sprint, then the problems these demands place upon the longer Sprints are even more severe.

Vertical Ground Forces: Ground Contact

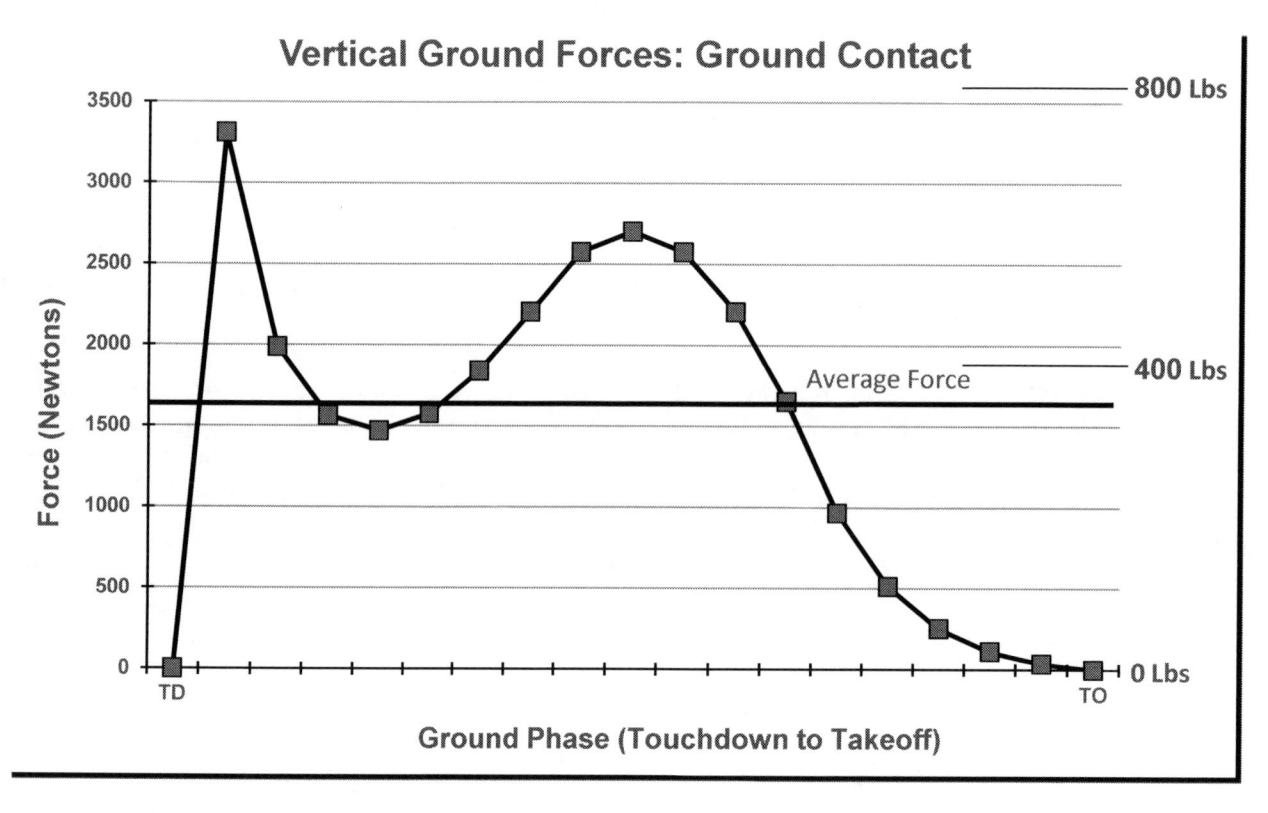

Figure 5-21: Vertical Ground Force During Ground Contact

The second problem is that, in the production of Vertical force, the athlete must deal with the magnitude of segment Velocity. As the Horizontal Velocity increases, the speed of the involved body segments increases. As discussed previously (see Figure 1-1a), if any of these high speed segment actions happen to be concentric in nature, the athlete will find it more and more difficult to produce the required forces since this high segment Velocity effectively decreases the concentric Vertical force potential of the performer.

Adding to the athlete's problems, the body position that the sprinter must assume to produce the required Vertical forces result in the production of unwanted braking forces in the Horizontal direction. As seen in Figure 5-22, to generate the range of motion required to produce the Vertical forces, the athlete is required to contact the ground with the foot in front of the body Center of Gravity (COG). Any time the foot position is placed in front of the COG (during the first half of the ground contact), it produces Horizontal braking forces. Since the athlete must endeavor to maintain maximum Horizontal Velocity, the sprinter is forced to produce a driving force during the second portion of ground contact to regain the Horizontal Velocity lost during the first half of ground contact. Thus, this is the reason why the Horizontal forces (both braking and driving), as previously shown in Figure 5-19, must be generated.

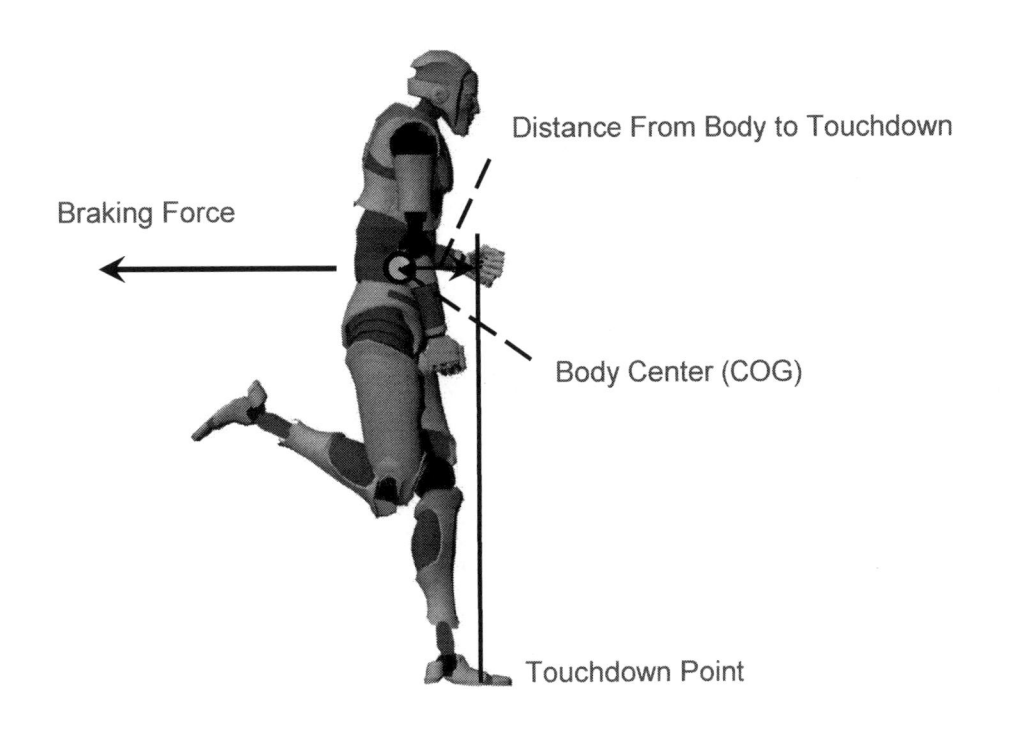

Figure 5-22: Horizontal Braking Forces at Touchdown

In summary, the forces generated in the entire Sprint are shown in Table 5-1:

	Lateral	Horizontal	Vertical	Total
Start	0 N (0 lbs)	1085 N (243 lbs)	1070 N (240 lbs)	1525 N (340 lbs)
Transition	0 N (0 lbs)			
Max Velocity	0 N (0 lbs)	0 N (0 lbs)*	1650 N (370 lbs)	1650 N (370 lbs)

*This force oscillates from braking to driving, which results in an average force of 0 Newtons

Table 5-1: Sprint Forces Generated in the Elite Sprint

This force chart points to three major conclusions:

1. **The sprinter has a finite amount of total force to work with. For elite 100 meter male sprinters, this force potential is about 1525-1650 Newtons (340-370 Pounds).**

2. **As long as the Vertical force demands of the Sprint are less than the total force, the sprinter can increase the Horizontal Velocity. This is possible during the Start and Transition.**
3. **Once the Vertical force demands reach the total available, the Maximum Velocity of the sprinter has been reached. Essentially, at this point, since all of the available force is needed in the Vertical direction, nothing is left to use in the Horizontal direction.**

Thus, the limiting element determining how fast an athlete can Sprint is the amount of total force that can be developed, and the Vertical force demands of the sprinter.

The Limitations of Force Production

The consequences of generating greater force can be demonstrated by assuming that a sprinter could actually decrease the ground contact to half of what is typical for an elite sprinter (from .087 to .045). To achieve this feat, which would increase the Horizontal Velocity by 30 percent, the Vertical force requirement would be:

$$\text{Vertical Force} = \text{Mass} * (\text{Change in Vertical Velocity}) / \text{Time}$$

and inserting the values:

$$\text{Vertical Force} = 77.5 * (1.0) / .045 = 1600 \text{ Newtons (360 Pounds)}$$

Finally, again assuming the athlete weighs 760 Newtons (170 Pounds), the total Vertical force would be:

$$\text{Total Vertical Force} = 1600 + 760 = 2360 \text{ Newtons (530 Pounds)}$$

It is evident that no Sprint athlete can currently produce this level of force production in such a small amount of time. However, an increase in force production is the way in which athletes have improved the performance times over the years.

There are a number of ways to increase the force potential in an athlete. The most common and effective way is to train the static, dynamic, and elastic(?) strength potentials of the performer. The research performed in the US High Performance Program has shown this to be a major performance enhancer.

Large amounts of Vertical force can also be quickly generated by having the athlete jam the landing leg vigorously into the ground at Touchdown, vaulting the body over the rigid segment as is successfully done in the high jump. This process is actually utilized by poorly trained sprinters, as well as by all sprinters as fatigue sets in. Unfortunately, this process generates large Horizontal forces that make it a major detriment to Sprint performance.

Finally, excellent Sprint Mechanics will ensure that all of the available Vertical force that the athlete can produce is effectively directed in the proper direction during ground contact.

The Available Total Force

In summary, a sprinter's ability to produce Horizontal Velocity is directly related to their ability to exceed the Vertical force demands of the activity. In both the Start and Maximum Velocity sections, it was concluded that the Vertical Velocity demands placed on the athlete are unavoidable. In the Start, Vertical force is required to raise the body to an upright position, support the body weight, and complete this action as quickly as possible. This is something that **must** be done, and cannot be avoided.

Likewise, at Maximum Velocity, Vertical force is required to stop the body's downward Velocity at Touchdown, launch the athlete in the air, and complete this action as quickly as possible. As in the Start, this is something that **must** be done and, again, cannot be avoided.

So, the difference between the Vertical demands of the Sprint, and the athlete's maximum force potential will result in their ability to produce Horizontal Velocity. Table 5-1 presented the forces (Lateral, Horizontal, Vertical, and Total) required for a world class Sprint performance. In contrast, Table 5-2 shows the force demands for a performance that is ten percent slower (a 10.45 second 100 meters for Men, or an 11.55 second 100 meters for Women).

	Lateral	Horizontal	Vertical	Total
Start	0 N (0 lbs)	904 N (199 lbs)	1008 N (221 lbs)	1353 N (298 lbs)
Transition	0 N (0 lbs)			
Max Velocity	0 N (0 lbs)	0 N (0 lbs)*	1476 N (324 lbs)	1476 N (324 lbs)

*This force oscillates from braking to driving, which results in an average force of 0 Newtons

Table 5-2: Sprint Forces Generated in the Non-Elite Sprint

In comparing the two performances (Table 5-1 and Table 5-2), note four major conclusions:

1. The Total Force difference is relatively small (172 Newtons (39 Pounds)) in the Start and at Maximum Velocity (174 Newtons (40 Pounds)). Thus, a small increase (or decrease) in an athlete's force levels can make a significant difference in performance.
2. The majority (75%) of the force decrement in the Start comes from the Horizontal direction. Since the Vertical force demands remain fairly constant, the only option is for the decrease in force to come from the Horizontal direction. Thus, the Non-Elite sprinter has a much less productive first three steps than the Elite performer.
3. Since the Horizontal force is balanced at zero at Maximum Velocity, the entire force decrement has to come from the Vertical direction. Thus, the Non-Elite sprinter runs out of the ability to produce sufficient force to cover the Vertical demands much sooner than the Elite sprinter. The result is that the poorer sprinter loses the ability to generate Horizontal force sooner that the Elite sprinter (it's all going to the Vertical direction), resulting in a lower top speed.
4. Due to poor Mechanics, the Braking/Driving forces are higher for the Non-Elite sprinter. This still results in an average Horizontal force of zero, but the greater effort required to generate these higher forces takes a toll on the Non-Elite athlete.

A lower Total Force production is not the only factor involved in producing a decrease in Sprint performance. An athlete can also lose productivity if they waste their available forces in an inefficient manner. This can take the form of wasting forces in the Lateral direction by moving the body sideways down the track, over-producing Vertical forces by projecting the body too high in the air, or generating excessive Horizontal braking forces at Touchdown. All of these problems are Mechanics based issues that can be devastating to a Sprint performance.

Special Topics

The Unavoidable Sprint Issues

From the discussion, it would seem that the way to improve performance would simply be to increase force production (get stronger) and run more efficiently. However, there are several additional Sprint Issues that are unavoidable, and must be confronted by all performers and their coach.

(1) The Importance of the Start Issue

The question must be asked, given the small amount of time the Start consumes during any Sprint race, just how important can it be? The fact is, what happens during the Start affects far more than just the first three steps of the race.

To demonstrate this, take the example of two athletes, with the exact abilities in all aspects of the 100 meter Sprint, with the exception of the Start. As shown in Figure 5-23, Athlete A has a more explosive Start, and reaches the end of the Start in 0.70 seconds at a Velocity of 7 meters per second.

In contrast, Athlete B has a poor Start, and reaches the end of the Start in 1.00 second at a Velocity of 5 meters per second.

Now, at this point in the race, it is obvious that Athlete A has a 0.3 seconds advantage over Athlete B. This may be impressive, but this is only the beginning. If, from the end of the Start to the finish, both Athletes accelerate at the same rate, reach the same Maximum Velocity, and perform identically in all respects, Athlete A will gain an even greater advantage over Athlete B by the time they both reach top Speed.

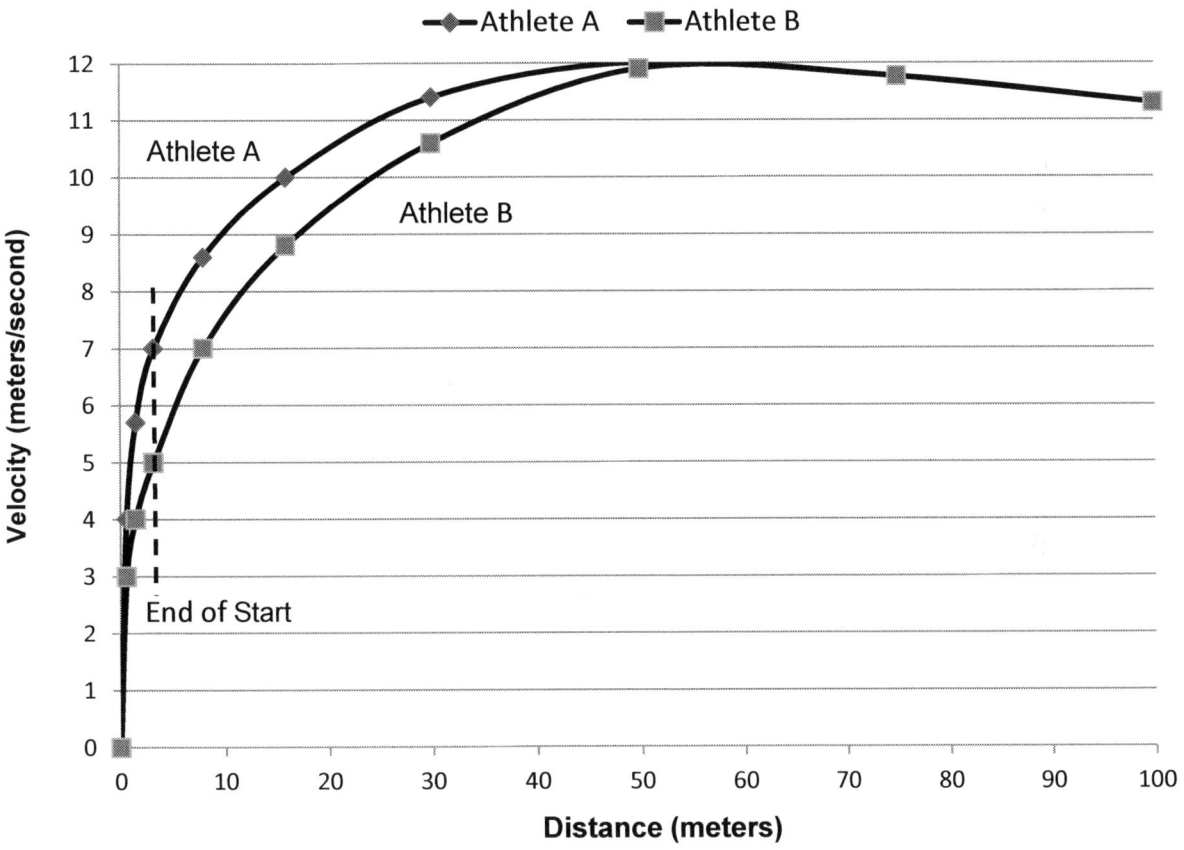

Figure 5-23: Effects of The Start on Horizontal Velocity in the Men's 100 Meters

As Figure 5-23 demonstrates, Athlete A has a Velocity advantage of 2 meters per second (7-5=2) at the end of the Start, and that advantage continues until Athlete B finally matches his opponent's Velocity at around the 60 meter mark. So, for more than half the race, Athlete A maintained a Velocity advantage that was generated during the brief Start time. So, at the end of the Start, Athlete A would be moving away from Athlete B at a rate of 2 meters per second. Although, as the Figure shows, this advantage decreases until both Athlete's velocities finally match at about 60 meters, **for more than half the race, Athlete A is moving away from Athlete B**. In this case, this would give athlete A an additional 0.7 second lead on Athlete B.

Thus, two athletes possessing the same abilities in everything but the Start, end up with final times that are a full second apart. It is difficult to believe that the Start has the ability to effect such major performance changes, but this is the reality. Any athlete that falls behind in the Start will be playing "catch-up" for the rest of the race.

(2) The Jump Start Verses the Shuffle Start Issue

There are two Start factions in Track: one that advocates a powerful, explosive start that seeks to jump out and make the steps as long as possible (Jump Start), and one that believes that the action should be a quick turnover action that makes the steps as short as possible (Shuffle Start).

In fact, both Starts can be effective. However, as is true with all human movements, the best way is always the one that is the MOST effective. In this case, **the Shuffle Start holds the definite advantage** due to the following reasons:

1. **Short Air Time**: Since force can only be applied when the athlete is in contact with the ground, the Start with the shortest Air Time (Shuffle Start) has a distinct advantage.
2. **More Effective Push Time**: Physics dictates that the athlete can best accelerate down the track when point of force application on the track is behind the Body COG. Since the Shuffle Start Touchdown position allows the athlete to achieve this goal throughout the Start, it allows the sprinter to apply effective Horizontal force as soon as ground contact occurs. In contrast, all Jump Start landings occur with the foot in front of the Body.
3. **Front Side Mechanics**: The emphasis on quick turnover dictates that the Shuffle Start must keep the legs in front of the body, and avoid any form of excessive push at Takeoff. This drives the body into Front Side Mechanics, which makes the transition to Maximum Velocity sprinting a seamless process. With emphasis on pushing off the blocks as long as possible, the Jump Start places the body into the unwanted Backside Sprint Mechanics position

(3) The Seven Step Hurdle Start Issue

For the past few years, most of the top Men and a few of the top Women in the Short Hurdle event have moved from the traditional eight step start to a seven step approach to the first hurdle. This change was driven by the fact that, as both races have become faster and faster, these athletes simply could not effectively get eight steps into the mandated distance. Since hurdlers recognize the importance of aggressively attacking the first barrier, and the task of jamming eight steps into the distance prior to the first hurdle compromised this goal, a change needed to be made.

For the traditional eight step start, the Mechanics of the Sprint Start is a perfect fit. For the seven step approach, however, some major changes must be made to the start Mechanics.

Stride Length: Since the distance to the first hurdle is a fixed number (13.72 meters for Men, 13.0 meters for Women), the Stride Lengths needed to reach the first hurdle are, except for small differences in block settings and Hurdle Takeoff distance, the same for all athletes. Thus, whether a hurdler is big or small in body height, long or short in leg length, or strong or weak in force production, the Stride Length demands are exactly the same. With the added fact that the lengths required to properly reach the first barrier are difficult for any size athlete, successfully incorporating this start into the Short Hurdle race is a daunting task.

Figure 5-24 identifies the Stride Length results that are being used by those elite hurdlers that have successfully incorporated the seven step pattern into their race.

Stride Lengths: Seven Step Hurdle Start

Step	Men	Women
Step 1	.76*	.71*
Step 2	1.42	1.35
Step 3	1.63	1.57
Step 4	1.78	1.70
Step 5	1.93	1.83
Step 6	2.08	1.98
Step 7	2.01	1.90

Critical Zone: Steps 1–3

* Measured from Starting line

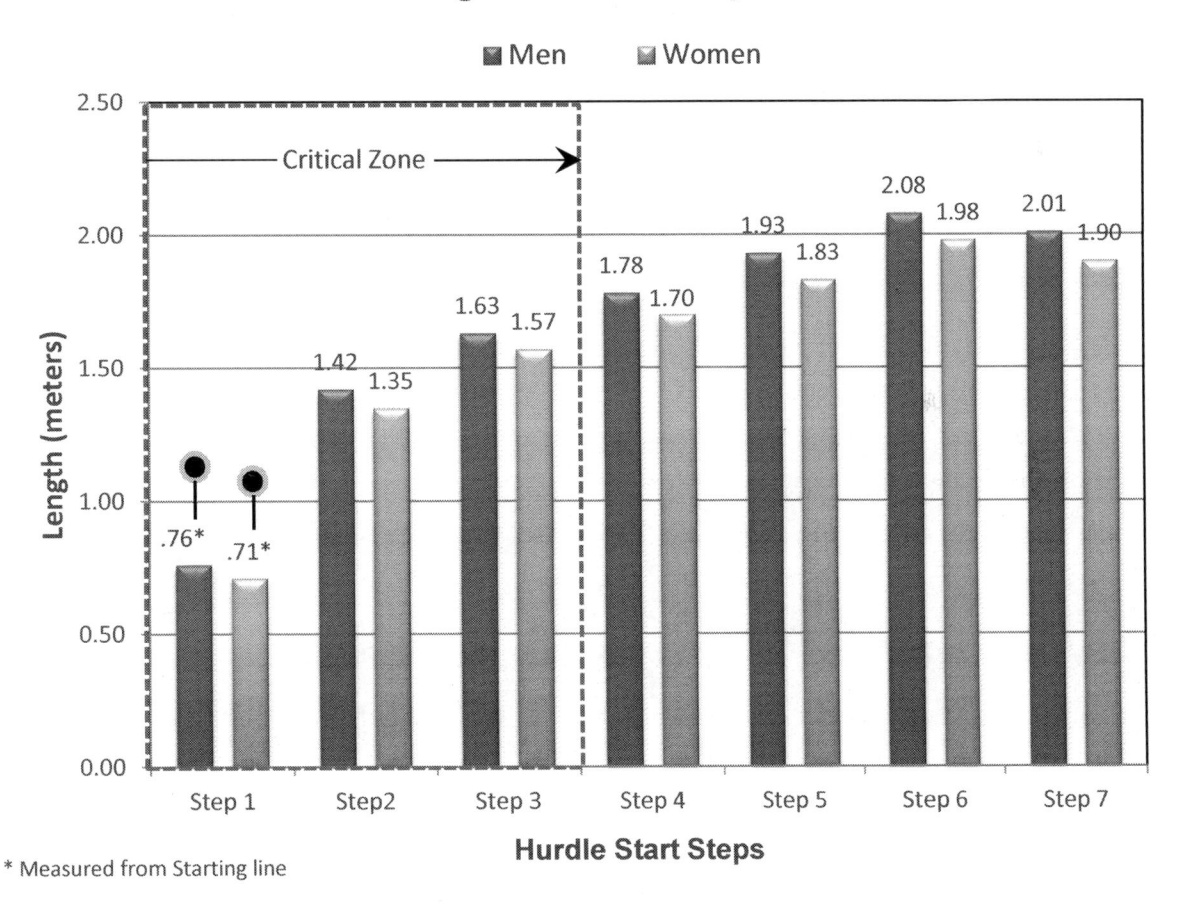

Figure 5-24: Stride Lengths for the Seven Step Hurdle Start

Note that Step One is measured from the Starting line, so the actual Stride Length is this length added to the distance from the Front Block to the Line (in the Figure, the total Length is identified by a dot (●)). Because Step One is so difficult to reach, when an athlete initially begins using this Start they tend to begin with the Front Block closer to the Line (as little as .28 meters). This crowded position creates several negative performance issues, however, since reaching the proper Stride Length is the most important goal, these sacrifices must be made. Later, when they become more proficient, they begin moving the block back toward the standard Sprint Start distance (about .50 meters).

Experience has shown that the critical zone for **successfully** performing this Start lies in the first three Steps (see the Figure). If the male hurdler cannot reach a mark set at 3.81 meters (3.63 for Women) from the Starting line on their third Step, they will not be able to land in the right place to properly attack the first barrier. Either they will have to over stride more than is already required, or they will land too far from the hurdle on Step Seven.

Figure 5-24 also shows that Step Seven is shorter than Step Six. This is necessary because, like all jumping events, the penultimate stride into the jump needs to be shorter than the rest of the approach strides.

Start Mechanics: Although some of the goals of the Shuffle Start, like quick turnover and short Ground Time, need to be modified to generate the necessary Stride Lengths, all of the Sprint Start Mechanics concepts are retained. As shown in Figure 7-24, in comparison to the Sprint Start, as the hurdler clears the Blocks the Stride Length is increased by producing a slightly larger total body Vertical emphasis while allowing the trunk to extend more, the recovery upper leg to flex more, the recovery leg toe to come through higher, and the Ground Leg to extend more.

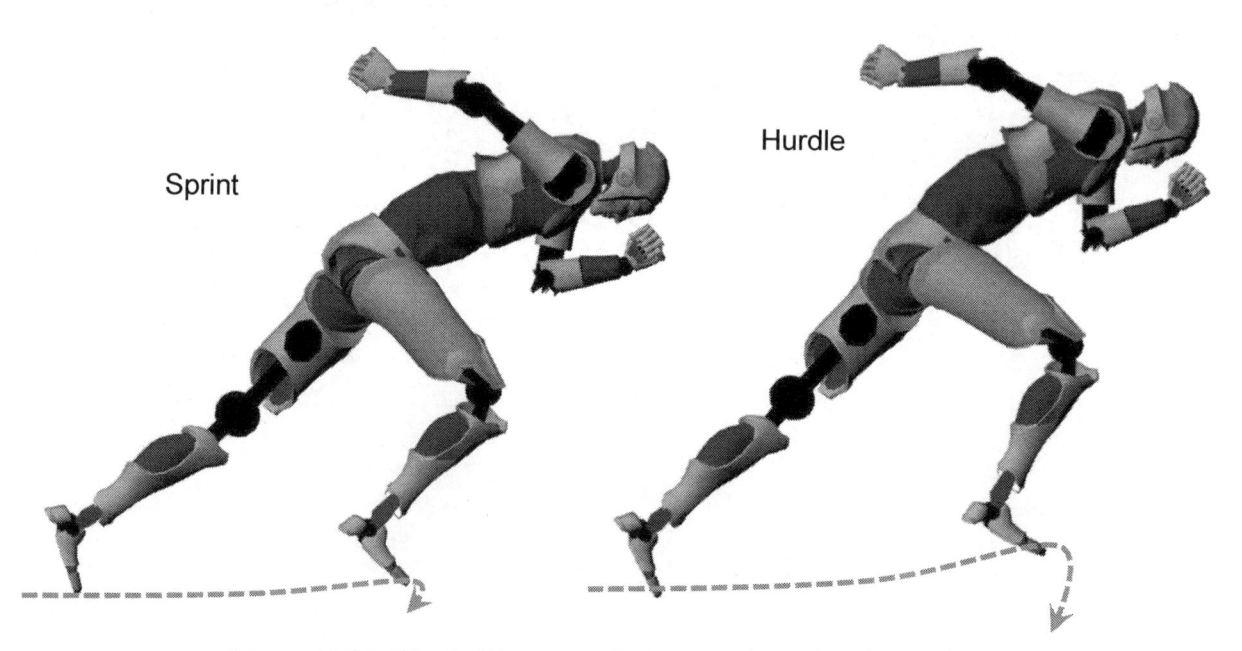

Figure 7-24: Block Clearance Stride Lengths for the Sprint Start and the Seven Step Hurdle Start

What doesn't change are the tendencies of the better performers to keep the trunk more flexed, the lower leg more extended during recovery, and the recovery leg toe lower to the ground while following a low-to-high path. These actions conclude with the Lead Leg toe driving down and back as Touchdown occurs, which places the Touchdown position closer to the Body COG.

These same modifications, from trunk position to foot Touchdown position, are seen in the remaining Steps of the Seven Step Hurdle Start. In fact, experience has shown that the only successful way to effectively perform this demanding Start is to utilize the approach described herein.

Selecting the Challenge: Due to the fact that virtually every one of the top caliber elite Men's 110 Meter Hurdlers, and more and more of the Women's 100 Meter Hurdlers, are moving to this Start, the big question is always "when does a hurdler switch from eight to seven steps?". The best answer is that the athlete will know when it is time. When they complain that they simply can't get eight steps into the first barrier without chopping every step, then they are ready. However, wanting to do this Start simply "because all the good ones do it" is not reason enough. Since this Start demands such a high level of mechanical and power proficiency, only those male athletes that have these capabilities, and are running under 13.5 seconds (12.7 for Women), have had success in incorporating this into their race.

(4) The Ground Time Issue

In the example above, it was assumed that an elite sprinter could actually produce a ground contact time of .045 seconds, which would produce a Stride Rate of almost 6 steps per second. However, in the more than 30 years of collecting data on sprinters, no sprinter (male or female) has ever produced a ground contact time of less than .075 seconds, or a **legitimate** Stride Rate of more than 5.1 steps per second. This may simply be due to the fact that the next super-elite athlete has not come along, or that the development of dynamic force on the track and/or in the weight room has not been maximized. Whatever the answer may be, the fact is that this Ground Time barrier of .075 seconds has become a real issue.

There is one solution to this problem, one that the current world record holder in the Men's Short Sprints used to redefine the event. The simple fact that tall sprinters with long legs naturally have lower Stride Rates (and longer Stride Lengths) gives them a distinct advantage in solving this Ground Time issue. In his world record 100 meter performance, the 1.95 meter (77 inches), long legged Usain Bolt produced a Ground Time of .092 seconds and a Stride Rate of 4.65 steps per second at Maximum Velocity. Although this Ground Time is well short of the .075 second barrier, for the average 1.77 meter (70 inches) typical leg length 100 meter male sprinter to match these numbers they would have to produce a Ground Time of .075 seconds and a Stride Rate of over 5.2 steps per second.

Thus, tall long legged sprinters have a distinct advantage in avoiding this Ground Time barrier. Sprinters of average or short stature, however, have a real problem. In fact, this issue effectively eliminates sprinters of less than 1.72 meters (68 inches) from ever reaching world record levels in the Men's Short Sprint races. For Women, the same restrictions come into play for sprinters of less than 1.60 meters (63 inches).

(5) The Air Time Issue

Early on in the research effort into Sprinting it became apparent that, since there was no difference in Air Times between elite and non-elite sprinters, it was not a viable means to alter performance. It is true that some sprinters have long or short Air Times, however, either direction has drawbacks that make it a poor choice for improvement:

1. **Long Air Time**: Increasing Air Time does increase Stride Length which, if everything else remains the same, will increase Velocity. Unfortunately, this change also unavoidably decreases Stride Rate, which is the most critical Mechanical factor in Sprint improvement. Research has shown, time and time again, that this is not the way to improve performance. The reasons behind this conclusion will be discussed in subsequent Chapters.
2. **Short Air Time**: If decreasing Stride Rate is the key to improvement, then it seems reasonable to conclude that a short Air Time should be the goal. In fact, this is exactly the case. Unfortunately, this approach can only be taken so far until further decreases begin affecting the athlete's ability to produce the proper Sprint Mechanics. For the Short Sprint this time is 0.123 seconds, while for the Long Sprint it increases slightly due to the fatigue factor.

Thus, the goal for Air Time should be to decrease it as long as Mechanics can be maintained. The problem comes when the idea of emphasizing Stride Rate leads to shortening this time just to drive down Rate. Stride Rates as high as 5.3 Steps per Second have been measured, but only due to an Air Time that had been reduced to the point where overall performance was compromised.

(6) The Stride Length Issue

With the commendable emphasis toward improving Sprint Mechanics and emphasizing Stride Rate, coaches have helped their athletes to drive the records lower and lower. In fact, elite sprinters are closing in on the inevitable problem of producing excellent Mechanics and Stride Rate results and still being unable to dominate their event.

It is not an issue of the inability to reach elite status with excellence in these two areas, but rather in reaching the top of the podium. So, in cases where significant additional improvements in Mechanics and Rate become difficult, the focus must begin to shift toward Stride Length. This poses a myriad of problems since the most obvious ways to increase Length is to increase Air Time, reach out farther at Touchdown, or push longer at Takeoff; all of which decrease Stride Rate and the quality of Mechanics. Since neither of possibilities these can be used, it comes down to **improving Length by getting more Horizontal projection out of the time spent on the ground.**

One tendency that is often present in athletes that emphasize Stride Rate is their inclination to project Vertically, rather than Horizontally, during ground contact. This emphasis gives the visual impression that they are "running in place". Coaches have developed excellent drills, concepts, and teaching strategies to produce high Stride Rates, now they need to do the same for Stride Lengths. The real challenge will be to develop this improved Length without decreasing Rate or compromising Mechanics.

(7) Tempo Training Issue

One focus that has been lacking in Sprint training has been Maximum Speed tempo training, with the focus on properly developing Stride Rate as well as Stride Length.

Stride Rate: Since Stride Rate is recognized as the key to improving Sprint performance, most programs utilize drills to develop this variable. What isn't being done, however, is pushing athletes to produce high Stride Rates while moving at top speed. Sprint training runs need to be developed that drive sprinters to 1) generate a goal of five steps per second (Men and Women) while at maximum effort, while 2) maintaining proper Sprint Mechanics, with immediate feedback on the success of reaching these two goals.

Stride Length: Since Stride Length is recognized as **not** being the key to improving Sprint performance, most programs do little to develop this variable. As discussed previously (see (6)), the Length component is beginning to receive greater emphasis. However, if Stride Length is to become a focus of change, **it can only be done successfully if improvement is done by exerting greater Horizontal Force during the Ground Phase**. In doing so, it is critical to insure that neither Air Time nor Mechanics are altered in this process.

Thus, Sprint training runs need to be developed that drive sprinters to 1) generate a goal of matching their Model Stride Length (if unavailable, use the results presented in Figure 8-3) while at maximum effort, while 2) maintaining proper Air Time and Sprint Mechanics, with immediate feedback on the success of reaching these two goals.

(8) Practice Velocity Verses Competition Velocity Issue

With an enormous base of data on elite Sprinters, both in practice and competition, it has become evident that the only time an athlete can produce maximum Horizontal Velocity is in a high stress competitive environment. In fact, the typical elite sprinter can only generate between 92 to 95 percent of their Maximum Velocity in any practice session. Thus, whether the training goal is the development of Maximum Velocity, or preparing the ability to handle multiple Maximum Velocity rounds in a Championship, the best place to do this is in competition.

This conclusion provides insight into why so many young athletes do well in the collegiate system, but fail to improve or even match these performance levels once they complete their eligibility. While in college, they compete in meets almost every week for six months a year, running up to three Sprint races a day, sometimes multiple days in succession. This gives them up to a hundred high intensity race intervals a year that no practice session can come close to matching. In addition, with the number of multiple races that the collegiate sprinter typically is expected to do, the sprint endurance component is also trained at the same intense levels. This type of quality training is so impactful that athletes with little or no between-meet training, or even poor coaching, can produce quality performance simply due to this training effect.

Once out of the collegiate system, an elite athlete may run in ten competitions a year, if they are lucky. In addition most of them involve, at the most, two races per meet. Thus, with an 80 percent drop in these high intensity workouts, and virtually no sprint endurance component, the athlete is at a distinct disadvantage. Unless they are lucky enough to find (or retain) a good coach, their performances will decline.

Good coaches must recognize the major training effect that competitions provide, and adjust their practice sessions accordingly. Too often, competitions are treated as "breaks between training", when they should be recognized as the pinnacle of this process. Finally, training strategies must be developed an attempt to achieve the same type of maximal training effect that is found in competition.

(9) Foot Stabilization at Touchdown Issue

Recent research has indicated that one way successful sprinters are decreasing Ground Time, as well as making it more productive, is by taking less time to stabilize the foot once Touchdown has occurred. They are accomplishing this task by using two methods.

1. **Proper Landing Position**: To put the foot in the correct position, better sprinters are landing with the foot aligned so that they have just enough range of motion to cushion the impact. As shown in Figure 5-25, the foot is placed in just under 10 degrees of plantar flexion at Touchdown. This allows the athlete sufficient time to stop the downward fall of the body, while not allowing the heel to crash into the ground and produce large, unwanted forces.
2. **Rigid Foot Segment**: To properly handle this foot small range of motion, the sprinter must be strong enough in the muscles that control the foot motion in both plantar/dorsal flexion and inversion/eversion

This Touchdown position can only be produced, as with so many other Sprint positions, with a combination of proper Mechanics and Strength levels.

If a sprinter lands with too much plantar flexion (toe landing), then too much time is spent waiting for the foot to rotate down into a stable position. If an athlete is not strong enough they may need this much time to stabilize the foot, and will be unable to improve unless they improve their strength levels in this area. On the other hand, if the athlete has the strength but, due to poor mechanics, they land in this poor position, they are wasting time for no reason. Regardless of the cause, lack of strength or mechanics, their performance will suffer.

Likewise, if the sprinter lands with insufficient plantar flexion, they will be unable to keep the heel from slamming into the ground, resulting in the production of large unwanted forces that will not only disrupt the controlled production of Ground Forces, but also delay the stabilization of the foot. Of the two errors, too much or too little plantar flexion, this is the one to avoid.

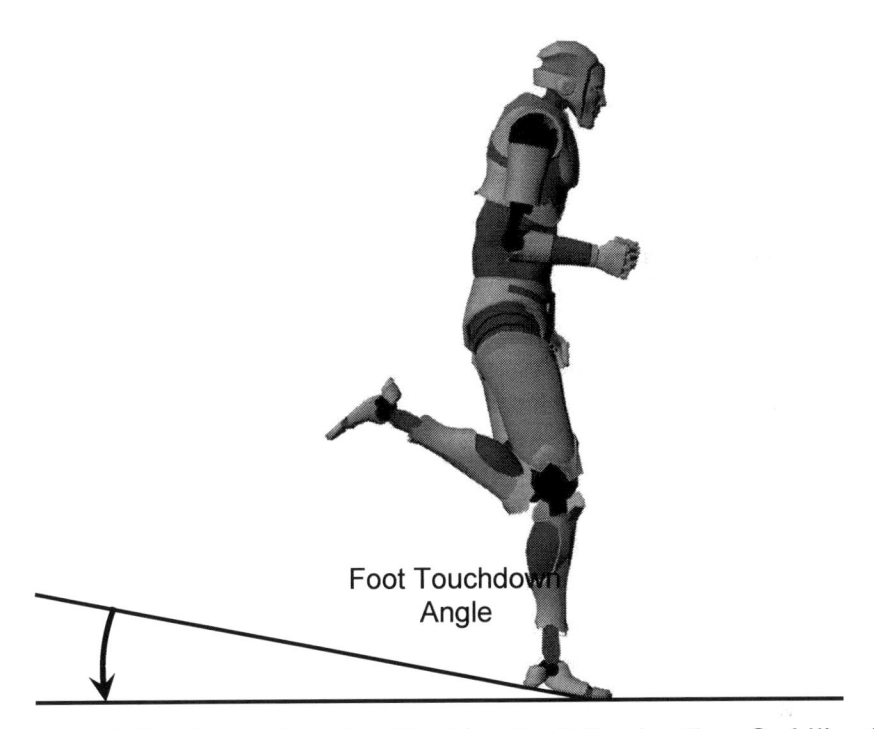

Figure 5-25: Proper Landing Position for Effective Foot Stabilization

The goal should be to develop the foot strength, especially in inversion/eversion, and then strive to decrease the amount of plantar flexion until heel strike becomes a problem.

(10) Timing the Upper and Lower Leg Action Approaching Touchdown Issue

The interaction of the upper and lower leg segments at the end of the Air Phase can affect performance positively or negatively depending on the timing of events. Suffice it to say that, as the recovery leg is swung forward, the moment when the lower leg begins its extension, it immediately produces a reaction that attempts to extend the upper leg.

If this lower leg extension begins too early, it halts the upper leg's motion as it strives to produce the sought-after "high knee" position. Instead, it produces an early upper leg extension, which drops the knee toward the track. This action, along with the early lower leg extension, presents a straight legged, heel first landing position at Touchdown. Along with a poor landing position, this action also produces poor upper leg extension and lower leg flexion velocities.

On the other hand, if the sprinter can delay the lower leg extension until the upper leg reaches the high knee position (Figure 5-26), then the lower leg extensor action will actually add to the upper leg's extension as it moves toward Touchdown. In addition, the explosive lower leg rotation will allow it to complete its extension, and allow it to begin flexion just before ground impact.

Producing this beneficial upper/lower leg action is not a matter of strength, but one of timing. If the lower leg is properly controlled, then the beneficial action occurs automatically. However, if the lower leg is allowed to begin its extension too early, no amount of leg strength will allow the athlete to avoid the unwanted early upper leg extension results.

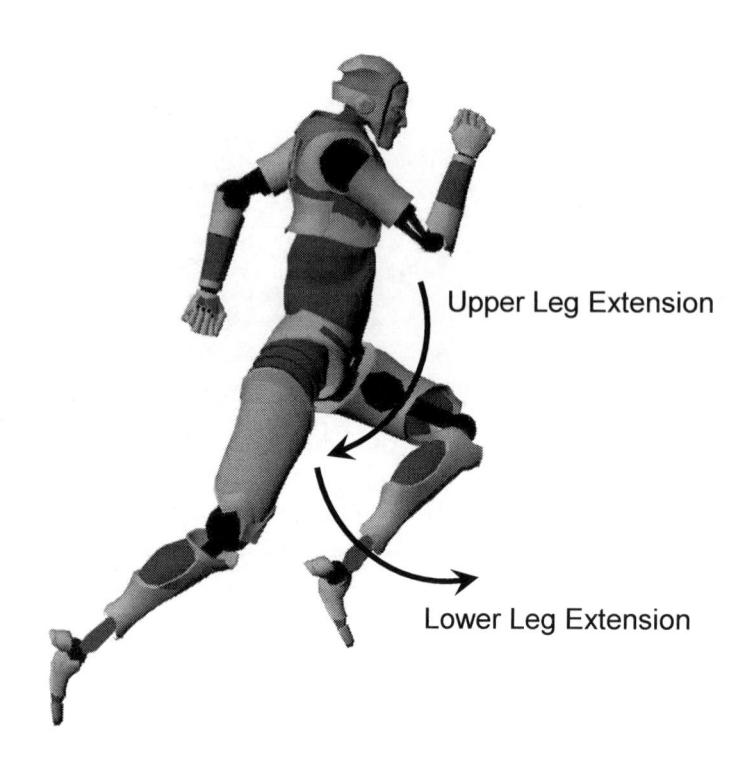

Figure 5-26: Proper Upper and Lower Leg Timing

(11) The Comfort Trap Issue

In the Long Sprints, the natural tendency for all sprinters, when they are trying to "run relaxed" or when fatigue sets in and they are struggling to get to the finish, is to reach out and jam their Touchdown leg in front of them and vault over the leg. This produces an excessively long Air Time and Stride Length, which feels "comfortable" to the athlete because this is the easiest method to get their body into the next Air Phase.

Unfortunately, this comfort feeling is also a trap because this sprinting technique produces several unwanted results:

Understanding the Sprint Performance

1. By crashing the Touchdown leg into the ground, the segment must withstand an enormous impact shock to the system, followed by a large Horizontal braking force.
2. The large braking force must be followed by a large driving force if the sprinter is to maintain their Horizontal Velocity.
3. The excessive Air Phase means that the athlete is airborne a large portion of the time, and unable to exert the ground forces required to counteract the detrimental effects of wind resistance. This large jump also means that the athlete will be falling from a greater height, which produces an even bigger crash during the next ground contact.

Besides the feeling of running comfortably, there is nothing productive about this "crash and jump" technique. The repeated shocks to the system negatively affect the nervous system, and make it less responsive when called upon. Couple this with the additional effort the athlete must exert to overcome the excessive braking forces and you have a recipe for disaster for the Long Sprint race.

Unfortunately, it is not easy for an athlete to overcome their natural tendency to crash and jump their way down the backstretch and home stretch. It takes a committed athlete to maintain their form down the backstretch, then focus on generating Stride Rate (as opposed to Length) coming home. Two of the most dominate 400 male athletes over the past 20 years, Michael Johnson and LaShawn Merritt, both developed this ability, which is one of the major reasons that made them so successful.

(12) The Weight Issue

How much weight an athlete must accelerate down the track is a much greater issue than most coaches and athletes realize. There are two situations where this issue becomes a major problem:

1. **The Overweight Athlete**: If a male sprinter is more than seven percent body fat, or a female sprinter is more than eleven percent body fat, than they are dragging too much weight down the track. In fact, the problem is much worse than was typically believed.

    Returning to the example of the Vertical Force demands of a typical 77.5 Kilogram (170 Pound) male sprinter, if the athlete becomes lazy and puts on ten percent more fat (7.75 Kilograms (17 Pounds)), then the amount of force needed to maintain the same Air Time would be:

    Vertical Force = 85.25*(1.0)/.087 = 980 Newtons (220 Pounds)

    and when you add the increased body weight (835 Newtons (187 Pounds)) into the equation, the Total Vertical Force becomes:

Total Vertical Force = 980+835 Newtons = 1815 Newtons (407 Pounds)

This points to the fact that, for this same sprinter with their added fat levels to sprint at the same elite level they achieved before they packed on the weight, they would need to generate **10 percent more Vertical Force during each ground contact** (1650 Newtons to 1815 Newtons). Now, since this additional weight was added as fat, and not muscle, there is no logical way that the athlete would be able to increase their force production. In fact, if you assume that the athlete can still produce their "pre-feasting" force levels at their new weight, then their Ground Time would go from .087 to .106 seconds, and their Stride Rate would go from 4.76 to 4.37 steps per second. This would drop the performance from world record level to that of a Poor quality elite athlete, simply due to the fact that **the sprinter added body weight that did not contribute to their ability to generate force**.

2. **The Bulked Up Athlete**: If an athlete adds body weight by adding muscle mass, it must be remembered that **for every one pound of muscle added to the body, two pounds of additional ground force is needed to offset the weight gain** for performance to improve. Thus, the goal of any strength improvement program must be to maximize the power of the lower body while minimizing the weight gain from adding additional muscle mass.

The biggest strength program mistake that athletes make is by bulking up the upper body. Adding ten pounds to the chest and arms by increasing their bench press levels may be aesthetically pleasing, but since this added weight is almost as worthless as putting on body fat, the resulting performance decrement is just a devastating. Physics doesn't care if the additional weight comes from muscle or fat; if the gain is not offset by additional force gains exerted on the ground then the performance will suffer.

(13) The Transition Issue

Although the Transition has been categorized as a non-critical Phase of the Sprint, it is affected by the athlete's ability to produce force. In fact, the greater the athlete's ability to generate force, the farther down the track that Maximum Velocity is achieved. Today's best sprinters don't reach peak Velocity until almost 60 meters into the race.

This tendency has been used as an argument that the top sprinters are actually not expending full effort during the Start and Transition, and saving something for the end of the race. In fact, when compared to all other sprinters, the best performers accelerate at a higher rate in both the Start and Transition. The reason why these superior athletes achieve top Speed later in the race is simply due to the fact that they have a greater ability to generate **productive** force for a longer period of time. This allows them to accelerate faster at the beginning of the race, and continue to produce the required amount of Vertical force demanded of the activity; with enough left over to produce the Horizontal force required to increase their peak Velocity well into the race.

Understanding the Sprint Performance

> **Chapter Summary:**
>
> In summary, the maximal Horizontal Velocity that a sprinter can produce is dependent upon the amount of effective total force that the athlete can apply during ground contact. In the Start, any forces beyond the required Vertical forces can be directed toward accelerating the athlete Horizontally down the track. The maximum Horizontal Velocity, as well as where it occurs in the race, again depends on the total amount of force the performer has at their disposal.
>
> If this force can be increased through either strength gain or efficiency improvement, the overall performance will improve.
>
> There are, however, several Sprint Issues, all related to the effective application of Effective Force, that are unavoidable and must be confronted by all performers and coaches.

Prelude To The Remaining Sprint Sections

Since the focus of this presentation is on Sprint Mechanics, the development of the athlete's strength potential will not be focused upon. It is assumed that the athlete and coach understand how to elicit the required improvements in this area, as well as the critical nature of the endeavor.

Instead, those mechanical factors that have been determined to be critical in the production of an elite Sprint performance will be scrutinized. These results will be presented for both Men and Women elite athletes. For each of the significant mechanical performance variables that are discussed, values for Poor, Average, and Good elite performers will be presented. In using this terminology, it must be realized that a poor performance for an elite sprinter would constitute an excellent performance for even a collegiate quality sprinter. However, since this is the level with which the elite performer must contend, even this level of performance must be improved upon.

In addition, the values presented are those results produced by an athlete of a typical elite sprinter body build. Thus, those athletes that are either taller or shorter than this typical build will require a slight revision in many of the results. For instance, if the athlete is extremely long legged, the performer has an advantage in producing length results like Stride Length and, thus, their results will be higher than an average size sprinter. On the other hand, long legs will hinder speed results like Stride Rate and, thus, their results will be lower than the average size sprinter. In contrast, if the sprinter is short legged, this will provide an advantage in producing speed results like Stride Rate and, thus, their results will be higher than an average size sprinter. Similarly, short legs will hinder length results like Stride Length and, thus, their results will be lower than an average size sprinter.

To properly compare results between all sprinters, leg lengths must be taken into consideration. Although the individual High Performance Reports that are generated for the participating athletes take leg length into consideration, the actual process is sufficiently complex to make it impossible to be either described or performed easily. Thus, the numerical results that are presented herein are done **only as a descriptive tool**.

Finally, since the Short Sprints and the Long Sprint are distinctively different events, the results will be separately presented. Initially the Short Sprints will be examined, followed by a brief description on how the Long Sprint results deviate from the shorter races.

PART THREE: START MECHANICS

INTRODUCTION

THE START GOLDEN POSITION

After analyzing thousands of athletes over many years, coupled with actual interactive, on-track teaching sessions with elite athletes, a single "Golden Position" has been identified as the benchmark to judge overall Start Mechanics. If an athlete can arrive at this position in the proper body position, at the right time, and at the required Velocity, then the Start will be successful.

The Figure below identifies the Golden Position as Ankle Cross during Step 1. If the athlete can reach this position, under control, in 0.42 seconds, touching down 0.12 meters from the starting line, while producing a Velocity of 5 meters per second, all criteria have been met.

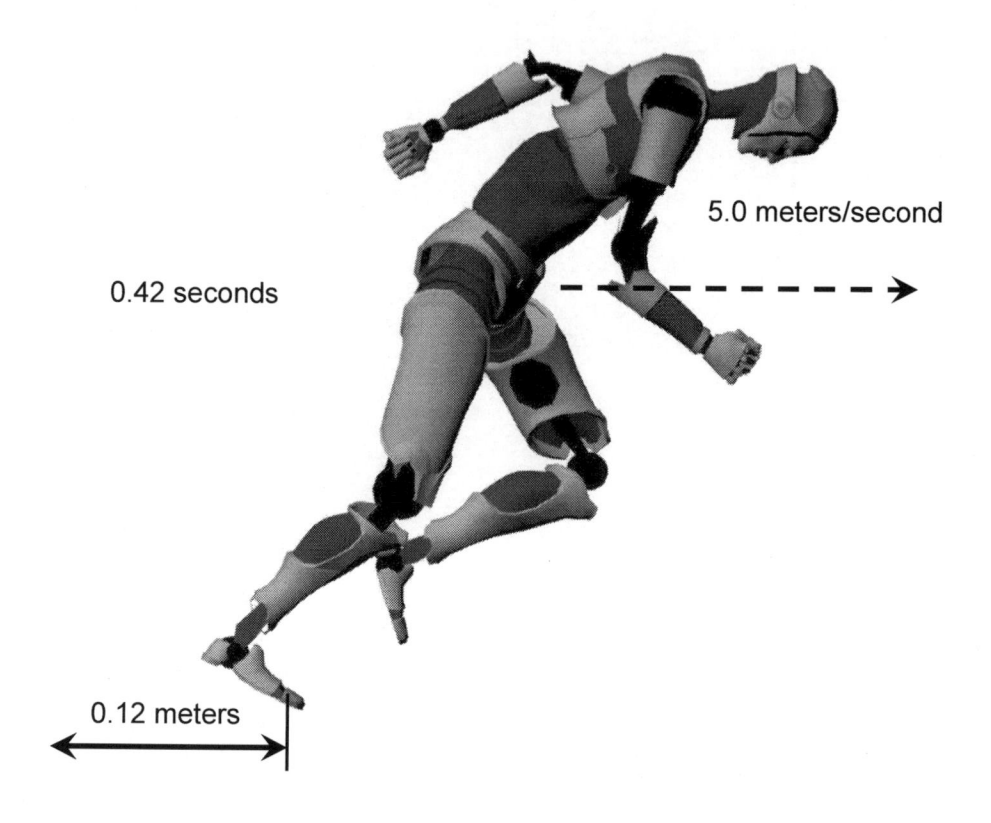

Step 1 Ankle Cross: The Start Golden Position

This single position has been termed "Golden" since, to achieve it, the athlete must perform all subsequent Mechanics properly, and possess the Flexibility and explosive Strength to make the most of the actions. In addition, matching this position is the only way to allow the athlete to successfully complete the remaining portion of the Start.

If there are any Mechanical flaws, or Flexibility/Strength deficiencies, this position simply cannot be produced, as well as insuring a decrement in the overall Start result.

These distance, time, and Velocity values will, of course, vary with body size as well as gender, but they are excellent goals for all performers.

The information contained in Part Three describes how elite sprinters achieve this goal.

CHAPTER 6

CRITICAL GENERAL PERFORMANCE DESCRIPTORS FOR THE START

In the Start, **General Performance Descriptors** identify the result of the athlete's effort. The nature of these descriptors identify how well the athlete is doing, however, they do not identify how the performer is mechanically producing the results. Those general descriptors that are directly related to Start performance include:

1. **Horizontal Velocity**
2. **Vertical Velocity**
3. **Stride Length**
4. **Stride Rate**
5. **Ground Time and Air Time**
6. **Time to 3, 5, 10, and 20 Meters**

Horizontal Velocity is a measure of the Speed the athlete is moving down the track, and is typically expressed in meters per second or feet per second. Stride rate is the turnover rate of the athlete (steps per second), while Stride Length is the distance covered with each step (meters or feet). Finally, ground contact time is the amount of time the athlete spends in contact with the ground (seconds) while Air Time is the amount of time spent airborne (seconds) during each stride.

Although these descriptors do not identify specifically how the elite athlete produces a successful starting performance, they will indicate the general areas that must be emphasized to accomplish this task.

Horizontal Velocity

The most obvious General Performance Descriptor in the Start is Horizontal Velocity. Most coaches agree, and the available research tends to confirm, that the goal of the Start is to maximize Horizontal Velocity.

As can be seen in Figure 6-1, during block contact, Horizontal Velocity is generated by exerting Horizontal force against the blocks (A) which, in turn, exerts the same force back on the athlete (B) driving the body down the track. There are no reasons to moderate or limit this effort, and it should be as explosive as possible. For the two steps of the Start after the blocks have been cleared, additional Horizontal Velocity is produced in the same manner.

Horizontal Push (A)   Horizontal Drive (B)

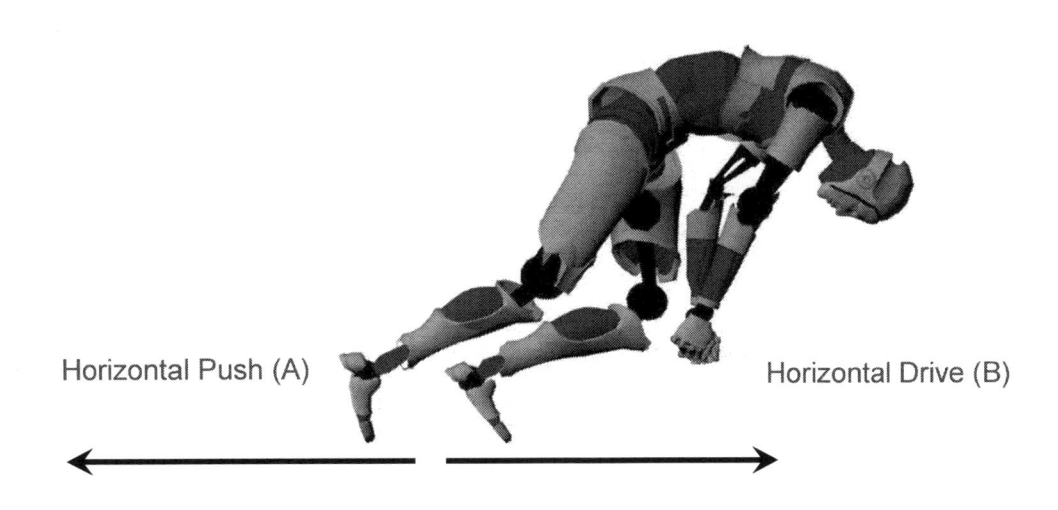

Figure 6-1: Horizontal Forces Generated While in the Blocks

Figure 6-2 shows the Horizontal Velocity generated during the initial portion of the Men's 100 meters, as well as the Maximum Velocity reached during the race.

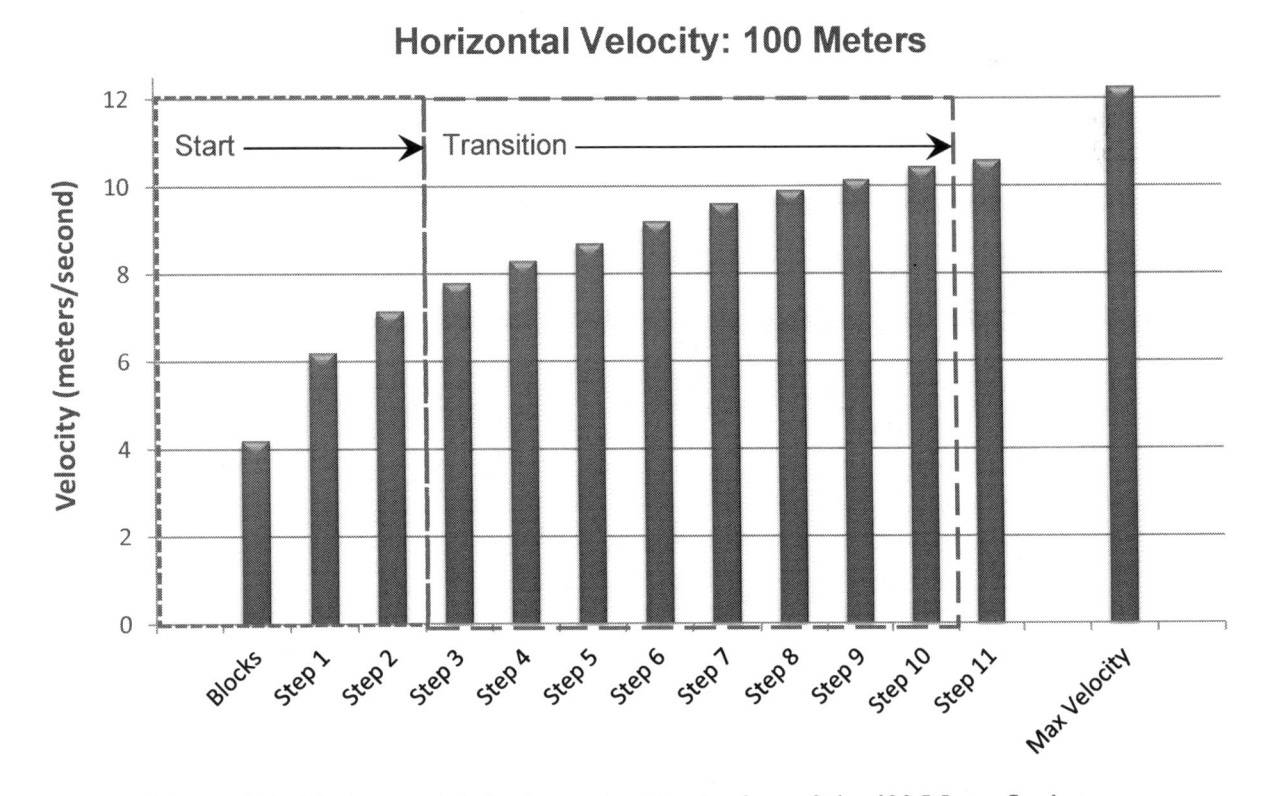

Figure 6-2: Horizontal Velocity at the Beginning of the 100 Meter Sprint

Critical General Performance Descriptors For the Start

As previously discussed, the Start generates more than half of the performer's maximum Horizontal Velocity. Figure 6-2 shows that, after the explosive effort of the blocks and first two steps, the Velocity increase becomes a gradual, controlled effort. This was one factor that led to defining the Start as occurring during the first 2 steps of the race.

Note that the Maximum Velocity phase threshold has been defined as when the performer reaches 80 percent of their Maximum Velocity. As shown in the Figure, this should be achieved around step 10 of the race, which occurs at about the 20 meter mark.

Since Horizontal Velocity is such a critical value, the results for the first three push efforts are displayed below for both Men and Women. Figure 6-3 shows the Poor, Average, and Good values at the end of Block Clearance (Touchdown of the rear foot out of the blocks), Figure 6-4 shows the Velocity at the end of Step 1 (Touchdown of the front foot out of the blocks), and Figure 6-5 shows the Velocity at the end of Step 2 (second Touchdown of the rear foot).

Horizontal Velocity: Blocks

☒ Poor   ▨ Average   ☐ Good

MEN
- Poor: 3.38
- Average: 3.78
- Good, 4.18

WOMEN
- Poor: 3.31
- Average: 3.51
- Good, 3.71

Velocity (meters/second)

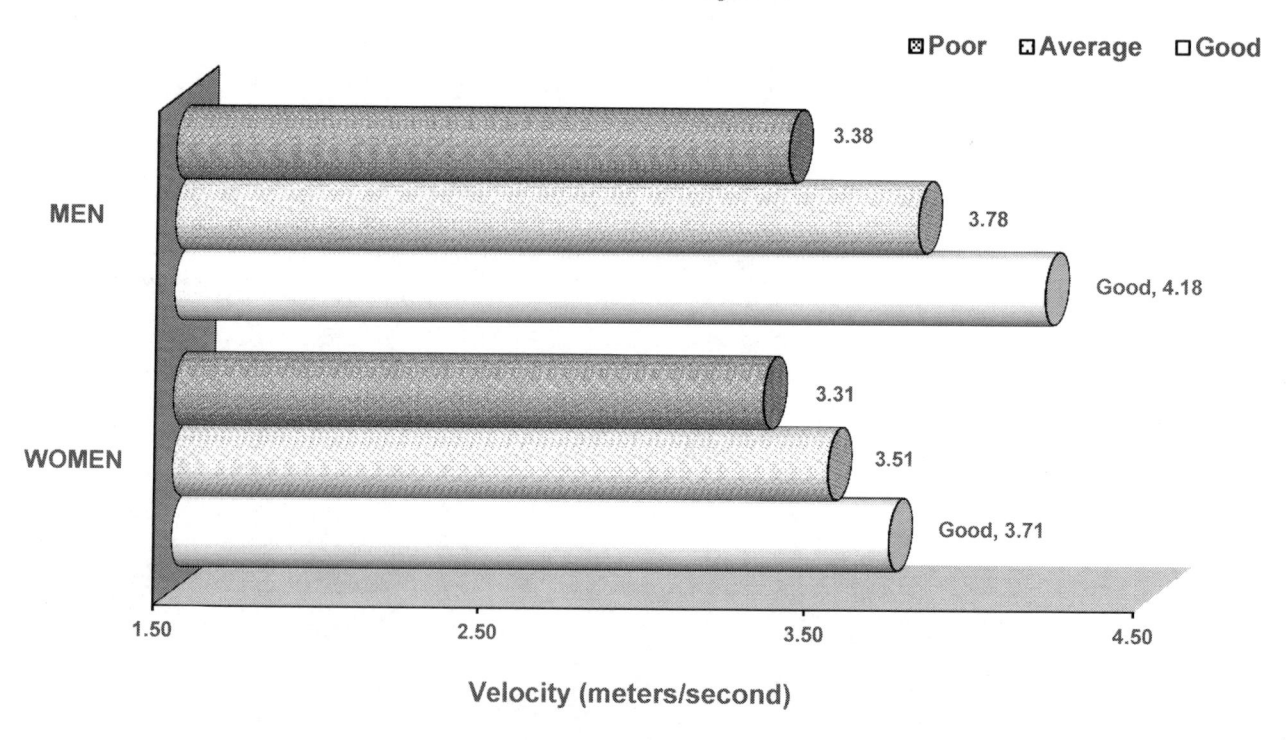

Figure 6-3: Horizontal Velocity at End of Block Clearance

Note: Throughout this document, results for Good, Average, and Poor Elite athletes are presented. These values are to be used as a guideline only, since the results may vary due to the athlete's body type.

Horizontal Velocity: Step 1

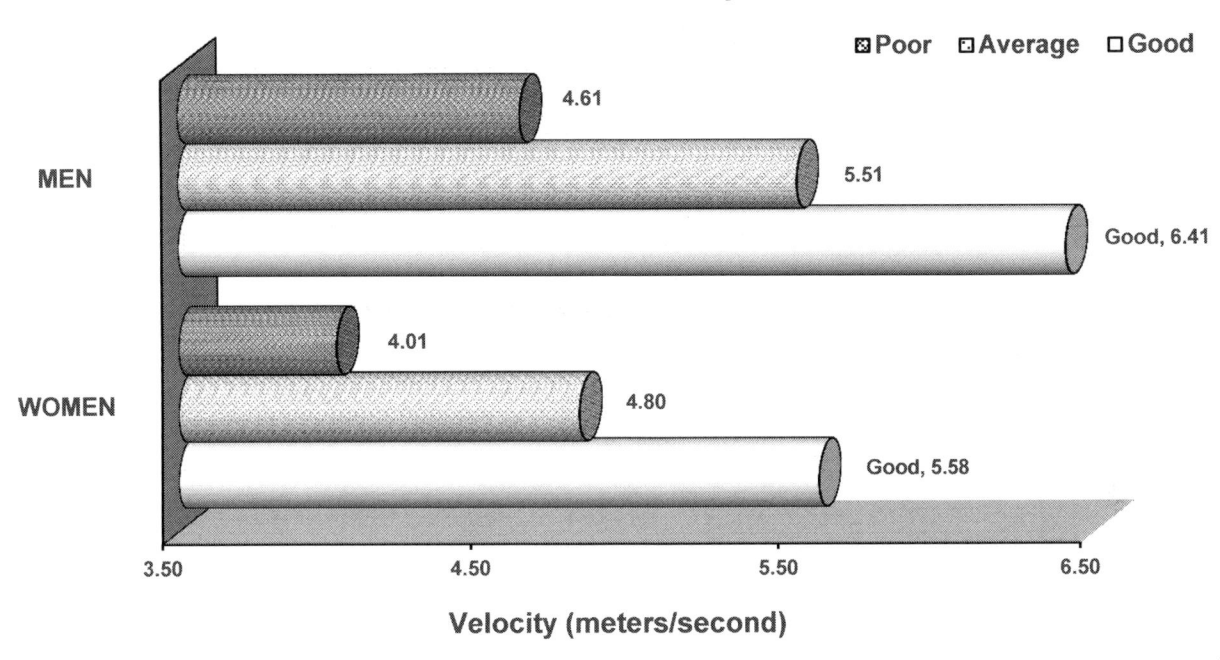

MEN
- Poor: 4.61
- Average: 5.51
- Good, 6.41

WOMEN
- Poor: 4.01
- Average: 4.80
- Good, 5.58

Velocity (meters/second)

Figure 6-4: Horizontal Velocity at End of Step 1

Horizontal Velocity: Step 2

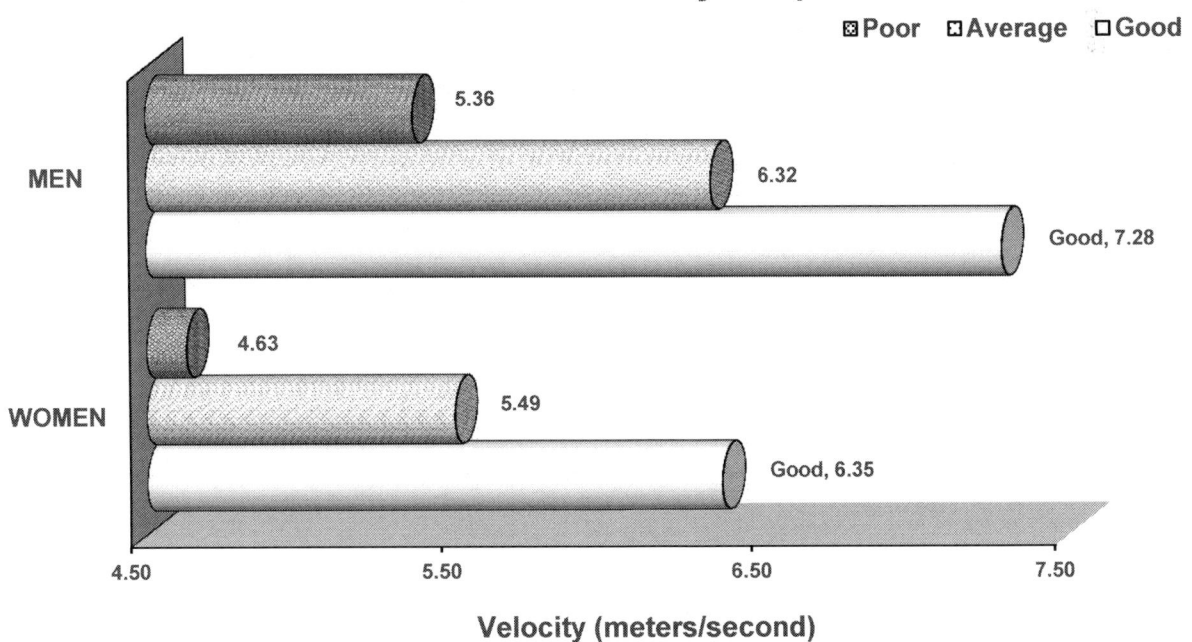

MEN
- Poor: 5.36
- Average: 6.32
- Good, 7.28

WOMEN
- Poor: 4.63
- Average: 5.49
- Good, 6.35

Velocity (meters/second)

Figure 6-5: Horizontal Velocity at End of Step 2

These results are the critical "bottom line" results that determine the level of success of the starting action. If sufficient explosive power and proper technique are applied, the sprinter can not only complete the Start in excellent position, but also set up the body position for a successful transition toward Maximum Velocity sprinting.

As discussed in Chapter 5, the key to generating Horizontal Velocity is to direct as much of the athlete's exertion in the Horizontal direction as possible. Figure 6-6 demonstrates the Horizontal force exerted during the block portion of the Start.

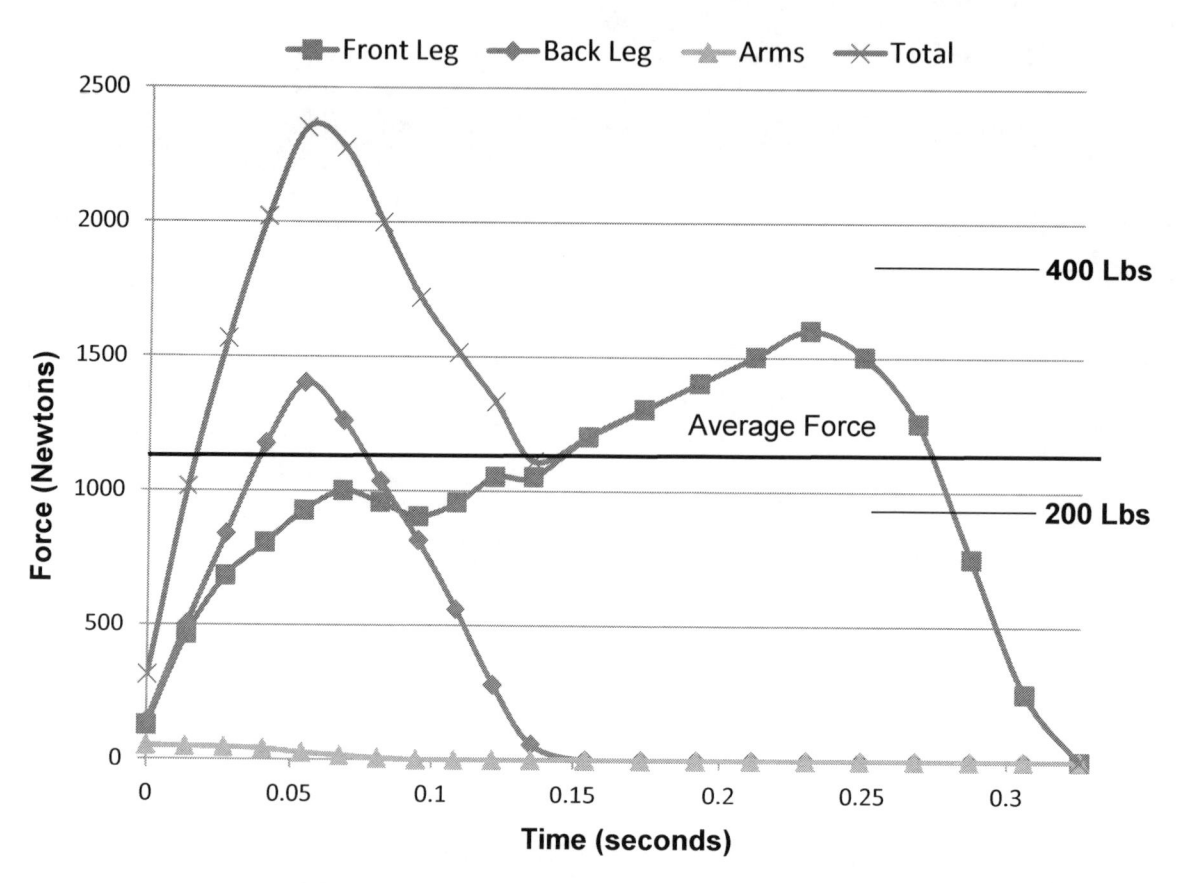

Figure 6-6: Horizontal Force in the Blocks

During the block time of about .32 seconds, the legs are able to exert an average of around 1085 Newtons (243 Pounds), which generates more than 4 meters per second of Horizontal Velocity at block clearance. At the end of the Start, almost 60 percent of the Maximum Horizontal Velocity has been created, which points to the critical nature of the Start in the success of the Sprint race.

Vertical Velocity

Since the purpose of the Start is to generate Horizontal Velocity, the amount of Vertical emphasis is expected to be minimal. Figure 6-7 shows the Vertical Velocity generated during each step of the initial portion of the 100 meters, as well as the Velocity reached during the maximum Speed portion of the race. Since the Vertical results are about 1/10 of the Horizontal (see Figure 6-2), it initially appears that the Vertical emphasis is a minor element in the Start. However, the summary previously presented in Table 5-1 indicates that this is an incorrect conclusion.

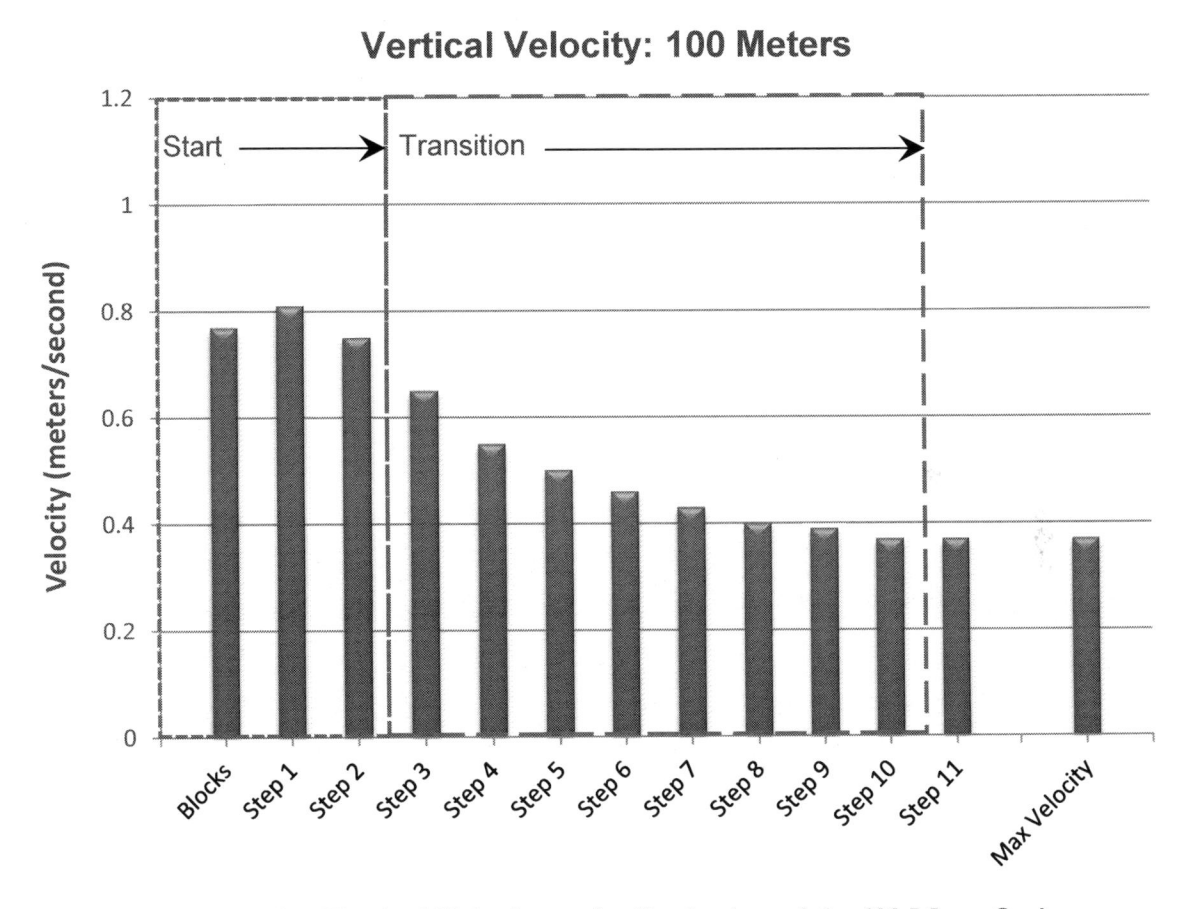

Figure 6-7: Vertical Velocity at the Beginning of the 100 Meter Sprint

The key to the Vertical demands of the Start begin with the required change in Velocity. The first reason the Vertical Velocity during the Start and the Transition is greater than Maximum Velocity is due to the need to raise the Body COG from the Start position to a full running position. Second, it is apparent that this goal has been achieved by Step 11 (about 20 meters) since the Velocity has been reduced to the Maximum Velocity value at this point. Finally, it appears that the majority of the

Vertical effort is done during the Start, with the greatest Vertical emphasis occurring during Step 1, followed by the block effort.

The Vertical effort during the Start is surprising since most coaches attempt to minimize Vertical projection. Even greater revelation occurs when the amount of actual Vertical force is examined. Figure 6-8 shows the Vertical forces produced during the Block portion of the Start.

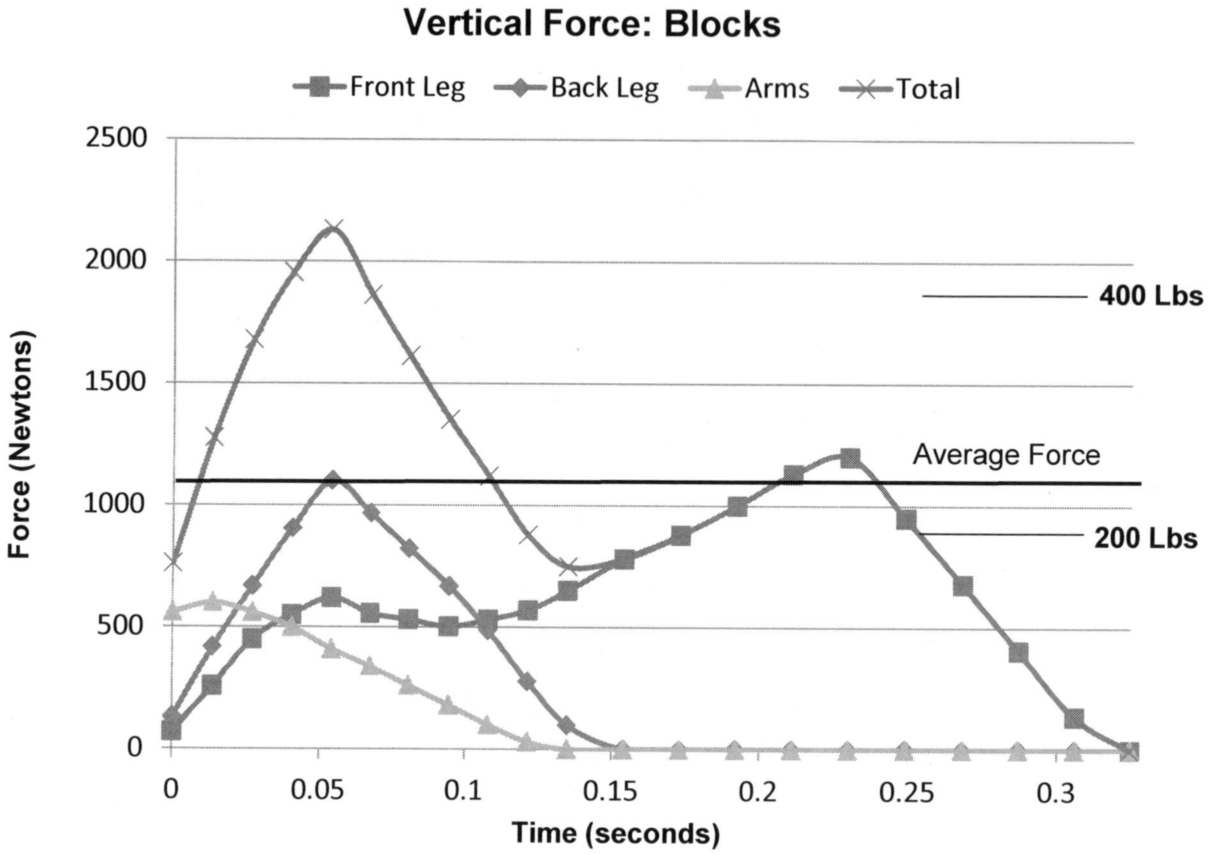

Figure 6-8: Vertical Force in the Blocks

Instead of the expected small force production, the amount of Vertical force produced during the Block portion of the Start (as well as Steps 1 and 2) is actually **virtually the same** as the Horizontal force.

There are two reasons for this surprising result. First, as shown in Figure 6-9, the production of Horizontal force during the Start produces a great deal of body rotation (R1) that, if unopposed, will quickly rotate the body around the Body COG to an upright position. The only way to control this rotation is to generate Vertical force, which will produce the counter rotation (R2) needed to control how the body rotates during the Start.

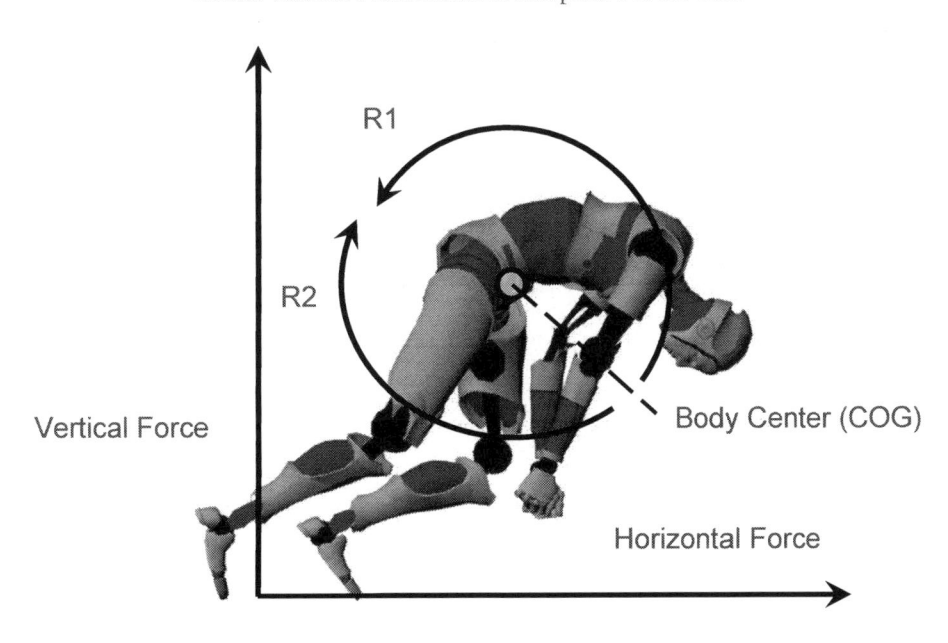

Figure 6-9: Controlling Body Rotation in the Start

Even more critical than rotation, the sprinter must deal with the problem imposed by gravity. As shown in Figure 6-10, as soon as the Start begins, the legs must generate sufficient Vertical force to not only support the athlete's body weight (WT), but also additional force to move the Body COG upward into a running position.

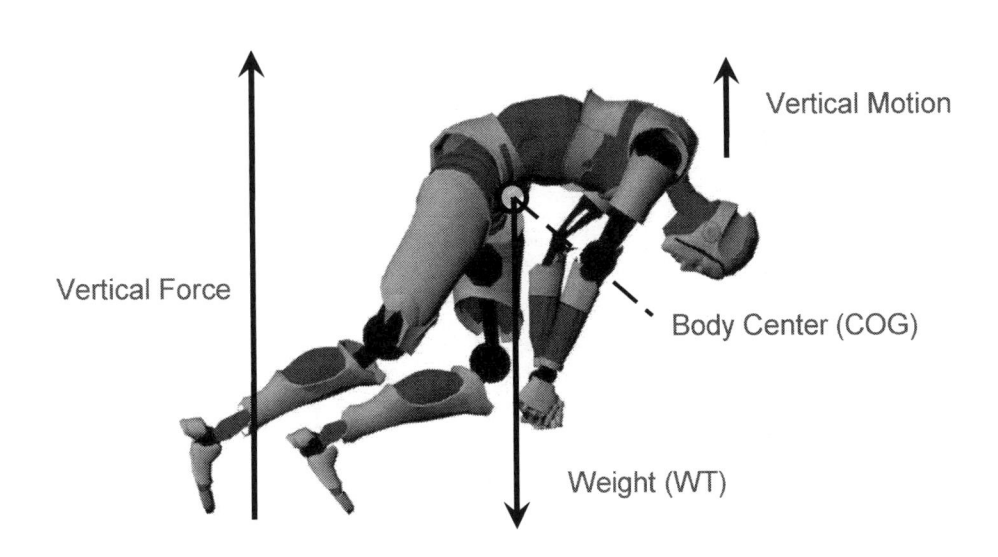

Figure 6-10: Vertical Force Required to Support and Move the Body

Contrary to popular belief, the Start involves the production of balanced levels of Horizontal and Vertical forces. As shown in Figure 6-11, the two forces produce a total force (Vertical and Horizontal combined as shown) that is directed **just under the Body COG**. This provides the forces required to properly move the body forward and upward, as well as producing a controlled rotation of the performer to an effective upright sprinting position.

The Total Force **must** be directed as shown. If the force is directed lower, the athlete will rotate upright too fast, not allowing a proper "low driving" Start. Even worse, if the Total Force is directed too high, the athlete will rotate forward, face down into the track.

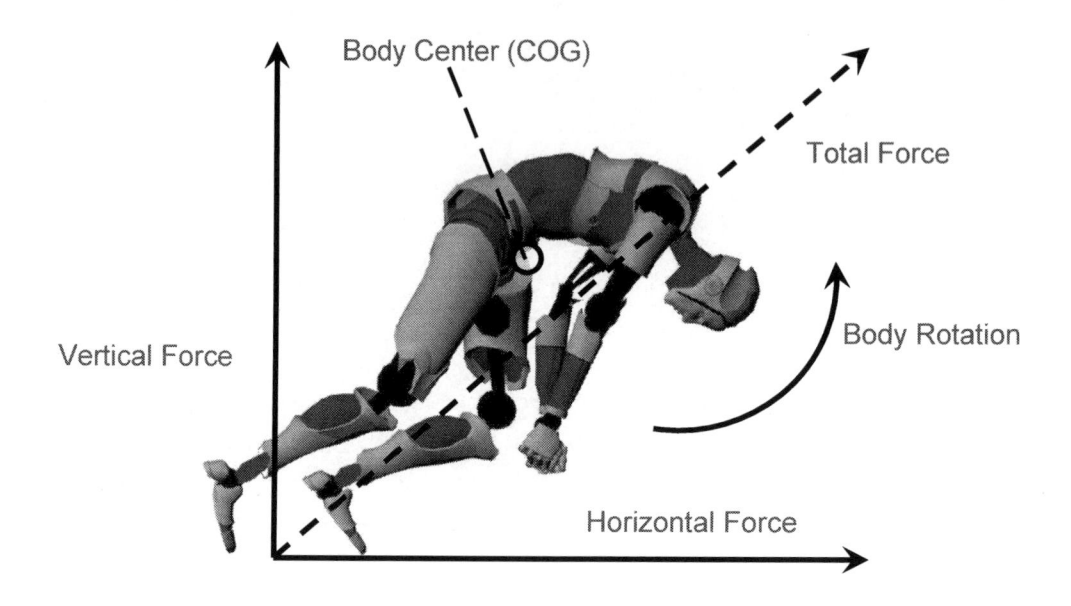

Figure 6-11: Total Force Direction During Block Contact

The role of Strength and Mechanics in the Start is more critical than originally believed. It is obvious that greater strength allows the performer to produce greater forces, however, the nature of the Start makes this only a part of the answer. The key to this conclusion is the fact that **the minimum Vertical force demands during the Start are essentially unalterable**. Since the majority of the Vertical demands are due to the fact that the athlete **must** support their weight (plus a little more to raise the body), this force demand is constant throughout the Start.

With this in mind, the way to increase the Horizontal force is to increase the total force. If the performer is stronger, or mechanically proficient, they can produce a larger total force as shown in Figure 6-12. Since the Vertical demands are constant, this increase in total force allows the athlete to produce a larger Horizontal force (in comparison to Figure 6-11).

Now, since the total force must be directed just below the Body COG, a larger Horizontal force allows the sprinter to keep the body even lower during the Start.

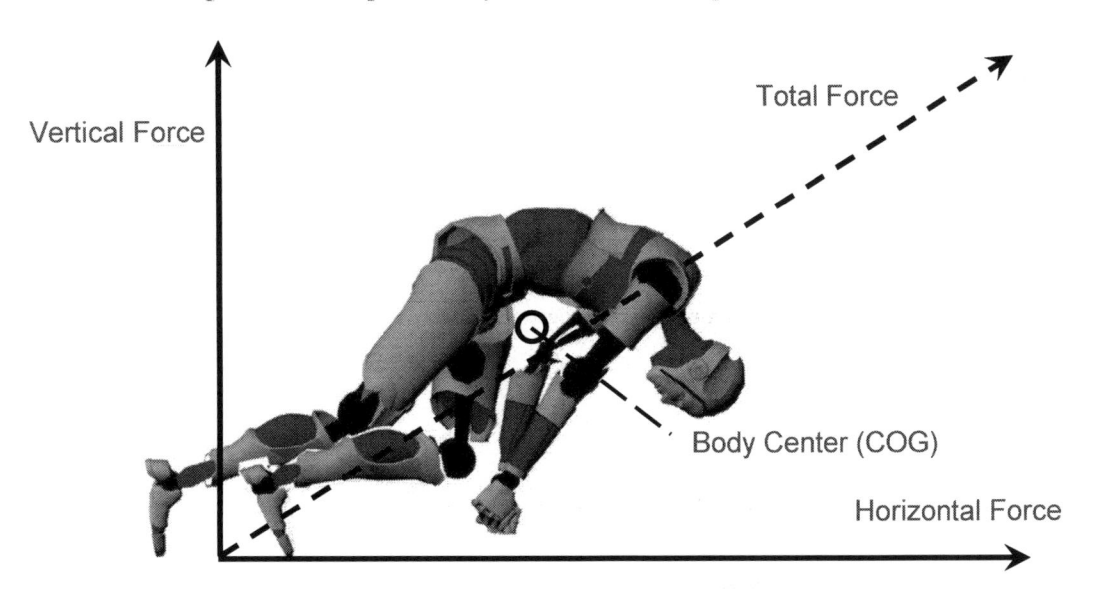

Figure 6-12: The Beneficial Effects of Increased Total Force

Unfortunately, this same situation can be just as detrimental to the weaker sprinter. As shown in Figure 6-13, if the performer's best effort produces a smaller total force, since the Vertical force cannot change, the result is a smaller Horizontal force. This shifts the total force toward the Vertical, and the athlete must project the body center more Vertical to keep it above the total force projection.

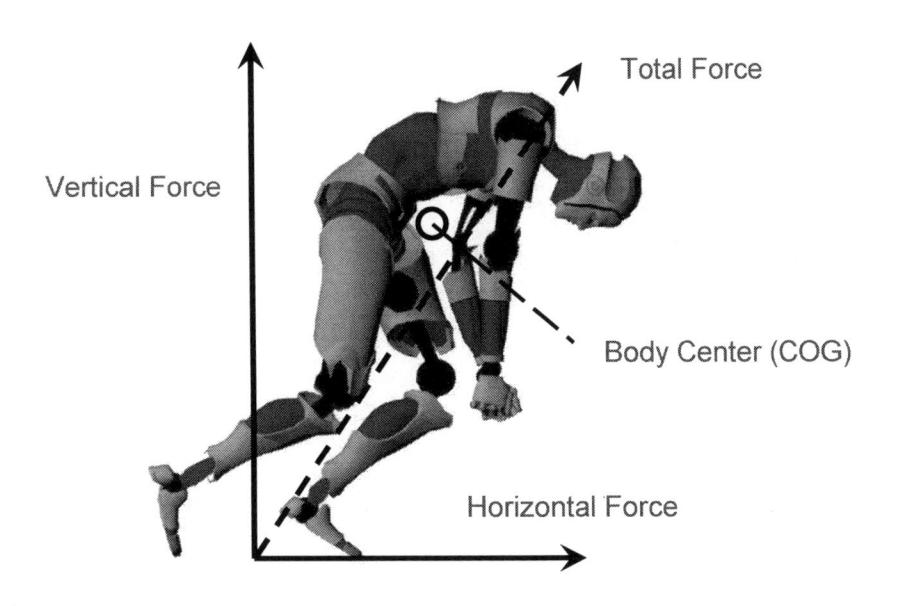

Figure 6-13: The Detrimental Effects of Decreased Total Force

This is why weaker, or less proficient sprinters "pop-up" during the Start. As in all phases of the Sprint, Strength and proper Mechanics allow the athlete to gain a performance advantage.

In conclusion, the key to creating a great Start is to generate as much Horizontal Velocity as possible during the first three steps of the race. Toward that end, since Horizontal Velocity is produced by Horizontal force, whatever must be done to maximize this effort has to be the primary goal of the Starting action. With that objective in mind, the information presented in this section indicates that **overcoming the required (and inescapable) Vertical force demands of the Start is the key to directing as much of the athlete's total force capacity as possible to the Horizontal direction**. As indicated, the best way to do this is for the athlete to be both mechanically proficient (so as not to waste any force) **and** be as strong as possible (to cover the Vertical demands and have a large remaining force left to direct Horizontally).

The elite athletes that excel in the Start also exploit one previously overlooked method to further decrease the Vertical force demands on the legs during the initial block portion of the activity. Unlike any other part of the race, during the first 30 percent of the time the athlete is in the blocks, both the legs **and the arms** can be in contact with the ground. This gives the athlete the ability to significantly decrease the Vertical force demand on the legs by supporting the body with the arms. In reviewing the Vertical forces of Figure 6-8 note that, at the Set position, the arms are producing about 560 Newtons (125 Pounds) of force. This means that, for the best Start athletes, they are supporting more than 70 percent of their weight on their arms when the gun is fired (Figure 6-14).

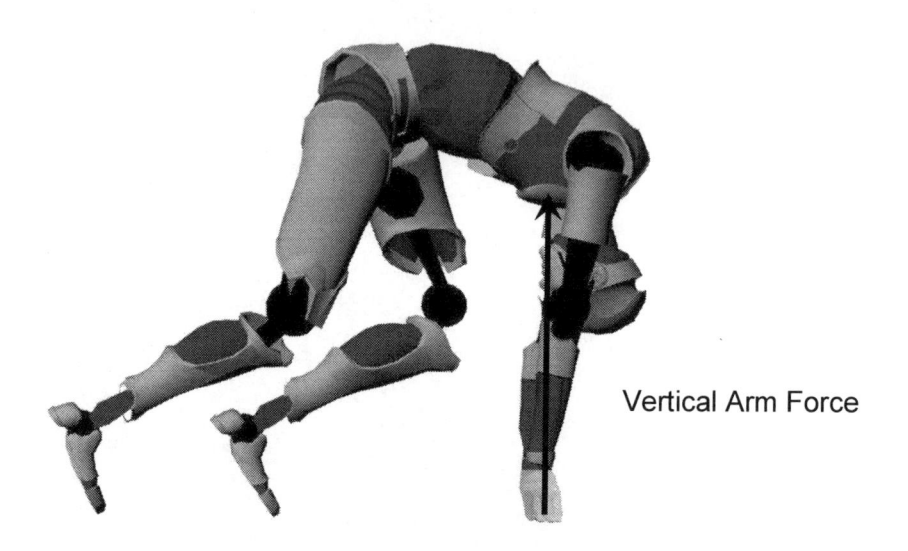

Figure 6-14: Vertical Force Production by the Arms at the Set Position

This arm force contribution continues into the initial portion of the Start. Instead of immediately lifting the arms off the track, as many coaches teach, the better performers actually drive the arms down and back after the gun. As previously shown in Figures 6-6 and 6-8, this action actually increases both the Vertical **and** Horizontal contribution.

Stride Rate and Stride Length

How fast a sprinter moves the legs (Stride Rate) and how far each stride covers (Stride Length) determine the success of the Start since the product of these variables equals Horizontal Velocity. Figure 6-15 shows the Stride Rate generated during each step of the initial portion of the 100 meters, as well as the rate and length reached during the maximum Speed portion of the race.

The most surprising Start result was found in these rate results. Once the blocks have been cleared, **the Stride Rate of the remaining portion of the race is virtually the same.** The only thing keeping the Stride Rate of the Block portion of the Start from matching the rest of the race is the strength of the performer. Thus, the goal should be to maximize the Stride Rate for the entire Start process.

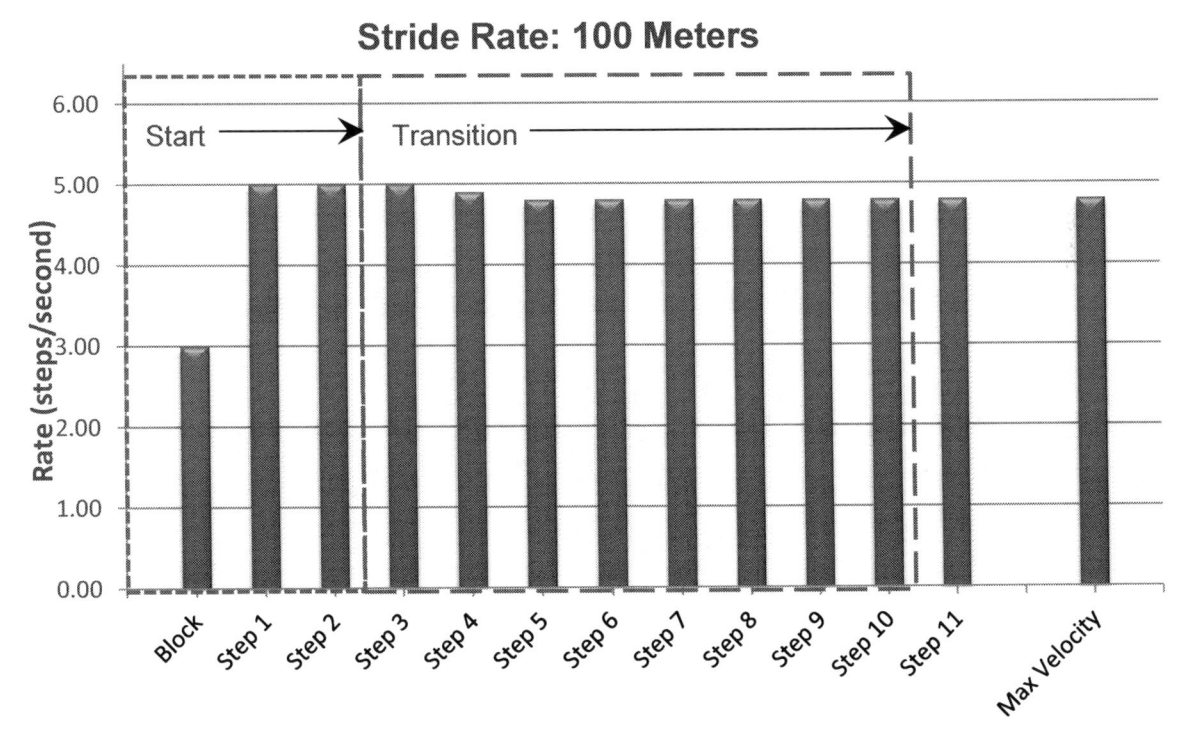

Figure 6-15: Stride Rate During the 100 Meter Sprint

The Stride Rate results for the first three strides are displayed in Figures 6-16, 17, and 18.

Critical General Performance Descriptors For the Start

Stride Rate: Blocks

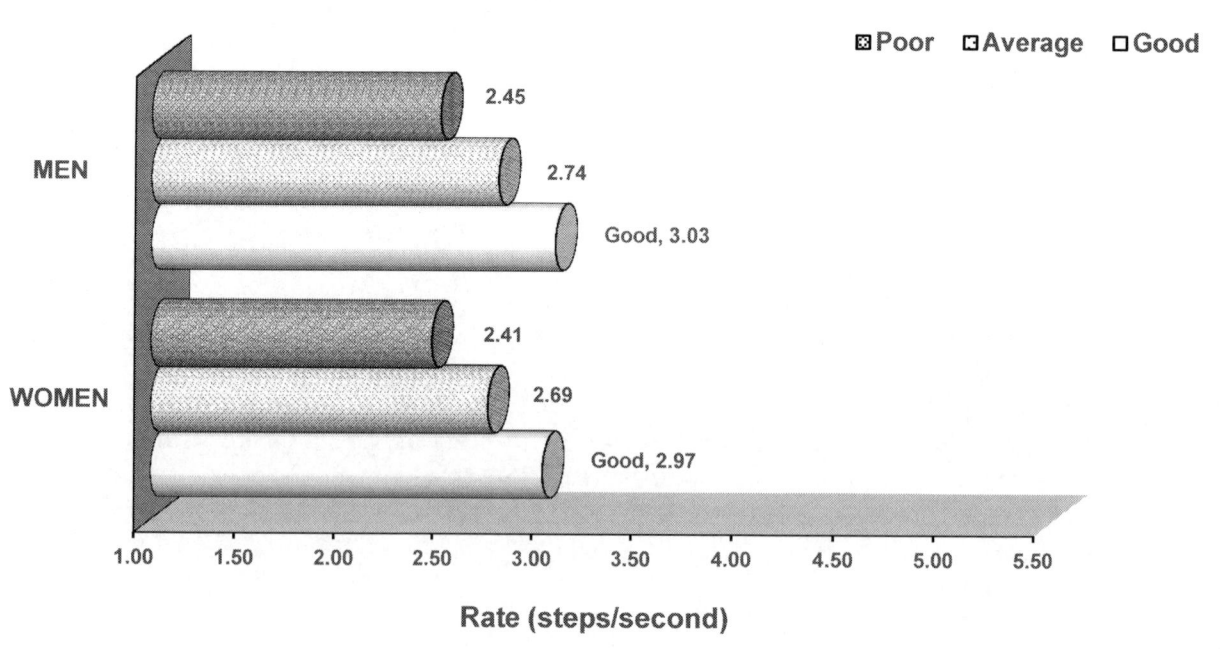

■ Poor ▨ Average □ Good

MEN
- 2.45
- 2.74
- Good, 3.03

WOMEN
- 2.41
- 2.69
- Good, 2.97

Rate (steps/second)

Figure 6-16: Stride Rate During Block Clearance

Stride Rate: Step 1

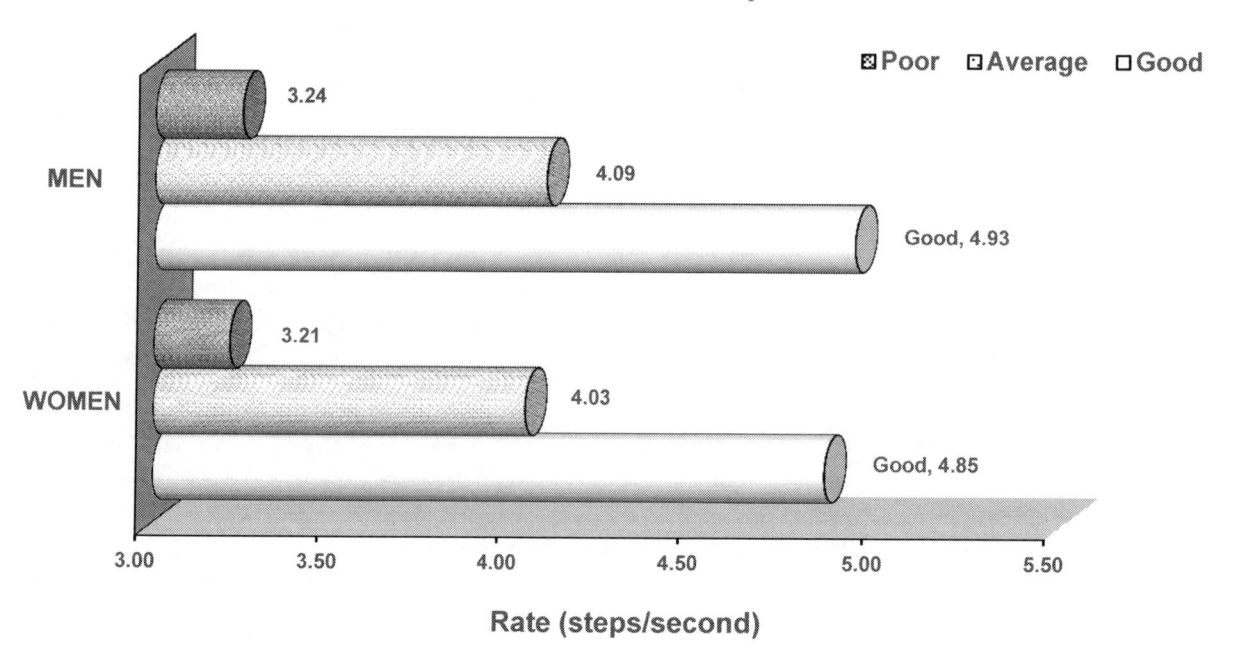

■ Poor ▨ Average □ Good

MEN
- 3.24
- 4.09
- Good, 4.93

WOMEN
- 3.21
- 4.03
- Good, 4.85

Rate (steps/second)

Figure 6-17: Stride Rate During Step 1

Stride Rate: Step 2

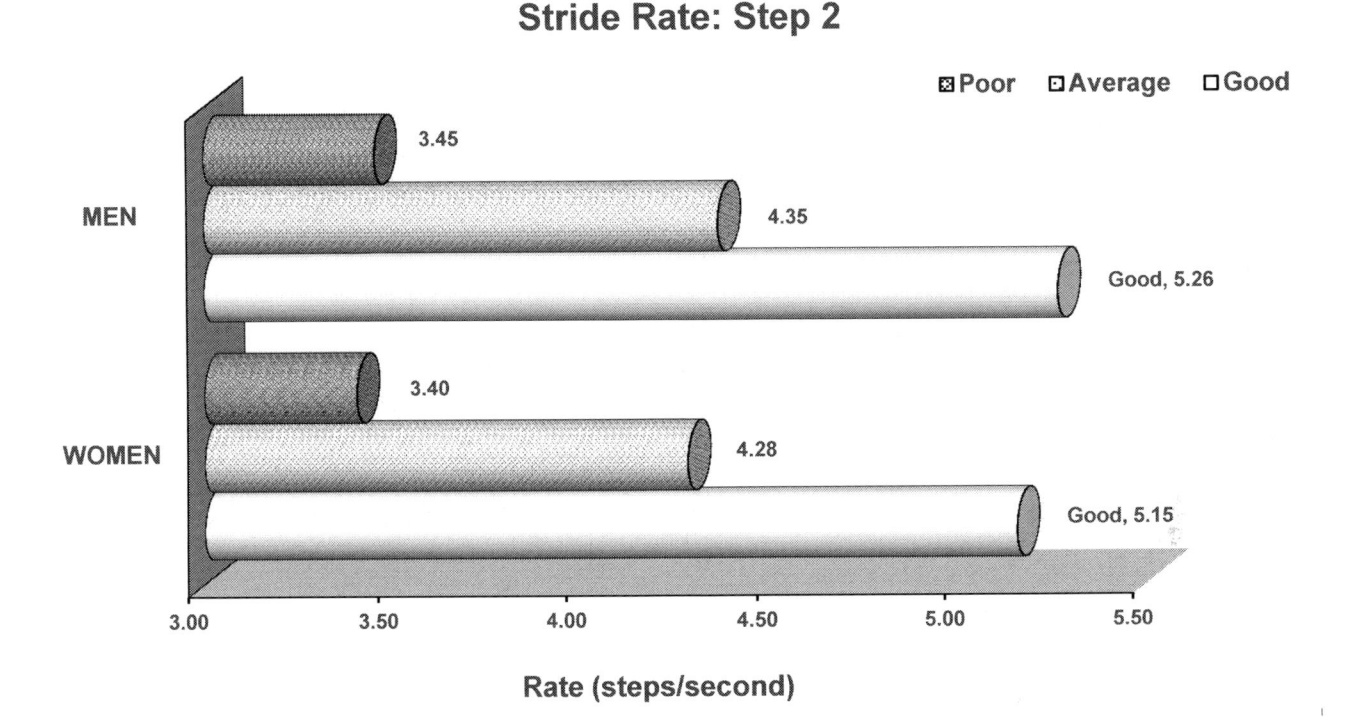

■ Poor　▣ Average　□ Good

MEN
- 3.45
- 4.35
- Good, 5.26

WOMEN
- 3.40
- 4.28
- Good, 5.15

Rate (steps/second)

Figure 6-18: Stride Rate During Step 2

In every case (as will be seen in the Full Speed Sprint action as well) the better performers maximize Stride Rate throughout the Start. These results refute the old concept that the best Start involves slow, long, driving strides coming out of the blocks. In fact, the limitations of this type of jump Start make it a poor choice in any situation, for any athlete.

The Stride Length results (Figure 6-19) underscore the differences, and difficulty, of block clearance and the first two steps of the Sprint race (the Start). The steps in the Start are the only steps where Touchdown takes place behind the Body COG. This, coupled with the fact that the body must be driven forward and up points to the difficulty of performing the Start effectively.

The entire Start sequence should emphasize turnover, not step length. The force demands upon the athlete are so high that the Vertical emphasis (Stride Length) should be minimized so that more of the available force can be directed Horizontally.

Once the second step is completed, half of the final Stride Length has been achieved, and the body is in a position to produce a smooth transition toward Maximum Velocity. By the time Step 11 is reached, 80 percent of the final Stride Length has been generated.

Stride Length: 100 Meters

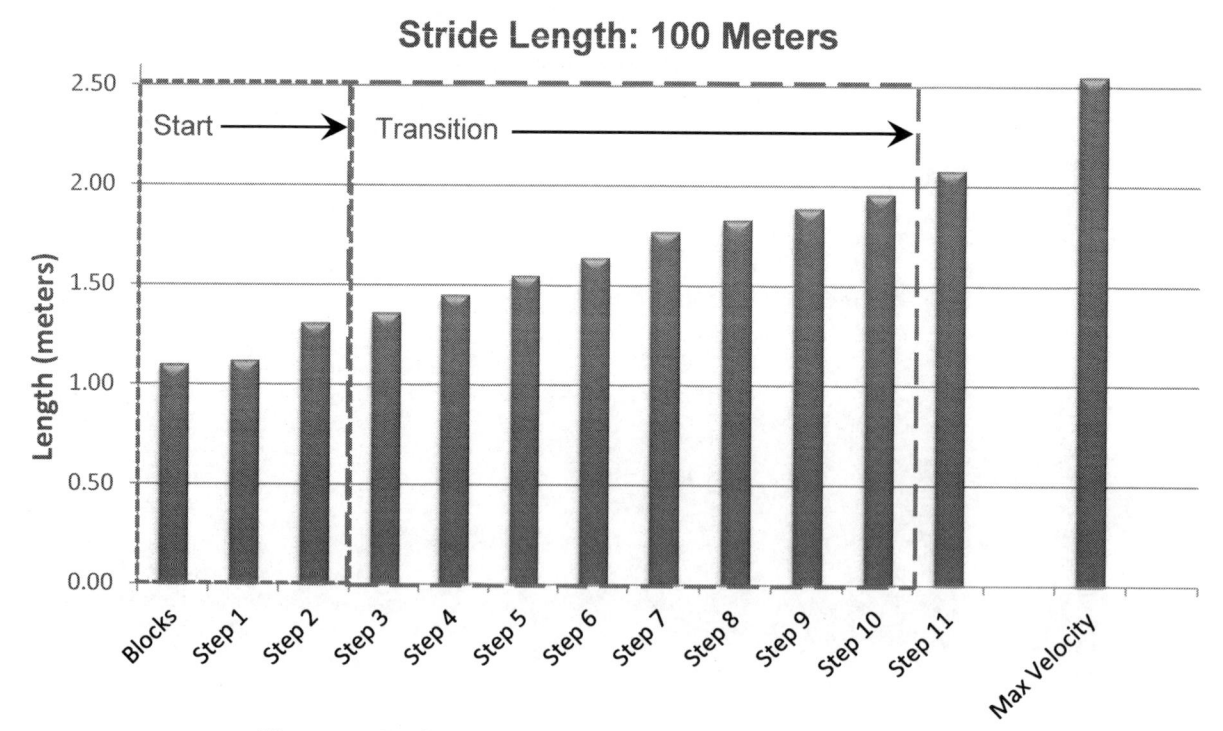

Figure 6-19: Stride Length During the 100 Meter Sprint

The Stride Length results for the first three strides are displayed in Figures 6-20, 21, and 22.

Stride Length: Blocks

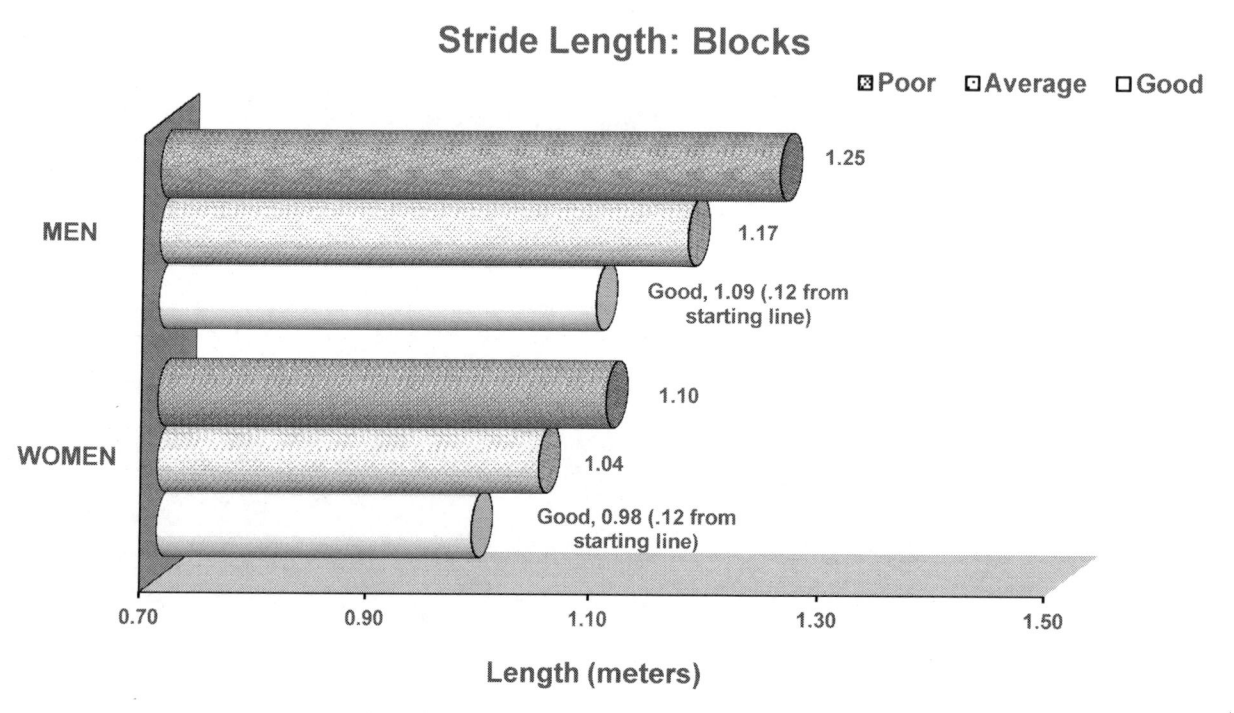

Figure 6-20: Stride Length During Block Clearance

Stride Length: Step 1

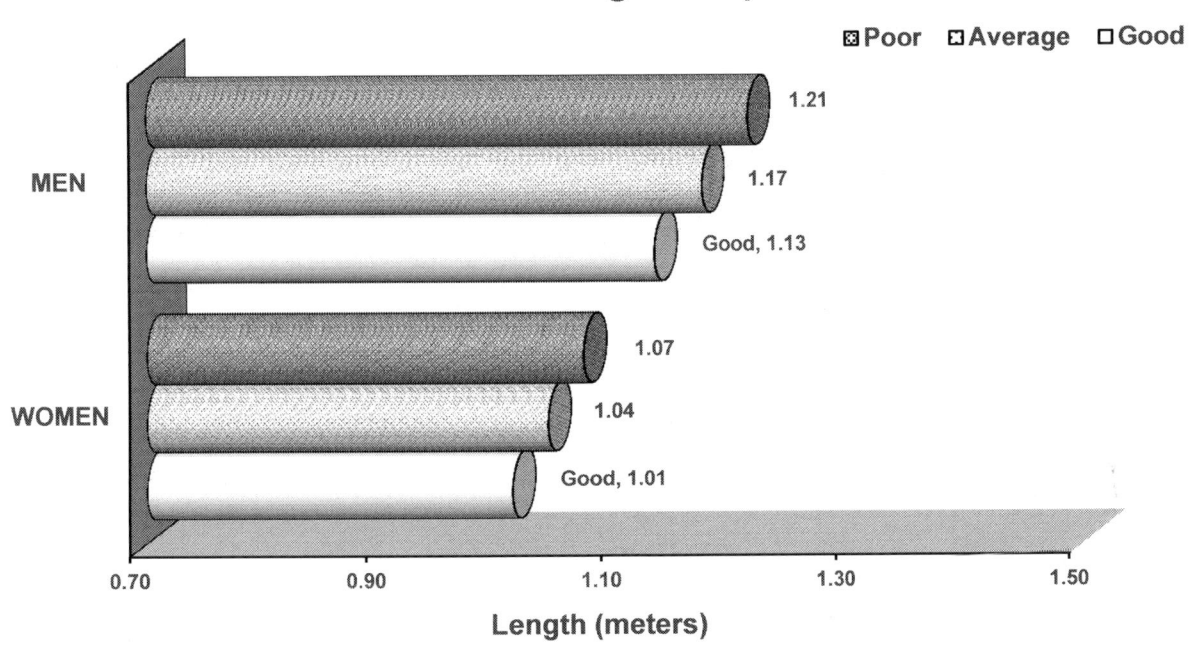

- MEN: Poor 1.21, Average 1.17, Good 1.13
- WOMEN: Poor 1.07, Average 1.04, Good 1.01

Figure 6-21: Stride Length During Step 1

Stride Length: Step 2

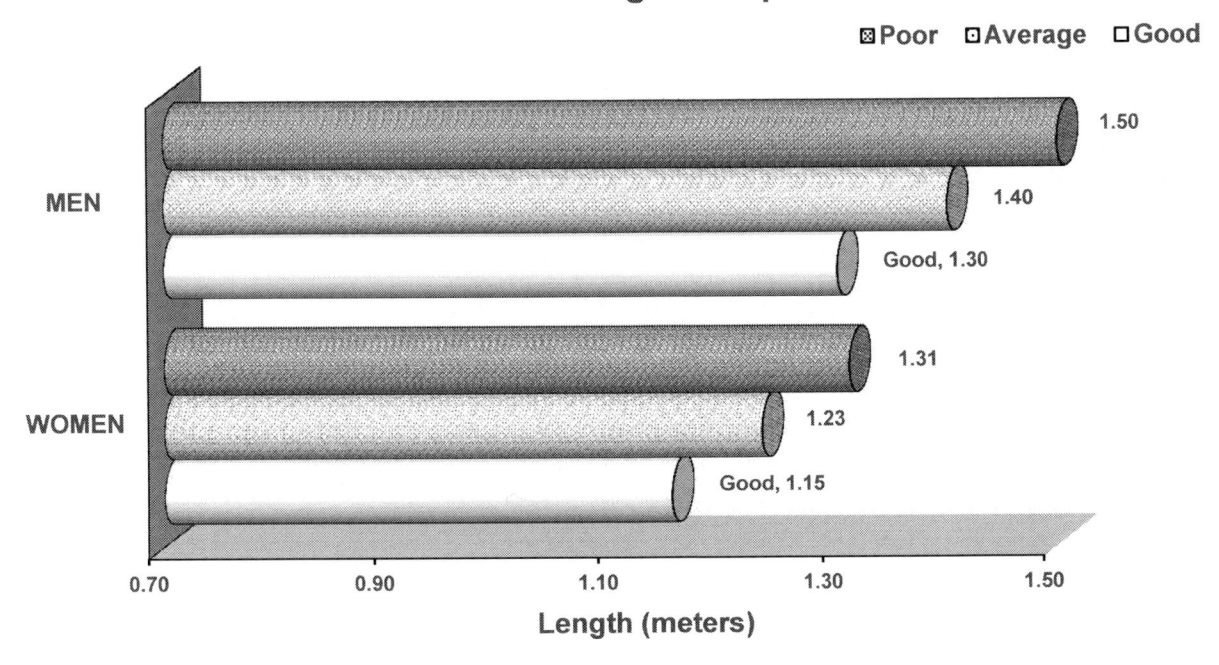

- MEN: Poor 1.50, Average 1.40, Good 1.30
- WOMEN: Poor 1.31, Average 1.23, Good 1.15

Figure 6-22: Stride Length During Step 2

Unlike the Maximum Velocity portion of the Sprint race, the better performers minimize Stride Length throughout the Start. The reason for this will be seen in the Ground and Air Time results.

Ground Time and Air Time

Of all of the General Performance Descriptors, Ground Time and Air Time provide the greatest insights into how the elite Start performance is accomplished. Since Air Time primarily dictates Stride Length, and the combination of Ground and Air Time dictate Stride Rate, these time results provide further information regarding how the sprinter is allocating resources to produce Horizontal Velocity.

Figure 6-23 shows the Ground and Air Times generated during each step of the initial portion of the 100 meters, as well as the times reached during the maximum Speed portion of the race.

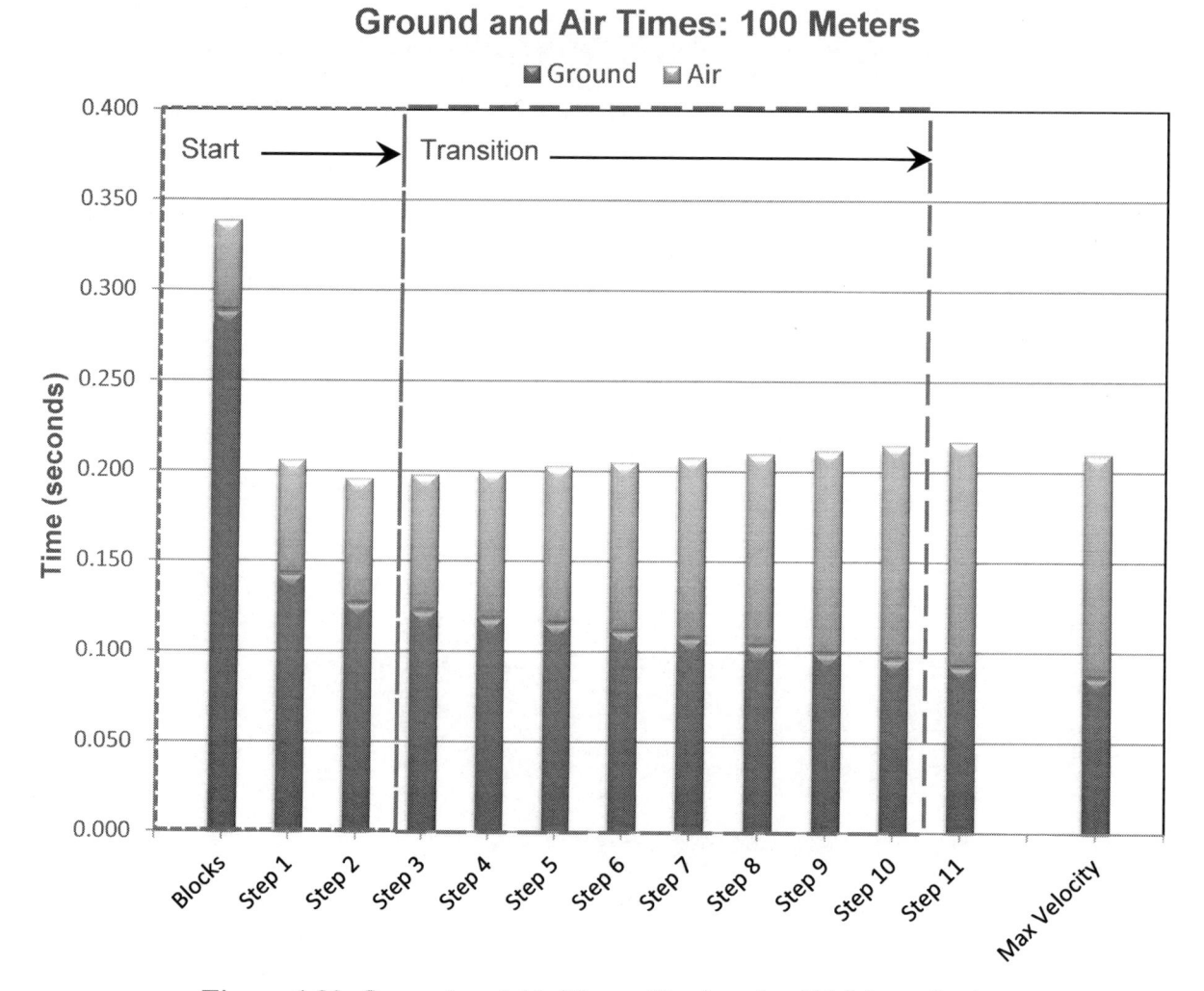

Figure 6-23: Ground and Air Times During the 100 Meter Sprint

The Figure demonstrates that, after the blocks are cleared, the total Ground and Air Time for each step is virtually constant. Although the ground contact time is largest during the Start, the better performers minimize this result. As will be seen, this goal will be continued into the Full Speed portion of the Sprint.

Unlike the Full Speed portion, however, the Start consists of three very short Air Phases. These are performed to minimize the Vertical emphasis while maximizing the time on the ground and, thus, the ability to produce the forces to accelerate the body down the track.

Once the Transition phase begins (Step 3), the Ground Time/Air Time ratio begins a gradual shift toward a smaller and smaller ground contact value. This trend will be further discussed in Part Four.

The Ground Time results for the first three strides are displayed in Figures 6-24, 25, and 26. As in the Maximum Velocity phase of the Sprint performance, the key to success in the Start is the ability of the sprinter to produce enormous levels of explosive force as quickly as possible, directed in a mechanically efficient manner.

Ground Time: Blocks

■ Poor ▨ Average ☐ Good

MEN
- Poor: 0.358
- Average: 0.319
- Good: 0.280

WOMEN
- Poor: 0.365
- Average: 0.326
- Good: 0.287

Time (seconds)

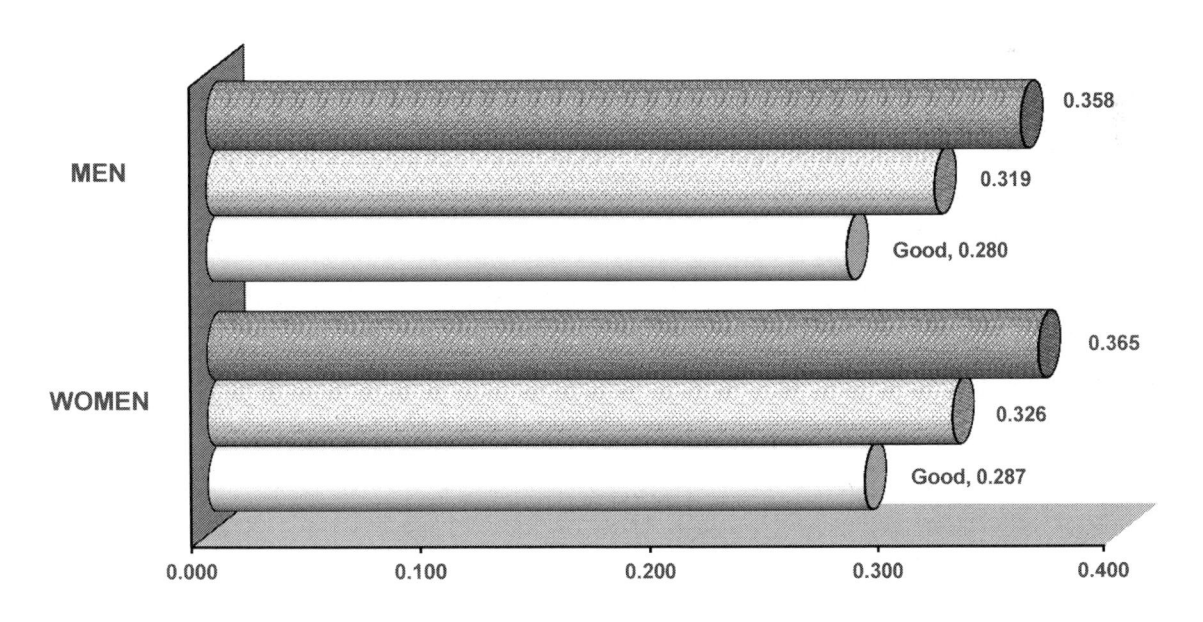

Figure 6-24: Ground Time During Block Clearance

Ground Time: Step 1

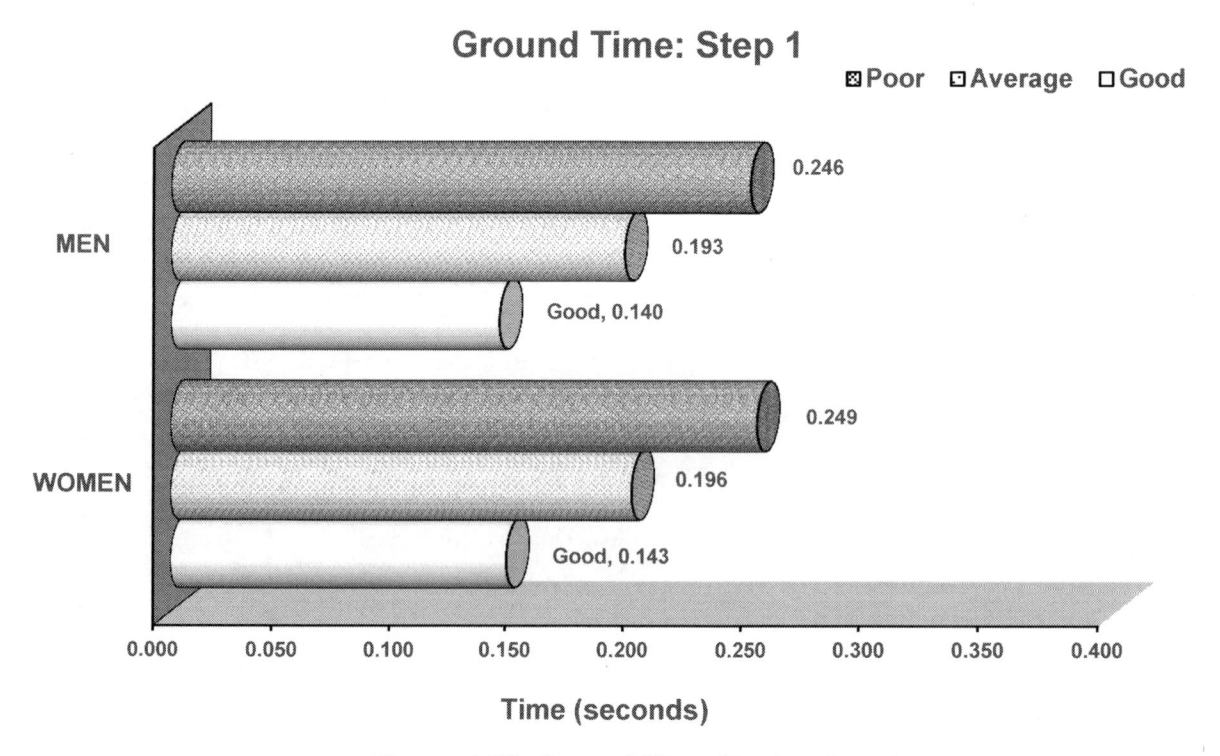

MEN
- Poor: 0.246
- Average: 0.193
- Good: 0.140

WOMEN
- Poor: 0.249
- Average: 0.196
- Good: 0.143

Figure 6-25: Ground Time During Step 1

Ground Time: Step 2

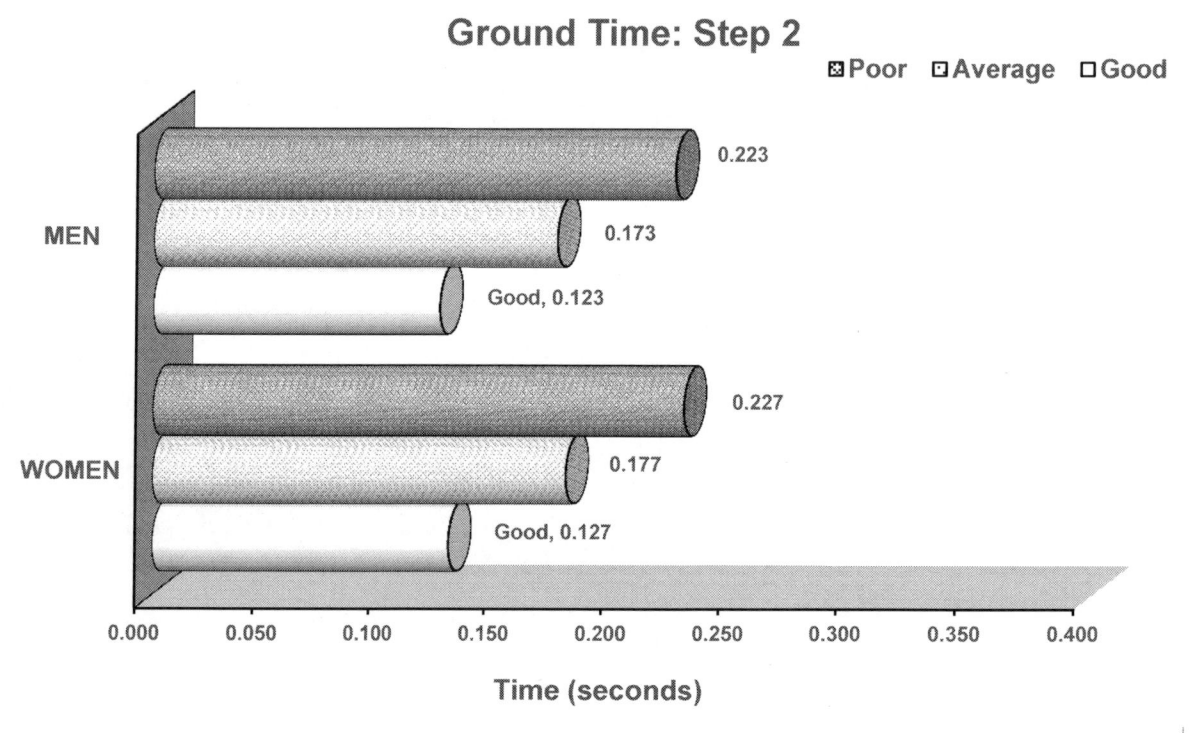

MEN
- Poor: 0.223
- Average: 0.173
- Good: 0.123

WOMEN
- Poor: 0.227
- Average: 0.177
- Good: 0.127

Figure 6-26: Ground Time During Step 2

Critical General Performance Descriptors For the Start

The Air Time results for the first three strides are displayed in Figures 6-27, 28, and 29.

Air Time: Blocks

⊠ Poor   ▣ Poor   ▢ Good

MEN
- 0.070
- 0.030
- Good, 0.050

WOMEN
- 0.070
- 0.030
- Good, 0.050

Time (seconds)

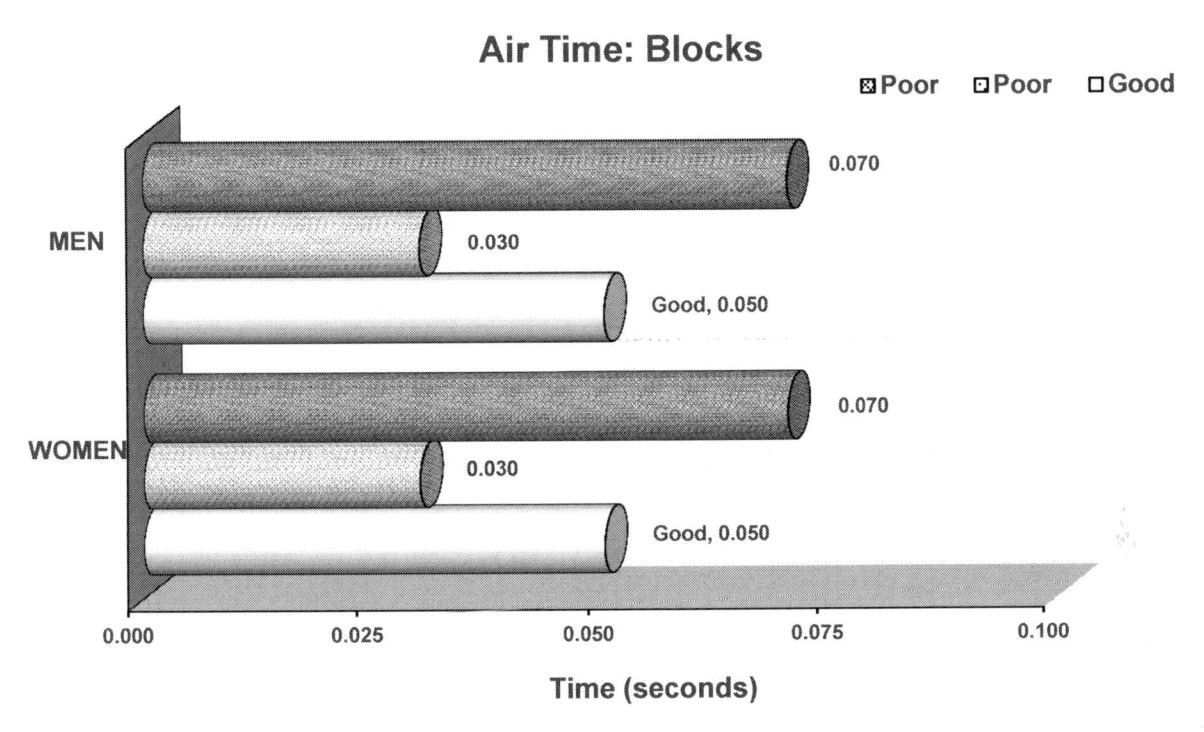

Figure 6-27: Air Time During Block Clearance

Air Time: Step 1

⊠ Poor   ▣ Poor   ▢ Good

MEN
- 0.080
- 0.040
- Good, 0.060

WOMEN
- 0.080
- 0.040
- Good, 0.060

Time (seconds)

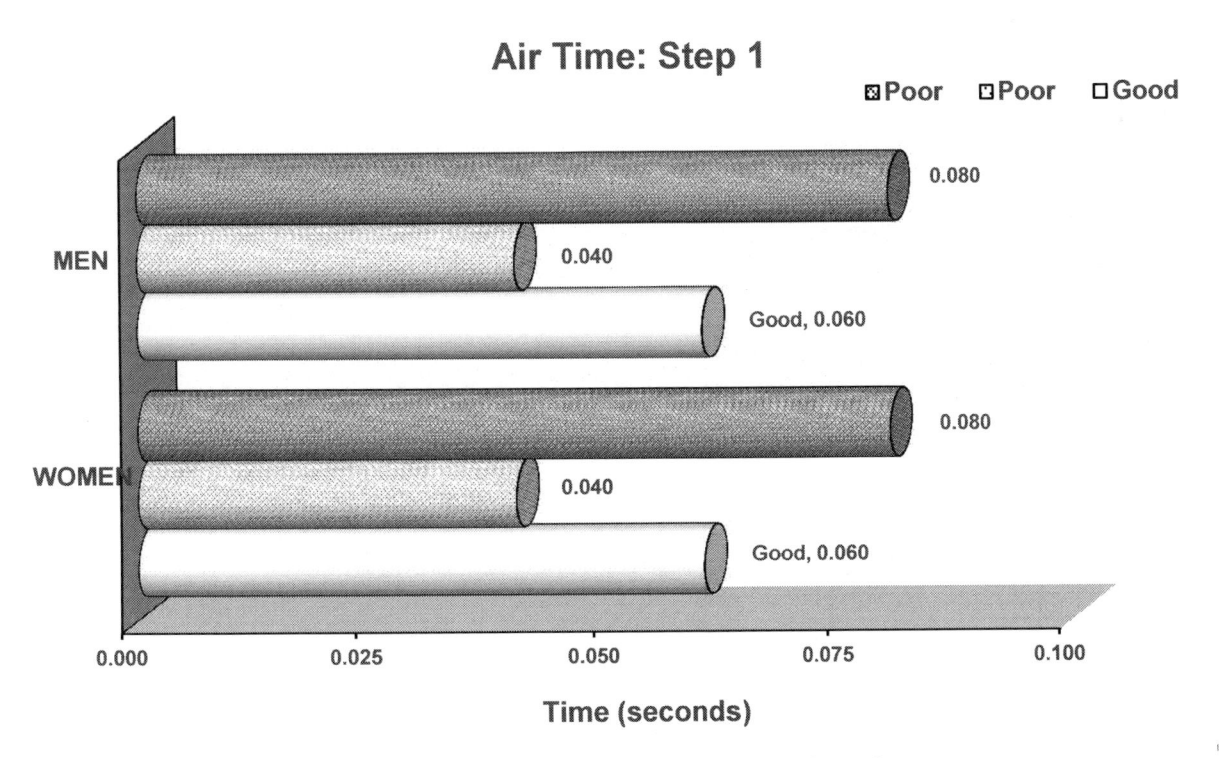

Figure 6-28: Air Time During Step 1

These results indicate that the emphasis of the Start is to produce a short Air Phase, and maximize the percentage of the time that is spent exerting forces on the ground.

Air Time: Step 2

Group	Poor	Poor	Good
MEN	0.087	0.047	0.067
WOMEN	0.087	0.047	0.067

Time (seconds)

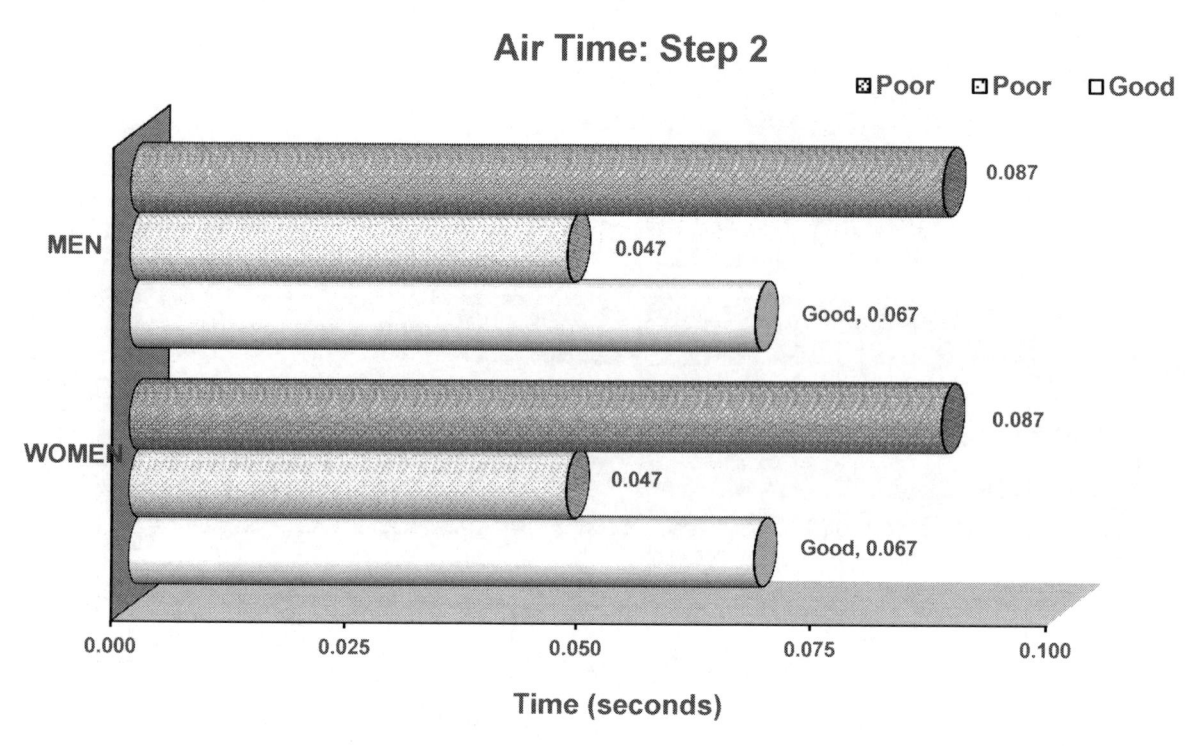

Figure 6-29: Air Time During Step 2

For all three subphases of the Start, the Air Time results for all levels of well coached sprinters are the same. Thus, Poor results can occur if the athlete produces Air Times that are either too short or too long. If the time is too short, the athlete does not have sufficient time to properly recover the body segments to the most efficient mechanical position. If the time is too long, then the athlete wastes time in the air that should be spent on the ground, driving the body down the track. It must be remembered that, whenever a sprinter is in the air, the strongest athlete is no more effective than the weakest athlete since there is nothing to push on. This is why, during the Start, **the best performers are on the ground almost 80 percent of the time**.

This same trend will be seen in the Maximum Velocity portion of the race.

It is apparent from the Ground and Air Time results that the key to the Start lies in minimizing ground contact by generating large amounts of ground force, while minimizing the Air Time by directing the action Horizontally (down the track) as much as possible.

How this is accomplished will be discussed in the next Chapter.

Time to 3, 5, 10, and 20 Meters

A direct final measure of the success of the Start are the times generated during the first 20 meters of the race. If the Start is properly performed, excellent results will be produced at 3, 5, 10, and 20 meters. Figure 6-30 shows the times required to reach each of these positions. Times are measured from the athlete's first movement to when the top of the head reaches each benchmark distance.

Pace Times: 100 Meters

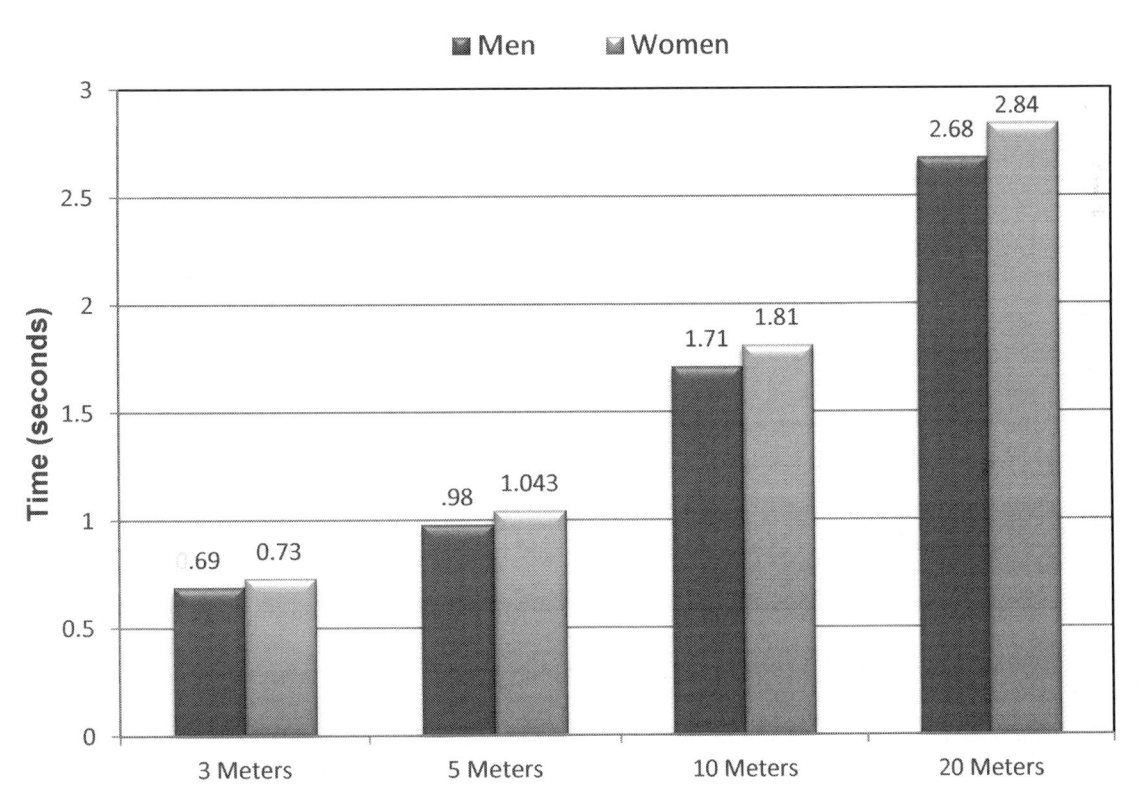

Distance	Men	Women
3 Meters	0.69	0.73
5 Meters	0.98	1.043
10 Meters	1.71	1.81
20 Meters	2.68	2.84

Figure 6-30: Times to 3, 5, 10, and 20 Meters of the 100 Meter Sprint

The Start sets the pace for the level of success over the initial 20 meters. Pure power can be used to produce a good 3 meter time, but proper Mechanics is necessary if the remainder of the race is to be completed successfully.

Chapter Summary:

Critical General Performance Descriptors For the Start

> The Start comprises the time spent to clear the blocks and complete the first two steps of the race. It is one of the most complex phases of any Sprint race, and success is dependent on proper Mechanics and explosive strength.
>
> It is evident that the General Performance Descriptors can be used to determine the overall success of the Start effort. These results point to the fact that success in the Start is achieved by generating high force levels, while properly managing these forces and the resulting body positions.
>
> Finally, small Velocity advantages gained during the Start will provide dividends over a large majority of the race.

Realizing that maximizing and managing force to produce Horizontal Velocity is the key to elite Sprint Start performance is one thing, understanding how the elite sprinters actually accomplish this task is another problem altogether. To resolve these questions, more specific performance variables must be investigated.

CHAPTER 7

CRITICAL SPECIFIC PERFORMANCE DESCRIPTORS FOR THE START

Chapter 6 concluded that success in the Start was tied to properly applying enormous amounts of explosive strength. The operative words here are "properly" and "enormous" because without Mechanics and Strength, success in this highly competitive environment is simply not possible.

The image shown in Figure 7-1 is a unique example how a very tall sprinter, at a definite disadvantage during the Start, can beat the entire field out of the blocks by using both Mechanics and Strength at high levels of competence.

Figure 7-1: How a Tall Sprinter Can Beat the Entire Field to the 10 Meter Mark in the 100 Meter Sprint Race

In the Start, **Specific Performance Descriptors** identify how the performer is mechanically producing the critical General Performance Descriptors identified in Chapter 6. Those specific descriptors that are directly related to performance include:

1. **Block Distances**
2. **COG Distance at the Set Position**

3. **Segment Angles at the Set Position**
4. **Segment Angles During Block Clearance**
5. **COG Distance at Step 1 Touchdown**
6. **Segment Angles During Step 1**
7. **COG Distance at Step 2 Touchdown**
8. **Segment Angles During Step 2**
9. **COG Distance at Step 3 Touchdown**

A complete understanding of these variables will provide a base around which to develop a mechanically sound sprinter, as well as focusing the talents of the athlete in the most productive manner possible.

Block Distances

The distance from the starting line and the front and rear blocks are dependent, unsurprisingly, on the leg length of the sprinter. A good rule of thumb to follow is that the front block should be placed so that, when, in the blocks, if the athlete places the front knee on the ground it is about 3 centimeters (≈1 inch) in back of the starting line. Once the front block distance is determined, the back block should be about 170% of this distance. Thus, if the front block is 56 centimeters from the line, then the back block should be around 94 (56*1.70) centimeters from the line (Figure 7-2).

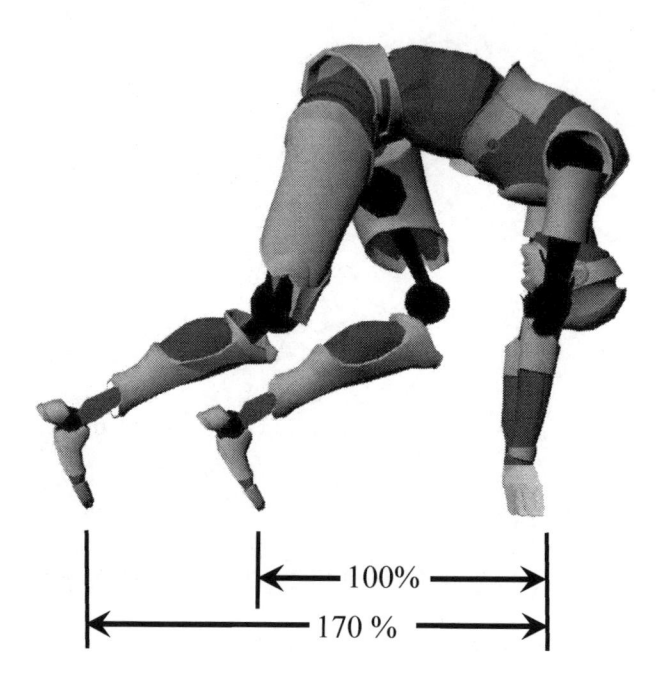

Figure 7-2: Block Distance Percentages

If these percentages are followed, and the Segment Angles at Set Position are properly produced, then the sprinter will look like the Model shown in Figure 7-2. This position places the trunk and legs into the best power position to deliver the maximum explosive force on the blocks.

COG Distance at the Set Position

The block distances dictate how the sprinter is able to drive through the Body COG and produce the starting action. As shown in Figure 7-3, at the Set position, the proper block position allows the sprinter to direct a large portion of the front and rear foot force Horizontally, down the track.

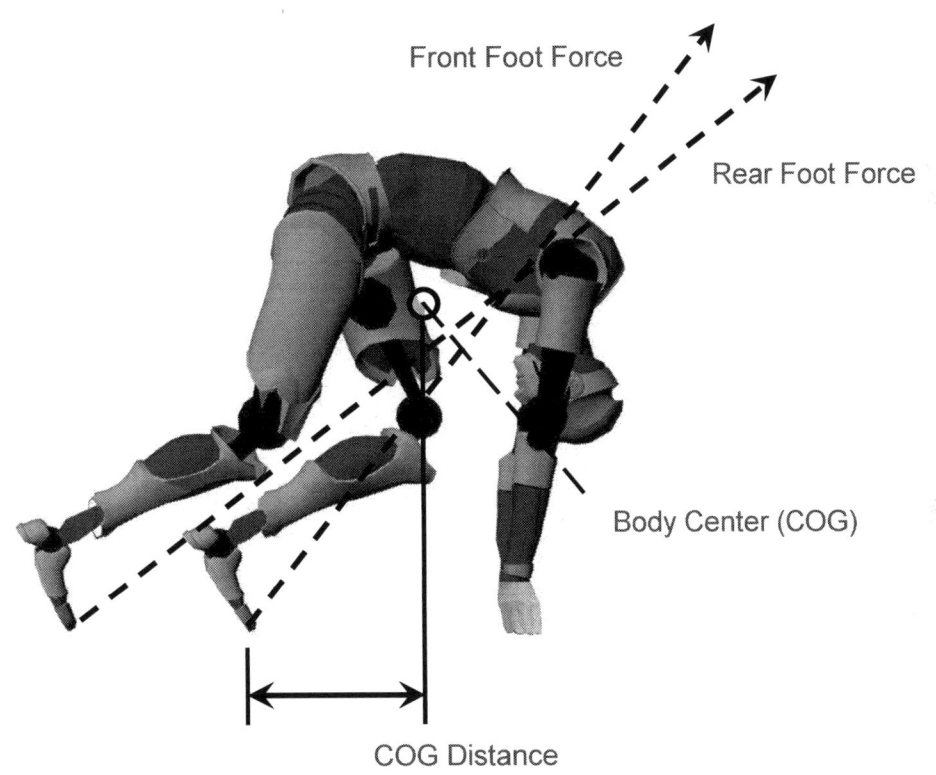

Figure 7-3: The Body COG Distance at the Set Position

For purposes of comparison, the COG Distance is measured Horizontally from the front foot to the Body COG. Obviously, if the feet are moved forward then the force tends to be more Vertically directed. Likewise, if the feet are moved back then the force tends to be more Horizontally directed.

The Body COG Distance results are displayed in Figure 7-4. These results indicate that there is a balance between placing the feet far enough back to drive the body down the track, but close enough to allow the legs sufficient range of motion as well as produce enough Vertical force to raise the Body COG to an upright sprinting position once the Start has been completed.

Body COG Distance: Set Position

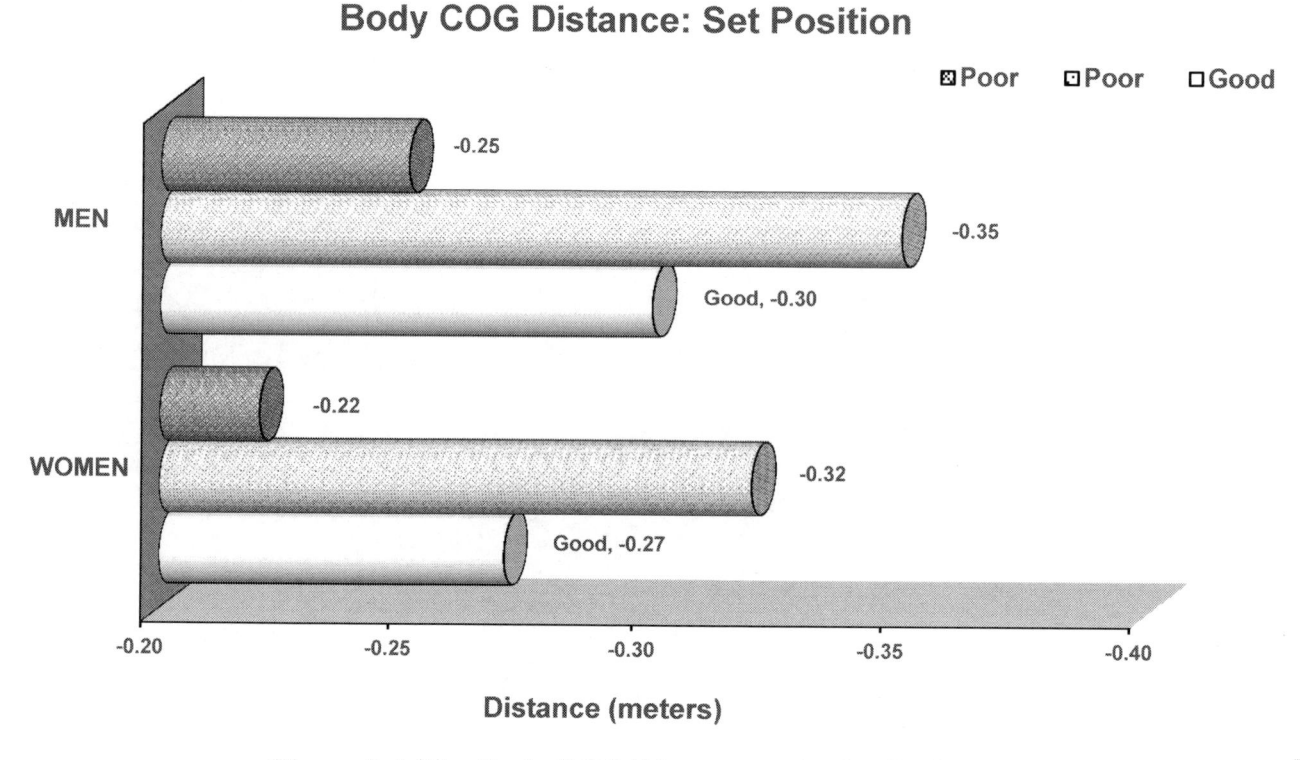

	Poor	Poor	Good
MEN	-0.25	-0.35	Good, -0.30
WOMEN	-0.22	-0.32	Good, -0.27

Distance (meters)

Figure 7-4: The Body COG Distance at the Set Position

Sprinters that do not have great strength levels and must focus most of their effort on getting the body up to a sprinting position, tend to place the body over the blocks (a smaller COG Distance). This makes it much easier for the athlete to produce the Vertical force required to raise the Body COG. Unfortunately, this Vertical emphasis reduces the ability to produce Horizontal force, which is what determines the success of the Start.

On the other hand, some athletes that have sufficient strength still place the block position too close (again a smaller COG Distance number), robbing them of the ability to produce the most efficient forces during the Start. Whether the problem is insufficient strength or poor Mechanics, the result is a significant decrease in performance.

Segment Angles at Set Position

If the blocks are set properly, then the sprinter can naturally produce the proper segment angles at the Set position (Figure 7-5). As seen, the critical angles are those at the trunk (in relation to the Horizontal), the rear and front upper legs (hips), and the lower legs (knees).

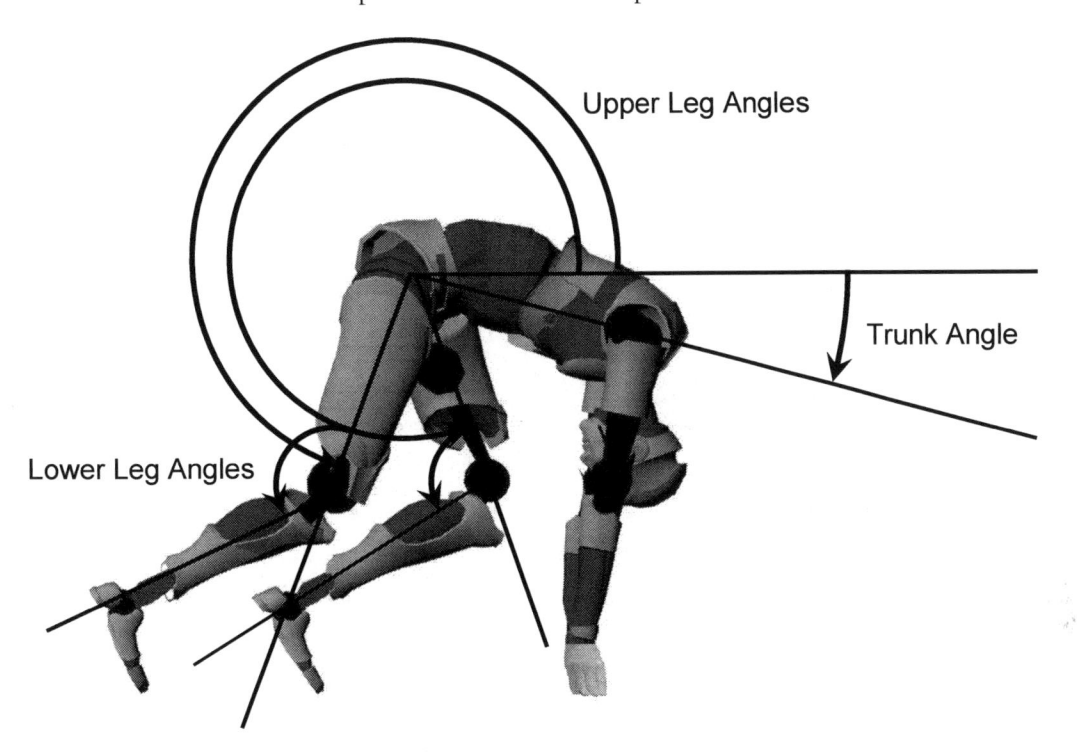

Critical Specific Performance Descriptors For the Start

Figure 7-5: The Trunk and Rear Leg Angles at the Set Position

Actual values for these angles are shown in Figure 7-6. Since the angles for both Men and Women are similar, they are presented as one. Note that, in every angle, there is a balance between too much or too little flexion/extension.

When the gun is fired at the Start, the body is in a static position. Thus, the entire body initial movement consists of low Velocity, high acceleration concentric motion. This action is best mimicked and, therefore, developed in the weight room. Full and Half Squats should be done to stop as close to the upper and lower leg angles as possible. Thus, Full Squats should stop at an upper leg angle of around 290 degrees and a lower leg angle of around 90 degrees. Half Squats should stop at an upper leg angle of about 250 degrees and a lower leg angle of 135 degrees. Likewise, for Power Cleans, the same two starting positions should be utilized as closely as possible.

This same concept should be used for all leg exercises – the upper and lower legs should all start at the two indicated angles and, if possible, rapidly accelerate from this static position. Whatever effort required to achieve these starting positions should be done since the greatest power development will only occur if these angles are closely achieved.

Trunk extensor strength must also be addressed. Since the trunk begins the Start at only about 55 degrees from the front leg, powerful extensor action must be performed from this tightly folded position.

Critical Specific Performance Descriptors For the Start

Segment Angles: Set Position

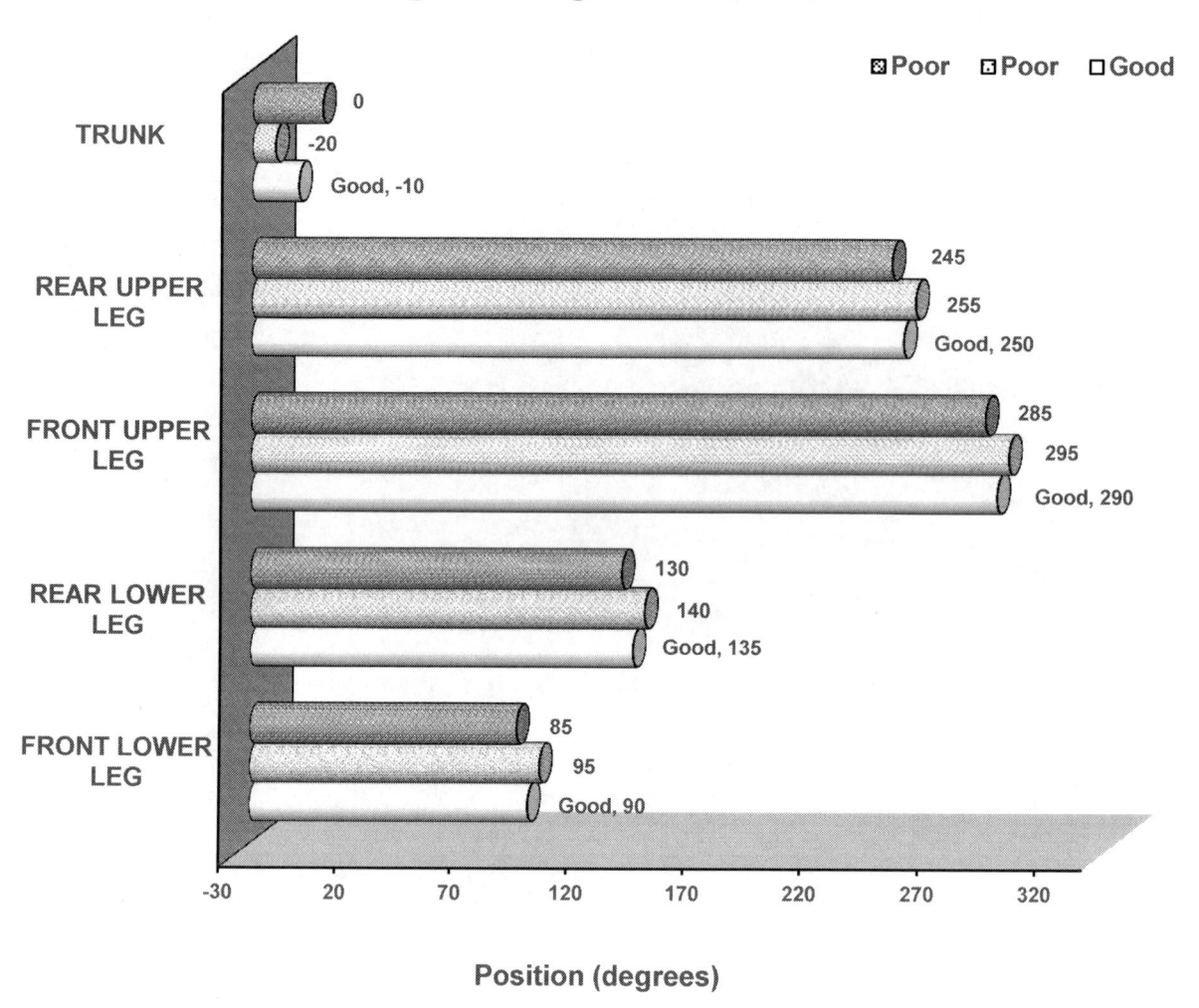

◼ Poor ▨ Poor ☐ Good

Segment	Poor	Poor	Good
TRUNK	0	-20	-10
REAR UPPER LEG	245	255	250
FRONT UPPER LEG	285	295	290
REAR LOWER LEG	130	140	135
FRONT LOWER LEG	85	95	90

Position (degrees)

Figure 7-6: The Segment Angles at the Set Position

At the gun, the explosive strength that the athlete can generate from this position will dictate, to a large degree, the success of the race since this starting position affects all aspects of the movement down the track.

Segment Angles During Block Clearance

During Block Clearance there are several critical positions. These include the lower leg (knee) angle as the rear foot clears the block (Figure 7-7), the lower leg (knee) angle as the rear ankle crosses the front knee (Figure 7-8), and the trunk and lower leg (knee) angles as the front foot clears the blocks (Figure 7-9).

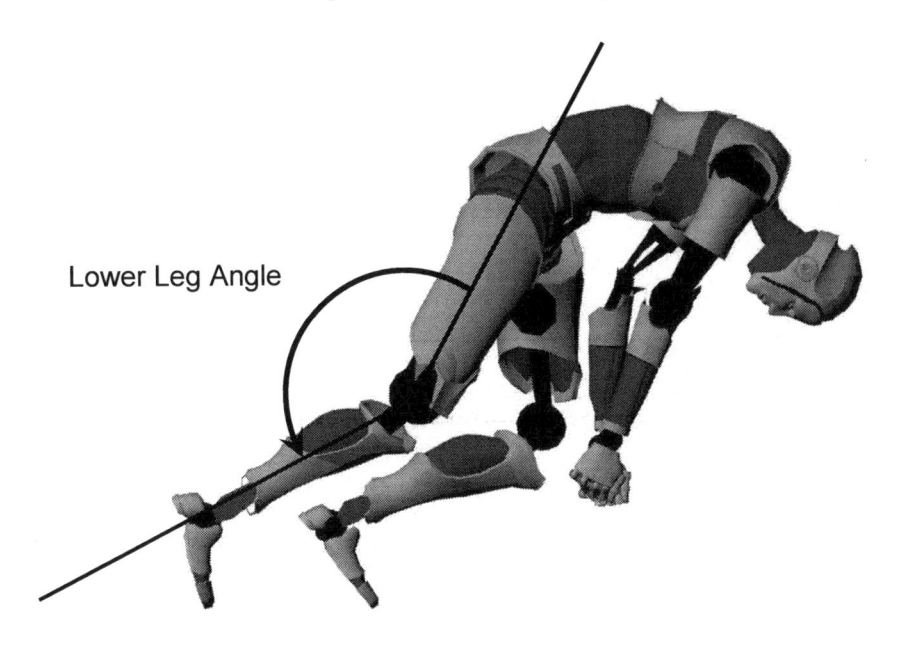

Critical Specific Performance Descriptors For the Start

Figure 7-7: The Segment Angles at Rear Foot Clearance

Figure 7-8: The Segment Angles at Rear Ankle Cross

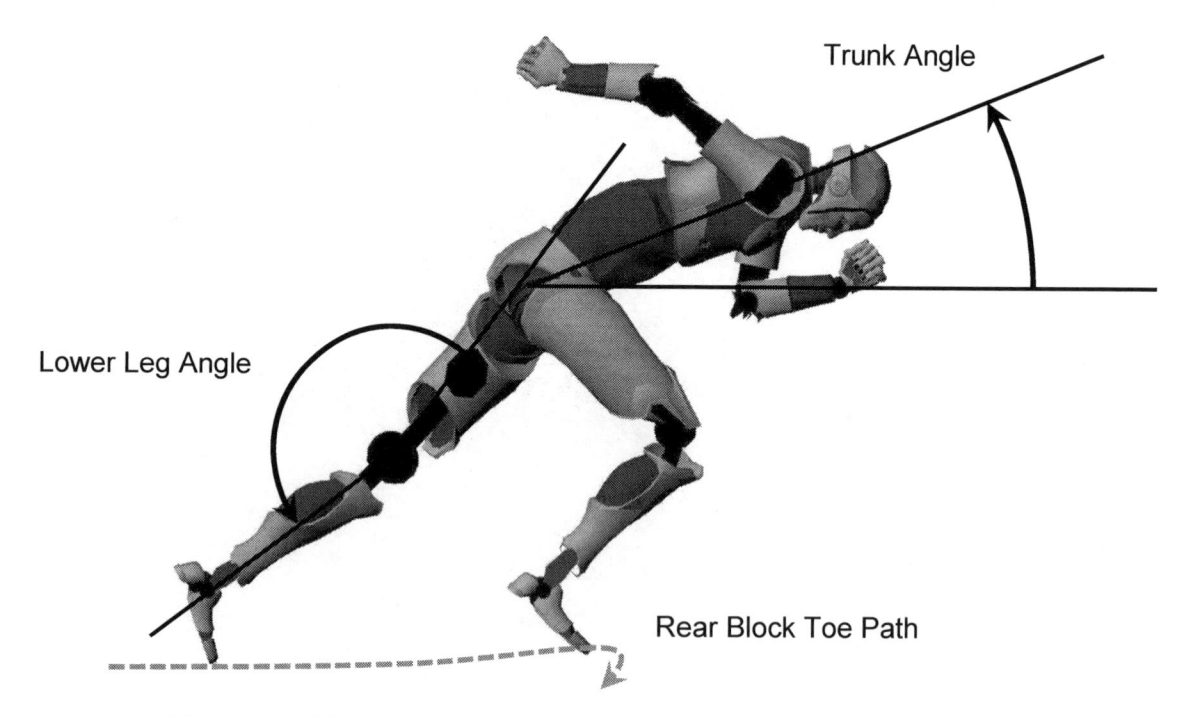

Figure 7-9: The Segment Angles at Front Foot Clearance

Actual values for these angles are shown in Figure 7-10. Since the angles for both Men and Women are similar, they are presented as one.

These dynamic block results point to the Start concept that the best sprinters are using to successfully clear the blocks. The key lies in the results of the trunk and lower leg angles. At the end of the push phase for both the rear foot (Figure 7-7) and front foot (Figure 7-9), note that the knee is not fully extended. This indicates that the athlete is not pushing the leg through full extension (just as will be seen in the Full Speed Sprint). This action of actively pulling the feet off the blocks prior to full knee extension is critical for the success of the Start because it does not waste time extending (and then flexing) the knee through the last 20-40 degrees of extension when the action produces only a small amount of additional driving force. The only thing an athlete must remember is that this recovery occurs at the **end** of the push effort, since some take this action to extremes and fail to get the most out of the initial leg extension action.

Furthermore, during the recovery of the rear leg, it is swung low to the ground with the lower leg extended to the point that the toe is barely off the ground (shown in Figure 7-8: compare this to the low foot the position of the taller sprinter in Figure 7-1). The key to success of this low recovery can be seen in the path of the toe of the foot as it clears the Back Block and moves toward the initial Touchdown. As can be seen, the toe path moves from a position of **low-to-high**, then powerfully drives **down and back** to the track.

This is coupled with the production of a low trunk angle as the blocks are cleared (Figure 7-9).

This starting action is the first indication that the Start should be dominated by the goal of keeping the body segments in the front of the body, while minimizing any action that occurs in the back of the body. This concept will be discussed in detail in Chapter 12.

Segment Angles: Blocks

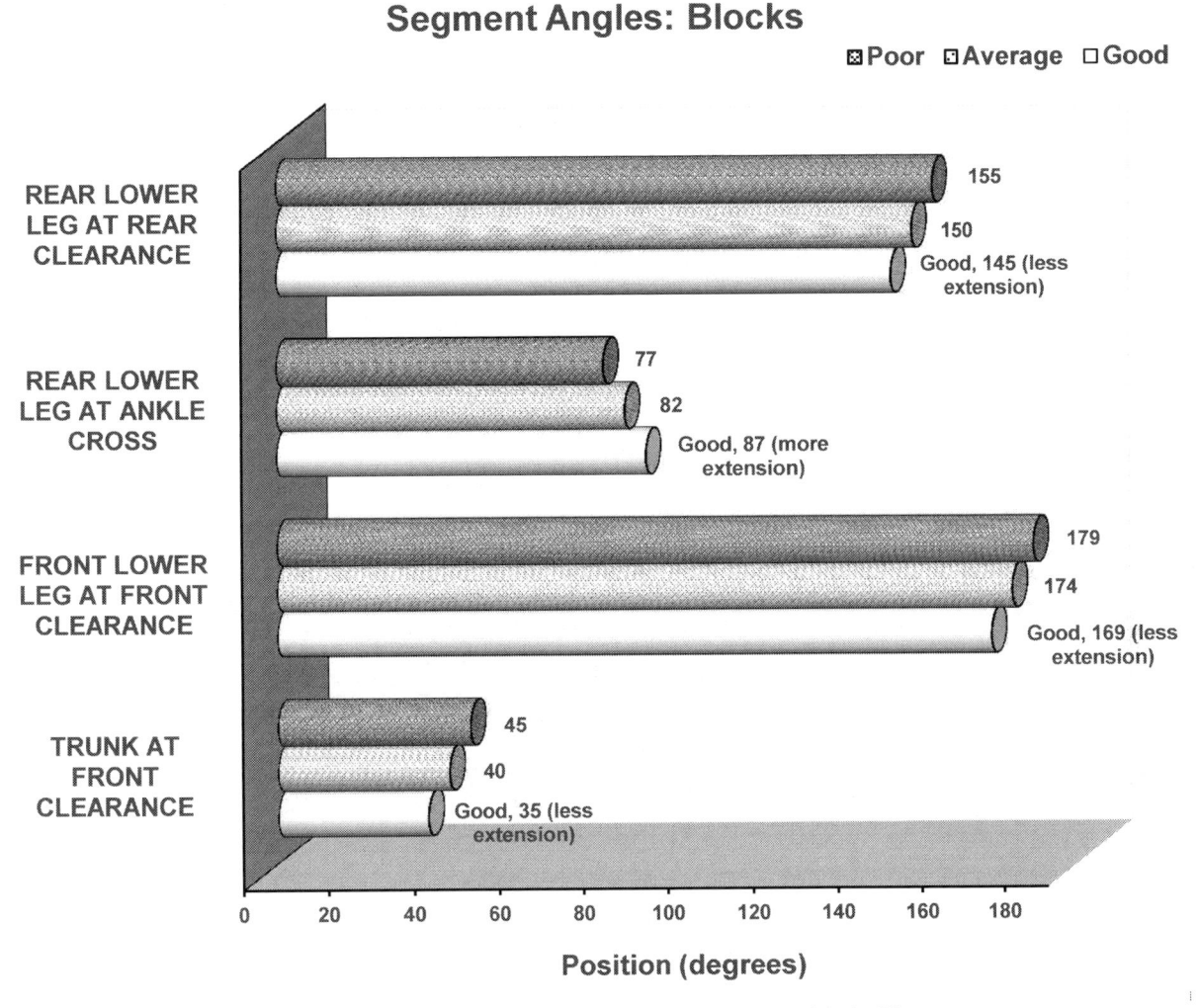

☒ Poor ☐ Average ☐ Good

Segment	Poor	Average	Good
REAR LOWER LEG AT REAR CLEARANCE	155	150	145 (less extension)
REAR LOWER LEG AT ANKLE CROSS	77	82	87 (more extension)
FRONT LOWER LEG AT FRONT CLEARANCE	179	174	169 (less extension)
TRUNK AT FRONT CLEARANCE	45	40	35 (less extension)

Position (degrees)

Figure 7-10: The Segment Angles During Block Clearance

COG Distance and Segment Angles During Step 1

During Step 1 there are several critical positions. These include the Body COG Touchdown distance (Figure 7-11), the lower leg (knee) angle as the rear ankle crosses the front knee (Figure 7-12), and the trunk and lower leg (knee) angles at Takeoff (Figure 7-13).

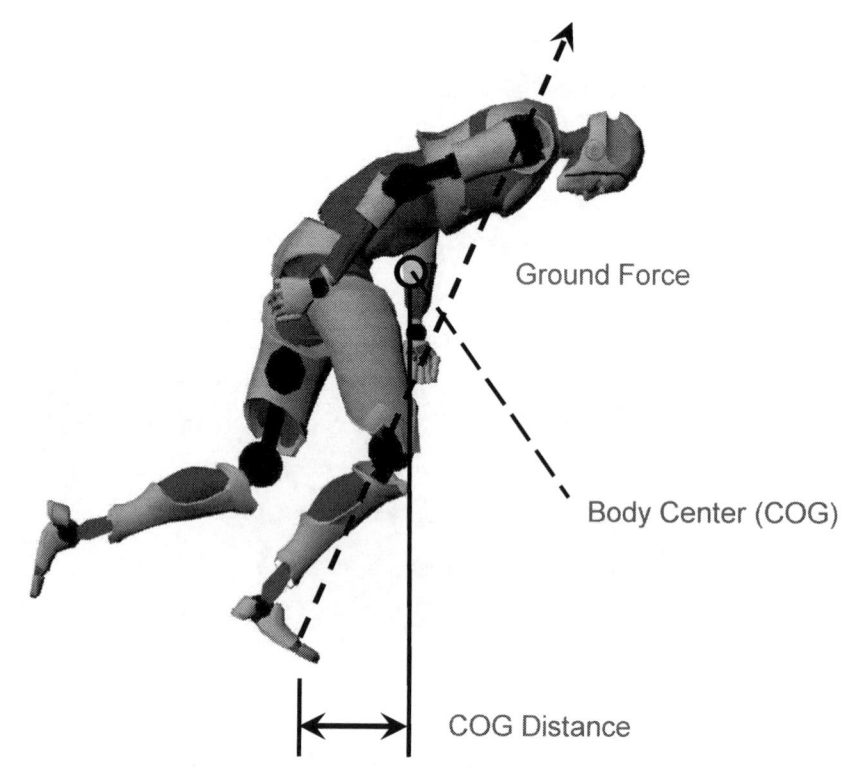

Figure 7-11: Step 1 Body COG Touchdown Distance

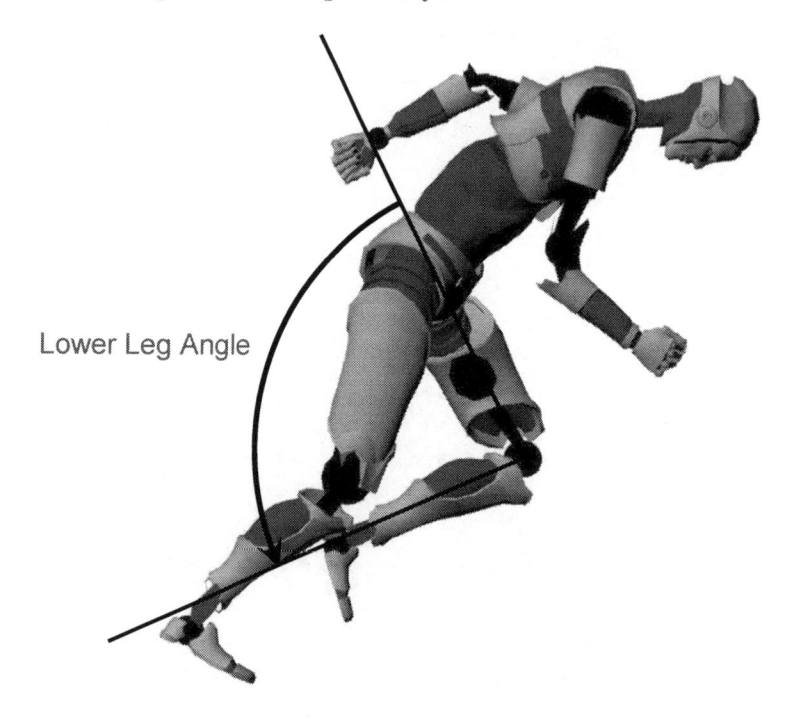

Figure 7-12: The Segment Angles at Step 1 Ankle Cross

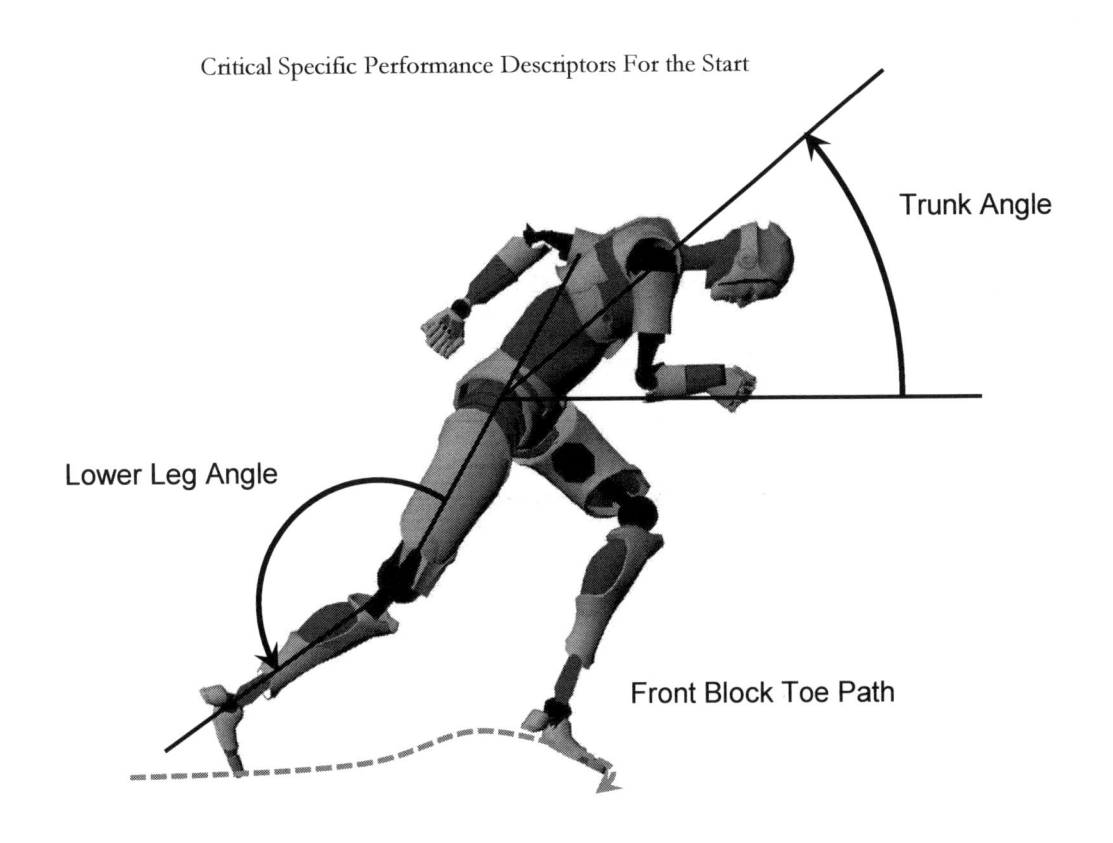

Figure 7-13: The Segment Angles at Step 1 Takeoff

Actual values for these results are shown in Figures 7-14 and 7-15.

As in the Block phase, Figure 7-14 indicates that, for the most proficient performers, the entire ground contact phase occurs behind the Body COG, placing the body in a position to produce maximum Horizontal (down the track) acceleration. However, the body is in an awkward, half crouched posture and must continue to raise the body to an upright position. This, combined with the challenge of maintaining body balance on one leg after a very brief Air Phase, **makes this step the most difficult stride in the entire Sprint race**. It is also the most dangerous since it is this step where, if not done properly, can cause the athlete to stumble forward, rise up too quickly, over stride, or otherwise lose body balance. If this occurs, then not only is the power of this single step lost, but it negatively affects the remainder of the Start as well as the transition into maximum sprinting Speed. It is, without a doubt, the most important single step in any Sprint race.

As seen in the numerical results shown in Figure 7-15, during the recovery of the rear leg, it is swung low to the ground with the lower leg extended to the point that the toe is barely off the ground (Figure 7-12). As was true in the Back Block toe recovery, the path of the Front Block toe moves from **low-to-high**, then powerfully drives **down and back** to the track (Figure 7-13). Also as in the Block phase, full extension of the lower leg does not occur as ground contact is dynamically ended, with the Ground Leg actually pulled off the ground. This is coupled with the production of a minimal trunk angle in an effort to maintain a low, forward driving position.

Critical Specific Performance Descriptors For the Start

Body COG Distance: Step 1

■ Poor ▨ Average ☐ Good

MEN
- 0.16
- 0.00
- Good, -0.14

WOMEN
- 0.19
- 0.03
- Good, -0.11

Distance (meters)

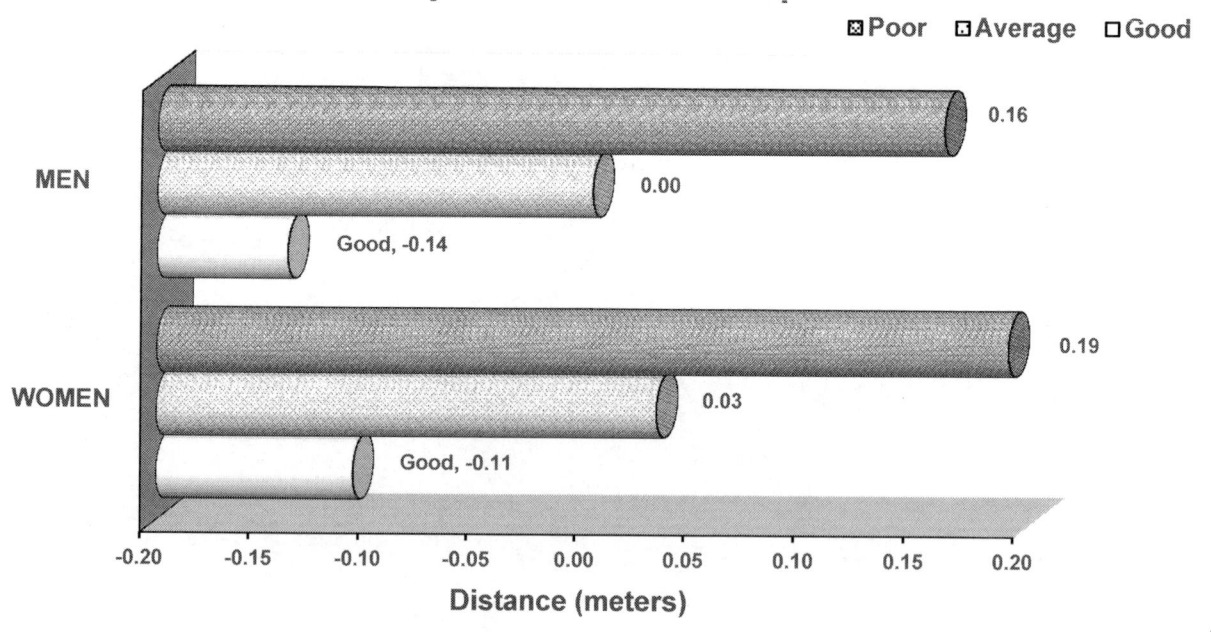

Figure 7-14: The Body COG Distance at Step 1 Touchdown

Segment Angles: Step 1

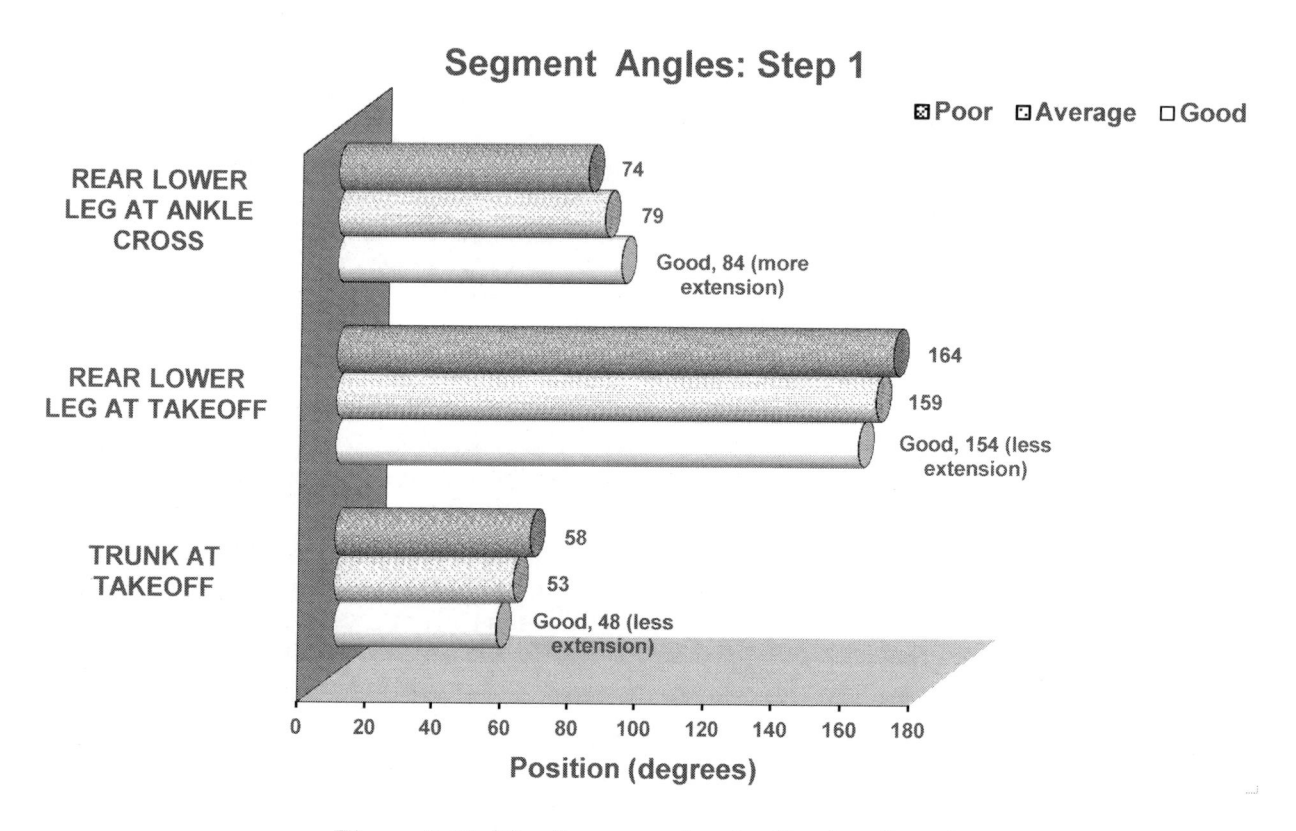

■ Poor ▨ Average ☐ Good

REAR LOWER LEG AT ANKLE CROSS
- 74
- 79
- Good, 84 (more extension)

REAR LOWER LEG AT TAKEOFF
- 164
- 159
- Good, 154 (less extension)

TRUNK AT TAKEOFF
- 58
- 53
- Good, 48 (less extension)

Position (degrees)

Figure 7-15: The Segment Angles During Step 1

COG Distance and Segment Angles During Step 2

The Mechanics of Step 2 are the same as Step 1 with the exception that, as the body is lifted and rotated toward the full sprinting position, it becomes more difficult to keep the Body COG behind the Touchdown position.

As in Step 1 there are several critical positions in Step 2. These include the Body COG Touchdown distance (Figure 7-16), the lower leg (knee) angle as the rear ankle crosses the front knee (Figure 7-17), and the trunk and lower leg (knee) angles at Takeoff (Figure 7-18).

Actual values for these results are shown in Figures 7-19 and 7-20.

These Figures demonstrate that, as was seen as the athlete moves from the Blocks through Step One, the entire ground contact phase occurs behind the Body COG, placing the body in a position to produce maximum Horizontal (down the track) acceleration.

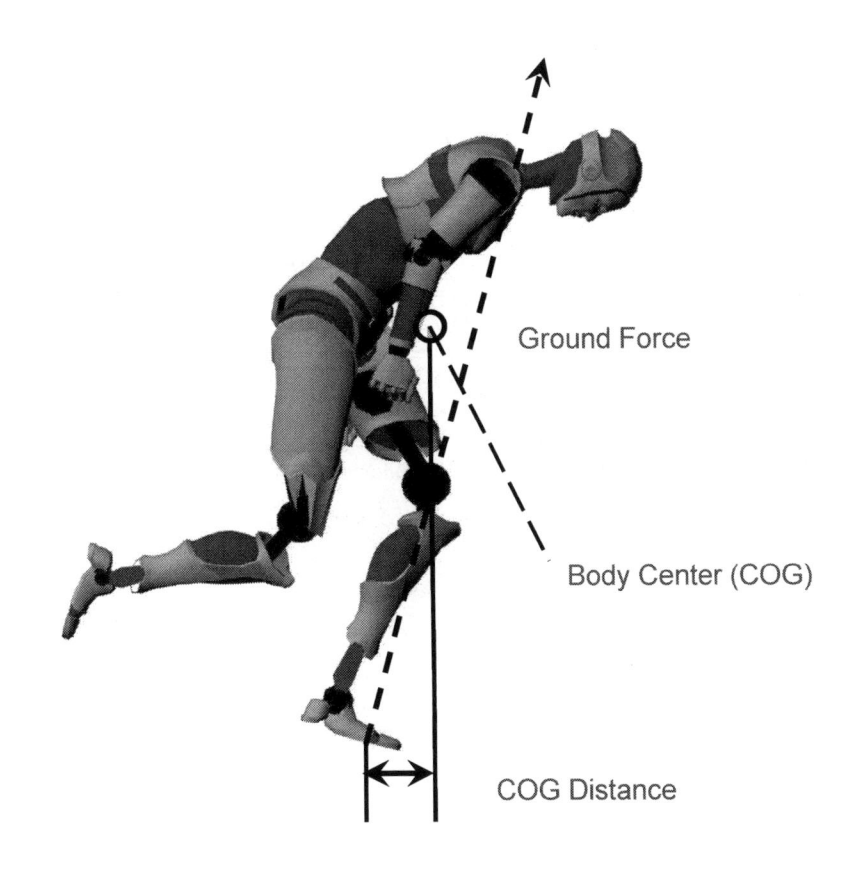

Figure 7-16: Step 2 Body COG Touchdown Distance

Critical Specific Performance Descriptors For the Start

Figure 7-17: The Segment Angles at Step 2 Ankle Cross

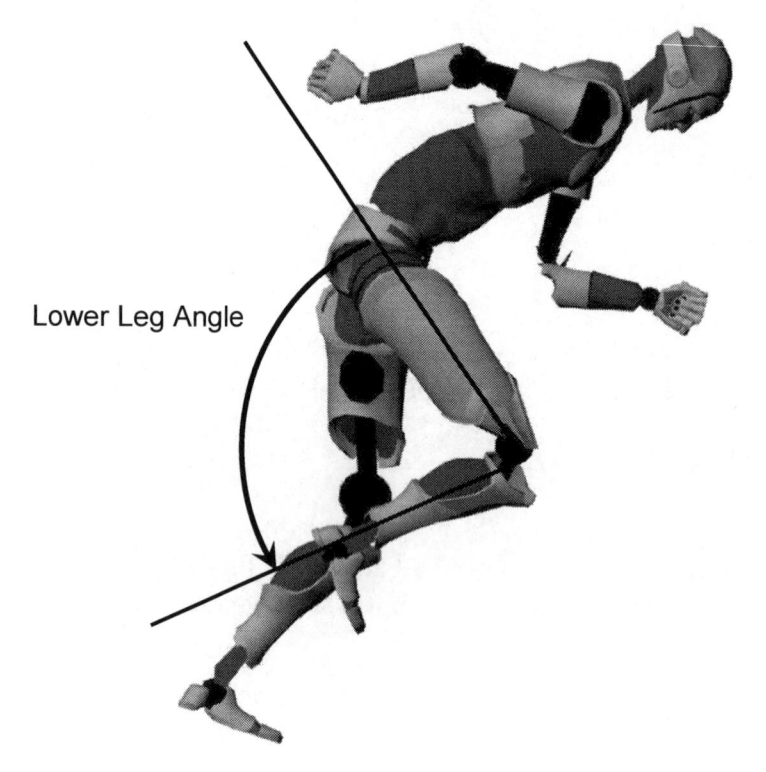

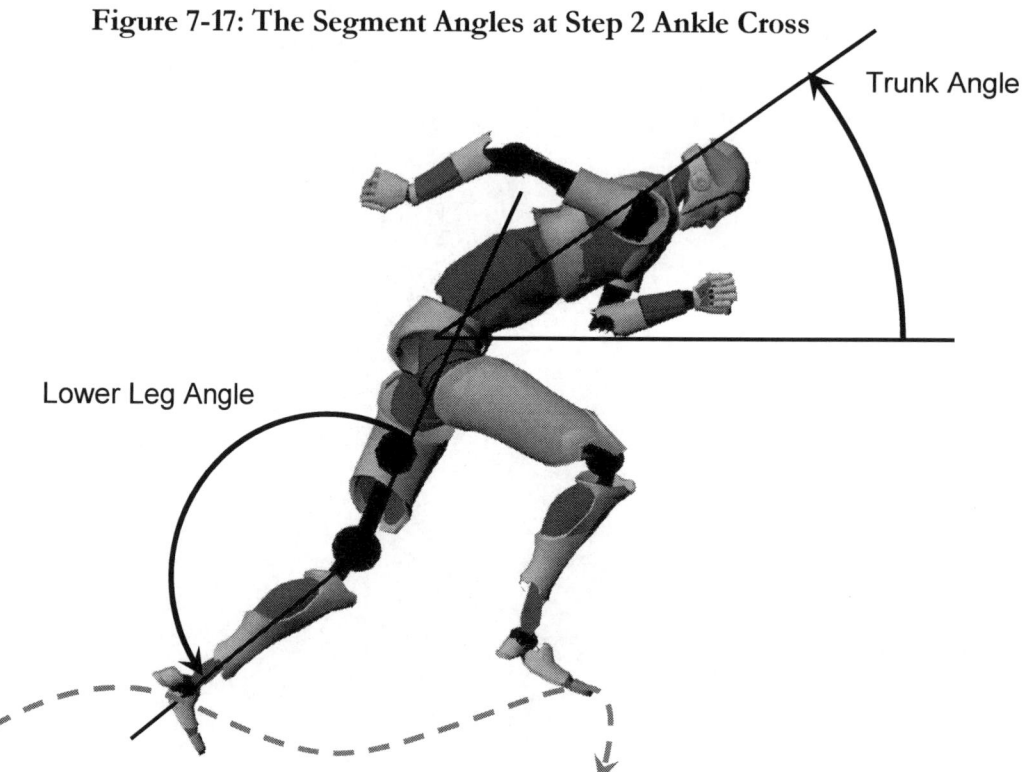

Figure 7-18: The Segment Angles at Step 2 Takeoff

Critical Specific Performance Descriptors For the Start

Body COG Distance: Step 2

Legend: ▨ Poor ▨ Poor ☐ Good

MEN:
- Poor: 0.08
- Poor: -0.04
- Good, -0.16

WOMEN:
- Poor: 0.12
- Poor: 0.00
- Good, -0.12

Distance (meters)

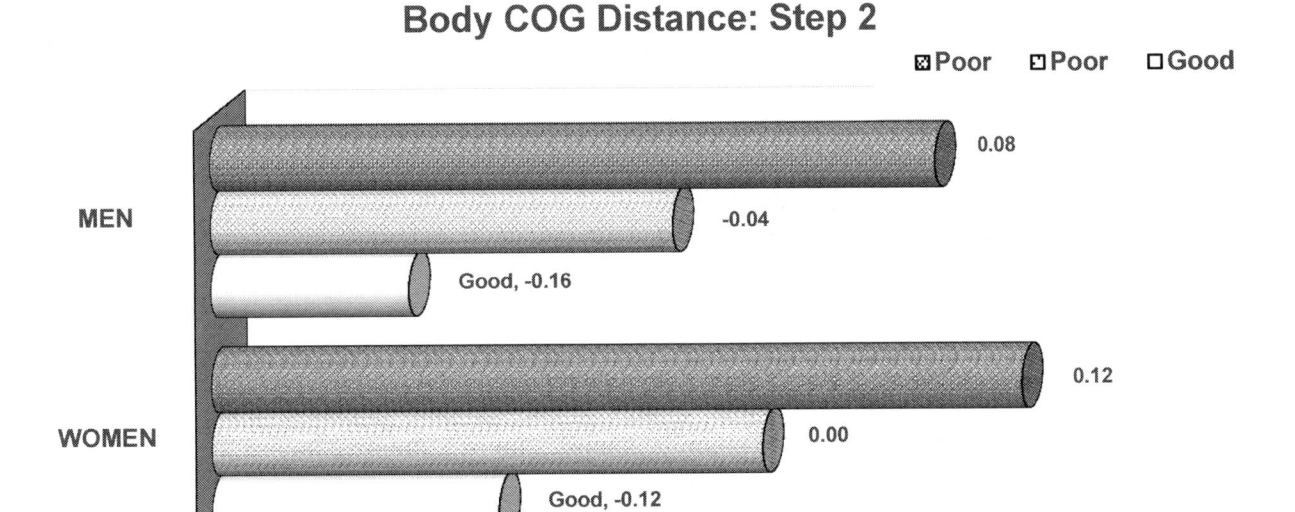

Figure 7-19: The Body COG Distance at Step 2 Touchdown

Segment Angles: Step 2

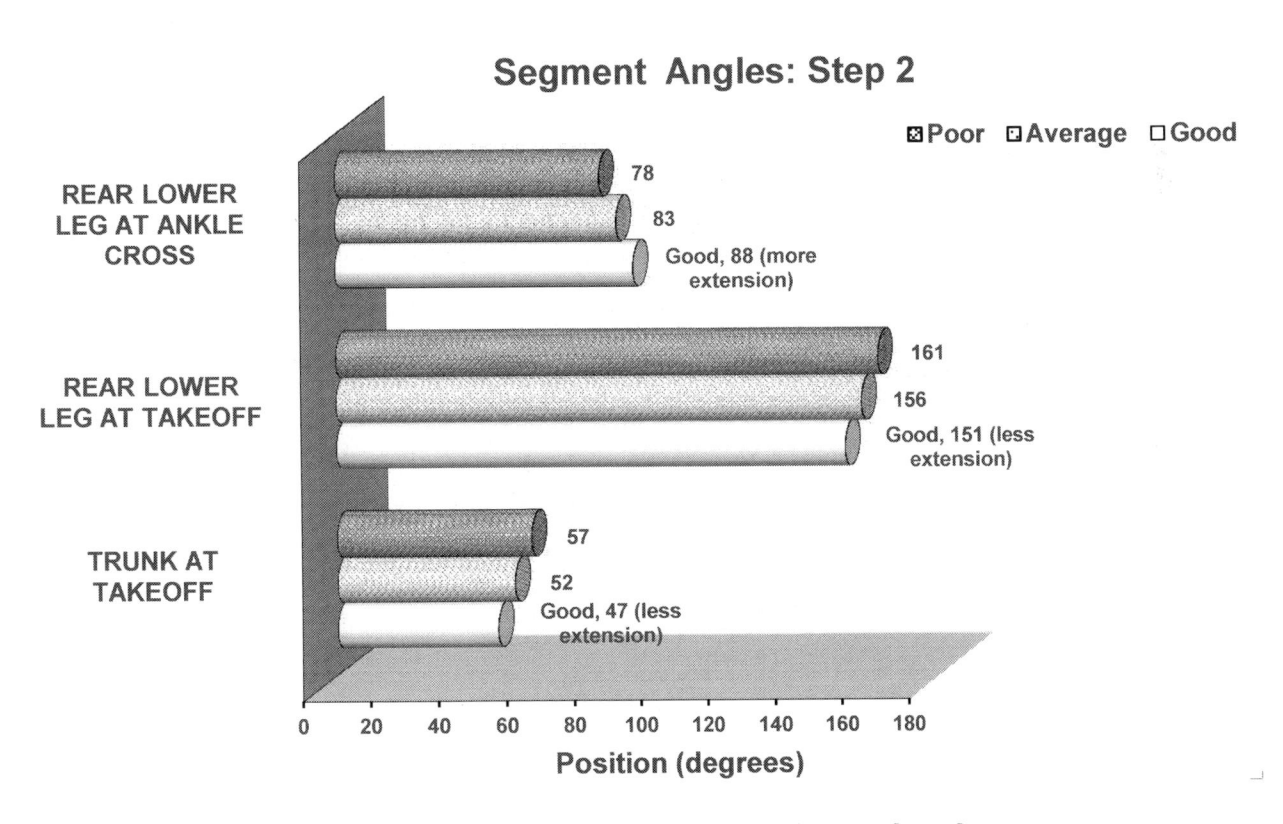

Legend: ▨ Poor ▨ Average ☐ Good

REAR LOWER LEG AT ANKLE CROSS:
- Poor: 78
- Average: 83
- Good, 88 (more extension)

REAR LOWER LEG AT TAKEOFF:
- Poor: 161
- Average: 156
- Good, 151 (less extension)

TRUNK AT TAKEOFF:
- Poor: 57
- Average: 52
- Good, 47 (less extension)

Position (degrees)

Figure 7-20: The Segment Angles During Step 2

In addition, Step Two mechanics demonstrate the same low-to-high toe path of the recovery leg and limited lower leg extension of the Ground Leg at Takeoff. Finally, the trunk continues to remain considerably flexed even this late in the starting process.

COG Distance During Step 3

The Touchdown Mechanics of the beginning of Step 3 are the same as Step 2 as the body is further lifted and rotated toward the full sprinting position (Figure 7-21).

Actual values for these results are shown in Figures 7-22. Note that, for both Men and Women, only the best athletes manage to keep their Body COG behind their Touchdown position.

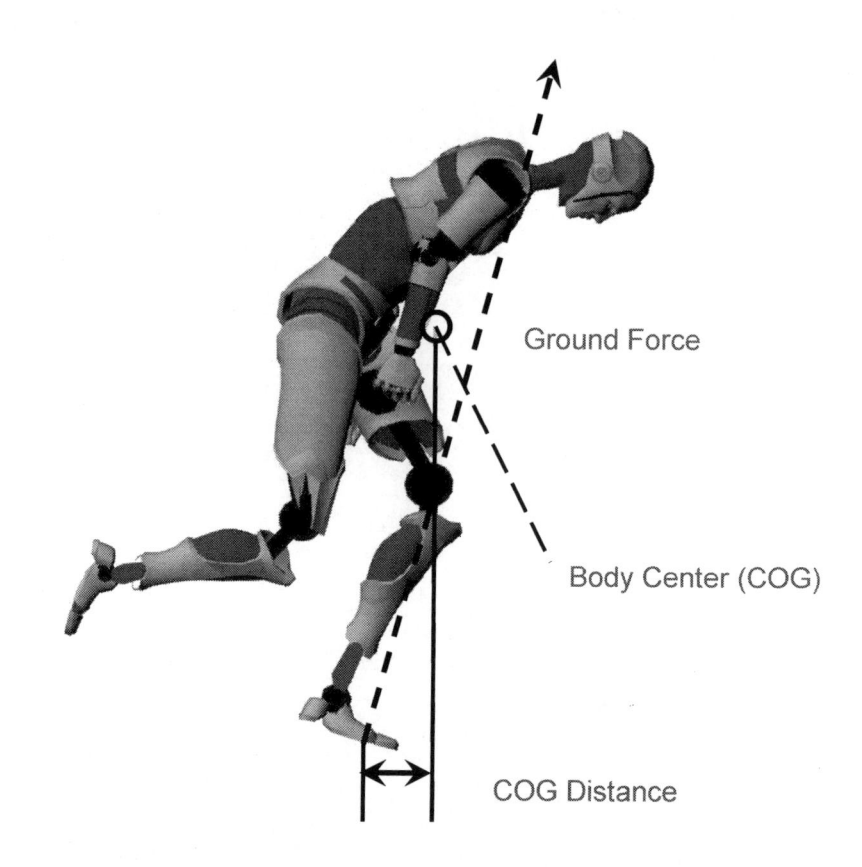

Figure 7-21: Step 3 Body COG Touchdown Distance

Body COG Distance: Step 3

Legend: ⊠ Poor   ▨ Poor   ☐ Good

MEN
- 0.12
- 0.00
- Good, -0.12

WOMEN
- 0.15
- 0.03
- Good, -0.09

Distance (meters)

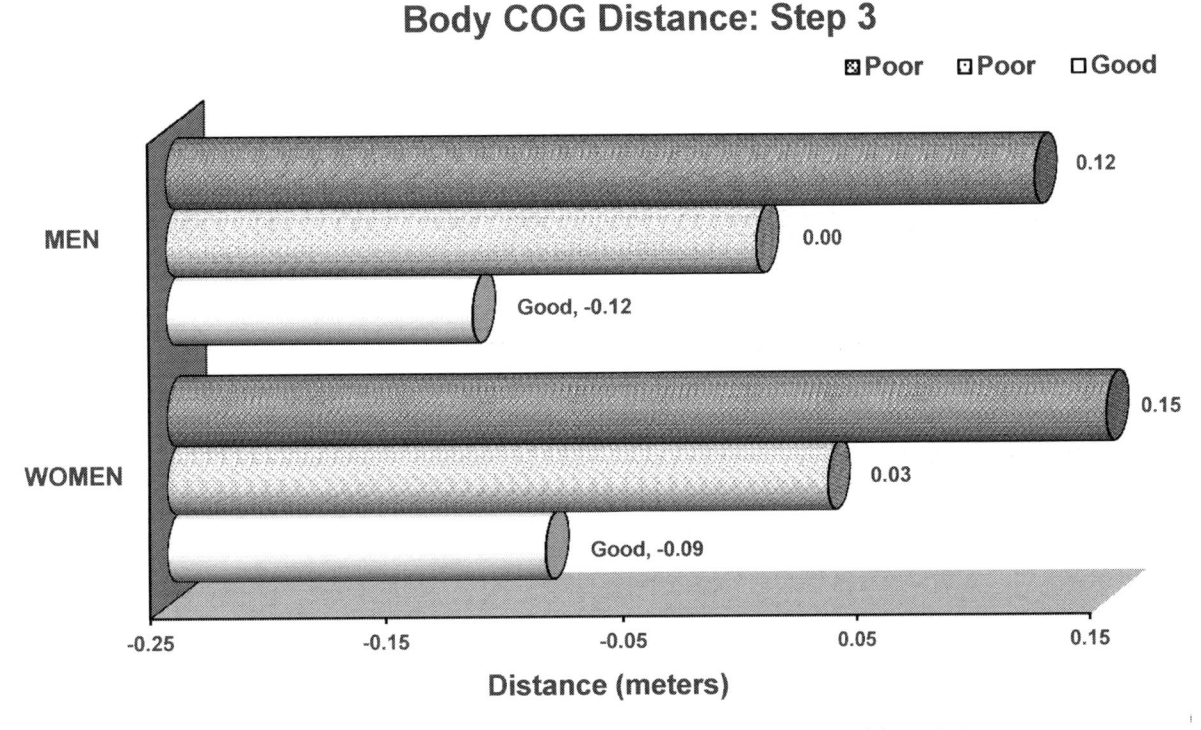

Figure 7-22: The Body COG Distance at Step 3 Touchdown

Once the Start is concluded and top Speed is approached, the foot Touchdown position moves forward, occurring in front of the Body COG. If the athlete can arrive at this step in control and in the proper position, the transition to Maximum Velocity becomes a more productive process.

The goal of the Start is to take the athlete from complete rest to almost 60 percent of Maximum Velocity by the end of the second step.

Chapter Summary:

The Specific Performance Descriptors point to the fact that success in the Sprint Start is determined by the ability of the athlete to generate great amounts of explosive strength at the proper time. Generally, the proper mechanical application of this strength results in an elite performance that is characterized by a high Stride Rate and low Air Times. Specifically, the superior performance is a product of emphasis on keeping the segments in front of the body and producing precise body control.

All of these factors lead to the conclusion that the Shuffle Start is the most effective way to produce the greatest amount of Speed in the shortest amount of time, while preparing the body for the proper Full Speed Mechanics portion of the race.

For those elite hurdlers that are so big and/or so fast that putting eight steps into the allotted distance to the first hurdle negatively affects their race, using a Seven Step Start can be beneficial. However, the extreme physical demands of this Start make it viable for only the best of the best.

PART FOUR: MAXIMUM VELOCITY MECHANICS

INTRODUCTION

THE SPRINT GOLDEN POSITION

After analyzing thousands of athletes over many years, coupled with actual interactive, on-track teaching sessions with elite athletes, a single "Golden Position" has been identified as the benchmark to judge overall Full Speed Sprint Mechanics. If an athlete can arrive at this position in the proper body position, at the right time, and at the required Velocity, then the Sprint will be successful.

The Figure below identifies this Position as the point of maximum upper leg flexion (high knee position). If the athlete can reach this position, under control, no sooner than 0.033 seconds after Takeoff, while producing a Velocity of 12.5 meters per second (10.9 meters/second for Women), all criteria have been met.

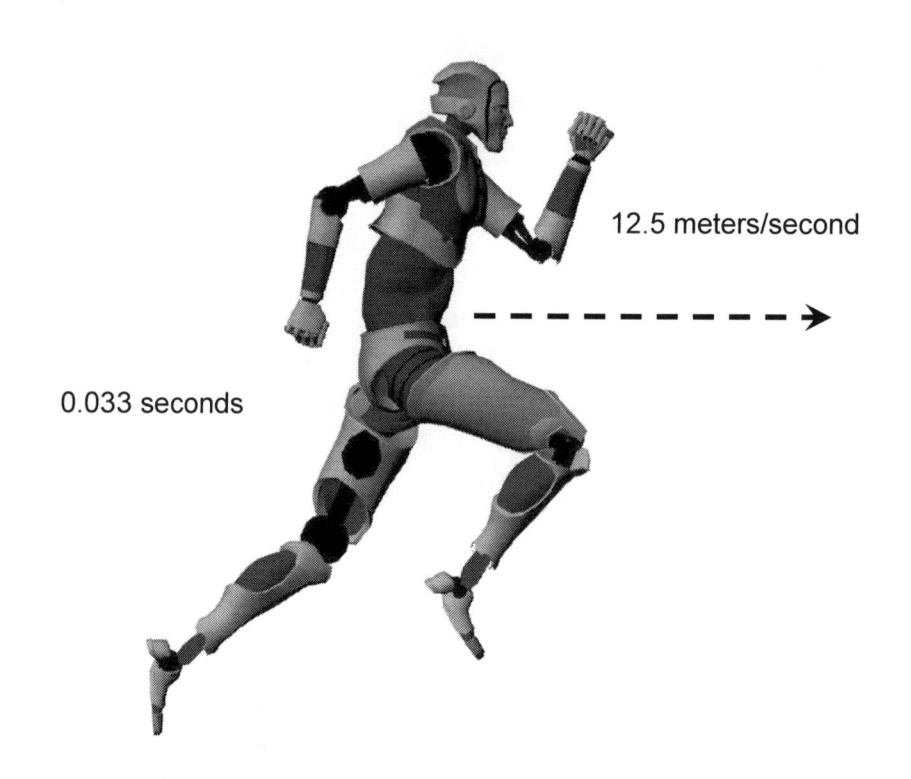

Maximum Upper Leg Flexion: The Sprint Golden Position

This single Position has been termed "Golden" since, to achieve it, the athlete must perform all subsequent Mechanics properly, and possess the Flexibility and explosive Strength to make the most of the actions. In addition, since the Sprint action is repeated over and over, matching this position is the only way to allow the athlete to successfully continue to produce the proper Mechanics during subsequent strides.

If there are any mechanical flaws, or Flexibility/Strength deficiencies, this Position simply cannot be produced, as well as insuring a decrement in the overall Sprint result.

These time and Velocity values will, of course, vary with body size as well as gender, but they are excellent goals for all performers.

The information contained in Part Four describes how elite sprinters achieve this goal.

CHAPTER 8

CRITICAL GENERAL PERFORMANCE DESCRIPTORS FOR THE SHORT SPRINTS AT MAXIMUM VELOCITY

In the Maximum Velocity Sprint performance, **General Performance Descriptors** identify the result of the athlete's effort. These descriptors identify how well the athlete is doing, however, they do not identify how the performer is mechanically producing the results. Those general descriptors that are directly related to performance include:

1. **Horizontal Velocity**
2. **Stride Rate**
3. **Stride Length**
4. **Ground Contact Time**
5. **Air Time**
6. **Time to Maximum Upper Leg Flexion**

Horizontal Velocity is a measure of the Speed the athlete is moving down the track, and is typically expressed in meters per second or feet per second. Stride rate is the turnover rate of the athlete (steps per second), while Stride Length is the distance covered with each step (meters or feet). Ground contact time is the amount of time the athlete spends in contact with the ground (seconds) while Air Time is the amount of time spent airborne (seconds) during each stride. Finally, Time to Maximum Upper Leg Flexion is the time, from Takeoff, that it takes for the recovery Upper Leg to reach its greatest flexion position.

Although these descriptors do not identify specifically how the elite athlete produces a successful Sprint performance, they will indicate the general areas that must be emphasized to accomplish this task.

Horizontal Velocity

The most obvious General Performance Descriptor in the Sprint is Horizontal Velocity. Ignoring the importance of the Start, the athlete that can produce the greatest amount of Horizontal Velocity will be the most successful. As simple as this seems, this result also points out the weakness in looking at these general descriptors for assistance in effectively evaluating the performance. Although the Velocity result will indicate how fast the athlete is moving, it gives no information regarding how the sprinter is producing the result. Thus, except for categorizing a sprinter, this result is of little use to a coach.

For the elite sprinters, the range of Horizontal Velocity values is presented in Figure 8-1.

Horizontal Velocity

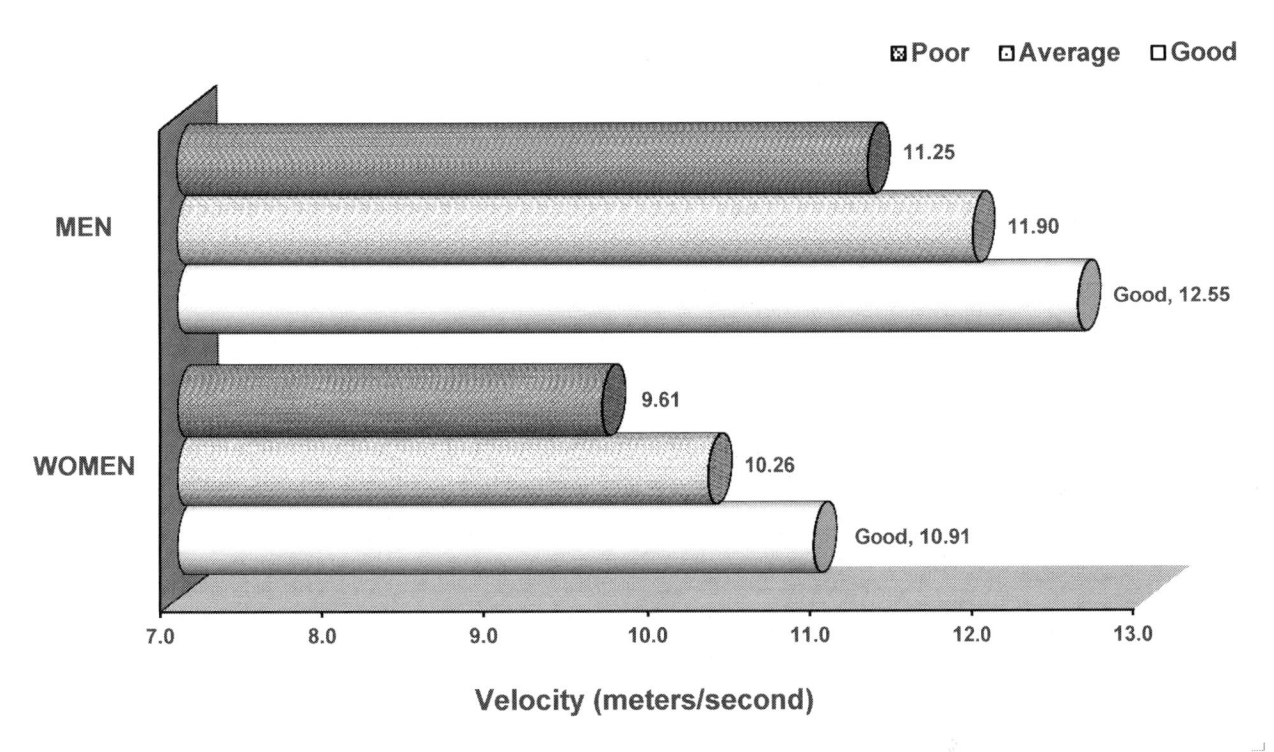

	Poor	Average	Good
MEN	11.25	11.90	12.55
WOMEN	9.61	10.26	10.91

Velocity (meters/second)

Figure 8-1: Horizontal Velocity Results

These Velocity results are interesting in that the result for the Poor elite Men sprinter is almost matched by the result of the Good woman sprinter. This indicates there is less performance difference between the sexes than often realized.

Stride Rate and Stride Length

How fast a sprinter moves the legs (Stride Rate) and how far each stride covers (Stride Length) determines the success of the performance since the product of these variables equals Horizontal Velocity. Although these results are also General Performance Descriptors, they do provide greater insight into how the athlete is producing the Horizontal Velocity.

An ideal performance situation, of course, involves a high Stride Rate coupled with a large Stride Length. Unfortunately, Stride Rate and Length are not mutually independent. Thus, Stride Rate can easily be increased by shortening the time in the air, however, this change will also decrease Stride Length. Likewise, Stride Length can easily be improved by increasing the time in the air, however, this will also serve to decrease Stride Rate.

As in many performance results, a compromise situation must be reached. In this case it involves determining the best tradeoff between Stride Rate and Length. The research on sprinting indicates unequivocally that **improvement in Stride Rate is the means by which the better sprinters improve their performance**. In fact, when the differences in body size and Horizontal Velocity are factored out, the Stride Length of the elite sprinter is no different than that of the typical collegiate sprinter. Thus, the superior elite sprinter will maintain an acceptable or slightly above average Stride Length, while producing an excellent Stride Rate.

The following Figures show the Stride Rate (8-2) and Stride Length (8-3) results for all elite athletes investigated to date. Although emphasis should be placed on Stride Rate, excellent scores in either result can be beneficial as long as the other result is not compromised. Thus, a high Stride Rate is good, but only if Stride Length is maintained at an acceptable level. Likewise, a large Stride Length is beneficial, but only if an excellent Stride Rate is maintained.

It is important to understand that, although the Stride Length results indicate that it is desirable to produce a larger Stride Length, this increase is due solely to factors that the sprinter cannot control (i.e. leg length) or by results that affect Stride Length without any effort on the part of the sprinter to actually increase the length result (i.e. Horizontal Velocity). Additional data on this conclusion will be presented in the discussion on Ground and Air Times.

Stride Rate

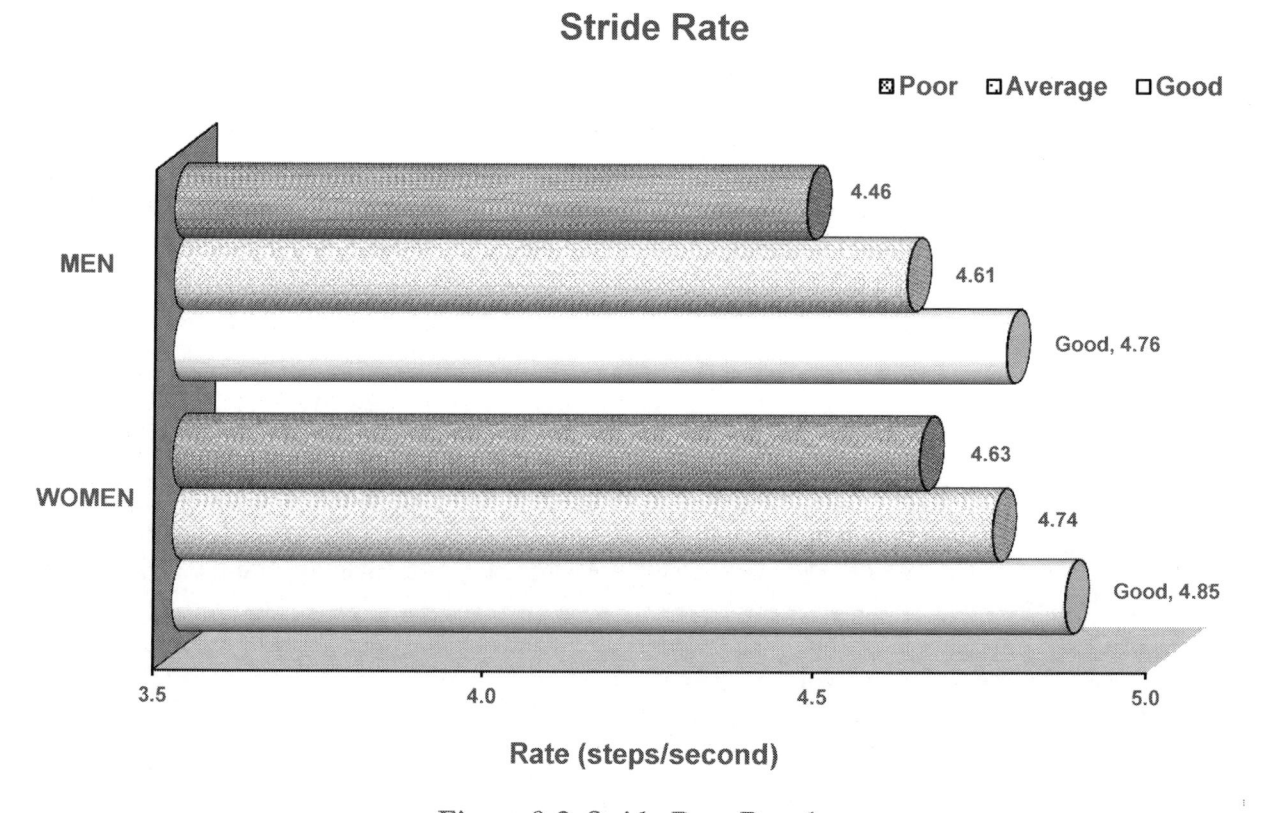

■ Poor ▨ Average ☐ Good

MEN
- Poor: 4.46
- Average: 4.61
- Good: 4.76

WOMEN
- Poor: 4.63
- Average: 4.74
- Good: 4.85

Rate (steps/second)

Figure 8-2: Stride Rate Results

Stride Length

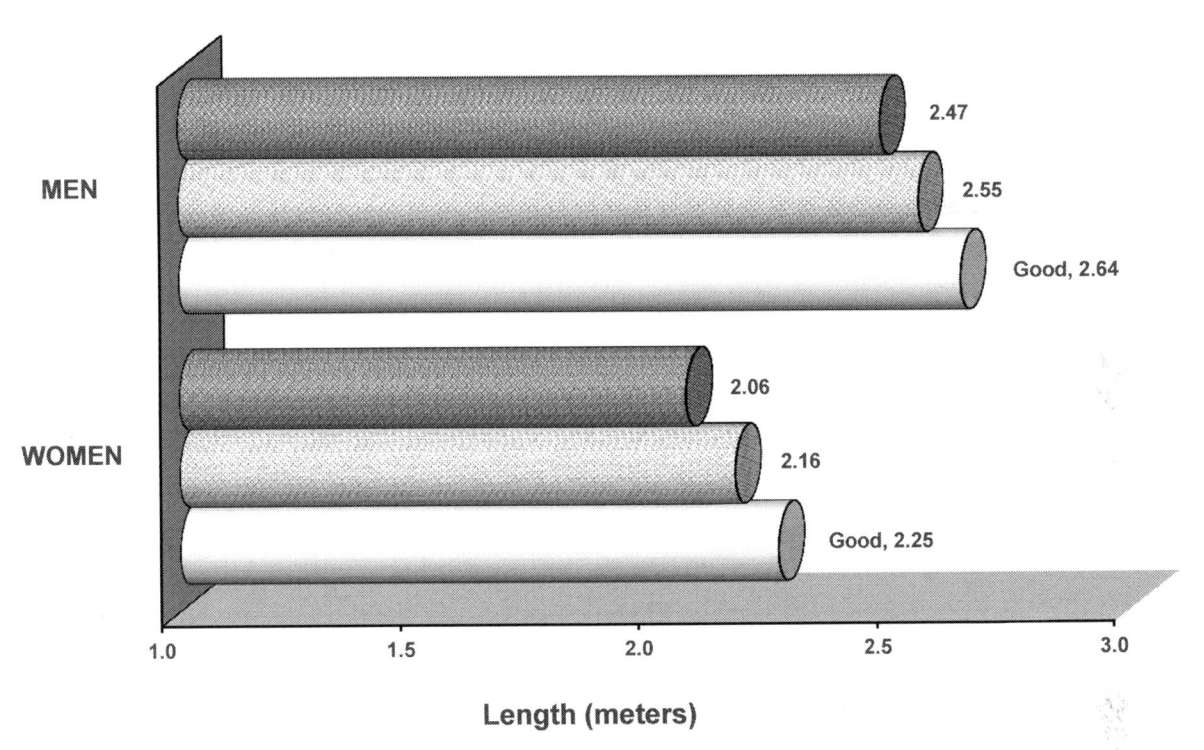

	Poor	Average	Good
MEN	2.47	2.55	2.64
WOMEN	2.06	2.16	2.25

Length (meters)

Figure 8-3: Stride Length Results

Ground Time and Air Time

Of all of the General Performance Descriptors, Ground Time and Air Time provide the greatest insights into how the elite performance is accomplished. Since Air Time primarily dictates Stride Length, and the combination of Ground and Air Time dictate Stride Rate, these time results provide further information regarding how the sprinter is allocating resources to achieve and maintain Horizontal Velocity.

The following Figures show the Ground Times (8-4) and Air Times (8-5) for all elite athletes investigated to date. Ground time is dependent upon how quickly the sprinter can produce the ground forces required to successfully project the body into the next Air Phase. As Figure 8-4 indicates, the better Short race Sprinters minimize this variable, resulting in an increase in Stride Rate and, therefore, an increase in Horizontal Velocity (assuming no other results are affected by this change).

Ground Time

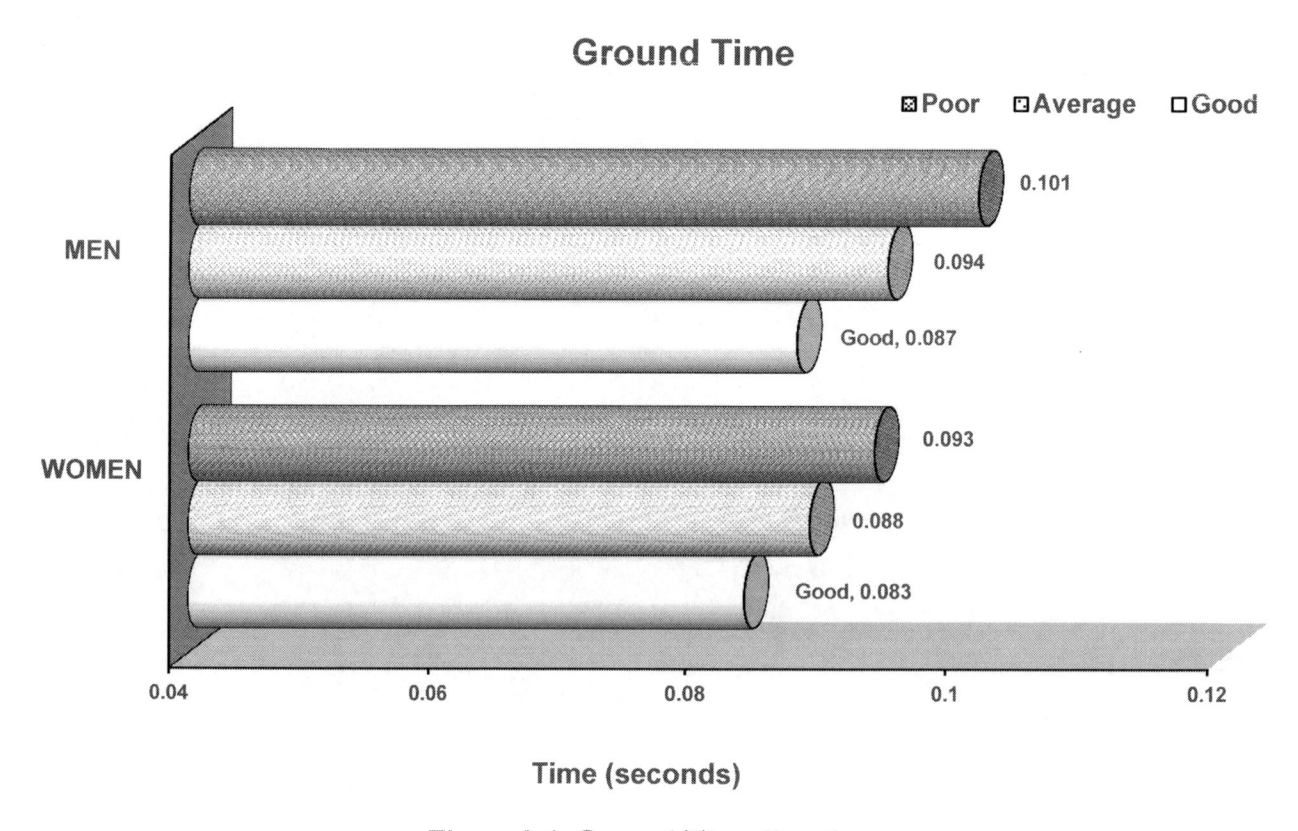

	Poor	Average	Good
MEN	0.101	0.094	0.087
WOMEN	0.093	0.088	0.083

Figure 8-4: Ground Time Results

The Air Time results (Figure 8-5) are unique in that there are only Good or Bad results. This is true since, regardless of the quality of the sprinter, there is **no difference in the Air Time results**. In fact, research has indicated that beginning High School sprinters have the same Air Time as elite sprinters. Thus, all sprinters need to strive toward an average Ground Time, and avoid being in the air either too short or too long.

Thus, the only acceptable Air Time result is the average result. Note that the Poor result indicates that an Air Time that is either too short or too long is unwanted.

The time the sprinter spends in the air is one of three variables that dictate how far the body will travel during the stride. The other two are leg length and Horizontal Velocity. Since the sprinter has no control over leg length, and Horizontal Velocity is only the result of properly (or improperly) performing the activity, Air Time is the only major contributor to alteration in Stride Length over which the athlete has direct control. Thus, if Stride Length is to be increased, it can be accomplished by simply increasing Air Time. Unfortunately, an increase in Air Time also results in a decrease in Stride Rate. Since, as previously indicated, elite sprinters place an emphasis on increasing Stride Rate, it is not surprising that there is no difference in the Air Time results of non-elite and elite sprinters.

Air Time

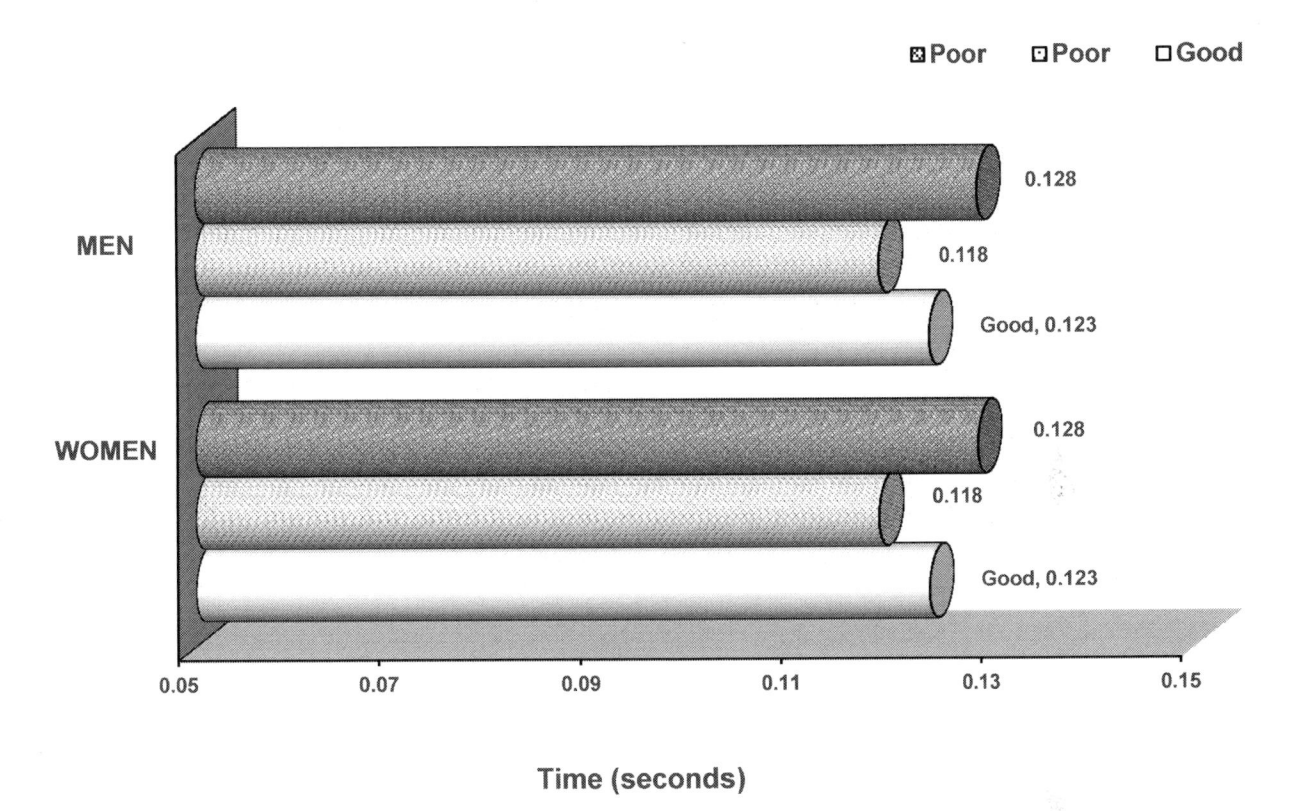

	Poor	Poor	Good
MEN	0.128	0.118	Good, 0.123
WOMEN	0.128	0.118	Good, 0.123

Time (seconds)

Figure 8-5: Air Time Results

Using the conclusion that increasing Stride Rate is beneficial, an argument could be made toward decreasing Air Time. Although this would decrease Stride Length, the resulting gain in Stride Rate should make the sacrifice justifiable. In fact, performance trends found in elite athletes actually support this conclusion. Unfortunately, it appears that the human body requires a minimum amount of Air Time to sufficiently recover the body segments in preparation for the next ground contact. In fact, regardless of the size, gender, or quality of the sprinter, this time is virtually the same. That being said, although the time remains the same, within this time the better sprinters produce a more proficient landing position as well as superior limb velocities and accelerations..

With the elimination of Air Time as a major contributor toward increasing Sprint performance, **ground contact and the time that this phase requires becomes the area that must be exploited to produce maximum performance**. Since the Ground Phase of the Sprint is the only time when the athlete can apply force to alter the Body's Velocity, it is not surprising that this is where great Sprint results are produced.

Time to Maximum Upper Leg Flexion

After 20 years of analysis, a new variable has been added to the General Performance Descriptors. Beginning at Takeoff, the time it takes a sprinter to move to the maximum upper leg flexion (high knee) position (Figure 8-6) is **the best overall measure of proper Sprint Mechanics**.

Unlike the other General Performance Descriptors, this result cannot be improved by simply getting stronger. In contrast, to properly generate this result the sprinter must execute the entire range of Sprint Mechanics in precisely the proper timing and sequence.

It has been shown time and time again that, if the athlete allows any unwanted action, especially in the back of the body, the proper timing of the upper leg simply cannot occur. This successful recovery is critical because, if not done properly, the sprinter cannot attack the next Ground Phase in the most effective manner.

Figure 8-6: The Maximum Upper Leg Recovery Position

The time to maximum flexion results are shown in Figure 8-7.

The results indicate that the better sprinters are reaching maximum flexion as late as possible in the recovery action. This allows the athlete to reach a higher knee position and delay Lower Leg extension. From this position, the sprinter can attack the track from a higher point, generating the maximum amount of total force during ground contact.

Upper Leg Recovery Time

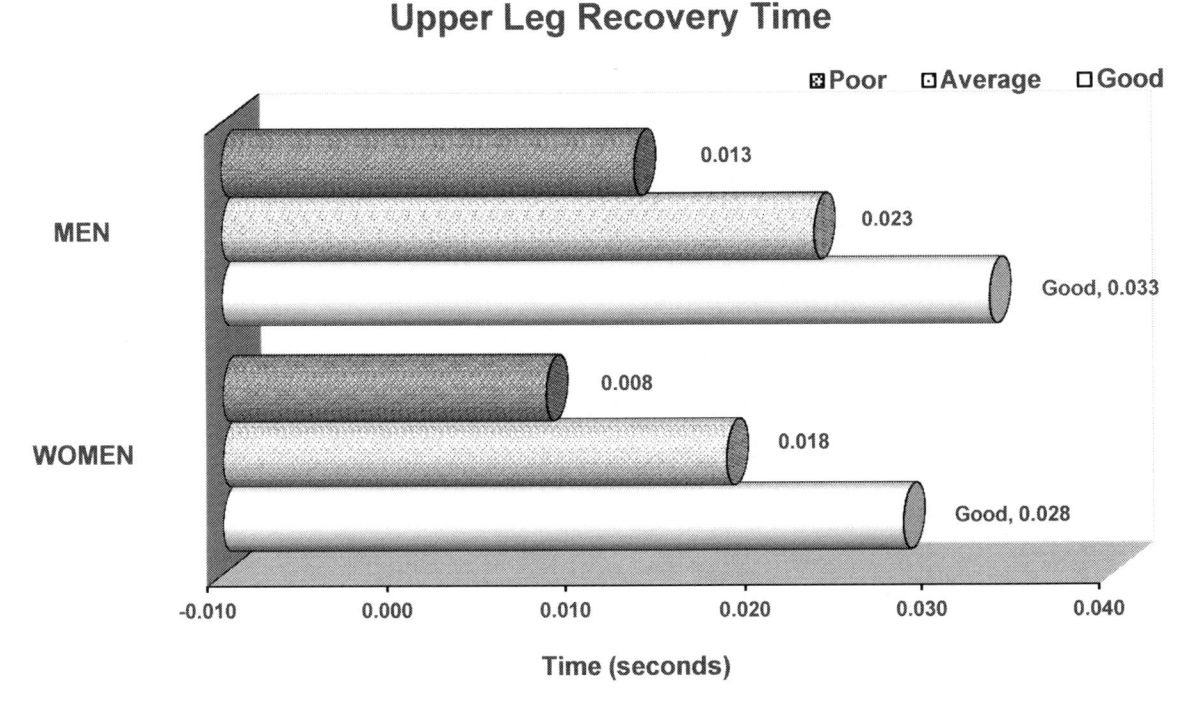

	Poor	Average	Good
MEN	0.013	0.023	0.033
WOMEN	0.008	0.018	0.028

Time (seconds)

Figure 8-7: Maximum Upper Leg Recovery Time Results

If there is a flaw in Mechanics, it will directly affect this variable. Any flaw will result in the athlete reaching full flexion earlier, a decrease in maximum flexion, and a premature extension of the lower leg.

Chapter Summary:

It is evident that the General Performance Descriptors can be used to determine the overall success of the Sprint effort. These results point to the fact that success in the Short Sprint is achieved through increasing Stride Rate by decreasing ground contact time. This must be done without compromising the Air Time of the stride, or the segment sequence of events.

Realizing that minimizing Ground Time and properly sequencing the Sprint Mechanics are the keys to elite Sprint performance is one thing, understanding how the elite sprinters actually accomplish these tasks is another problem altogether. The additional question of how this Rate increase is achieved without a decrease in Stride Length must also be answered. To resolve these questions, more specific performance variables must be investigated.

CHAPTER 9

CRITICAL SPECIFIC PERFORMANCE DESCRIPTORS FOR THE SHORT SPRINTS AT MAXIMUM VELOCITY

In the Sprint performance, **Specific Performance Descriptors** identify how the performer is mechanically producing the critical General Performance Descriptors previously identified. Those specific descriptors that are directly related to performance include:

1. **Arm Action**
2. **Horizontal Foot Speed at Touchdown**
3. **Horizontal Foot Distance at Touchdown**
4. **Trunk Angle at Touchdown**
5. **Knee Separation at Touchdown**
6. **Upper Leg Motion**
7. **Upper Leg Rotational Speed**
8. **Lower Leg Motion**
9. **Lower Leg Rotational Speed**

A complete understanding of these variables will provide a base around which to develop a mechanically sound sprinter, as well as focusing the talents of the athlete in the most productive manner possible.

Arm Action

Contrary to popular belief, superior arm speed does not produce a superior Sprint performance. In fact, regardless of the quality of the sprinter, there is no significant difference in the arm speed. If a sprinter could improve the Horizontal Velocity simply by moving the arms faster, then even old, out of shape coaches could run as fast as the elite sprinter since virtually everyone has the ability to move their arms fast enough to produce an elite level Stride Rate of five steps per second.

What the coaches, and most other people, cannot do is produce the leg action required to produce an elite Sprint performance. It is the legs that must not only move their own considerable bulk, but also contend with large ground forces during each successive ground contact. In comparison, the arms must only move their own rather meager bulk, without any other external hindrance.

Thus, **it is the legs, not the arms, that primarily dictate success in sprinting**. Whatever motion demands that are made upon the arms can easily be produced by the performer. That is not to say, however, that the arms are not important in the Sprint run. They are critical in the maintenance of balance, as well as providing a slight Vertical lift during each stride. The balance factor makes the arms a good coaching check to determine if the athlete is producing an economical sprinting action since any unbalanced motion will show up in the arm movement. Finally, the arms must be sufficiently conditioned so that they do not become a detrimental factor in the fatigue state.

Perhaps the most important contribution that the arms make is their ability to lead the entire body in its effort to shift the body movements to the front of the body during the Sprint (Front Side Mechanics). As shown in Figure 9-1, the upper arm range of motion is shifted slightly toward the front of the body (by almost 10 degrees).

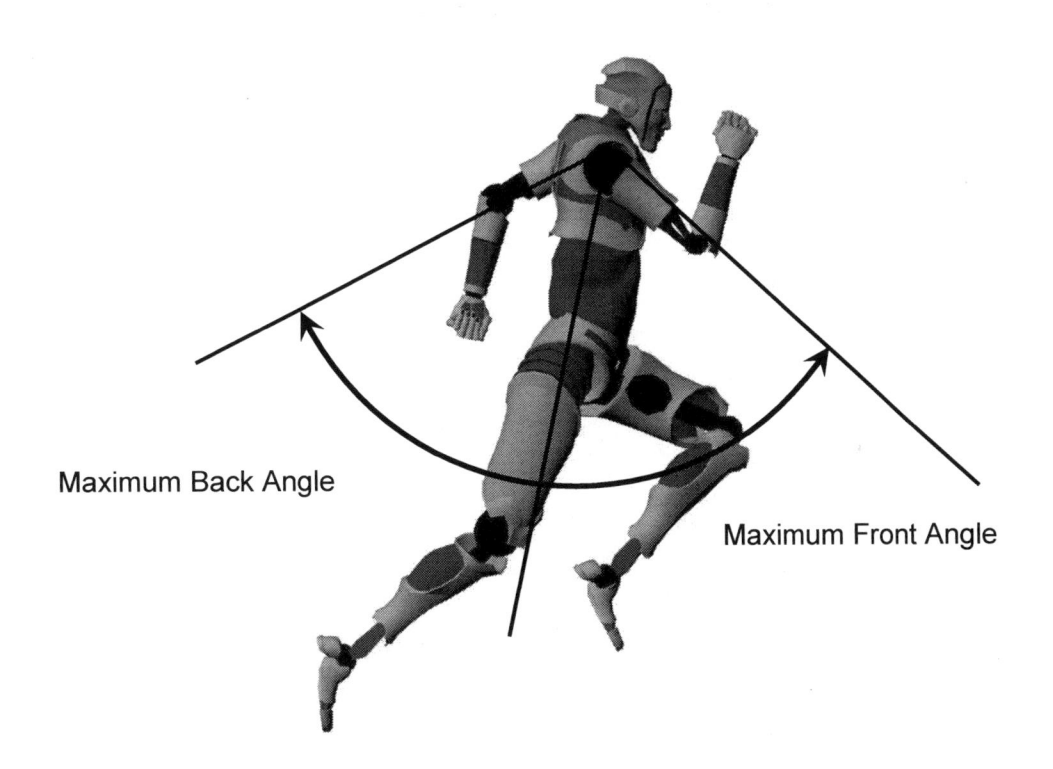

Figure 9-1: Upper Arm Action

Contrary to some coaching beliefs, the lower arm (elbow) does not maintain the same angle during sprinting. Instead, it ranges from a minimum of about 75 degrees at the full front position, to a maximum of about 155 degrees at the midpoint of the arm swing (see Figure 9-2). Note that, since the opposite arm is used to balance the opposite leg, the lower arm is placed in maximum extension when its opposite leg is on the ground. This serves to slow the extended arm to allow the Ground Leg to remain in synch with the arms.

In addition, as with the upper arm, the lower arm assists in the effort to shift the body movements to the front of the body. This is done by not allowing the minimum angle (Figure 9-2) to flex past 75 degrees. If this happens, Ground Time becomes excessive and the leg segments are shifted behind the body – both unwanted actions.

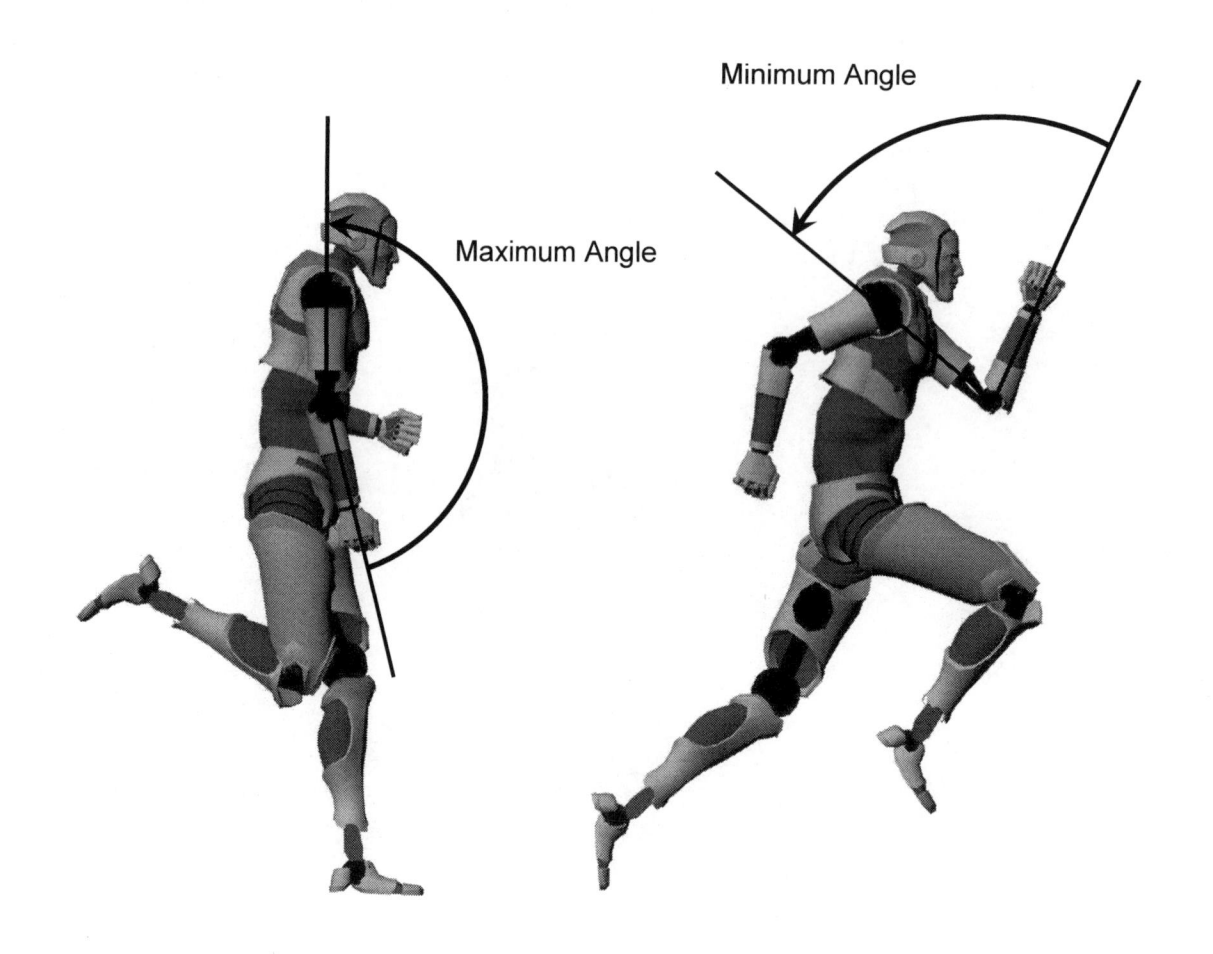

Figure 9-2: Lower Arm Action

Horizontal Foot Speed at Touchdown

To avoid slowing down when the foot hits the ground, the sprinter must have the foot moving backward as fast as possible at ground contact. In fact, the faster the sprinter can move the foot backward, the faster and more economical the performance. This action is important since, to sprint faster, the performer must somehow push backward on the ground. The problem is, when a sprinter is running at an elite rate of 12 meters per second forward, to have the foot moving backward at ground contact the foot must be moving more than 12 meters per second backward with respect to the sprinter.

This concept may be difficult to follow, but assume you are in a car, traveling 30 miles per hour. As you approach a telephone pole you stick your hand out. Although the pole is not moving, your hand strikes the pole at 30 miles per hour since that is how fast the car is moving. Now, if you are foolish enough to move your hand forward an additional 10 miles per hour (in relation to the car) just before you reach the telephone pole, your hand will now be traveling 40 miles per hour as it strikes the pole (30+10=40).

If, instead of moving your hand forward, you move it backward at 10 miles per hour (in relation to the car), your hand will strike the pole at only 20 miles per hour (30-10=20). Better yet, if you could move your hand backward at 30 miles per hour (in relation to the car), the car's forward speed and the hand's backward speed would offset each other and the hand would touch the pole at 0 miles per hour (30-30=0), causing no damage to your hand.

This, in essence, is the problem facing the sprinter. Moving forward at 12 meters per second means that, to avoid hitting the ground with the foot moving forward, the leg motion must be such that the foot is moving backward (in relation to the sprinter) at a speed of at least 12 meters per second (see Figure 9-3).

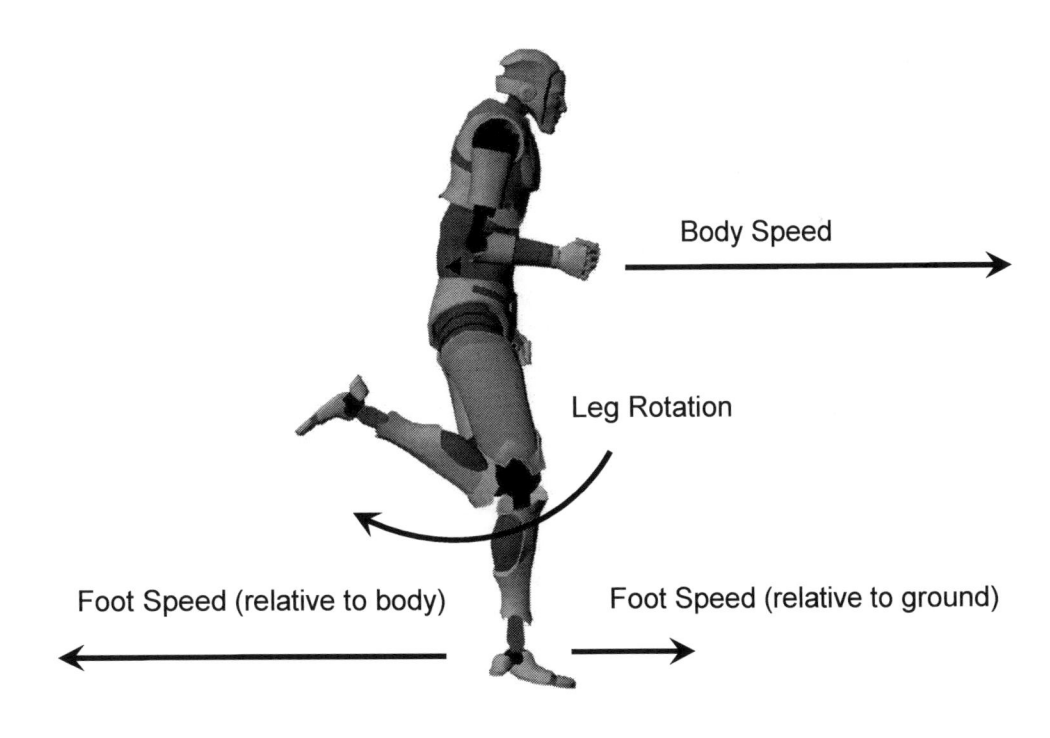

Figure 9-3: The Relationship Between Foot Speed at Touchdown and Horizontal Braking Force

If the sprinter cannot produce a backward foot speed equal to the forward Body Velocity then, as in the case of the hand hitting the pole, the foot will receive a backward push or braking force, slowing the sprinter. In fact, regardless of the quality of the sprinter, it is impossible to avoid producing this braking force. The better sprinters, however, minimize the problem by producing backward foot speeds that are close to their forward sprinting Speed.

Figure 9-4 shows the Horizontal foot speed at Touchdown, in relation to the sprinter, for all elite athletes analyzed to date. Referring back to Figure 8-1, note that, even for the good performer, the foot speed does not equal the Horizontal Velocity result.

Horizontal Foot Speed at Touchdown

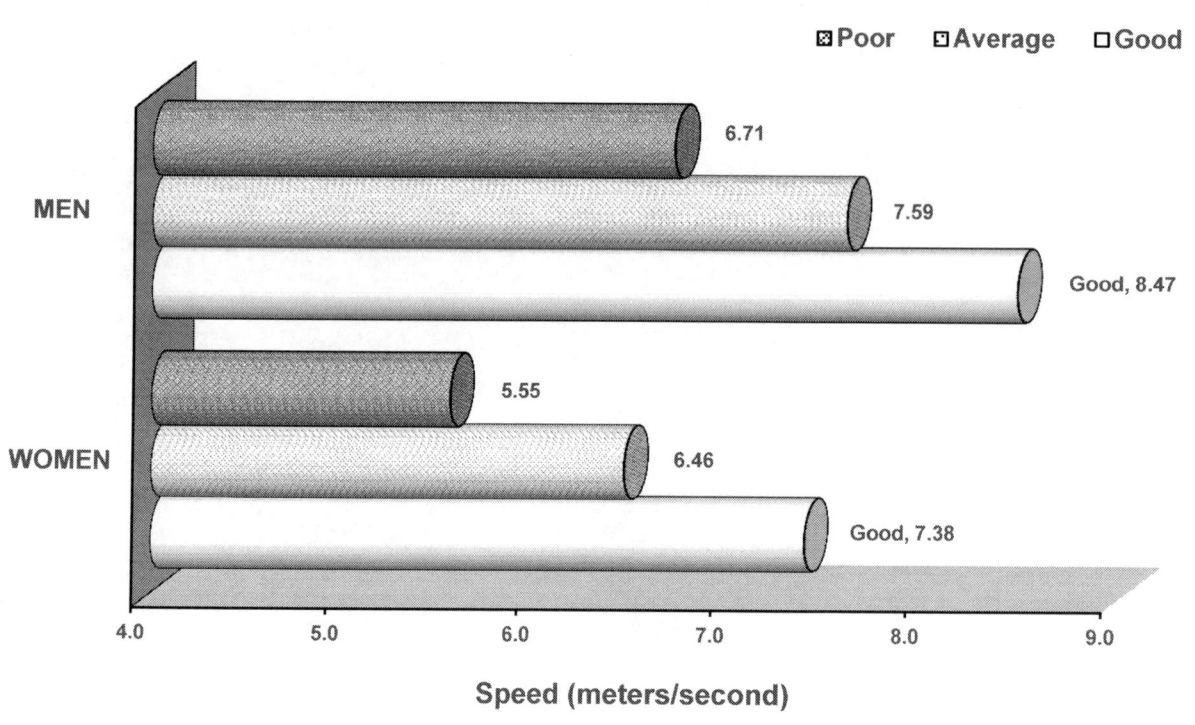

Poor   Average   Good

MEN
- 6.71
- 7.59
- Good, 8.47

WOMEN
- 5.55
- 6.46
- Good, 7.38

Speed (meters/second)

Figure 9-4: Horizontal Foot Speed at Touchdown (Relative to Body)

For example, the best elite athlete Women's Short race Sprinters can produce a backward foot speed of 7.38 meters per second. However, since Figure 8-1 indicates that the same athlete is moving forward at 10.9 meters per second, even the best Women's sprinters are striking the ground with the foot moving forward at 3.52 meters per second (10.9-7.38). This difference between foot speed and Horizontal Velocity is always about 3.5 meters per second, which points to the importance of increasing this variable if the performer is to improve.

Horizontal Foot Distance at Touchdown

As shown in Figure 9-5, to Sprint properly, the foot must Touchdown in front of the body. This is a very important action since it increases the Stride Length, as well as giving the leg sufficient range of motion to produce the necessary Vertical projection and maintain the forward motion while on the ground. On the other hand, the farther out the sprinter lands the greater the Horizontal braking force, which slows the sprinter.

Any additional landing distance also increases the range of motion of the Ground Leg, which increases the Ground Time. Thus, a tradeoff situation occurs since sufficient leg range of motion is needed to produce the necessary ground forces and produce an acceptable Air Time (and Stride Length), while the Ground Time must be reduced to a minimum to maximize Stride Rate.

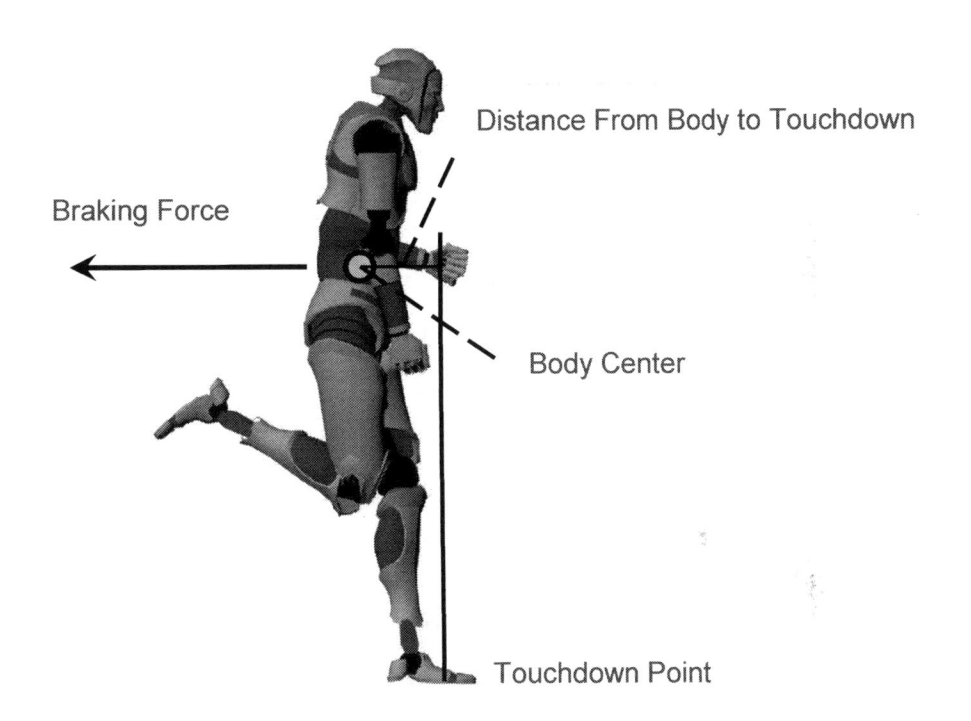

Figure 9-5: Horizontal Distance From the Foot to the Body Center at Touchdown

As previously indicated, the research on sprinting indicates that the better elite athlete sprinters are favoring a decrease in Ground Time, which rules out any increase in leg range of motion. Thus, they are actually minimizing the Horizontal Touchdown distance in an effort to minimize the Ground Time and maximize Stride Rate.

This result raises a number of questions concerning how the better sprinters are successfully minimizing this Touchdown distance while, as shown by the Stride Length results (see Figure 8-3), not sacrificing Stride Length in an effort to minimize Ground Time. From the available data, it is evident that the sprinters are accomplishing this in two ways:

1. Properly preparing the Ground Leg for Touchdown (this will be discussed in the leg motion and speed results).

2. Developing sufficient leg strength to generate the necessary Velocity changes during a shorter Ground Time. As previously discussed, the biggest problem in sprinting is to stop the downward fall of the body and produce upward projection into the next Air Phase. To accomplish this, large Vertical forces must be produced during ground contact. The example presented in Chapter 5 indicated that the elite sprinter is able to generate an average Vertical force of 1650 Newtons (370 Pounds) during ground contact, which is sufficient to produce the required 1.0 meter per second change of Vertical Velocity during the elite Ground Time of .087 seconds.

If, however, the athlete is unable to produce this large amount of ground force, the performance will not be elite in caliber. This can best be explained by assuming that the same sprinter used in the previous example was only able to generate 1310 Newtons (294 Pounds) of Vertical ground force. After subtracting the amount of force required to simply support the athlete's weight (760 Newtons), the force remaining to alter the Vertical Velocity would be:

Vertical Force = 1310-760 = 550 Newtons (124 Pounds)

Now, with less than elite level of Vertical force, some compromises in performance must be made. Remembering that Newton's second law states:

Vertical Force = Mass*Change in Vertical Velocity/Ground Time

then, as force decreases, the possible compromises must come from either Mass, Change in Vertical Velocity, or Ground Time. Since the mass of the athlete cannot be changed, this factor is not a possibility. Likewise, unless the sprinter is willing to severely decrease the Stride Length of the Sprint, the change in Vertical Velocity cannot be altered since this will result in a decrease in Air Time. This leaves only Ground Time as the variable that can be altered. In fact, if the Ground Time is increased from .087 to .12 seconds, then the athlete can produce the required Vertical Velocity with the decreased force potential.

The penalty for this increase in Ground Time is a decrease in Stride Rate sufficient to take the performance out of the elite level. In fact, the force and Ground Time values presented in this example are typical for a collegiate level sprinter.

Thus, by developing the ability to produce greater ground forces, the elite sprinters are then able to decrease Ground Time (which increases Stride Rate) without affecting the other performance results (like Stride Length).

Figure 9-6 shows the results for the Horizontal distance the foot is in front of the body at Touchdown for all elite athletes analyzed to date. Note that although even the best sprinters cannot land directly over the Touchdown point, it can be decreased to less than 0.3 meters (12 inches). This translates to a 0.12 meter (5 inch) advantage over the Poor category.

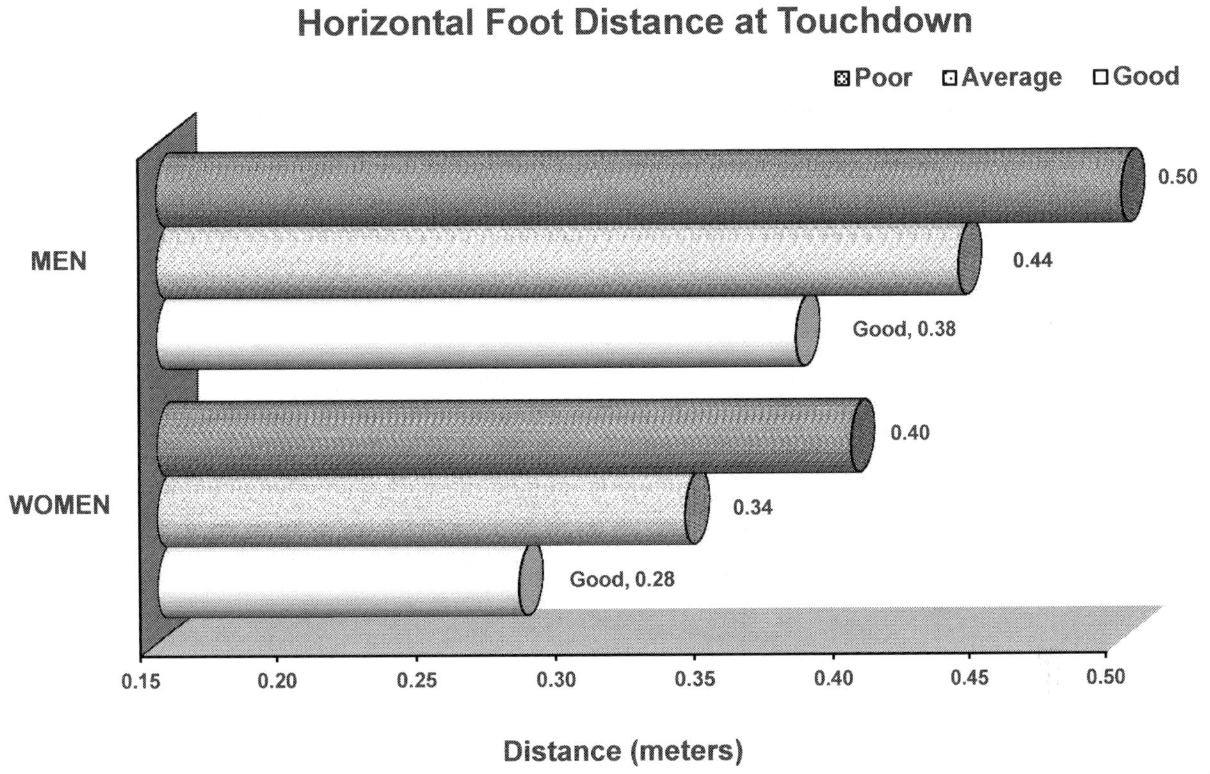

Horizontal Foot Distance at Touchdown

■ Poor   ▨ Average   □ Good

MEN
- 0.50
- 0.44
- Good, 0.38

WOMEN
- 0.40
- 0.34
- Good, 0.28

Distance (meters)

Figure 9-6: Horizontal Foot Distance at Touchdown

It is evident that, to minimize the Touchdown distance, and get the most out of this action, the sprinter must be very strong in those muscle groups that are active during this phase of the Sprint. These groups include the **hamstring and gluteal muscles** since these are needed to accelerate the leg and pull the body over the Touchdown point during the initial portion of ground contact. More than any other factor, the strength of these muscle groups dictate the success of a sprinter.

Trunk Angle at Touchdown

By a large margin, the trunk of the sprinter is the biggest and heaviest body segment that must be moved down the track. With this in mind, the performer wants to limit any unnecessary trunk rotation to avoid not only the additional energy cost, but also the time required to move the trunk back to the starting position. It must be remembered that, since the Sprint consists of a series of repeated strides, if the trunk is moved at one part of the stride, it must be returned to the same starting position during the next stride.

As shown in Figure 9-7, the trunk angle of the best sprinters remains almost constant at Full Speed. After Takeoff occurs, the effort to recover the Takeoff leg has the effect of shifting the hips slightly back at the next Touchdown position. Then, during ground contact, the hips are driven forward. Even in the best sprinters, there is a small forward-and-back trunk rotation during each stride.

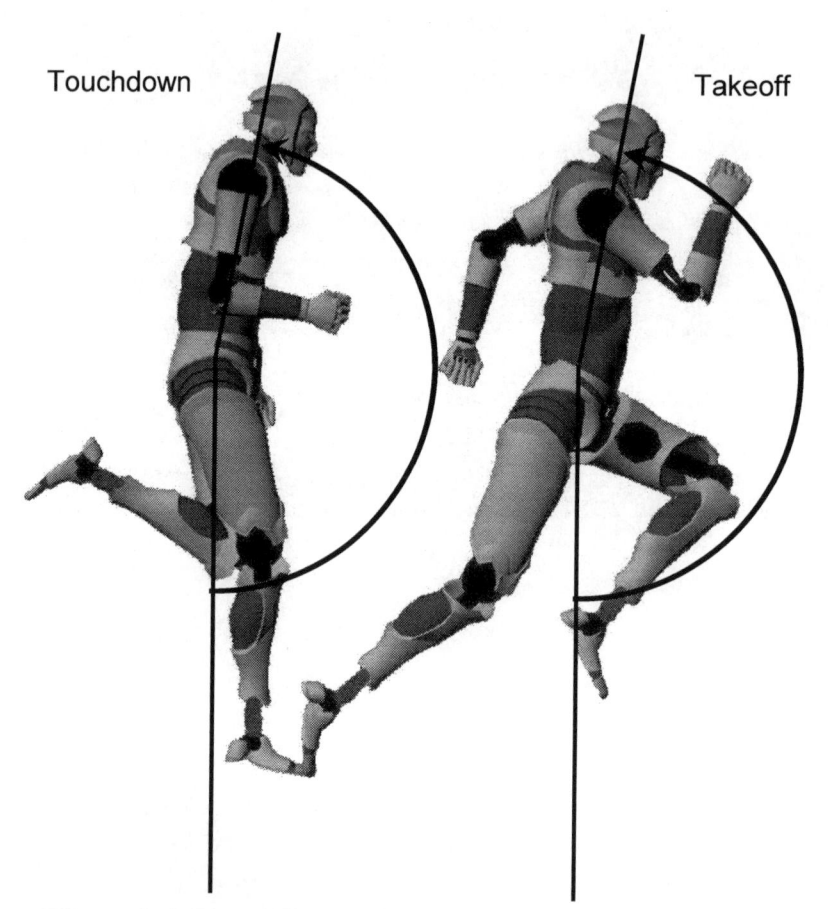

Figure 9-7: Trunk Angle During Ground Contact

If an athlete does not have strong core strength, they lack sufficient leg strength to handle the large ground forces, or their Mechanics are poor, they tend to use the trunk to help them move down the track. The problem with this is that it takes considerable effort to rotate the trunk back and forth, especially at a rate of around 5 times per second. In addition, this increased trunk range of motion demands greater Ground Time, which is the last thing that an elite sprinter wants to produce.

All elite sprinters can achieve the proper trunk position at Takeoff, which is a consistent 83 degrees for both Men and Women. If there is a problem, the variability always shows up at Touchdown. As shown in Figure 9-8, the best sprinters limit this trunk rotation to a few degrees during each stride.

Trunk Angle at Touchdown

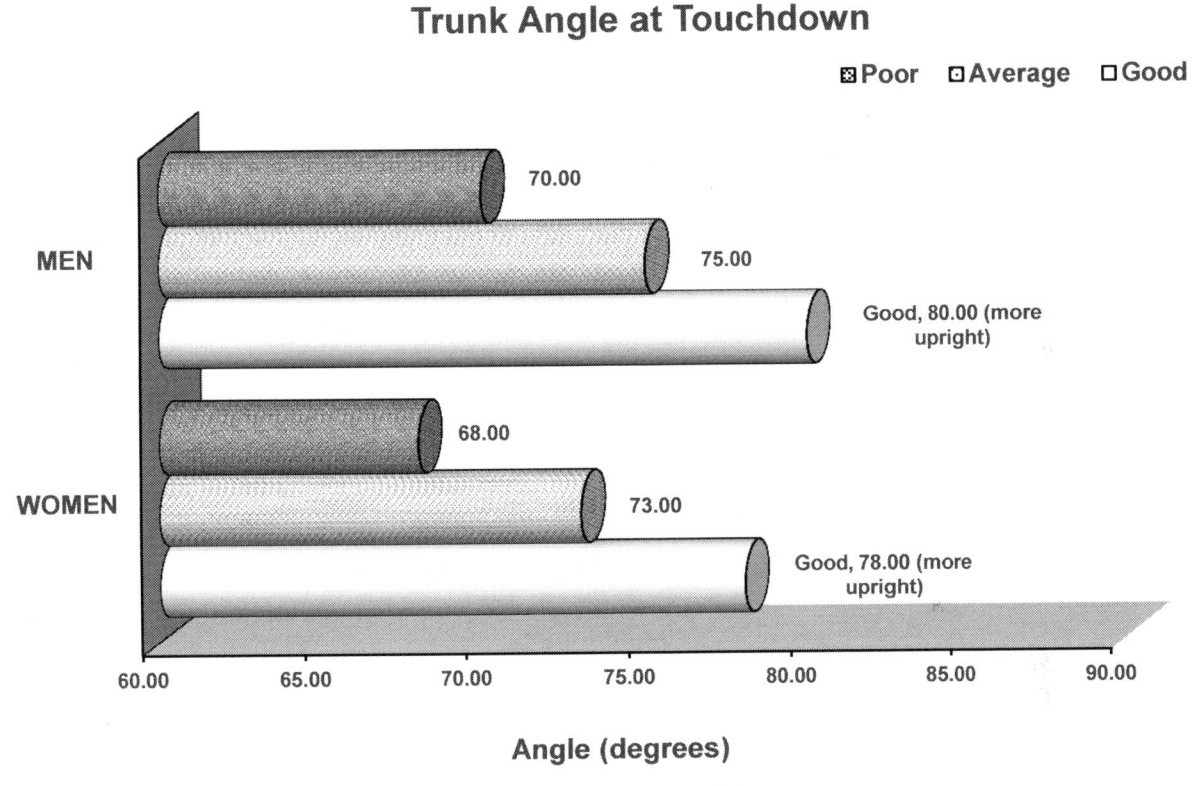

■ Poor   ▫ Average   ▫ Good

MEN
- 70.00 (Poor)
- 75.00 (Average)
- Good, 80.00 (more upright)

WOMEN
- 68.00 (Poor)
- 73.00 (Average)
- Good, 78.00 (more upright)

Angle (degrees): 60.00 – 90.00

Figure 9-8: Trunk Angle at Touchdown

In contrast to the 10 degrees of trunk rotation found in less competent sprinters, the level of energy and time savings is considerable. When this difference is multiplied by the number of strides in the 100 (40-50), 200 (70-100), or 400 (130-200), it becomes evident that controlling the trunk can make a major difference in the Sprint performance.

Knee Separation at Touchdown

There is no better indicator of proficient Sprint Mechanics than the amount of knee separation at Touchdown. Both coaches and researchers use it as a visual benchmark indicating how well an athlete is shifting their movements toward the front of the body as ground contact is initiated.

Figure 9-9 indicates how close the recovery knee should be to the ground knee at Touchdown. It is evident that, as a quick check benchmark, the knees should be even to best handle the high force demands while in contact with the ground.

In fact, it is not uncommon for those sprinters who are very powerful to actually land with the recovery knee in front of the ground knee. If the Sprint Golden Position is to be reached, then this minimal knee separation must be present.

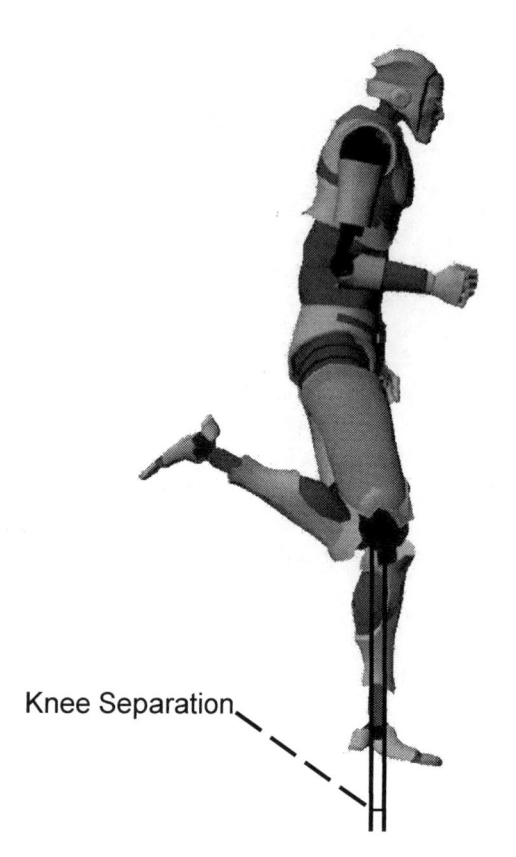

Figure 9-9: Knee Separation at Touchdown

If an athlete fails to bring the knees together at Touchdown, then not only will the Sprint performance suffer, but the potential for injury dramatically increases. Since all elite sprinters strive to reach the "high knee" position found in the Sprint Golden Position, if their recovery leg is behind when ground contact occurs (large knee separation) then they must try to "catch up" by increasing the speed of the leg. Unfortunately, when the athlete attempts to rapidly reverse this increased recovery Velocity and then bring the leg down toward Touchdown, the additional stress on the hamstring group can be increased to the point where injury occurs.

The actual values for knee separation for elite sprinters can be seen in Figure 9-10. Note that although the results for Men and Women are similar, the Women do have a tendency to have more difficulty in getting the knees together.

Knee Separation at Touchdown

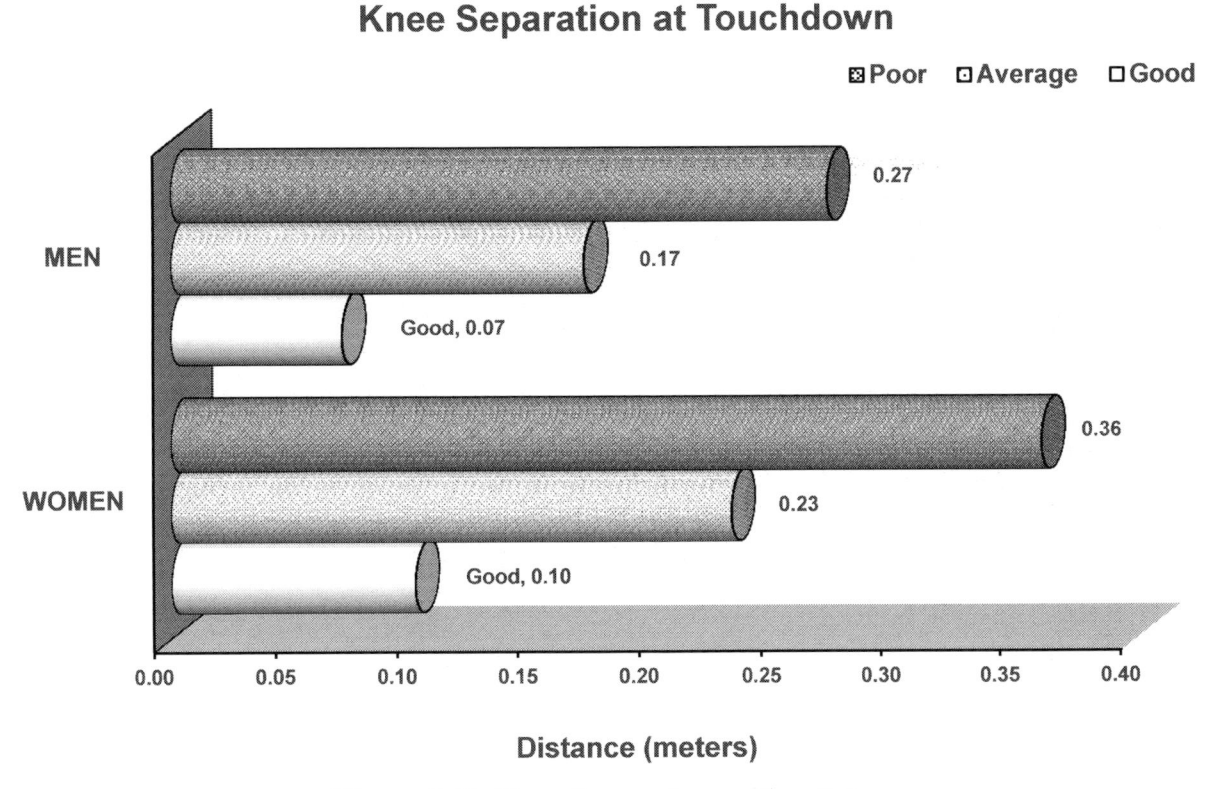

	Poor	Average	Good
MEN	0.27	0.17	0.07
WOMEN	0.36	0.23	0.10

Distance (meters)

Figure 9-10: Knee Separation at Touchdown

Upper Leg Motion

There are three critical positions for the upper leg during sprinting; the position at Takeoff, the Full Extension position, and the Full Flexion position (see Figure 9-11).

The better sprinters tend to minimize upper leg extension at Takeoff (on the runner shown, this would produce a larger angle) and full extension (again, a larger angle). This is contrary to the coaching adage that the leg should be fully extended to get the most out of ground contact. The fact is, the small increase in ground force gained is not worth the increase in Ground Time (and decrease in Stride Rate). Instead, these leg motions are produced to minimize Ground Time and make leg recovery as efficient as possible.

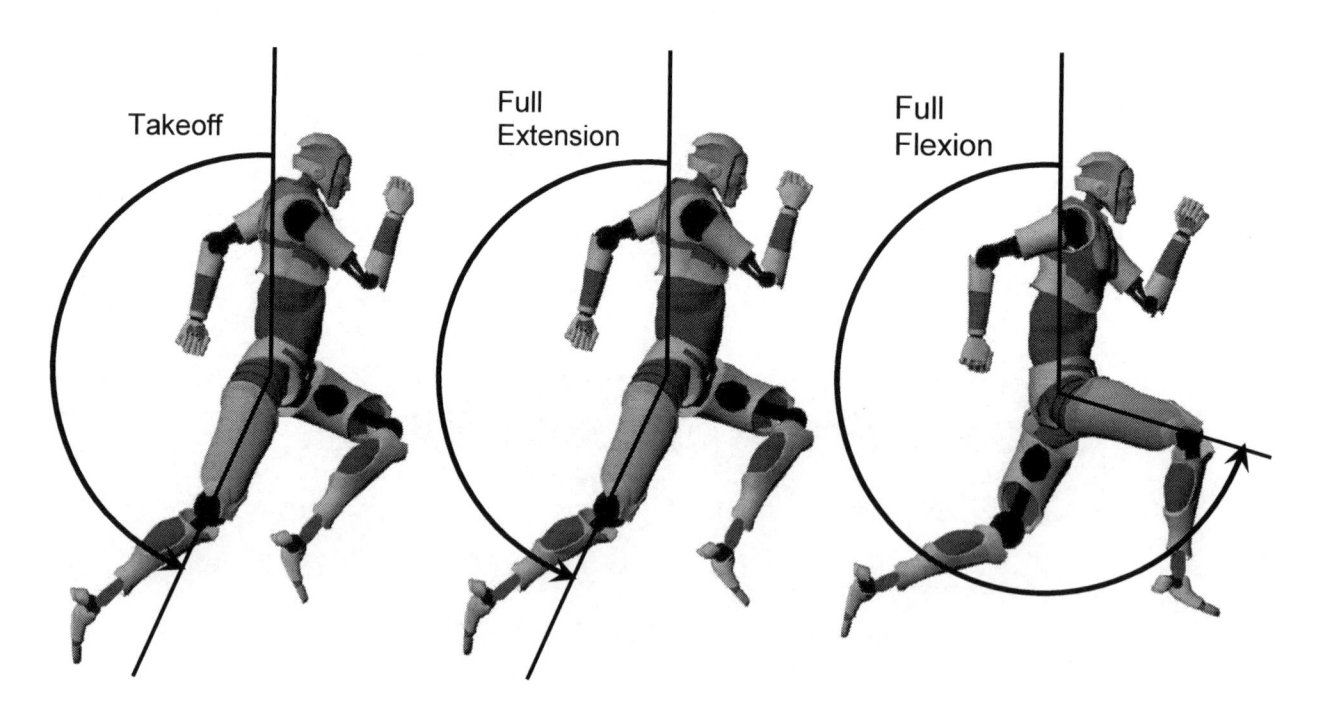

Critical Specific Performance Descriptors For the Short Sprints at Maximum Velocity

Figure 9-11: Upper Leg Motion

Finally, an effort is made to maximize upper leg flexion at full flexion (larger angle). This "high knee" position gives the athlete a greater range of motion through which to accelerate the leg toward ground contact.

Much of the coaching literature is replete with justifiable praise of this "high knee" position in sprinting. It should be noted that **there is little difference in the overall leg recovery range of motion between elite and non-elite sprinters**. Thus, the key to high knee recovery is to limit the leg extension (back of the body) action after Takeoff. Therefore, a decrease in leg extension of ten degrees will result in an increase in "knee lift" by ten degrees without placing any additional performance demands on the athlete.

Figure 9-12 shows the results for the Upper Leg Motion for all elite athletes analyzed to date (refer to Figure 9-11 for angle measurement direction information.)

It must be emphasized, however, that a very good angle at one position is only beneficial if the other results are acceptable. Poor results here commonly indicate a lack of leg strength (indicated by excessive extension at Takeoff and full extension), or an inability of a performer to properly recover the leg (indicated by insufficient flexion at full flexion).

Upper Leg Motion

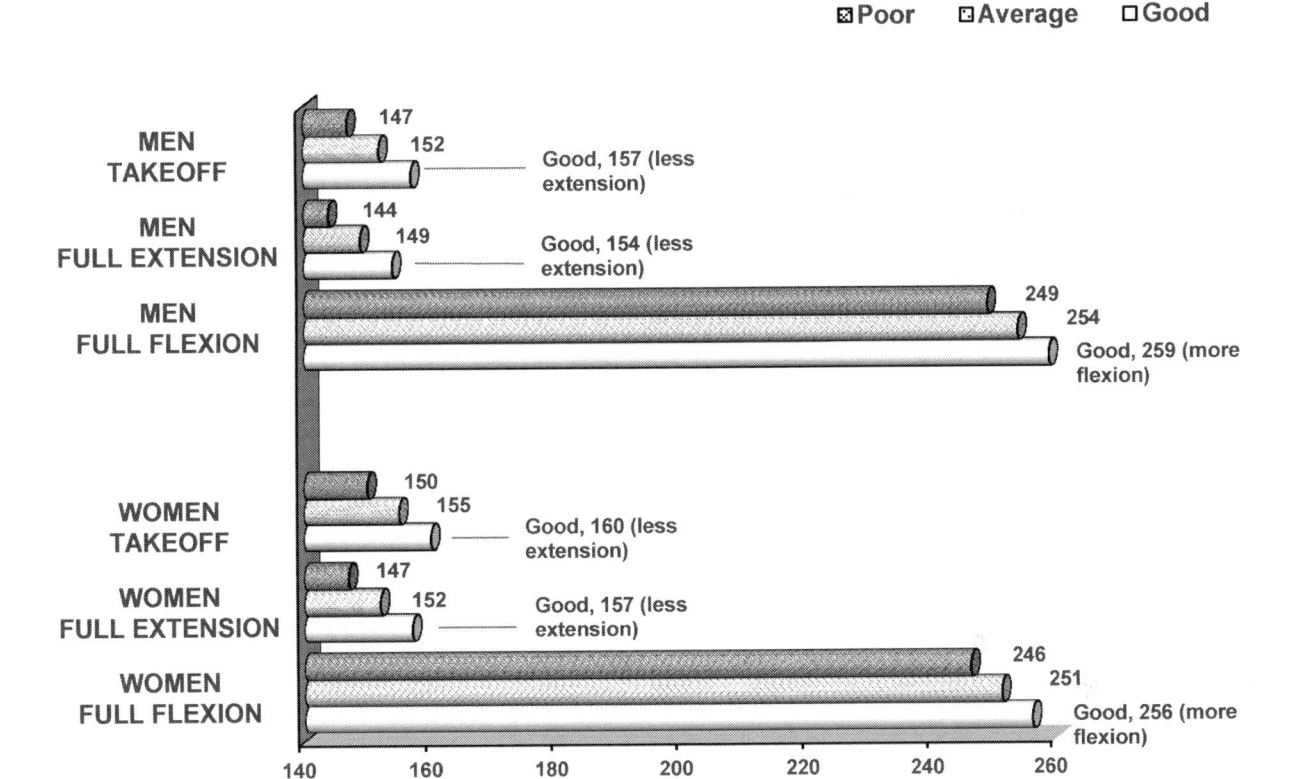

	Poor	Average	Good
MEN TAKEOFF	147	152	Good, 157 (less extension)
MEN FULL EXTENSION	144	149	Good, 154 (less extension)
MEN FULL FLEXION	249	254	Good, 259 (more flexion)
WOMEN TAKEOFF	150	155	Good, 160 (less extension)
WOMEN FULL EXTENSION	147	152	Good, 157 (less extension)
WOMEN FULL FLEXION	246	251	Good, 256 (more flexion)

Position (degrees)

Figure 9-12: Upper Leg Motion Results

All of these results are interesting, however, it was the combination of the trends of this data that led to something greater than all of the parts. In fact, the importance of the upper leg position cannot be overstated since it was the source of the breakthrough in re-defining the conceptual emphasis in Sprint development. It was the actions in this area that led to the emphasis in what has been termed **Front Side Mechanics**, while eliminating (as much as possible) what has been termed **Back Side Mechanics**. These concepts are covered in Chapter 12.

Upper Leg Rotational Speed

Of all of the specific performance variables, Upper Leg Rotational Speed is the most critical of the Specific Performance Descriptors in the production of an elite Sprint performance. This leg speed is critical in recovering the leg after Takeoff and producing the beneficial "high knee" position (see Upper Leg Motion) required for the athlete to properly prepare for ground contact. If properly positioned, the upper leg can then produce a large amount of upper leg extension speed at Touchdown, and continue the extension rotation during ground contact (see Figure 9-13).

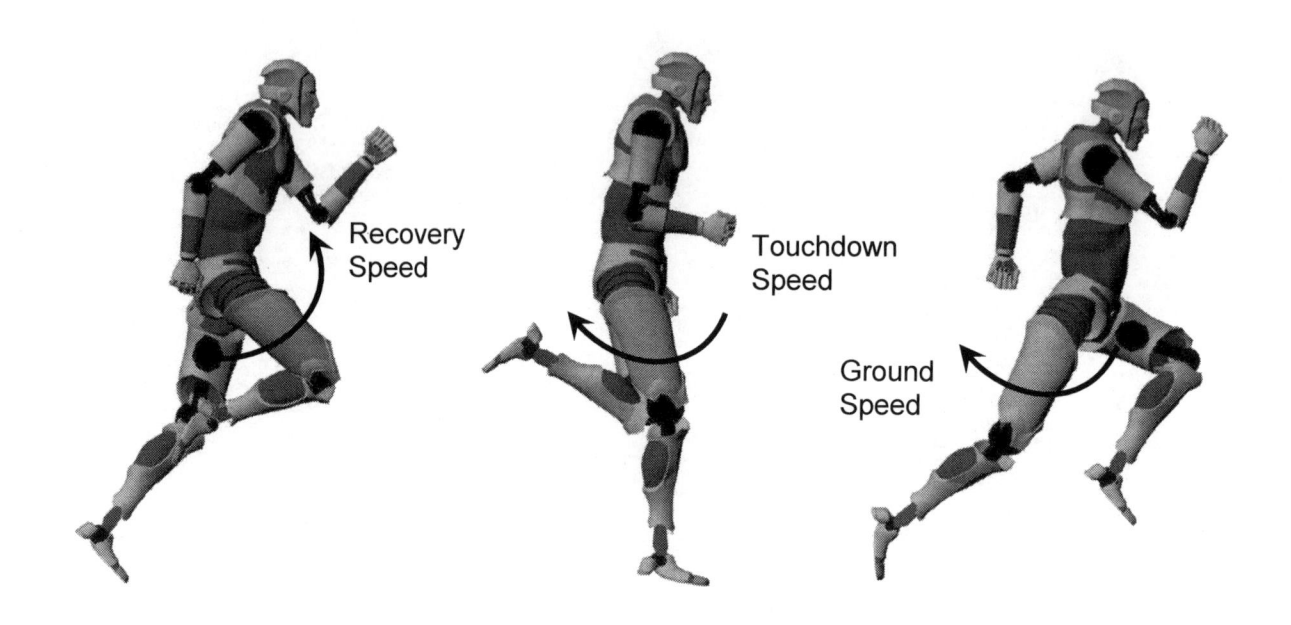

Figure 9-13: Upper Leg Rotational Speed

The better sprinters maximize the leg recovery and Touchdown rotation speeds, while maintaining or actually increasing (larger than Touchdown) leg speed during ground contact. As in upper leg position, these values indicate the degree of upper leg strength, as well as the quality of the sprinting Mechanics. Production of sufficient leg speed is of such great importance that, without this ability, an athlete has no chance of becoming an elite sprinter.

Figure 9-14 shows the average rotational flexion speed of the upper leg during recovery, the extension speed at Touchdown, as well as the average extension speed during the Ground Phase for all elite athletes analyzed to date.

Of all the upper leg results, the upper leg speed at Touchdown is the most critical since it affects both the amount of forward braking and the amount of ground contact time. Since decreasing

Ground Time is the means by which elite sprinters maximize Stride Rate, properly preparing the leg for Touchdown is a critical movement.

Upper Leg Rotational Speed

■ Poor   ▨ Average   □ Good

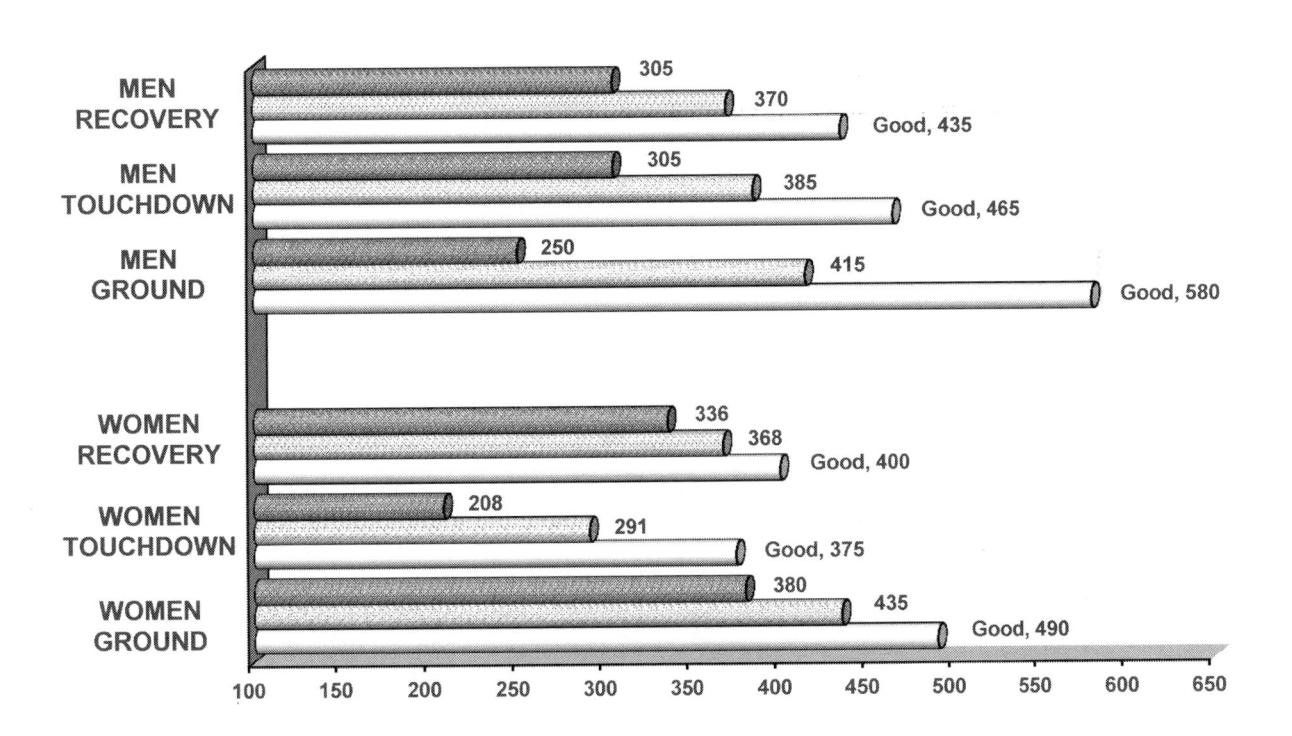

Category	Poor	Average	Good
MEN RECOVERY	305	370	435
MEN TOUCHDOWN	305	385	465
MEN GROUND	250	415	580
WOMEN RECOVERY	336	368	400
WOMEN TOUCHDOWN	208	291	375
WOMEN GROUND	380	435	490

Rotational Speed (degrees/second)

Figure 9-14: Upper Leg Rotational Speed Results

If the sprinter can properly attack the ground with large upper leg rotation, the next key is to maintain, or increase, the leg rotation during the contact phase. Proper preparation is a critical factor, but it must be followed with the dynamic strength ability to build on this foundation.

Finally, the level of upper leg rotation must not be decreased by spending any unnecessary extension effort during the end of the Ground Phase. This concept will be further discussed in Chapter 12.

Lower Leg Motion

There are three critical positions for the lower leg during sprinting; the position at Takeoff, the maximum flexion during recovery, and the position when the ankle crosses the opposite leg during recovery (see Figure 9-15).

The better sprinters tend to minimize lower leg extension at Takeoff (on the runner shown, this would produce a smaller angle). As in the case of the upper leg position at Takeoff, this lack of full lower leg (knee) extension is done to actively minimize the ground contact time (to increase Stride Rate).

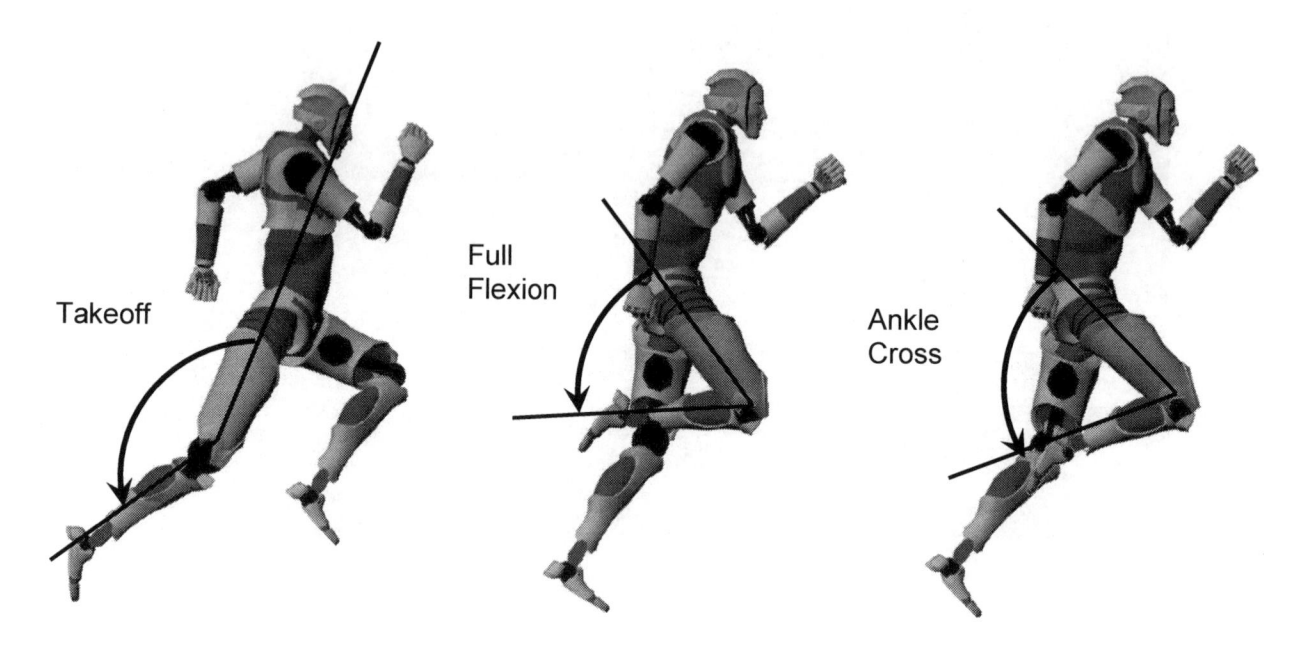

Figure 9-15: Lower Leg Motion

Properly controlling the lower leg during recovery is one of the most difficult tasks in sprinting. This is true because successful lower leg recovery can only occur if all other Sprint Mechanics are done both correctly and at the right time. Invariably, this is the last mechanical problem a sprinter must face.

To control the lower leg, the better elite sprinters do not allow the lower leg to go into excessive flexion during the initial portion of the recovery process. In addition, the proficient sprinter ensures that the full flexion position is reached as close to the ankle cross position as possible. In fact, these two positions (maximum flexion and ankle cross) have occurred at the same time for some of the greatest sprinters of all time.

Critical Specific Performance Descriptors For the Short Sprints at Maximum Velocity

By the time the ankle passes the opposite leg (ankle cross), the lower leg has already started to extend toward ground contact. However, if the sprinter wants to recover the upper leg to a "high knee" position to better attack the ground, the timing of this lower leg extension must be delayed as long as possible. The key to this is limiting the amount of flexion after Takeoff, then controlling the flexion during lower leg recovery – not too little and not too much.

The key to producing this position is the active recovery of the lower leg, as will be discussed in Chapter 12.

Figure 9-16 shows the lower leg angle at Takeoff, maximum flexion, and the point where the ankle crosses the opposite leg for all of the elite athletes analyzed to date. Refer to Figure 9-15 for angle measurement direction information.

Lower Leg Motion

■ Poor ▨ Average ☐ Good

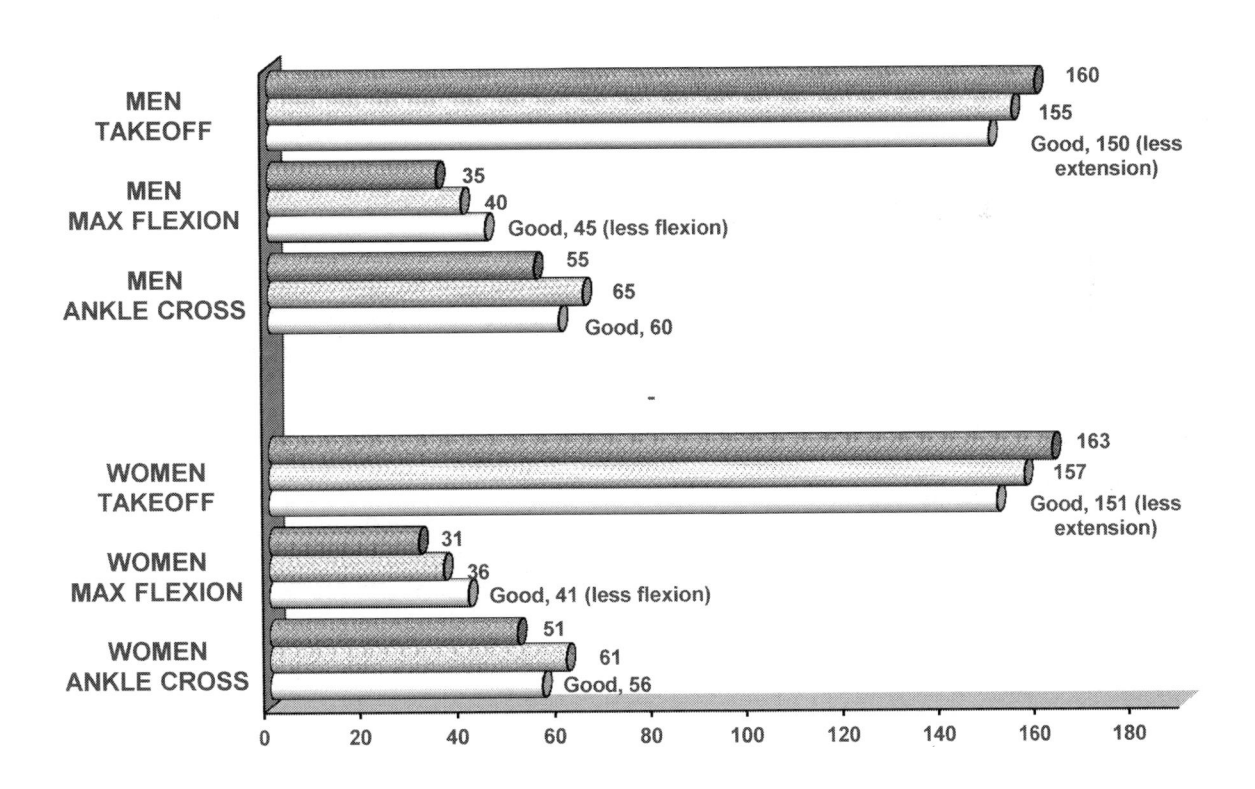

Category	Poor	Average	Good
MEN TAKEOFF	160	155	150 (less extension)
MEN MAX FLEXION	35	40	45 (less flexion)
MEN ANKLE CROSS	55	65	60
WOMEN TAKEOFF	163	157	151 (less extension)
WOMEN MAX FLEXION	31	36	41 (less flexion)
WOMEN ANKLE CROSS	51	61	56

Position (degrees)

Figure 9-16: Lower Leg Motion Results

The trends presented can be seen in the fact that the better sprinters extend around 10 degrees less at Takeoff, while coming within a few degrees of matching their maximum flexion and ankle cross values.

Lower Leg Rotational Speed

Lower leg rotational speed is critical as Touchdown occurs since it contributes to the Horizontal foot speed result. As with upper leg extension speed, lower leg flexion speed at Touchdown can reduce the amount of forward braking during the initial portion of ground contact (see Figure 9-17). As with the production of upper leg speed, this effort must be produced primarily by the hamstring group.

In addition, the extension speed of the lower leg as it crosses the ankle is another excellent indicator as to the quality of the leg recovery action. In this case, however, it is the lack of rotation at this point that is desired. After Takeoff, if the lower leg extension is minimized, the lower leg recovery occurs more in front of the sprinter, allowing the extension to start later in the recovery process. The goal of the sprinter is to wait until ankle cross occurs to begin the lower leg extension action toward the next ground contact.

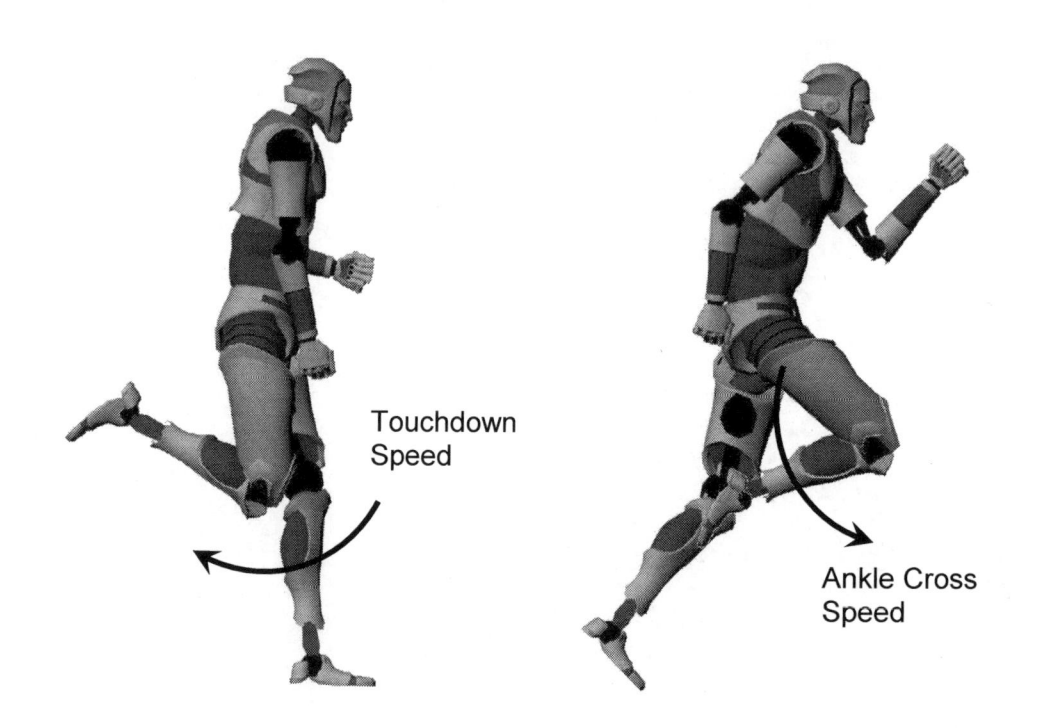

Figure 9-17: Lower Leg Rotational Speed

Figure 9-18 shows the average rotational speed of the lower leg at Touchdown for all elite athletes analyzed to date.

Lower Leg Rotational Speed

■ Poor　　▨ Average　　□ Good

- MEN TOUCHDOWN (FLEXION): Poor 30; Average 190; Good 350
- MEN ANKLE CROSS (EXTENSION): Poor 125; Average 62; Good 3
- WOMEN TOUCHDOWN (FLEXION): Poor 3; Average 120; Good 238
- WOMEN ANKLE CROSS (EXTENSION): Poor 175; Average 95; Good 40

Rotational Speed (degrees/second)

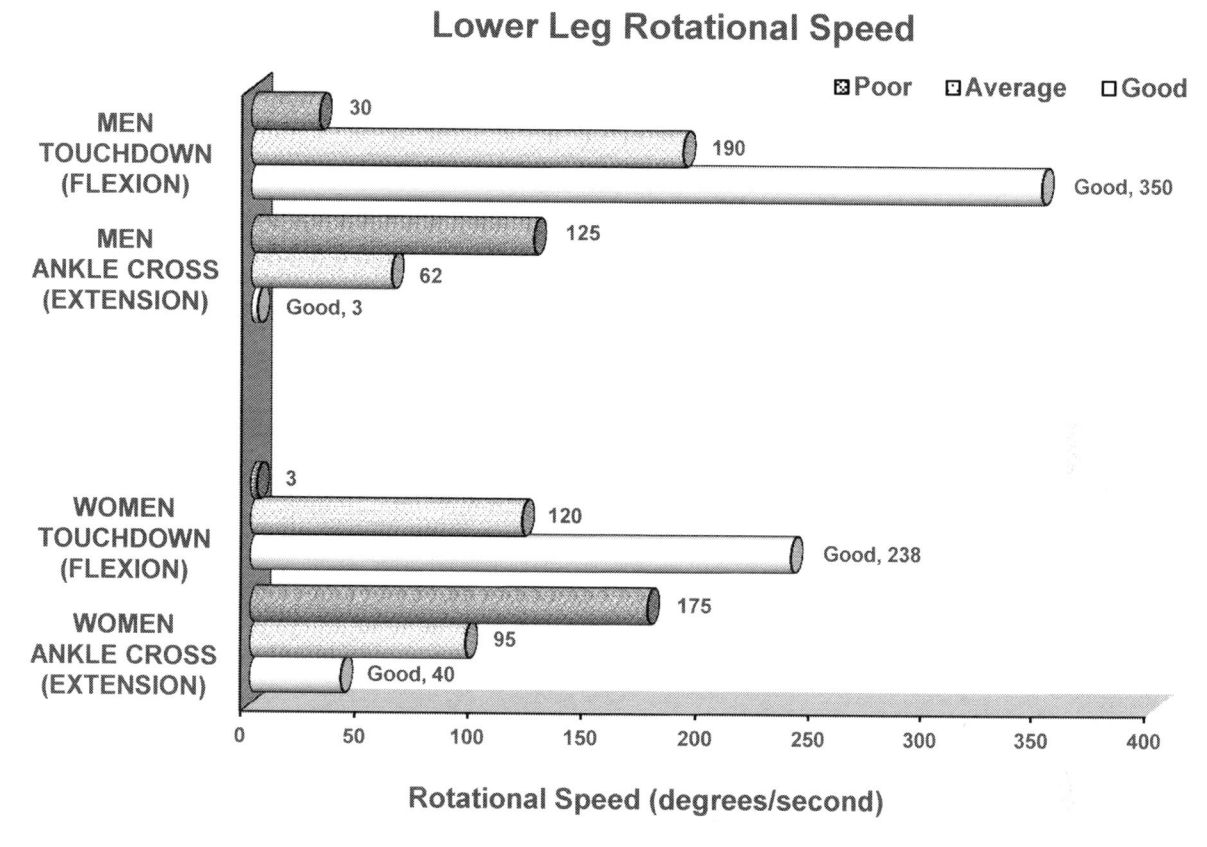

Figure 9-18: Lower Leg Rotational Speed Results

The dramatic way the better sprinters attack the ground is evident in the Touchdown results, while the less able performers are simply presenting a non-rotating lower leg. This result is set up by the superior performer by delaying the lower leg extension until the leg moves in front of the body during recovery. This concept will be further discussed in Chapter 12.

Chapter Summary:

The Specific Performance Descriptors point to the fact that success in the Short Sprint is determined by the ability of the athlete to generate great amounts of explosive strength at the proper time. Generally, the proper mechanical application of this strength results in an elite performance that is characterized by a high Stride Rate and moderate Stride Length. Specifically, the superior Stride Rate is a product of proper leg positioning, high leg speed, and exact timing; resulting in as small a Ground Time as possible.

Critical Specific Performance Descriptors For the Short Sprints at Maximum Velocity

> It is critical to understand that for the best Sprint performance to occur, **all** of these results must be produced properly, in the correct sequence, **and** at the right time. Any error in Mechanics will result in a decrease in the production of the General Performance Descriptors identified in Chapter 8.

CHAPTER 10

CRITICAL GENERAL PERFORMANCE DESCRIPTORS FOR THE LONG SPRINTS

Although all of the trends that were found in the Short Sprints are also evident in the Long Sprint, due to the length of the race, some compromises are made to account for the fatigue factor.

Horizontal Velocity

Since the Long Sprint covers more than 300 meters, the body cannot complete the event solely on the anaerobic systems. This compels even the elite athlete to compromise in the areas of speed and energy expenditure. As the elite Sprint results of Figure 10-1 indicate, this results in a decrease in Velocity, in the non-fatigue state, of approximately 11 percent as compared to the Short Sprint results (Figure 8-1).

Horizontal Velocity: Non-Fatigue

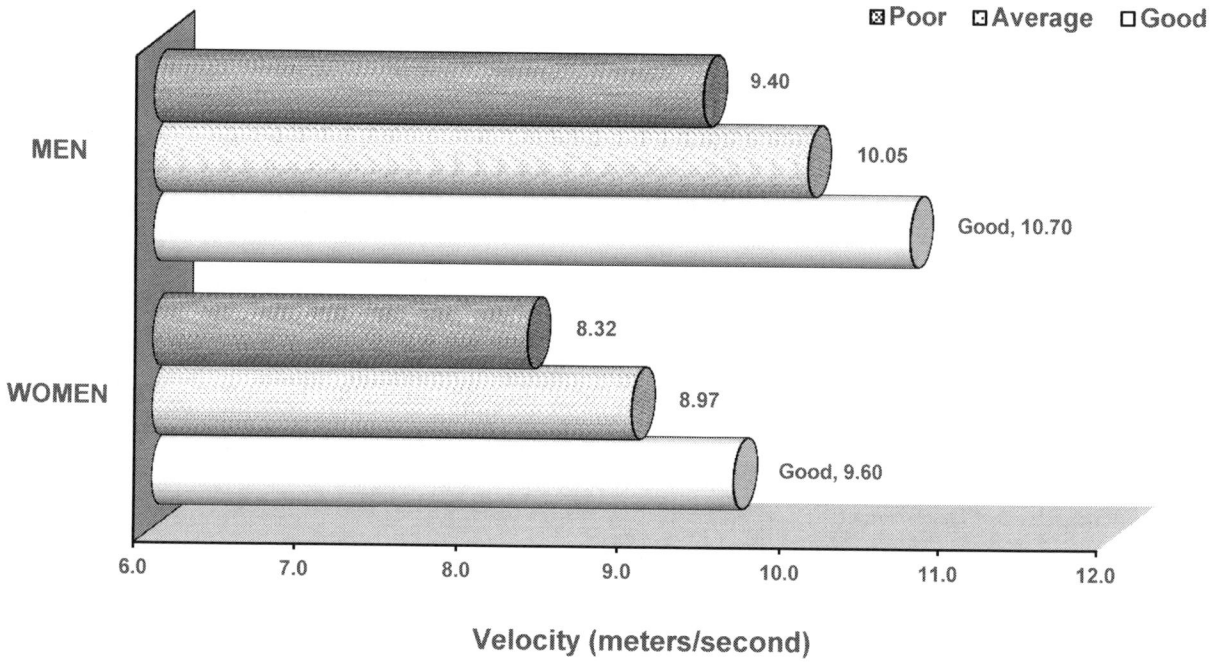

	Poor	Average	Good
MEN	9.40	10.05	10.70
WOMEN	8.32	8.97	9.60

Velocity (meters/second)

Figure 10-1: Non-Fatigue Horizontal Velocity Results

Regardless of the quality of the elite sprinter, some decrement in Velocity occurs as fatigue sets in. As shown in Figure 10-2, the decrement in Velocity is approximately 17 percent as compared to the non-fatigue state.

Horizontal Velocity: Fatigue

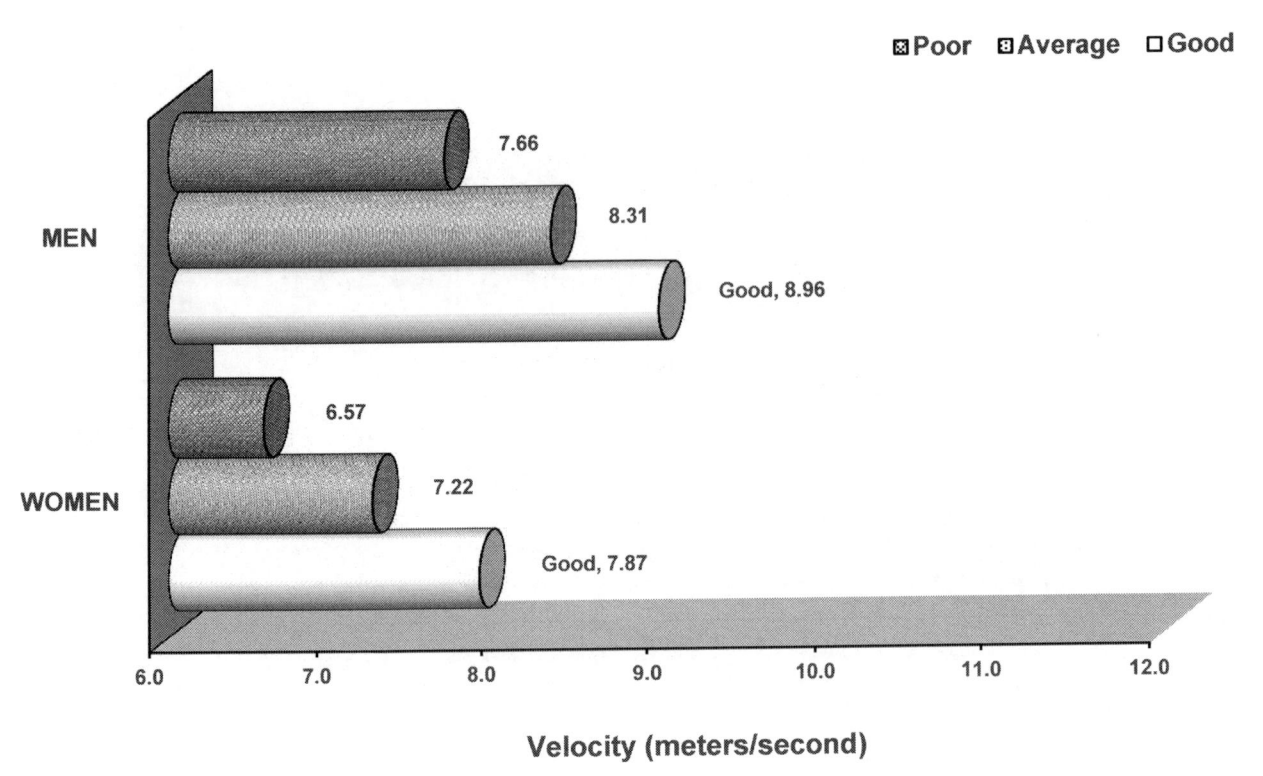

☒ Poor ▨ Average ☐ Good

MEN
- 7.66
- 8.31
- Good, 8.96

WOMEN
- 6.57
- 7.22
- Good, 7.87

Velocity (meters/second)

Figure 10-2: Fatigue Horizontal Velocity Results

In an event where coaches are looking to improve their athlete by that critical one or two percent, this seventeen percent decrement produced by fatigue looms as a major area of improvement potential. As will be seen, all of the compromises that the elite Long race Sprinters make are directed toward minimizing the devastating effects of fatigue.

Stride Rate and Stride Length

The same trend toward Stride Rate emphasis, as found in the Short Sprint, is found in the Long Sprint, with one major difference. Since the Short Sprint doesn't have to worry about fatigue, as much effort as possible can be directed toward producing the high turnover rate necessary to maximize Stride Rate. Since fatigue plays a critical part in the 400, the trend toward greater Stride Rate can only be taken as far as the sprinter can go without producing excessive fatigue at the close of the race. Thus, the 400 becomes a tradeoff between Speed at the beginning (more Speed produces much more fatigue), and Speed at the end (more fatigue produces much less Speed). This is why training is such a factor in the Long Sprint: it gives the sprinter the ability to Sprint faster at the beginning, and still handle the fatigue at the end.

In the Long Sprint, therefore, the fatigue factor must be taken into account when Stride Rate and Length are evaluated. An increase in Stride Rate is good in non-fatigue as long as the effort to produce the result does not severely affect the Stride Rate in fatigue. Likewise, a large Stride Length is acceptable in non-fatigue only if it can be reasonably maintained during fatigue. If these values drop significantly during fatigue, then either the initial Speed must be reduced (lower Stride Rate or Length), or greater training must be developed.

Figures 10-3 and 10-4 present the non-fatigue Stride Rate and Stride Length results for all of the elite Long race Sprinters analyzed to date.

Stride Rate: Non-Fatigue

☒ Poor ☐ Average ☐ Good

MEN
- Poor: 4.15
- Average: 4.25
- Good: 4.35

WOMEN
- Poor: 4.12
- Average: 4.22
- Good: 4.32

Rate (steps/second)

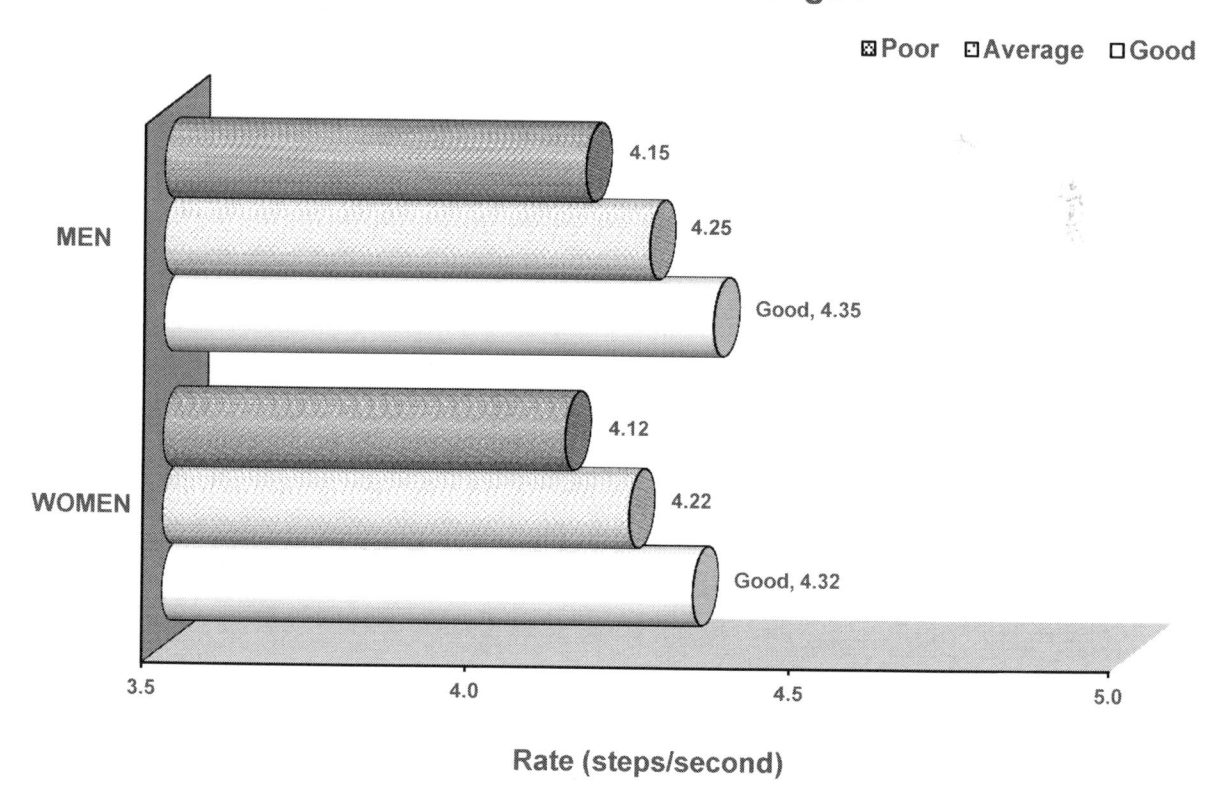

Figure 10-3: Non-Fatigue Stride Rate Results

Stride Length: Non-Fatigue

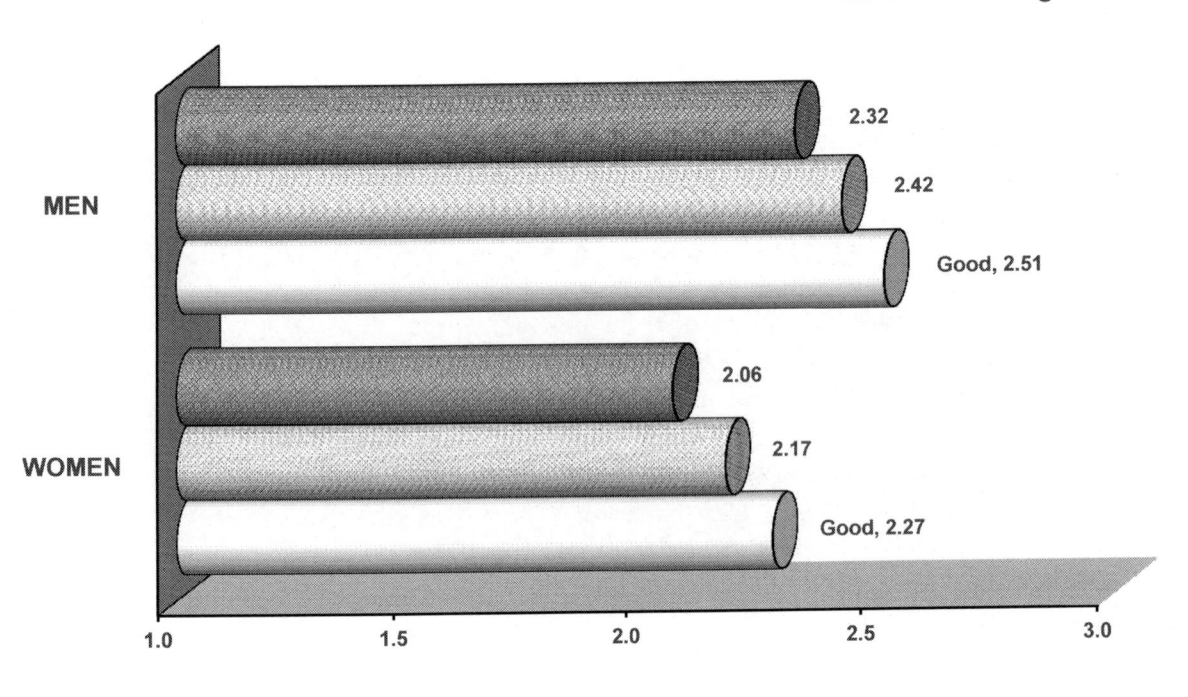

☒ Poor ☒ Average ☐ Good

MEN
- 2.32
- 2.42
- Good, 2.51

WOMEN
- 2.06
- 2.17
- Good, 2.27

Length (meters)

Figure 10-4: Non-Fatigue Stride Length Results

It is interesting to note that, while the Stride Rate results are 12 percent less than the Short Sprint results, the Stride Length results (see Figure 8-3) are virtually the same, in spite of the fact that the Long race Sprinters are moving at a lower Horizontal Velocity. This result further supports the fact that these athletes are compromising the Stride Rate result due to the fatigue factor.

In the fatigue state, as shown in Figures 10-5 and 10-6, both Stride Rate and Length suffer approximately a 10 percent decrement. Since the decrease in Stride Length is solely due to the decrease in Horizontal Velocity, it is not the critical factor in the loss of performance. This again points to the critical importance of striving to maintain Stride Rate both in the non-fatigue and fatigue situations.

Additional data on this conclusion will be presented in the discussion on Ground and Air Times.

Stride Rate: Fatigue

☒ Poor ▨ Average ☐ Good

MEN
- Poor: 3.58
- Average: 3.71
- Good, 3.86

WOMEN
- Poor: 3.58
- Average: 3.72
- Good, 3.86

Rate (steps/second)

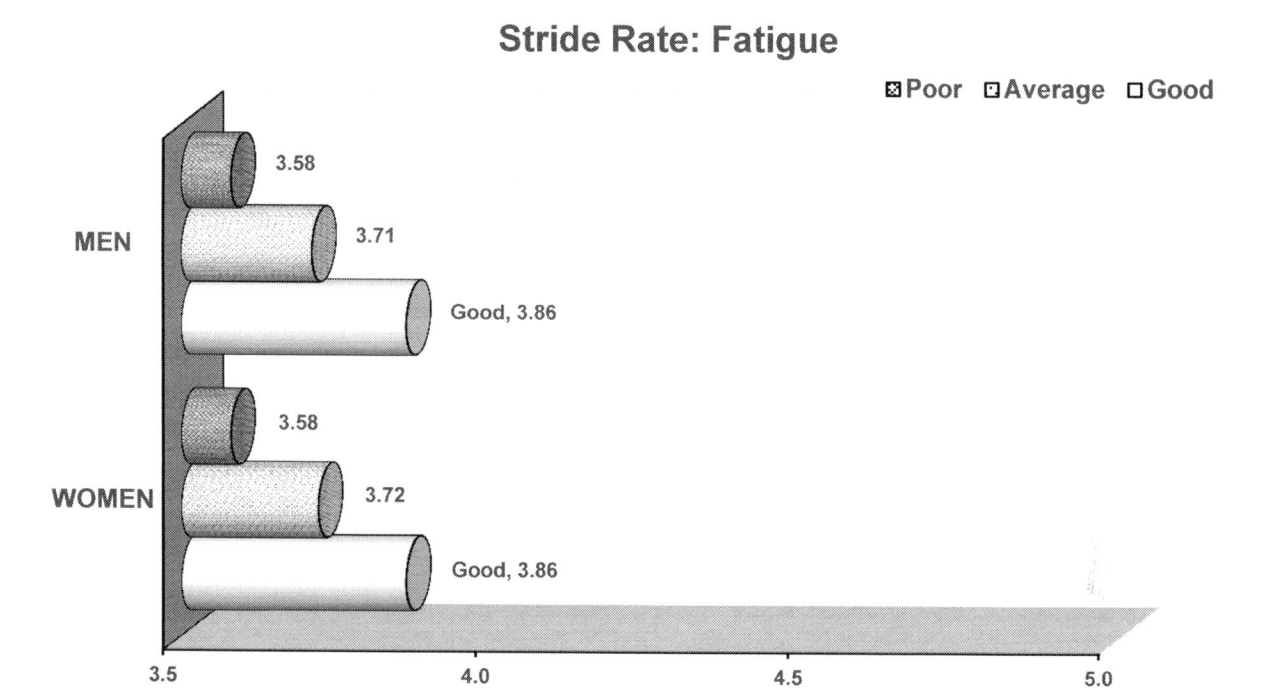

Figure 10-5: Fatigue Stride Rate Results

Stride Length: Fatigue

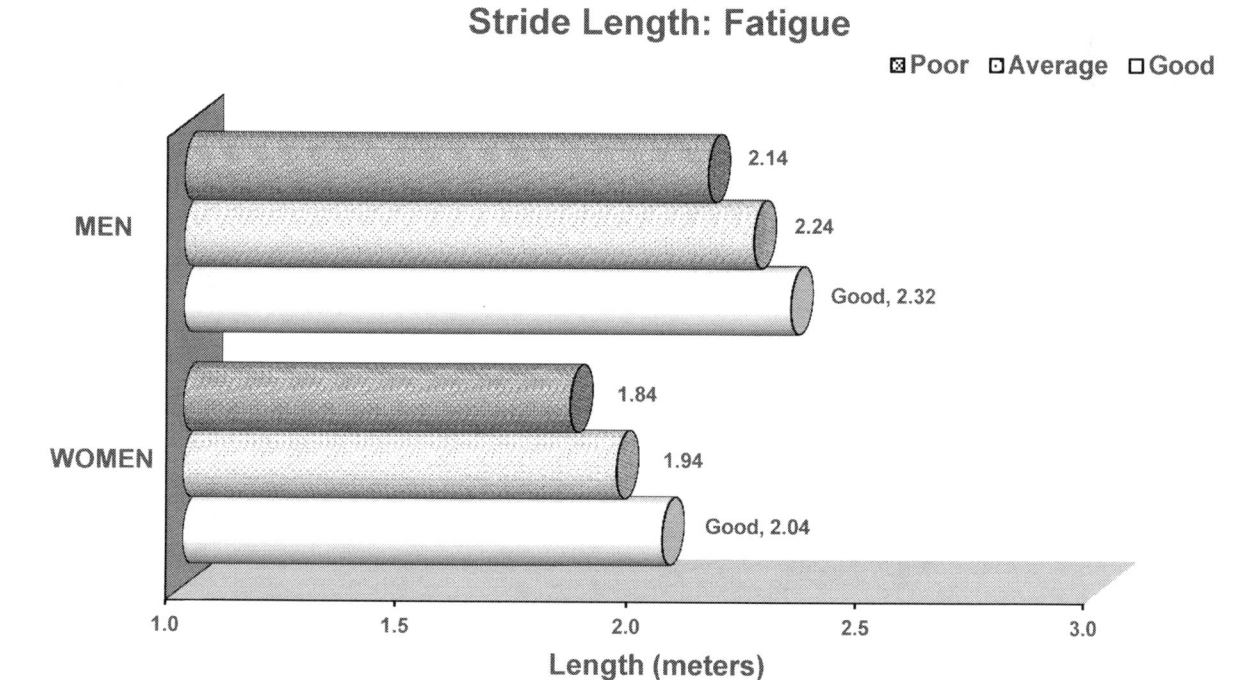

☒ Poor ▨ Average ☐ Good

MEN
- Poor: 2.14
- Average: 2.24
- Good, 2.32

WOMEN
- Poor: 1.84
- Average: 1.94
- Good, 2.04

Length (meters)

Figure 10-6: Fatigue Stride Length Results

Ground Time and Air Time

The following Figures show the non-fatigue Ground (10-7) and Air Times (10-8) for all Long Sprint elite athletes investigated to date. As in the Short Sprint, since Air Time dictates Stride Length, and the combination of Ground and Air Time dictate Stride Rate, these time results provide further information regarding how the sprinter is allocating resources to achieve and maintain Horizontal Velocity.

Ground Time: Non-Fatigue

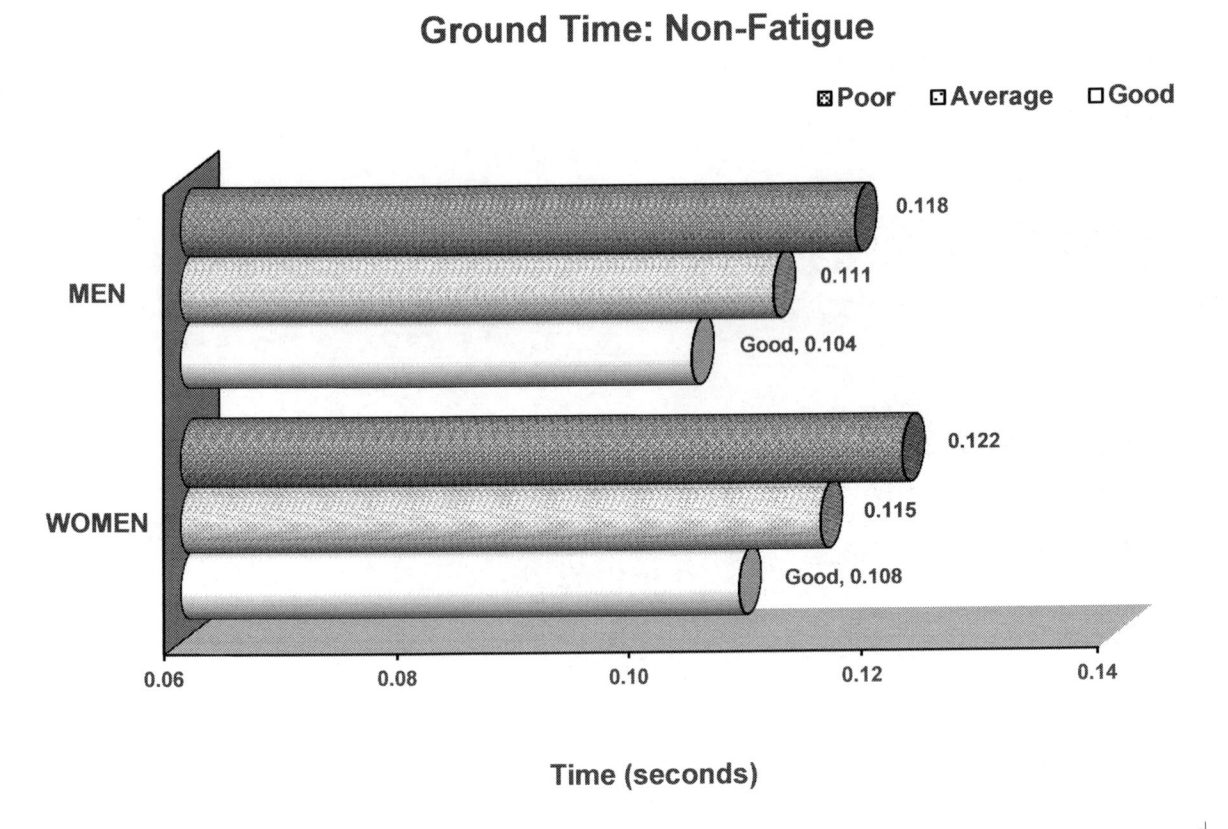

MEN
- Poor: 0.118
- Average: 0.111
- Good: 0.104

WOMEN
- Poor: 0.122
- Average: 0.115
- Good: 0.108

Time (seconds)

Figure 10-7: Non-Fatigue Ground Time Results

As was true in the Short Sprint, minimizing the Ground Time is the key to producing higher Stride Rates and, therefore, greater Horizontal Velocity. In fact, the 10 percent decrement in Horizontal Velocity between the Short and Long Sprints can be entirely attributed to the change in the ground contact time. Unfortunately, to reduce this time requires the expenditure of large amounts of strength and, therefore, energy. Thus, the compromise that must be in the Long Sprint is balancing the Speed of the race with the available Speed endurance.

Likewise, as in the Short Sprint, the Air Time results are unique in that, regardless of the quality of the sprinter, there is **no difference in the Air Time results**. Thus, the only acceptable Air

Time result is the average result. Also, as in the Short Sprint, the Poor result indicates that an Air Time that is either too short or too long is unwanted.

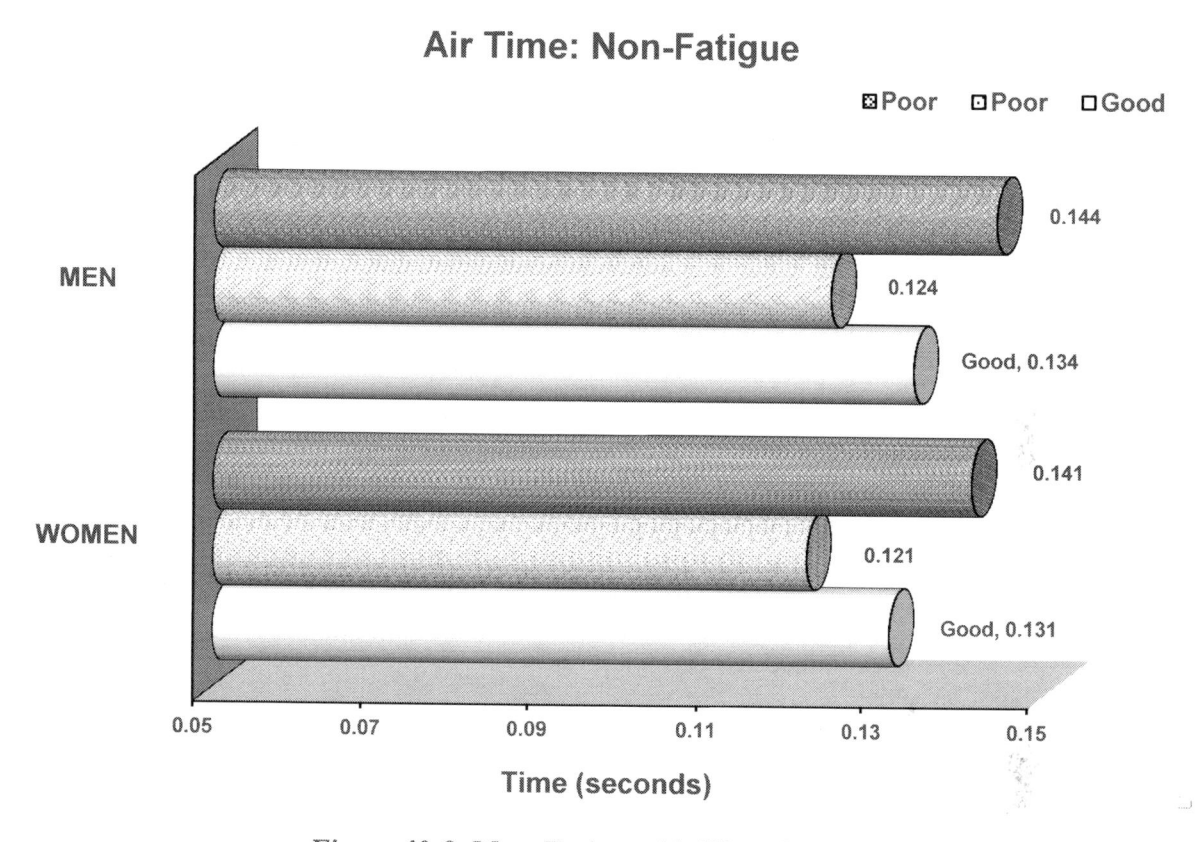

Air Time: Non-Fatigue

☒ Poor   ☐ Poor   ☐ Good

MEN
- 0.144
- 0.124
- Good, 0.134

WOMEN
- 0.141
- 0.121
- Good, 0.131

Time (seconds): 0.05 – 0.15

Figure 10-8: Non-Fatigue Air Time Results

In comparison to the Short Sprint, the Air Time for the Long Sprint is about 8 percent longer. This is due to the fact that the leg segments are moving slower, and need slightly longer to complete their recovery action. Thus, as in the Short Sprint, the Air Time for the longer race should be only as long as needed for proper leg recovery – but no shorter or longer.

In comparison, Figures 10-9 and 10-10 show the fatigue Ground and Air Times for all elite athletes investigated to date.

Note that all of the trends found in both the Short Sprint and non-fatigue portion of the Long Sprint are also found in these results. The Ground Time result continues to be the key to performance, while the Air Time result remains constant regardless of the quality of the performance. In fact, the 17 percent decrement in Horizontal Velocity between the non-fatigue and fatigue states can be entirely attributed to the change in the ground contact time.

Ground Time: Fatigue

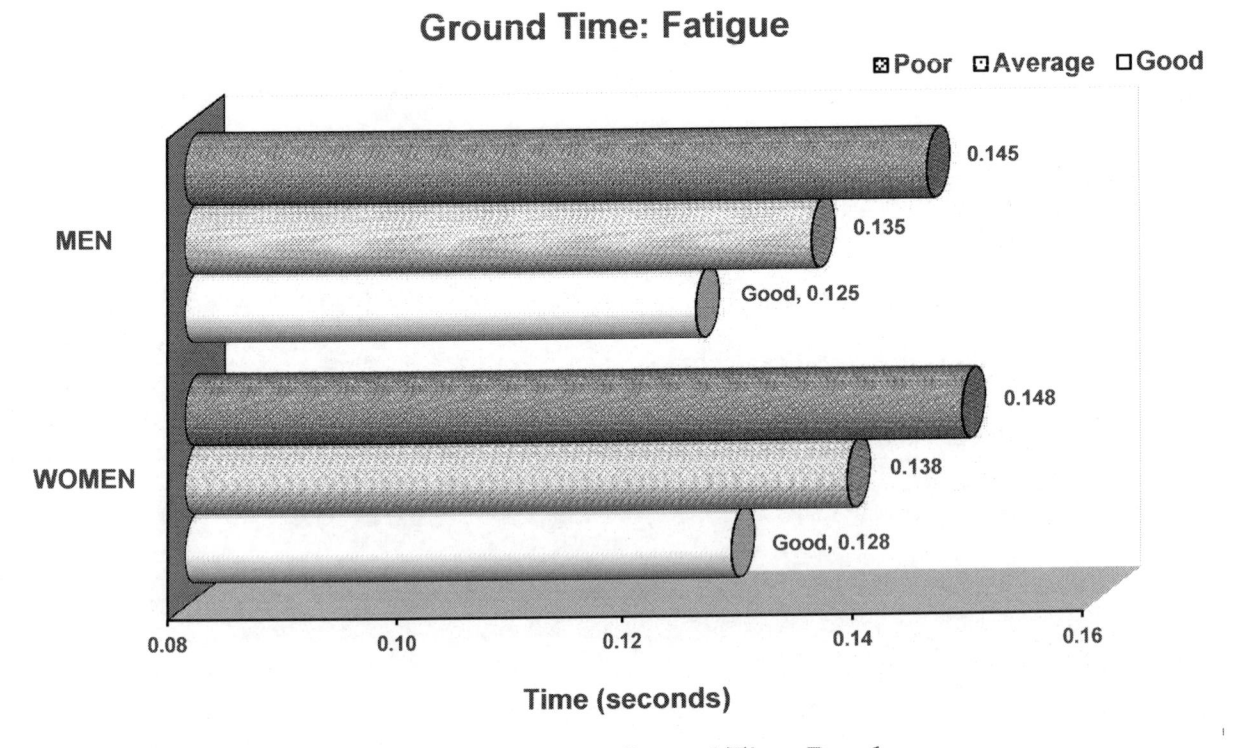

MEN
- Poor: 0.145
- Average: 0.135
- Good, 0.125

WOMEN
- Poor: 0.148
- Average: 0.138
- Good, 0.128

Time (seconds)

Figure 10-9: Fatigue Ground Time Results

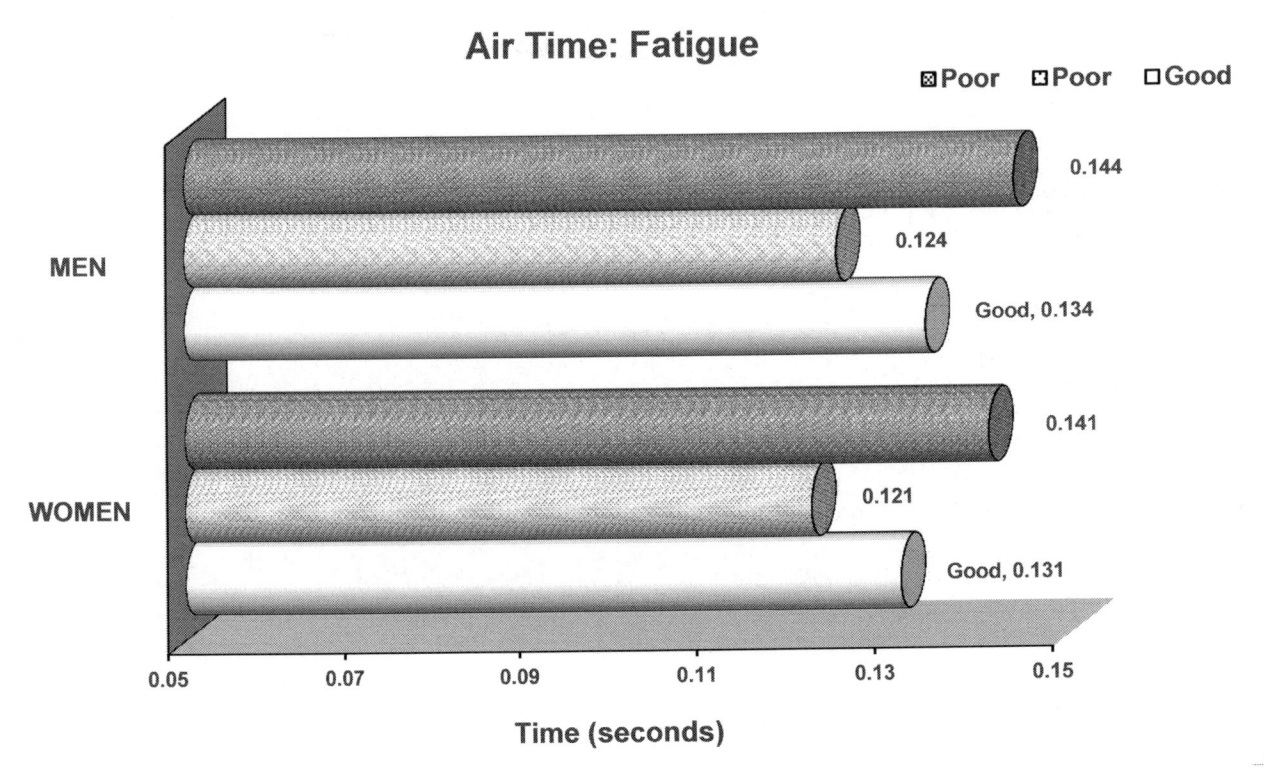

Air Time: Fatigue

MEN
- Poor: 0.144
- Poor: 0.124
- Good, 0.134

WOMEN
- Poor: 0.141
- Poor: 0.121
- Good, 0.131

Time (seconds)

Figure 10-10: Fatigue Air Time Results

The fact that Air Time does not change in fatigue has been seen in other running events. It is postulated that a certain amount of Air Time is required to recover the body segments for the next Ground Phase, so the time must be maintained. This further points to the critical need for the athlete to be able to produce and maintain the large ground forces during the Sprint performance.

Time to Maximum Upper Leg Flexion

As in the Short Sprint, the time to maximum upper leg flexion should happen as late in the Air Phase as possible (see Figure 8-6). Due to the fact that the Long Sprint Air Phase is longer and (as will be seen) the upper leg does not recover as high, this action is not as aggressive as in the Short Sprint, but the concept is the same. The better Long race Sprinters delay the upper leg flexion so that a more effective Touchdown position can be created.

Chapter Summary:

With several compromises in the General Performance Descriptors due to the fatigue factor, the key to the Long Sprint performance, like the Short Sprint, is achieved through increasing Stride Rate by decreasing ground contact time.

The next section investigates how the elite Long race Sprinters actually accomplish this task.

CHAPTER 11

CRITICAL SPECIFIC PERFORMANCE DESCRIPTORS FOR THE LONG SPRINTS

In presenting the Specific Performance Descriptors for the Long Sprint, comparisons will be made with the Short Sprint results. Since the only difference between the non-fatigue and fatigue results is in the magnitude, only the non-fatigue values are presented.

It is important to realize that every Descriptor that was significant in the Short Sprint performance is also significant in the Long Sprint. To review the specifics of each of the Descriptors, refer to the corresponding Short Sprint result in Chapter 9.

Arm Action

In the Long Sprint, as in the Short Sprint, the arms are used primarily for balance and to help the athlete shift the running Mechanics to the front side of the body. The only difference is that the arm action in the Long Sprint is less vigorous, with a smaller range of motion for both the upper and lower arms. Since fatigue is a factor, the Long Sprinter cannot afford to expend the extra energy required to get the small beneficial effects that a vigorous arm action provides.

Horizontal Foot Speed at Touchdown

The foot speed at Touchdown for the Long Sprinter is just as critical, if not more, as for the Short Sprinter. For the Short Sprinter, a superior result equates to greater Speed. For the Long Sprinter, the same result means not only better Speed, but better economy. This results not only in improved non-fatigue results, but the delay of the onset of fatigue. This is true primarily due to the fact that the better performer minimizes the braking forces during each Touchdown phase. This not only decreases the jarring impact that is highly fatigue producing, but also minimizes the effort that will be required to regain the forward Velocity that was lost. Multiply this benefit times the hundreds of strides involved in the Long Sprint and the overall gain is obvious.

Every Long Sprinter knows the term "Relax the Backstretch". One major difference between the better performers and the poorer performers is how this action is executed. The poorer sprinter's idea of relaxation is one of letting the recovery leg drop to the track with as little effort as possible, then vaulting over the leg once it hits the ground. The better sprinter's idea of relaxing consists of continuing to work the recovery leg so that it cycles normally, then relaxing once the leg strikes the ground

Although the lazy recovery action of the lesser sprinter "feels" easier, the impact shock that the resulting ground contact produces, along with the loss of forward Speed, greatly increases the total workload, as well as producing greater muscular fatigue at the end of the race. In contrast, although the extra work the better sprinters exert to properly prepare the recovery leg for Touchdown doesn't "feel" as easy as just letting the leg crash to the ground, the resulting energy savings during ground contact makes this approach better in the long run.

Figure 11-1 shows the Horizontal foot speed at Touchdown, in relation to the sprinter, for all elite athletes analyzed to date. For a visual description of this Variable, see Figure 9-3.

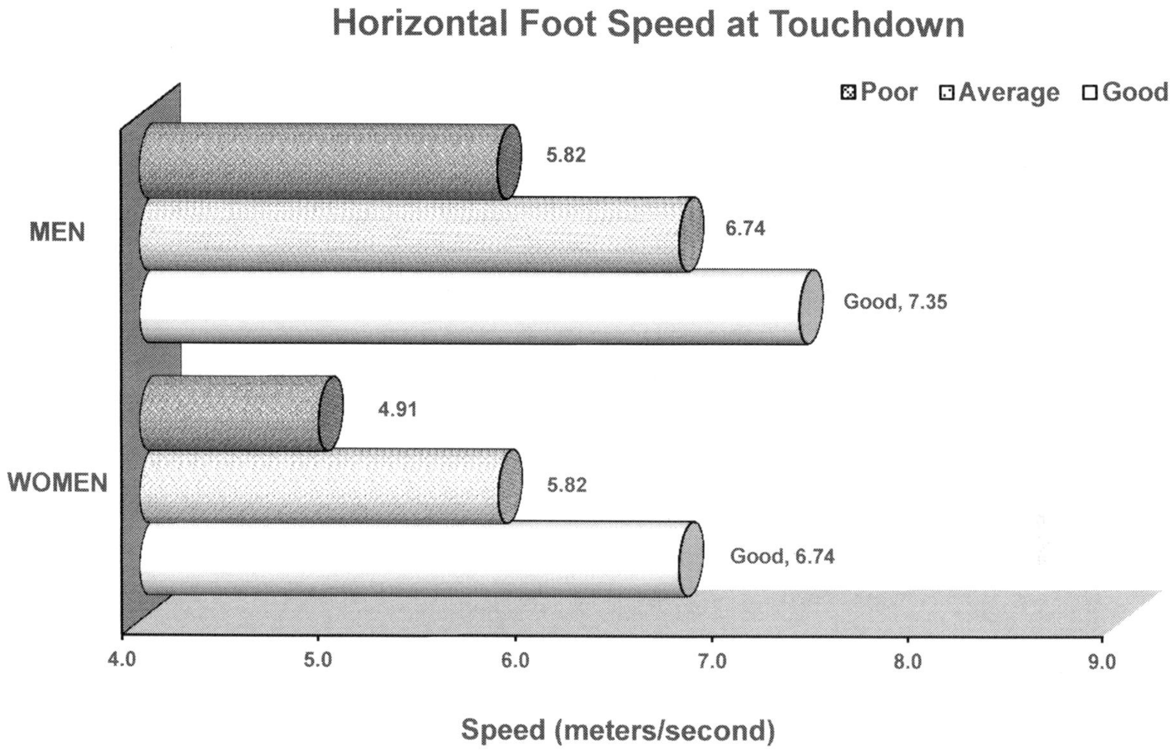

Horizontal Foot Speed at Touchdown

☒ Poor ☐ Average ☐ Good

MEN
- 5.82
- 6.74
- Good, 7.35

WOMEN
- 4.91
- 5.82
- Good, 6.74

Speed (meters/second)

Figure 11-1: Horizontal Foot Speed at Touchdown Results

Note that the approximate 3 meter per second difference between the foot speed and the Horizontal Velocity (Figure 10-1) for the Long Sprints is about the same as the Short Sprints (Figures 8-1 and 9-4). This points to the importance of generating as high a foot speed as possible since the resulting Speed down the track is directly related to this result.

Horizontal Foot Distance at Touchdown

Horizontal foot distance results are another area where compromises must be made due to the fatigue factor inherent in the Long race. Long race Sprinters land approximately 20 percent farther in front of the body center as compared to the Short race Sprinters. Although this action produces Horizontal braking and greater ground impact shock to the leg, it serves to help produce the critical Vertical Velocity by vaulting the sprinter over the extended leg. The better sprinters, however, have the strength endurance to minimize this less-than-beneficial reliance.

Figure 11-2 shows the results for the Horizontal distance the foot is in front of the body at Touchdown for all elite athletes analyzed to date. For a visual description of this Variable, see Figure 9-5.

Horizontal Foot Distance at Touchdown

☒ Poor ☐ Average ☐ Good

MEN
- Poor: 0.54
- Average: 0.48
- Good: 0.42

WOMEN
- Poor: 0.44
- Average: 0.38
- Good: 0.32

Distance (meters)

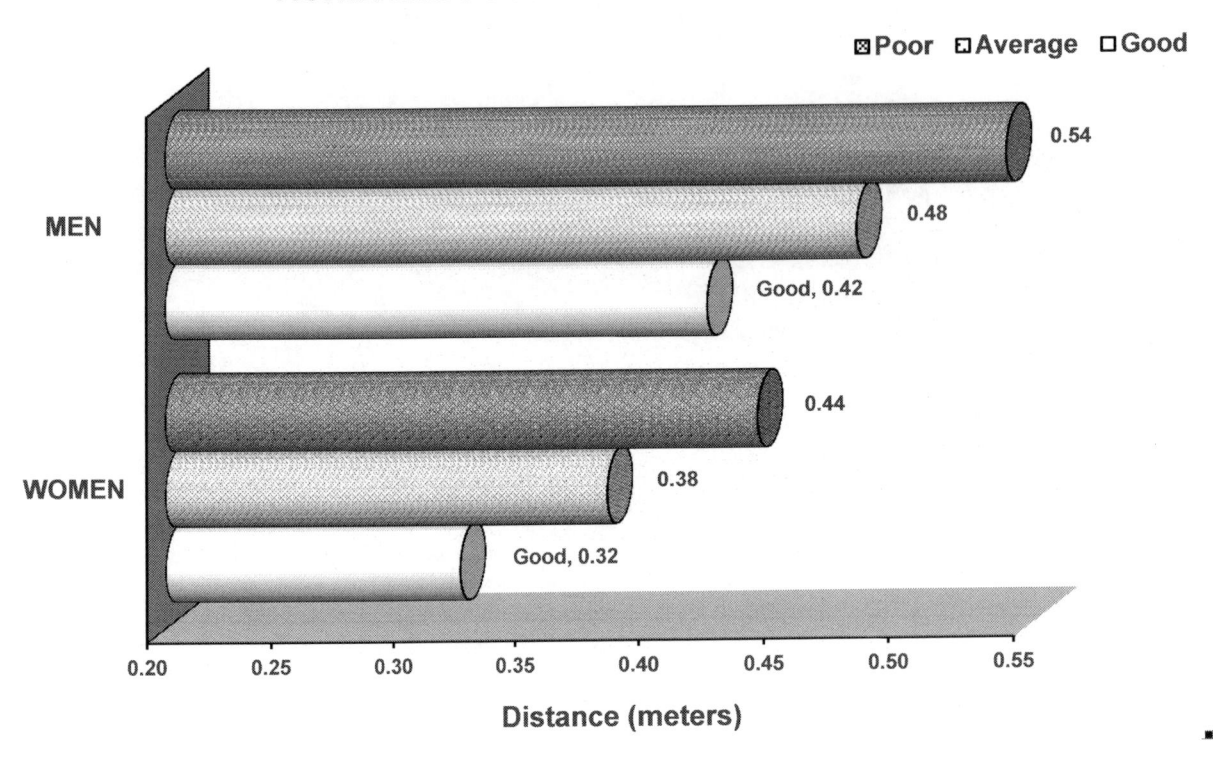

Figure 11-2: Horizontal Foot Distance at Touchdown

In comparing the fatigue and non-fatigue results for the Long Sprint, it has been found that fatigue forces the sprinter to increase the foot distance. This is done because the performer has less muscular force due to fatigue, and must rely more on vaulting over the leg to get the body into the air. It is interesting to note, however, that if the result can be improved in non-fatigue, it will carry over into the fatigue portion of the race.

Trunk Angle at Touchdown

In non-fatigue, the better Long race Sprinters continue to Takeoff with a trunk angle of around 83 degrees (see Figure 9-7 for measurement information), then limit the trunk forward rotation to under 5 degrees during ground contact. As fatigue sets in, however, athletes begin to use additional trunk extension to help them bring the recovery leg forward during ground contact, resulting in a more upright trunk angle at Takeoff. More proficient performers limit this trunk action because it increases both Ground and Air Times, which serves to decrease Horizontal Velocity.

Athletes in extreme fatigue can rely on the trunk to the extent that it is actually leaning backwards at Takeoff. When a sprinter reaches this level of fatigue, the race has been effectively lost. In contrast, the best athletes are fit enough to maintain their upper body Mechanics and produce a superior finish.

Knee Separation at Touchdown

As in the Short Sprint (see Figure 9-9 for measurement information), the amount of knee separation at Touchdown is an excellent measure of the quality of the Long Sprint Mechanics. As shown in Figure 11-3, although a little more separation is evident, the best still minimize this value.

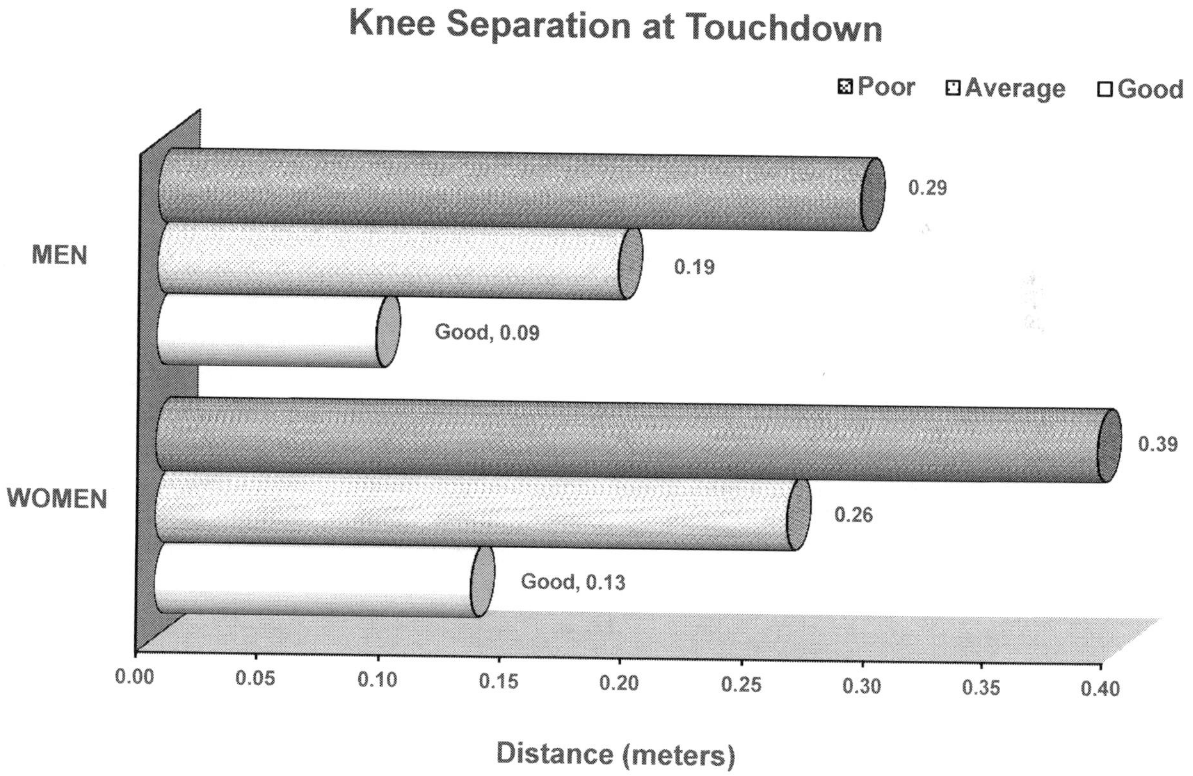

Knee Separation at Touchdown

Poor   Average   Good

MEN
- Poor: 0.29
- Average: 0.19
- Good: 0.09

WOMEN
- Poor: 0.39
- Average: 0.26
- Good: 0.13

Distance (meters)

Figure 11-3: Knee Separation at Touchdown

Both in non-fatigue and fatigue, the amount of separation is directly related to how well the sprinter is at keeping the leg segments in front of the body, providing the most effective and efficient Sprint form.

Upper Leg Motion

Since the Long Sprinter must increase the Ground Phase to conserve energy, the range of motion for the upper leg while on the ground is slightly increased. Figure 11-4 shows the results for the upper leg motion for all elite athletes analyzed to date. Refer to Figure 9-11 for angle measurement direction information.

Upper Leg Motion

Legend: ⊠ Poor ▨ Average ☐ Good

Category	Poor	Average	Good
MEN TAKEOFF	152	157	162 (less extension)
MEN FULL EXTENSION	142	147	152 (less extension)
MEN FULL FLEXION	245	250	255 (more flexion)
WOMEN TAKEOFF	152	157	162 (less extension)
WOMEN FULL EXTENSION	144	149	154 (less extension)
WOMEN FULL FLEXION	246	251	256 (more flexion)

Position (degrees)

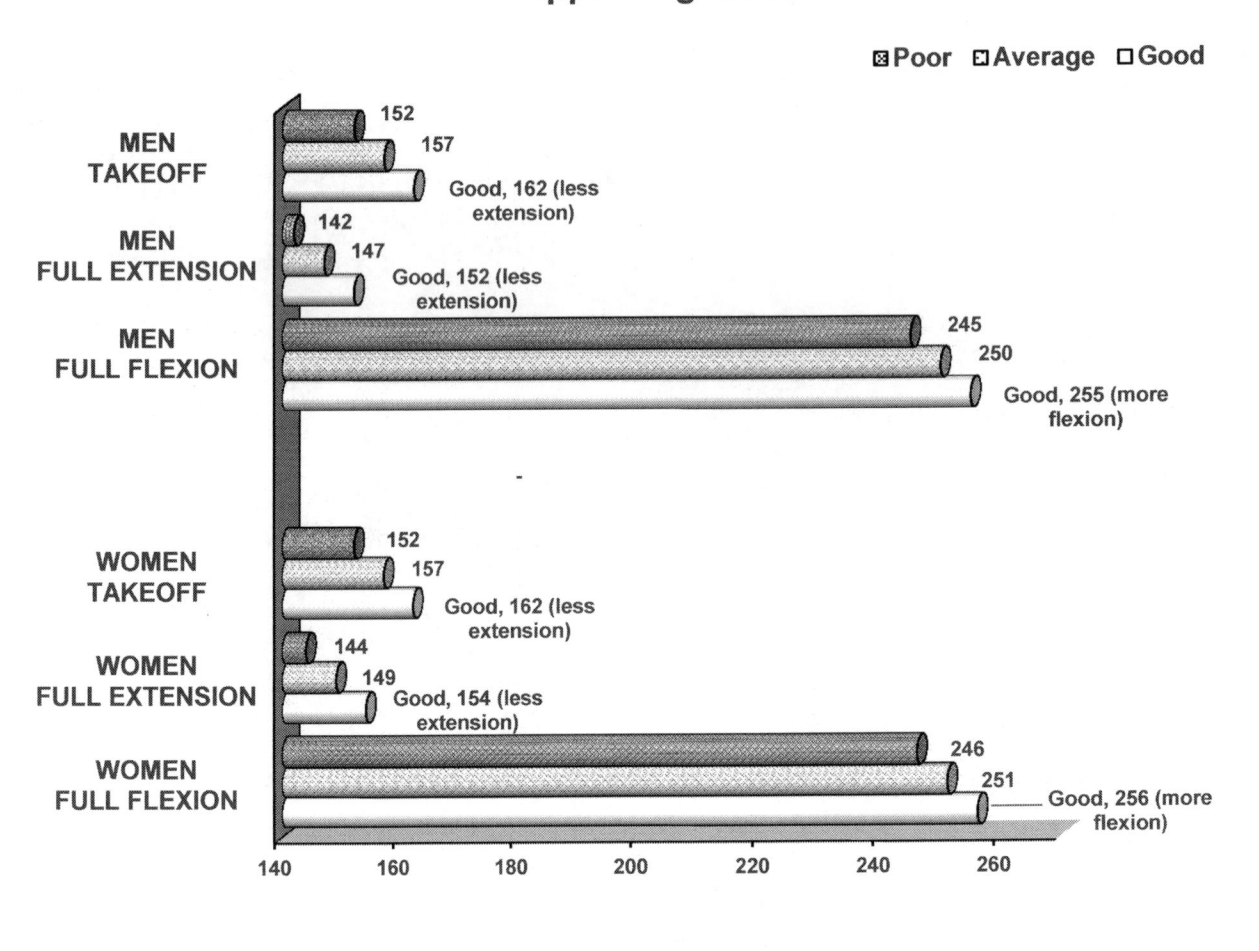

Figure 11-4: Upper Leg Motion

In fact, the Long Sprinter increases the leg extension at Takeoff by approximately 8 degrees compared to the Short Sprint (see Figure 9-12). Although this increases Ground Time (which decreases Stride Rate), leading to a lower Horizontal Velocity, it must be done to improve the efficiency of the performance. Once again the compromise required due to the fatigue factor can be seen.

In the full flexion position, however, no compromise is required since this action occurs in the Air Phase, which does not have the energy demands of the Ground Phase. Thus, the Long and Short Sprint results for this variable are similar as the athlete prepares for the next ground contact.

Upper Leg Rotational Speed

Figure 11-5 shows the average rotational speed of the upper leg during recovery, the extension speed at Touchdown, as well as the average extension speed during the Ground Phase for all elite athletes analyzed to date. For a visual description of this Variable, see Figure 9-13.

Upper Leg Rotational Speed

Category	Poor	Average	Good
MEN RECOVERY	320	360	400
MEN TOUCHDOWN	101	170	260
MEN GROUND	350	415	460
WOMEN RECOVERY	290	340	380
WOMEN TOUCHDOWN	75	150	223
WOMEN GROUND	340	390	430

Rotational Speed (degrees/second)

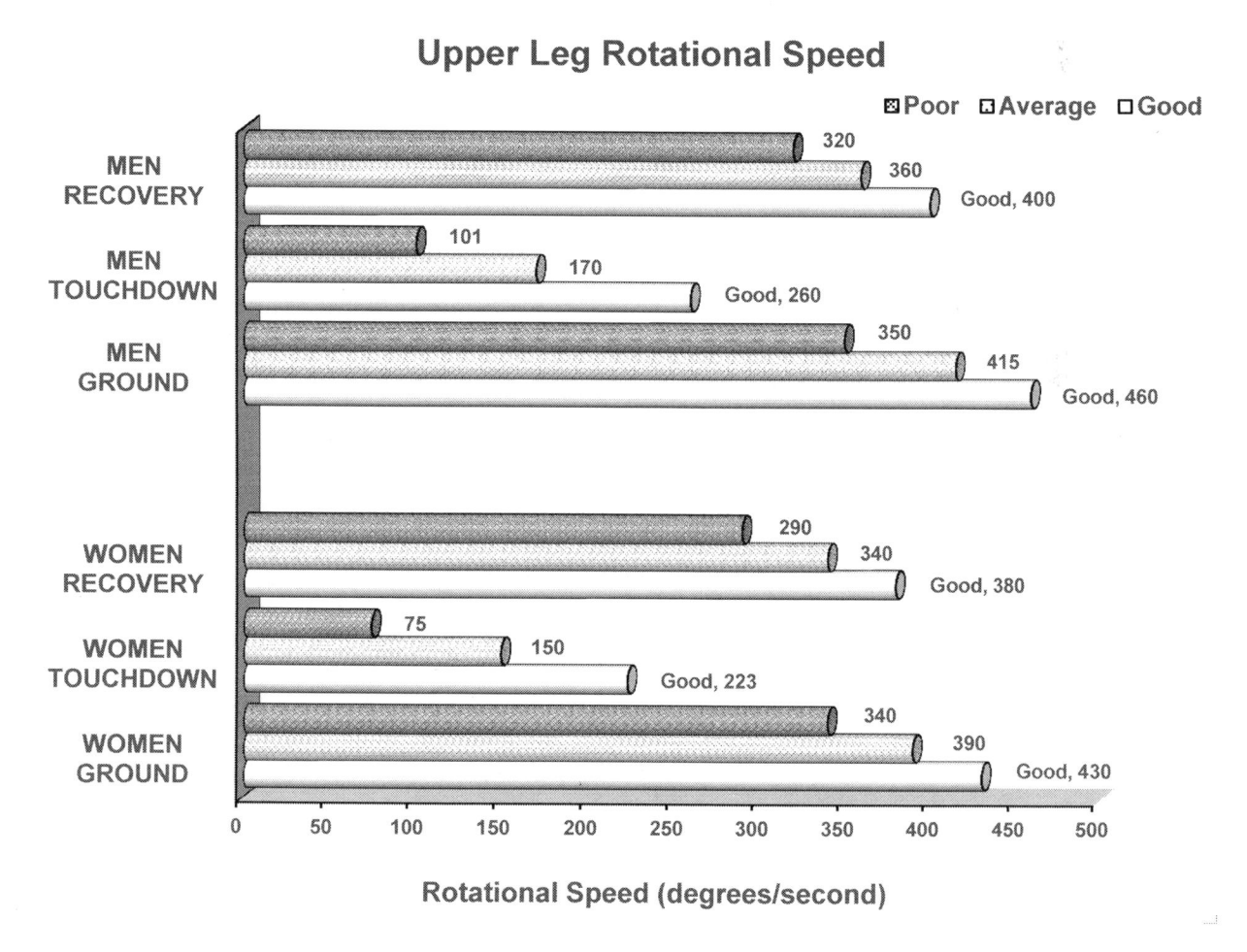

Figure 11-5: Upper Leg Rotational Speed

Since upper leg speed results are the most critical variable in Speed production, it is not surprising that the Long Sprint results are lower than those found in the Short Sprint (see Figure 9-14). It is also not surprising to note that the better sprinters produce significantly larger values in the Long Sprint as well.

As in the Short race, the better sprinters tend to maximize the leg recovery and Touchdown rotation speeds, while maintaining or actually increasing (larger than Touchdown) leg speed during ground contact. As in upper leg position, these values indicate the degree of upper leg strength and endurance, as well as the quality of the sprinting Mechanics.

Lower Leg Motion

Figure 11-6 shows the lower leg angle at Takeoff, maximum flexion, and the point where the ankle crosses the opposite leg for all of the elite athletes analyzed to date. Refer to Figure 9-15 for angle measurement information.

Lower Leg Motion

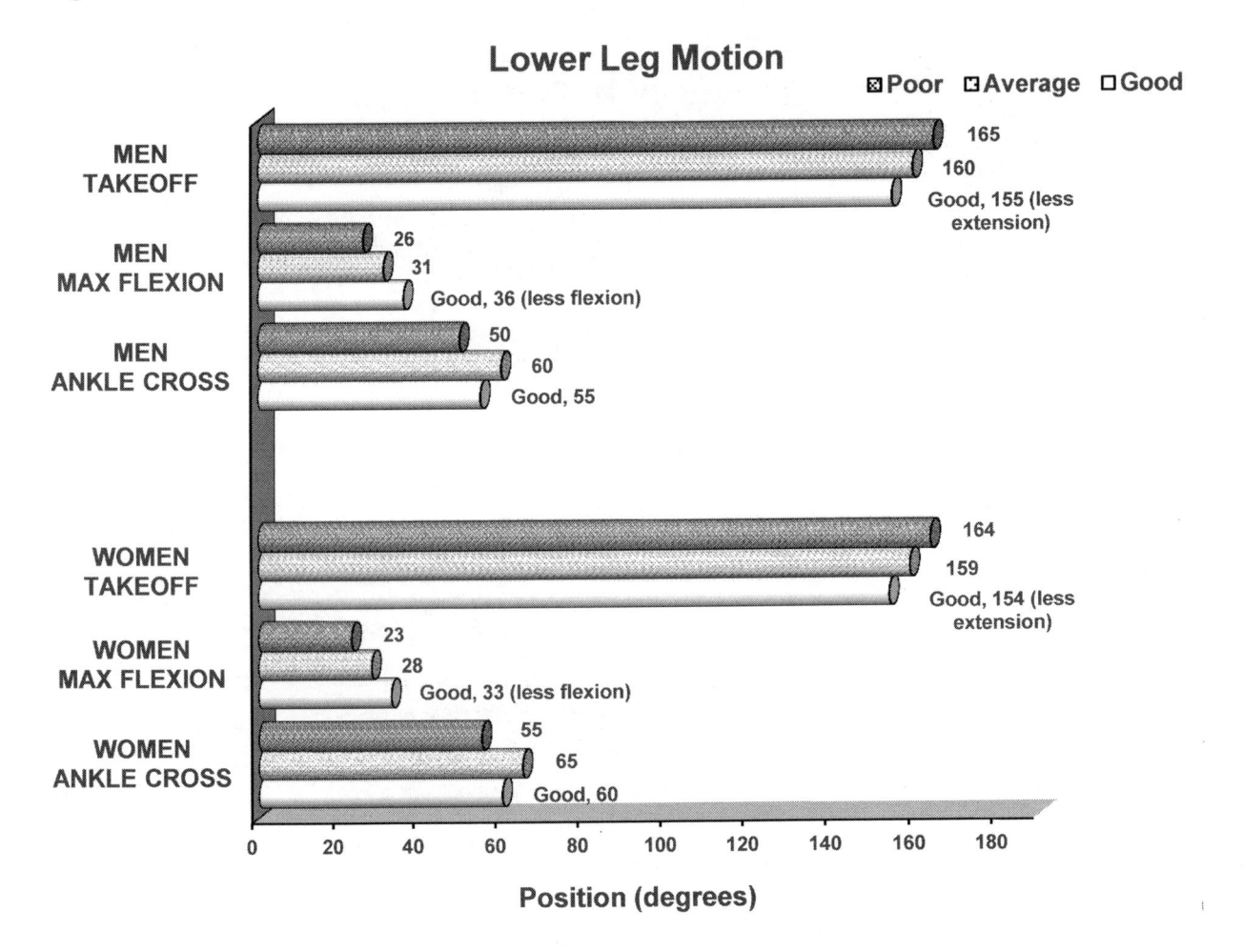

Poor / Average / Good

Category	Poor	Average	Good
MEN TAKEOFF	165	160	155 (less extension)
MEN MAX FLEXION	26	31	36 (less flexion)
MEN ANKLE CROSS	50	60	55
WOMEN TAKEOFF	164	159	154 (less extension)
WOMEN MAX FLEXION	23	28	33 (less flexion)
WOMEN ANKLE CROSS	55	65	60

Position (degrees)

Figure 11-6: Lower Leg Motion

As with upper leg motion, when compared to the Short Sprinter (see Figure 9-16) the ground contact action of the lower leg must be compromised by the Long Sprinter to produce a more economical Ground Phase, resulting in a greater (more extended) Takeoff angle.

As in the Short Sprint, by the time the ankle passes the opposite leg (ankle cross), the lower leg has already started to extend toward ground contact. However, if the sprinter wants to recover the upper leg to a "high knee" position to better attack the ground, the timing of this lower leg extension must be delayed as long as possible. The key to this is limiting the amount of flexion after Takeoff, then controlling the flexion during lower leg recovery — not too little and not too much. Since this action must be created using proper Mechanics and perfect timing, fatigue makes this even more difficult to achieve.

Lower Leg Rotational Speed

Figure 11-7 shows the average rotational speed of the lower leg at Touchdown for all elite athletes analyzed to date (see Figure 9-17 for angle measurement information)..

Lower Leg Rotational Speed

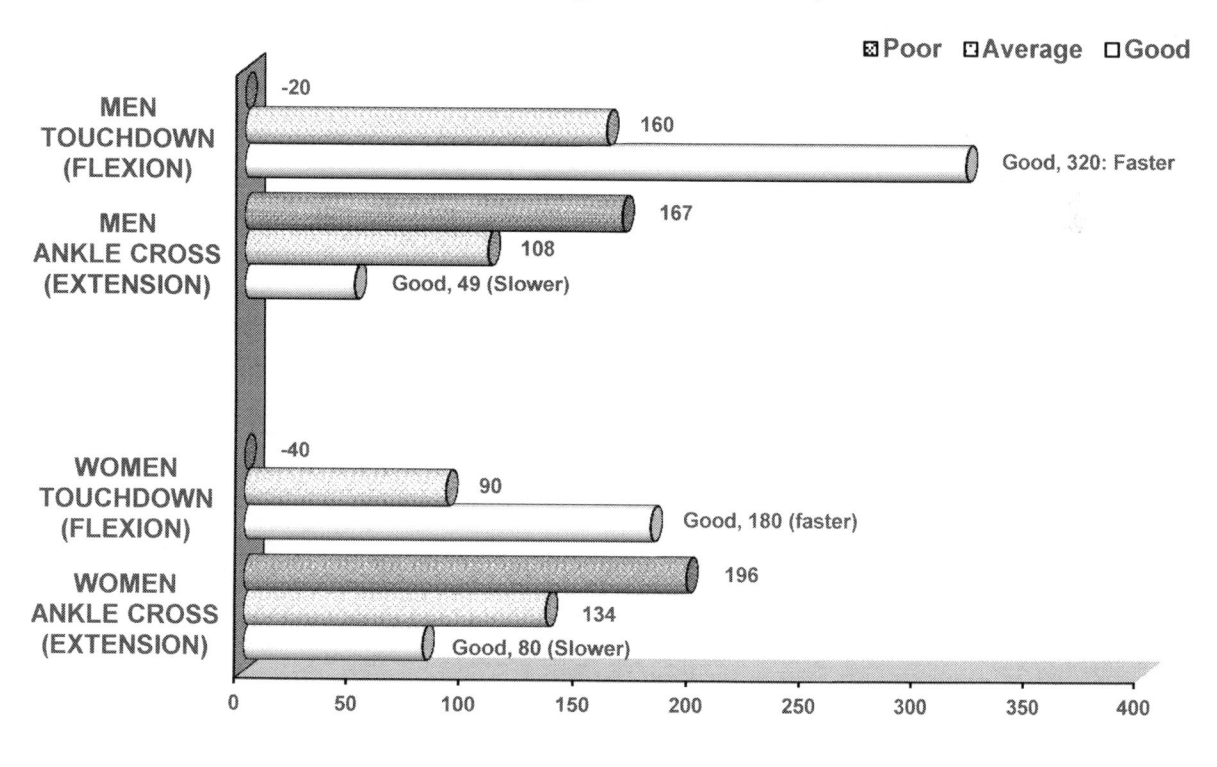

Legend: ⊠ Poor　▨ Average　☐ Good

Category	Poor	Average	Good
MEN TOUCHDOWN (FLEXION)	-20	160	320: Faster
MEN ANKLE CROSS (EXTENSION)	167	108	49 (Slower)
WOMEN TOUCHDOWN (FLEXION)	-40	90	180 (faster)
WOMEN ANKLE CROSS (EXTENSION)	196	134	80 (Slower)

Rotational Speed (degrees/second)

Figure 11-7: Lower Leg Rotational Speed

There is only minor decrement in the lower leg rotation results at Touchdown when compared to the Short Sprint (see Figure 9-18). These result further points to the tendency for the better Long race Sprinters to follow the running techniques of the Short race Sprinters. This concept will be further discussed in Chapter 12.

Section Summary:

As in the Short Sprints, it is evident that both the General and Specific Performance Descriptors point to the fact that success in the Long Sprint is determined by the ability of the athlete to generate great amounts of explosive strength at the proper time. It is also apparent that, due to the fatigue factor, the Long Sprinter must compromise every Ground Phase related variable in an effort to economize the Sprint effort. The most successful Long Sprinter is the one who is able to produce the most economical performance, while having the training level to minimize the compromises to the greatest extent possible.

Generally, the proper mechanical application of this approach results in an elite performance that is characterized by a high Stride Rate and a moderate Stride Length. Specifically, the superior Stride Rate is a product of proper leg positioning, high leg speed, and exact timing.

PART FIVE: FRONT SIDE AND BACK SIDE SPRINT MECHANICS

CHAPTER 12

FRONT SIDE AND BACK SIDE SPRINT MECHANICS

Early in the research effort in the elite Sprint events, it became apparent that the successful athletes were focusing their efforts on the leg action that took place in front of the body. The results presented in Chapters 5-11, as well as research done by many others, support this conclusion. In fact, **the more the sprinter can shift the critical ground contact efforts to the front of the body, the more successful the Sprint performance**.

For more than 20 years, the best Sprint coaches have been trying to shift the leg action of their athletes to the front side of the body. This emphasis became such a critical aspect of every Sprint evaluation that the term "Front Side Mechanics" became a term used by all knowledgeable coaches. In contrast to the desirable goal of maximizing Front Side Mechanics, the term "Back Side Mechanics" became a concept that was to be avoided at all costs.

As shown in Figure 12-1, these two Variables can be easily identified during any portion of the Sprint race by simply drawing a straight line through the upper body (trunk). Segments in front of the line are in the Front Side while segments in back of the line are in the Back Side.

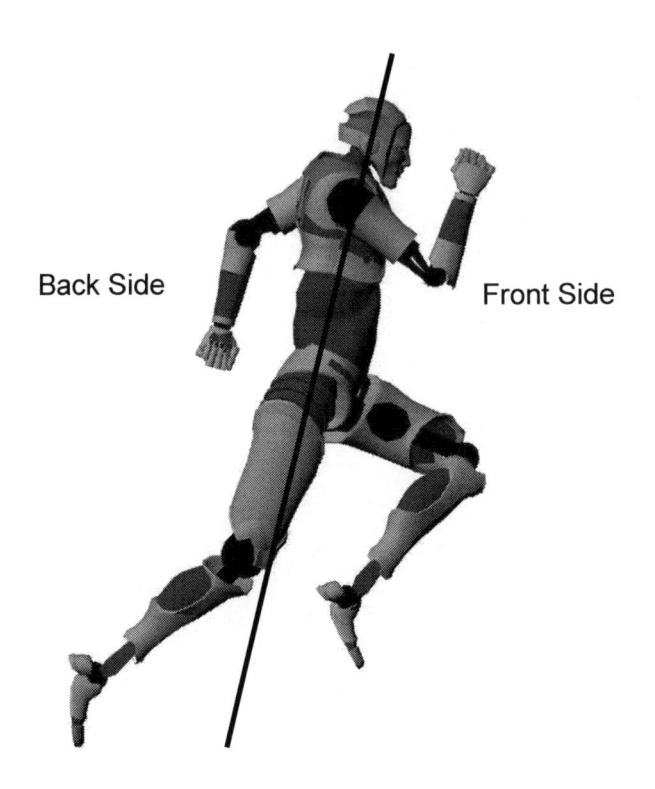

Figure 12-1 Front Side and Back Side Mechanics at Maximum Velocity

Initially the teaching goal was to get the Sprint athletes to emphasize, develop, and execute Front Side Mechanics at maximum Sprint Speed. Experience quickly identified that, to achieve proper Front Side Mechanics, it had to be properly set up during the Start, continued through the Transition, and into Maximum Velocity.

Traditionally, it has been assumed that the Start, or the acceleration phase of the Sprint race, was dominated by Back Side Mechanics. Recent research has determined that, contrary to this belief, **the entire Sprint, from gun to finish, should be Front Side oriented**. This is critical for two reasons, both directly related to Sprint success.

First, to achieve world class Sprint Acceleration and Velocity, an athlete must be Front Side dominate during ground contact to generate the most effective ground forces. The simple fact is that, at today's competition level, a sprinter cannot be competitive without performing in this manner. Thus, achieving this Sprint technique coming out of the starting effort is the first performance goal.

Second, it has become painfully evident that, **if a Sprint athlete fails to achieve Front Side dominance at the beginning of the race, they are unable to shift from that point forward**. Thus, if Back Side Mechanics are dominant during the Start, then the sprinter will finish the race with Back Side dominance.

Likewise, when fatigue sets in, **if a sprinter falls out of their Front Side dominant Mechanics, they cannot recover**. Once the shift moves from Front Side to Back Side, the athlete is stuck with the inferior performance situation.

Maximum Velocity Front Side Mechanics

The reason Front Side Mechanics is successful can be easily explained by looking at what happens during the brief, explosive ground contact phase of sprinting. Figure 12-2 shows the critical Vertical forces during ground contact of an elite level Sprint performance at Maximum Velocity.

It is evident that the force results during the first half (Front Side) of ground contact is greater than the last half (Back Side). In fact, the average force during the Front Side example shown is 2000 Newtons (about 450 Pounds), while the Back Side average is 1000 Newtons (about 225 Pounds). Since this constitutes a 100 percent difference in force production, it should not be surprising that the sprinter that spends more time in Front Side sprinting will have a major advantage.

More importantly, as the Figure shows, the force generated during the last fifteen percent of ground contact is minimal at best (about 100 Newtons or 20 Pounds). The best sprinters discovered that, if they ended this unproductive portion of ground contact early, they could get back to the productive side of the activity (Front Side) sooner. Given two sprinters of equal abilities, the one that spends more time on the Front Side of sprinting will prevail every time.

Vertical Ground Forces

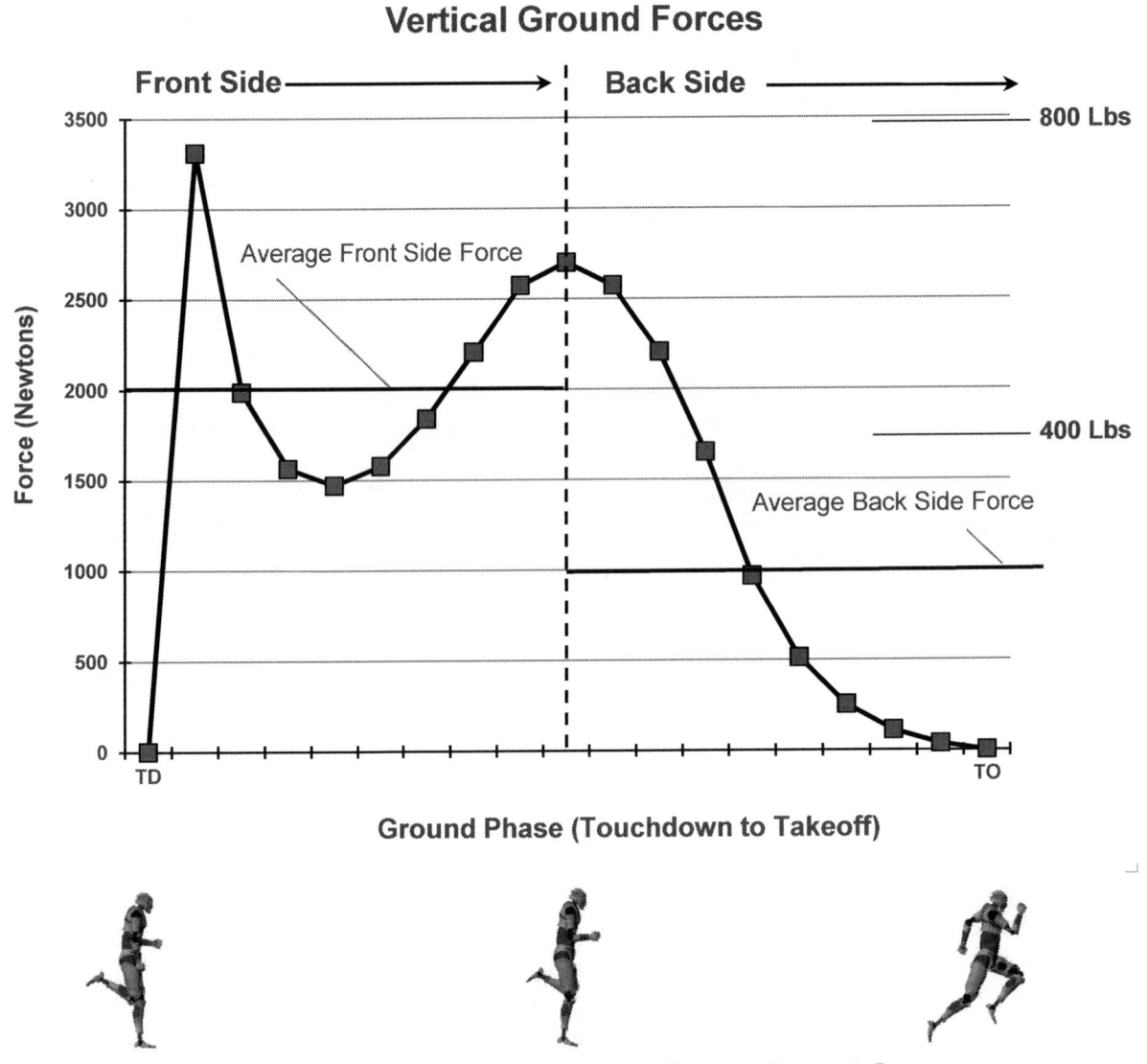

Figure 12-2: Vertical Ground Forces During Ground Contact (Touchdown (TD) to Takeoff (TO))

The act of emphasizing Front Side Mechanics ended the notion that elite sprinting is a natural action. In fact, the natural Mechanics of all runners is to allow Back Side Mechanics to just happen. It is much easier to allow the legs to simply rotate behind the body, then allow the natural range of motion and gravity to stop the rotation, and then begin the forward recovery.

To actually voluntarily try to minimize the Back Side motion of the legs is decidedly unnatural. This process has been termed "active recovery" by the coaches since it conveys the concept that the sprinter must feel if the proper action is to be produced.

The main goal of all Sprint development must be to maximize Front Side Mechanics. To accomplish this, an understanding of both the concept and the force (muscular) demands of this action is needed. Figure 12-3 shows the dominant demands of the muscles around the ankle to move an elite sprinter through ground contact.

Ankle Muscle Moment

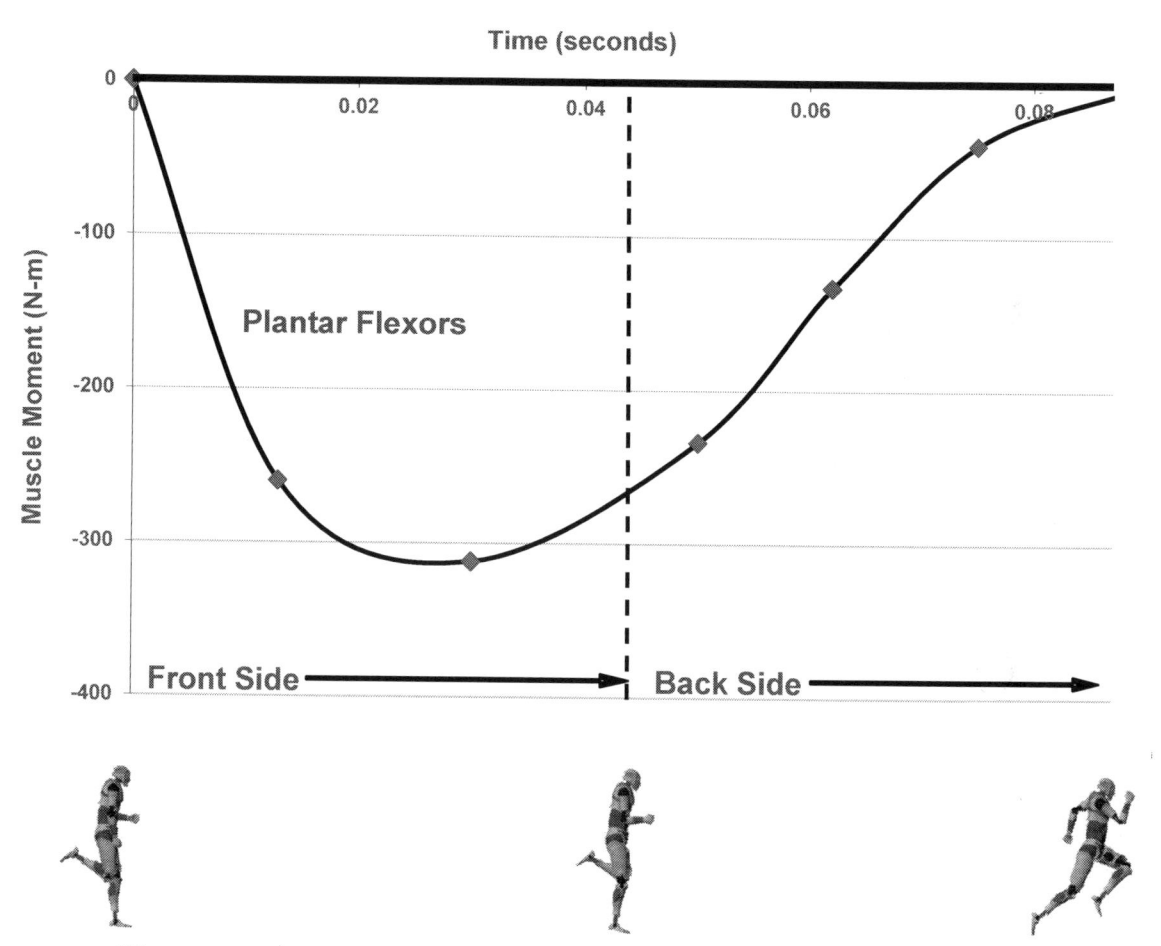

Figure 12-3: Muscular Demands At The Ankle During Ground Contact

Developing the muscular action at the ankle is easy since it is a simple, natural, and manageable action. The muscular force demands required to rotate the foot around the ankle joint consists solely of plantar flexion (negative values), and is well within the ability of any elite sprinter. In addition, using the powerful plantar flexors to exert force on the ground is a natural action, the athlete does this without thinking.

In this basic, one muscle group action, note that the majority of the force production occurs during the Front Side portion of ground contact. In addition, since most of the effort in Front Side is highly eccentric in nature, the muscular demands at the ankle are well below the maximum abilities of an elite sprinter.

What is not shown here are the muscular demands on the foot inverters and everters, which are required to help stabilize the foot at Impact. Unlike the plantar flexors, these muscles are being stressed to their limit during ground contact, and can be a limiting performance factor.

Moving up the leg, Figure 12-4 shows the dominant demands of the muscles around the knee during ground contact.

Knee Muscle Moment

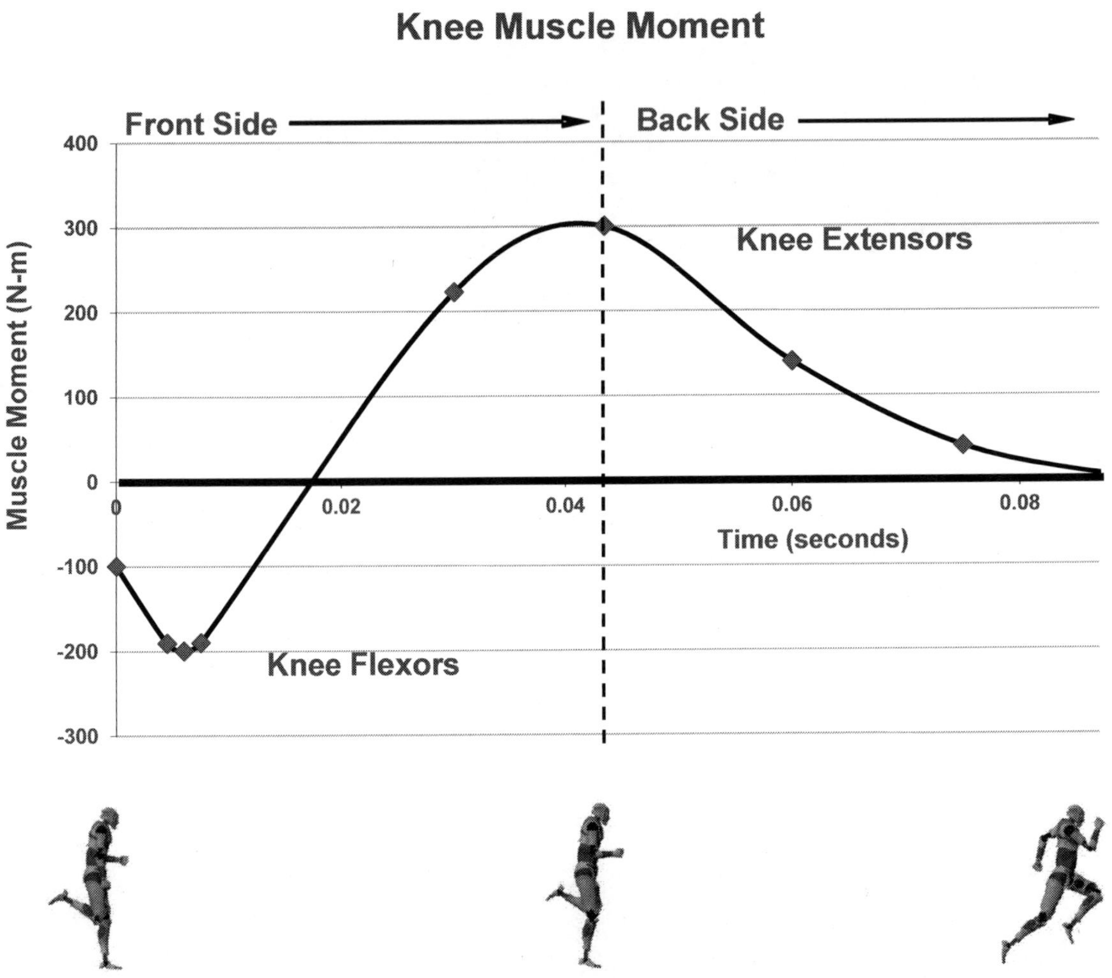

Figure 12-4: Muscular Demands At The Knee During Ground Contact

The action at the knee is more complex, and requires a solid concept of how the ground contact is initiated. Note that, when ground contact occurs, the elite sprinter is actually trying to rotate the knee into flexion (negative values). This flexion action was begun prior to contact, and serves to minimize the Horizontal braking action at ground contact.

Immediately after contact, the sprinter uses the knee extensors (positive values) to stop the downward motion of the athlete, and drive the body upward into the next Air Phase. Note that the majority of this effort occurs during the Front Side portion and, since most of the effort during this time is eccentric in nature, the muscular demand at the knee is within the range of any elite sprinter. As in the Ankle action, productive effort drops rapidly as soon as the Back Side phase is entered.

If the Air Phase Mechanics are properly executed, **and** the athlete possesses sufficient strength, **and** if they understand that ground contact must begin with an active lower leg flexion action, then this result can be achieved with relative ease.

Moving to the final leg joint, Figure 12-5 shows the dominant demands of the muscles around the hip during ground contact.

Hip Muscle Moment

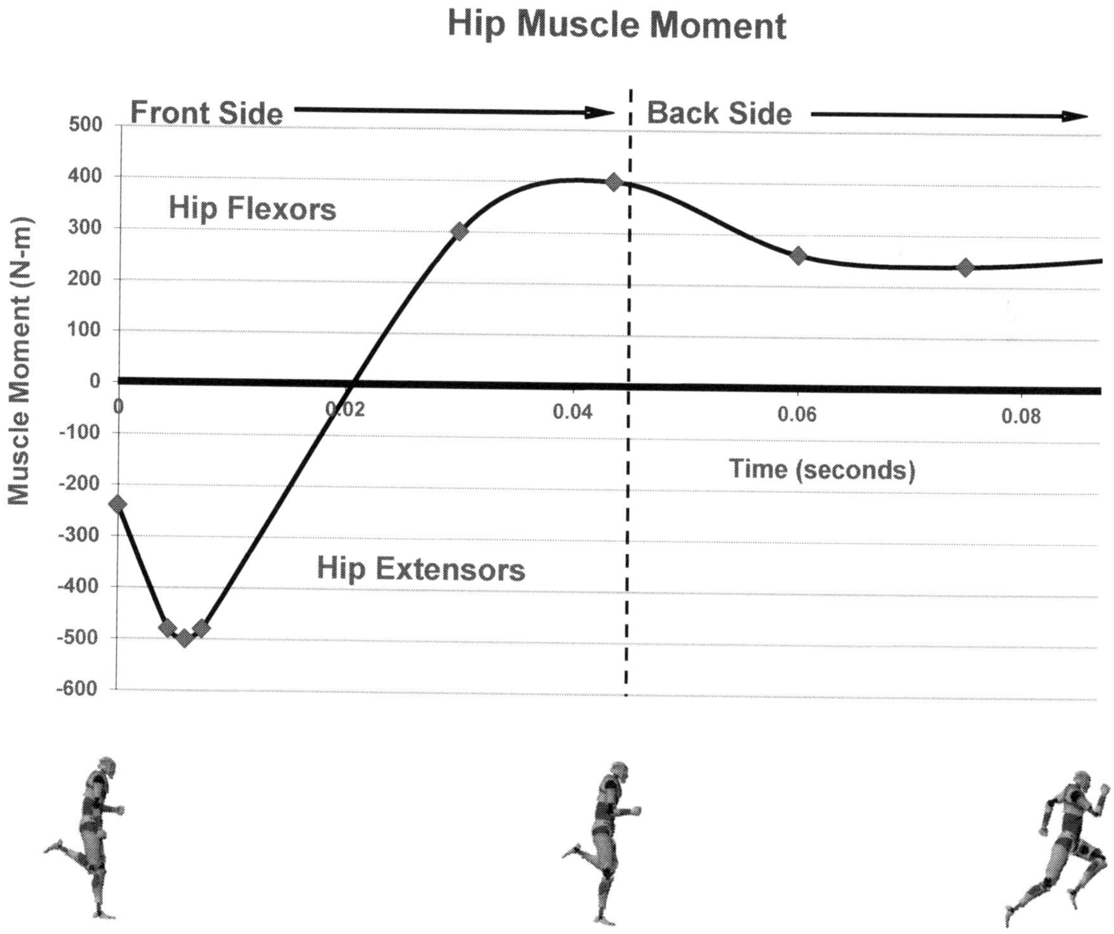

Figure 12-5: Muscular Demands At The Hip During Ground Contact

The muscular demands around the hip are complex, demanding, and counter-intuitive. This is the action that makes elite sprinting difficult to achieve for the athlete and to teach for the coach.

The first challenge lies in the magnitude of the demands. The peaks shown in the Figure are near the limits of human performance, especially for the hip extensors (negative values). At ground contact, the upper leg is rotating at about 500 degrees per second (Figure 9-14), allowing only the most powerful of athletes the ability to produce the **concentric** leg extension forces needed to produce an effective action.

The next challenge again involves force demands as the emphasis shifts from hip extensors to hip flexors (positive values). Once again, producing forces at rotational speeds of over 500 degrees per second is difficult, but manageable since the muscular demand is eccentric. As with the ankle and knee, the greatest hip forces are produced during the Front Side of the Sprint action.

The final challenge is one of concept, and has proven to be the most difficult. Whereas it is commonly believed, and intuitively supported, that a sprinter should use their hip extensors to drive the body down the track during ground contact, the data indicate otherwise. **In fact, the best of the elite sprinters only emphasize leg extension for the first 25 percent of ground contact.** It is true that this 25 percent is critical, and a great strain on the hip extensors, but this effort is short lived. For the last 75 percent of ground contact, the elite sprinter is actually using high levels of hip flexor activity to pull the hips and upper body forward toward the Takeoff position, as well as stopping the backward rotation of the upper leg.

It is not an easy conceptual change to make for a sprinter who is used to driving the leg backward during the entire ground contact phase. To move to the feeling of beginning an active recovery of the upper leg during ground contact is a major effort of re-education. It has been shown to be the most difficult aspect of Mechanics improvement, on the part of both the athlete and the coach.

The proof is, of course, in the performance results. The bestselling point is always a successful example. Carl Lewis, who possessed perhaps the best Sprint Mechanics to date, never let his upper leg pass behind a Vertical line dropped down from his hip when in top form. In his case, he essentially eliminated upper leg Back Side Mechanics.

The most critical component of Sprint Mechanics lies in the management of the upper leg Mechanics. It makes the most demands on both strength and proper movement. All performance components are vital, but this is where the major difference is made in elite Sprint performance.

Start and Transition Front Side Mechanics

As previously stated, the most current research has shown that, contrary to popular coaching belief, both the Start and the Transition to Maximum Velocity are dominated by Front Side

Mechanics. The reason that this emphasis is superior is due to the same reason found at Maximum Velocity. The only difference is that the body is tilted forward. However, if the trunk is again used as the reference (Figure 12-6), then the same Front Side/Back Side concept can be utilized.

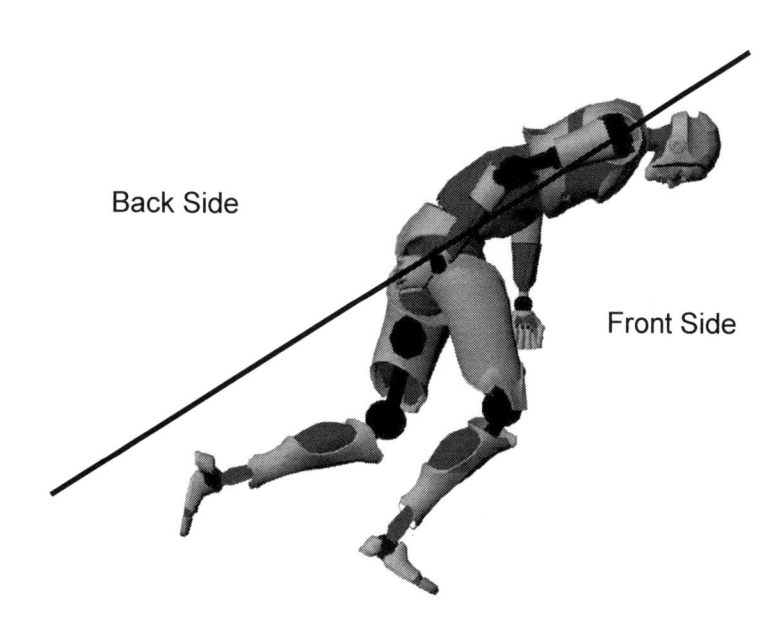

Figure 12-6 Front Side and Back Side Mechanics at the Start and the Transition

Thus, regardless of the phase of the race or the tilt of the trunk, the elite sprinters strive to keep the movements of the legs in front of the body to as great a degree as possible.

Chapter Summary:

The key to producing elite Sprint performance is emphasizing Front Side Mechanics, while minimizing Back Side Mechanics. To accomplish this, the athlete must understand the proper concept, including an active Touchdown and an active Takeoff.

It is critical to initially achieve Front Side Mechanics coming out of the Start. If this is not accomplished, then it cannot be regained later in the race. As fatigue sets in, if the Front Side emphasis is lost, it cannot be regained.

The force production at the ankle, knee, and hip are the keys to Sprint success, with the importance and complexity of the effort increasing from ankle to knee to hip.

PART SIX: UNDERSTANDING THE HURDLE PERFORMANCE

CHAPTER 13

UNDERSTANDING THE HURDLE PERFORMANCE

As in the Sprint event, in the attempt to understand the Mechanics of the Hurdle performance, and how the critical Limiting Factors are involved, a basic understanding of the physics of the activity is crucial. Remembering that the purpose of the race is to cover the required distance in as short a time as possible while negotiating the required number of barriers, it is reasonable, therefore, to assume that this requires the production of as great a Horizontal Velocity as possible. From this conclusion, it then becomes evident that, to produce this Horizontal Velocity, a great amount of Horizontal effort or force must be produced by the hurdler. Thus, it is universally believed that the Mechanics of a successful Hurdle performance must be based around this goal of producing large amounts of Horizontal force while in contact with the ground.

Whenever the Hurdle races are discussed in technical terms, all focus is placed on the Mechanics of clearing the barriers. In the past, the Start (to the first hurdle), the Finish (from the last hurdle to the Finish), and the Steps between the barriers have been either ignored or treated as Sprint related training issues. It is now known that this long-held assumption is, for the most part, wrong. In order of when they are encountered in the race, the revised thinking is as follows:

1. **The Hurdle Start**: For the Long race, and those athletes that use an Eight Step Start, the standard Sprint Start Model works extremely well. However, if the hurdler adopts the Seven Step Start, then a new Model must be followed. These differences were presented in Chapter 7 (see Figure 7-23).
2. **The Steps Between the Hurdles**: It has become apparent that the Steps between the hurdles are not standard Sprint strides. For too long they have been ignored, to the detriment of both Short and Long races. Models for both of these races will be discussed in these Hurdle Chapters.
3. **The Hurdle Finish**: Once the last barrier has been negotiated, since the sprint to the Finish has no further jumping demands, the concepts in the standard Sprint Model can be used.

So, with so many new concepts to address, which should take precedence? Should the focus remain on Hurdle Mechanics since the barriers are, by far, the most challenging part of the race? Or, should it be the Steps between the hurdles since there are far more of these than hurdle strides? In the end, it was decided that the best approach was to **focus on Hurdle Mechanics, and demonstrate how the remaining components are executed to allow proper Mechanics to happen.**

The Mechanics of Hurdle Clearance

As in the Sprint, although the production of Horizontal Velocity is the key to Hurdle performance, the production of Horizontal force is **not** the critical mechanical factor in achieving this goal. It is true that, during the Start or acceleration phase of the Hurdle race (covering the first 20 meters and the initial barrier of the race), the production of Horizontal ground force is of critical importance. In addition, the Maximum Velocity that an athlete can produce is dependent upon how long Horizontal forces can be applied. The question is, what limits the performer's ability to generate greater Horizontal forces in the Start and at Full Speed required to improve Maximum Velocity?

As will be seen, the key to successful hurdling is dependent on the ability to properly manage the force capability of the athlete, with these two goals:

1. **Produce Horizontal Velocity: To produce the greatest Maximum Horizontal Velocity, the goal must be to minimize forces in all other directions (primarily the Vertical) so that some productive Horizontal force can still be produced. As long as this is done, Horizontal Velocity will increase.**
2. **Maintain Horizontal Velocity: Once Maximum Velocity is reached, the goal must be to produce the large level of Vertical force required to maintain proper Mechanics while continuing to produce the small amount of Horizontal force needed to maintain Maximum Velocity.**

To understand these goals, the concept of force needs to be reviewed. Newton's first and second laws indicate that, to change Velocity, a force must be applied in the direction in which the Velocity is to be altered. In the Hurdle performance, this concept can be stated as:

$$\text{Force} = \text{Mass} * \text{Change in Velocity} / \text{Ground Time}$$

where **Force** is the effort the athlete pushes on the ground to drive the body down the track (forward, upward, or sideways), **Mass** is essentially the weight of the hurdler, **Change in Velocity** is the alteration in the Speed moving down the track (forward, upward, or sideways), and **Ground Time** is the time the hurdler is in contact with the ground during the force application.

Using this concept, the force demands for the hurdles can be determined in all possible directions.

Lateral Force

Since Lateral (sideways, across the track) movement is not productive at any time during the Hurdle race, the Lateral change in Velocity should be kept to zero at all times. Thus:

$$\text{Lateral Force} = \text{Mass} * (0) / \text{Ground Time} = 0 \text{ Newtons (0 Pounds)}$$

Any portion of an athlete's force potential that is wasted in the Lateral direction will detract from the effort required in the other two directions. This is particularly difficult during hurdle clearance since the Trail Leg must be moved Laterally to negotiate the barrier. However, the best athletes balance this leg action with the trunk and arms without the need to produce unwanted Lateral ground forces.

Horizontal Force

During the starting phase of the race, the athlete must apply large amounts of Horizontal force to change the Velocity of the body from a resting position (Velocity=0) to as high a value as possible (Velocity=Maximum). As the Maximum Velocity is reached, however, the change in Horizontal Velocity approaches zero since the athlete cannot further increase the Hurdle Speed. Thus, since the hurdler is no longer changing the Horizontal Velocity, the Horizontal force that the hurdler is producing approaches zero.

$$\text{Horizontal Force} = \text{Mass}*(0)/\text{Ground Time} = 0 \text{ Newtons (0 Pounds)}$$

The question that then must be asked is why the athlete is unable to produce additional Horizontal force and, therefore, increase the Maximum Velocity of the race. A plausible argument can be made that, at Maximum Velocity, the hurdler simply cannot move the body segments fast enough to produce any additional Horizontal force. Unfortunately, this assumption cannot be supported since Hurdle athletes can, and do, produce Horizontal forces even while operating at maximum Horizontal Velocity. Thus, the limiting mechanical factor does **not** lie in the Horizontal direction.

Vertical Force

Although the force demands in the Horizontal direction decrease as Maximum Velocity is attained, there are no similar decrements in the force requirements in the Vertical direction. Due to the presence of gravity, the Sprint and Hurdle action must consist of a series of alternating ground and Air Phases. To negotiate the 110 meter Hurdle, the athlete must increase the Vertical Velocity of the body from a downward Velocity of approximately 0.37 meters per second at Touchdown to a value of approximately 1.86 meters per second upward at the point where the foot leaves the ground. Thus, at Maximum Velocity, although the Horizontal Velocity is not changing, the Vertical Velocity is changing at the rate of 2.23 meters per second (from 0.37 meters per second downward to 1.86 meters per second upward) during each Hurdle ground contact phase.

To understand the consequences of this required change in Vertical Velocity, Newton's first and second laws must be quantified to the following equation:

$$\text{Vertical Force} = \text{Mass}*(\text{Change in Vertical Velocity})/\text{Ground Time}$$

Realizing that the mass of the typical hurdler is approximately 73 Kilograms (160 Pounds), and the Ground Time is approximately .124 seconds, the amount of Vertical force that the athlete must produce to make a change of 2.23 meters per second during ground contact can be calculated at:

Understanding the Hurdle Performance

Vertical Force = 73*(2.23)/.124 = 1310 Newtons (294 Pounds)

Now, if this were the only demand that gravity extracted from the hurdler, the world record would be under eleven seconds. Unfortunately, the gravitational attraction requires that, while simply standing on the Earth, a person must exert a Vertical force equal to their body weight simply to support themselves. Thus, the total Vertical force that the hurdler must exert to stop the downward Velocity and produce the upward Velocity to project the body into the hurdle must include the effort required to support the hurdler's own body weight. Thus, assuming the hurdler weighs 714 Newtons (160 Pounds), the total Vertical force during **each** ground contact moving into the hurdle would be:

Total Vertical Force = 1310+714 Newtons = 2024 Newtons (454 Pounds)

As can be seen, the Vertical force demands upon the athlete are impressive. Upon closer inspection, the reasons why this demand is the limiting element in Hurdle performance are evident.

To understand the unique problems presented to the hurdler in their attempt to produce force, the limitations of the body's force production capabilities must be examined. As can be seen in the Figure 13-1, due to mechanical efficiency and body position, an athlete is unable to produce a level, steady Vertical force during ground contact.

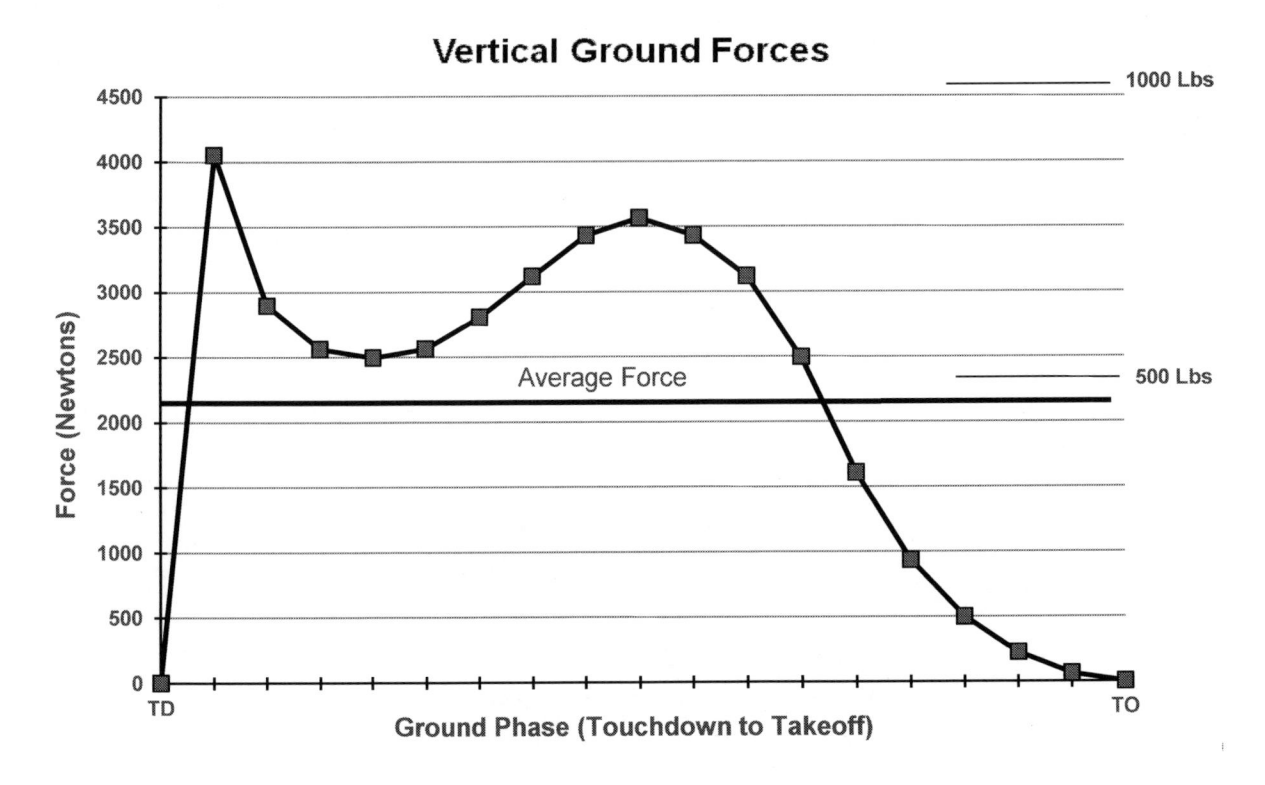

Figure 13-1: Vertical Ground Force During Ground Contact

Thus, if an average Vertical force of 2024 Newtons is required (as in the example), the force must be achieved by producing large values during certain phases of the Ground Phase to compensate for other portions where the Vertical force potential is lower. Thus, this situation actually demands that the athlete be able to produce a maximum Vertical force that is significantly greater than the average force required.

The Vertical demand becomes more apparent when it is realized that, during the 110 meter Hurdles, the athlete must complete 10 hurdle strides and over 40 Sprint strides: each demanding a Vertical force that is at the limit of the athlete's capability. It is evident that, with these repetitive demands, that fatigue does play a factor in even the shortest of the Hurdle races. If this conclusion can be made for the Short Hurdles, then the problems these demands place upon the Long Hurdles become even more apparent.

The second problem that the athlete must overcome in the production of Vertical force is the magnitude of body segment Velocity. As the Horizontal Velocity increases, the speed of the involved body segments also increases. As discussed previously (see Figure 1-1a), this high segment Velocity effectively decreases the concentric Vertical force potential of the athlete.

Adding to the athletes problems, the body position that the hurdler must assume to generate the required Vertical forces result in the production of unwanted braking forces in the Horizontal direction. As seen in Figure 13-2, to generate the range of motion required to produce the Vertical forces, the athlete is required to contact the ground with the foot in front of the body center of gravity.

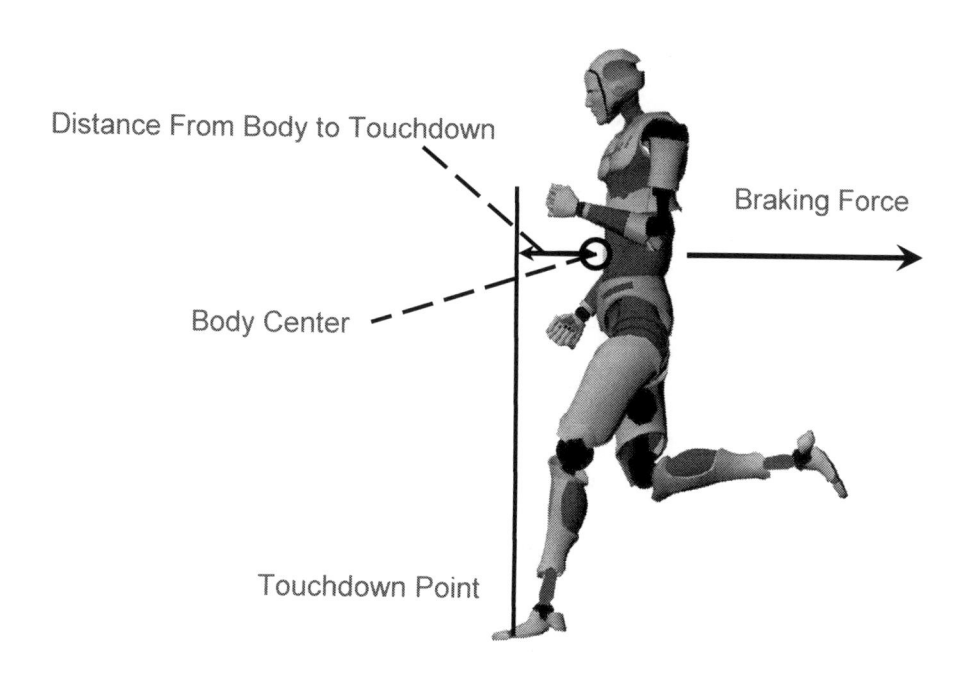

Figure 13-2: Horizontal Braking Forces at Touchdown

This forward foot position produces an initial braking force during the first half of the ground contact. Since the athlete must endeavor to attain maximum Horizontal Velocity, the hurdler is forced to produce a driving force during the second portion of ground contact to regain the Horizontal Velocity lost during the first half of ground contact.

Thus, as can be seen, the limiting element determining how fast an athlete can hurdle is the production of the Vertical force required to make the necessary change in the body Vertical Velocity during ground contact. This conclusion can be further demonstrated by assuming that a hurdler could actually decrease the ground contact to half of what is typical for an elite hurdler (from .124 to .062). To achieve this feat, which would increase the Horizontal Velocity by 30 percent, the Vertical force requirement would be:

Vertical Force = Mass*(Change in Vertical Velocity)/Time

and inserting the values:

Vertical Force = 73*(2.23)/.062 = 2625 Newtons (589 Pounds)

Finally, again assuming the athlete weighs 714 Newtons (160 Pounds), the total Vertical force would be:

Total Vertical Force = 2625+714 Newtons = 3339 Newtons (750 Pounds)

It is evident that no hurdler (or any human) can currently produce this level of Vertical force production in such a small amount of time; however, an increase in Vertical force production is the way in which hurdlers have improved their performance times over the years.

There are a number of ways to increase the Vertical force potential in an athlete. The most common, and effective way is to train the static, dynamic, and elastic (?) strength potentials of the performer. Large amounts of Vertical force can also be quickly generated by having the athlete jam the landing leg vigorously into the ground at Touchdown, vaulting the body over the rigid segment as is successfully done in the high jump. Unfortunately, this process generates large Horizontal forces that make it an unusable approach in the Hurdle performance. Finally, excellent Hurdle Mechanics will ensure that all of the available Vertical force that the athlete can produce, is effectively directed in the proper direction during ground contact.

Special Topics

The Unavoidable Hurdle Issues

From the discussion, it would seem that the way to improve performance would simply be to increase force production (get stronger) and run more efficiently. However, there are several additional Issues that are unavoidable, and must be confronted by all performers.

(1) The Total Body Rotation Issue

Sometimes traditional teaching concepts get in the way of progress in an Event and, unfortunately, this is true in the hurdles. The concept of "upper body dive into the hurdle" has gone a long way in limiting some of the best elite hurdlers. This ill-conceived concept produces an overall body rotation that wreaks havoc with an athlete's ability to quickly clear the barrier and efficiently move toward the next hurdle.

Coaches need to move beyond this detrimental concept and embrace the neutral body rotation, hip and lower body dominated Mechanics Model presented herein.

Once airborne, the athlete has no control over their body trajectory, and they must live with how they have prepared their body position and motion during the ground contact going into the hurdle. If their preparation is good then the hurdle clearance becomes much easier, and they can use each barrier as a springboard toward the next obstacle.

On the other hand, if their preparation is poor, they are forced to make numerous in-flight (or pre-flight) adjustments that are **always** detrimental to a successful hurdle clearance, which then detracts from their ability to move toward the next barrier.

The Vertical projection an athlete produces at Takeoff moving into the barrier dictates the time it takes to clear the hurdle. That being said, since all athletes realize that nothing good comes from excessive Air Times, elite hurdlers do not willingly jump too high over the barriers. Without exception, hurdlers that produce long Air Times do so to accommodate errors in their Hurdle technique. The most common of these are:

1. **Bad Touchdown Position**: As discussed previously, if an athlete touches down too far or too close to the barrier, they have no other option except to jump higher over the hurdle.
2. **Bad Body Position Over the Hurdle**: If an athlete will not (or cannot) fold their body into a tightly compressed position over the barrier, then they are forced to jump higher over the hurdle to accommodate this higher Body COG position.
3. **Bad Segment Position**: If the athlete's technique results in one of their segments being too low when that segment reaches the hurdle, then the hurdler will either hit the barrier or (as is

almost always the case) learn to jump higher in the air to clear this errant segment position. These segments are typically the foot of the Lead Leg, or the knee or ankle of the Trail Leg.

The first two problems are, for an elite hurdler, inexcusable. A little discipline and commitment is all that is needed to ensure that the correct Touchdown position is consistently achieved, and a good body position generated over the barrier.

The last problem (#3) is created when a performer generates **too much forward body rotation at Takeoff going into the Hurdle**. This is usually a case of the athlete being taught to 'dive' the upper body into the barrier going into the hurdle. This popular coaching concept has produced more problems in hurdlers, from beginners to elites, than any other misguided coaching belief. The myriad of problems created by this concept are shown in Figure 13-3.

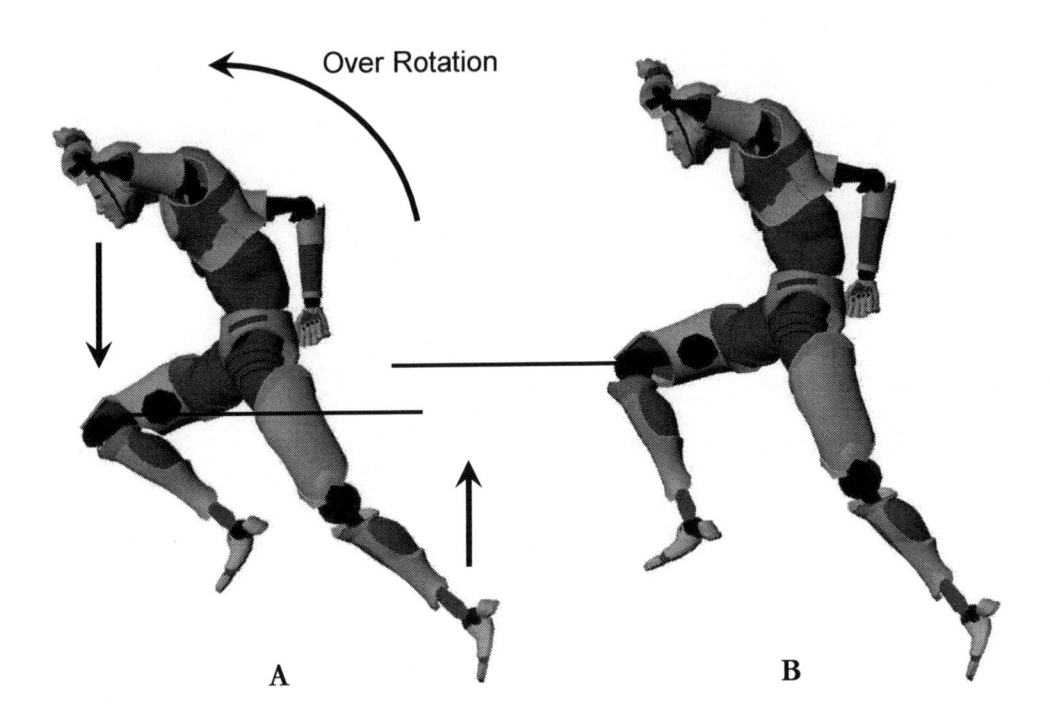

Figure 13-3: Problems Due To Excessive Forward Body Rotation Going Into the Hurdle

The biggest problem this technique causes is, due to the forward Body rotation, the segments in front of the body are rotated down and the segments in back of the Body are rotated up. Compared to the proper Mechanics of Athlete B, the over rotation of Athlete A drives the shoulders, Lead knee, and Lead foot down; while driving the hips, Trail knee and Trail foot up going into the hurdle. Although the lowered shoulder position could be deemed beneficial (and probably the reason this concept was developed), the effect on the rest of the segments are all detrimental.

As can be seen in Figure 13-3, forward rotation significantly drops the lead knee down, making it very difficult for the hurdler to get the leg up in time to clear the barrier. To offset this position, the athlete has to over-flex the lower leg (as shown) in an attempt to get the heel up and over the barrier. In addition, the rotation throws the back segments upward which, as will be seen, creates problems during the Air Phase.

Once airborne, the athlete has no control over the body rotation, and must contend with any over-rotation for the entire Air Phase (Figure 13-4).

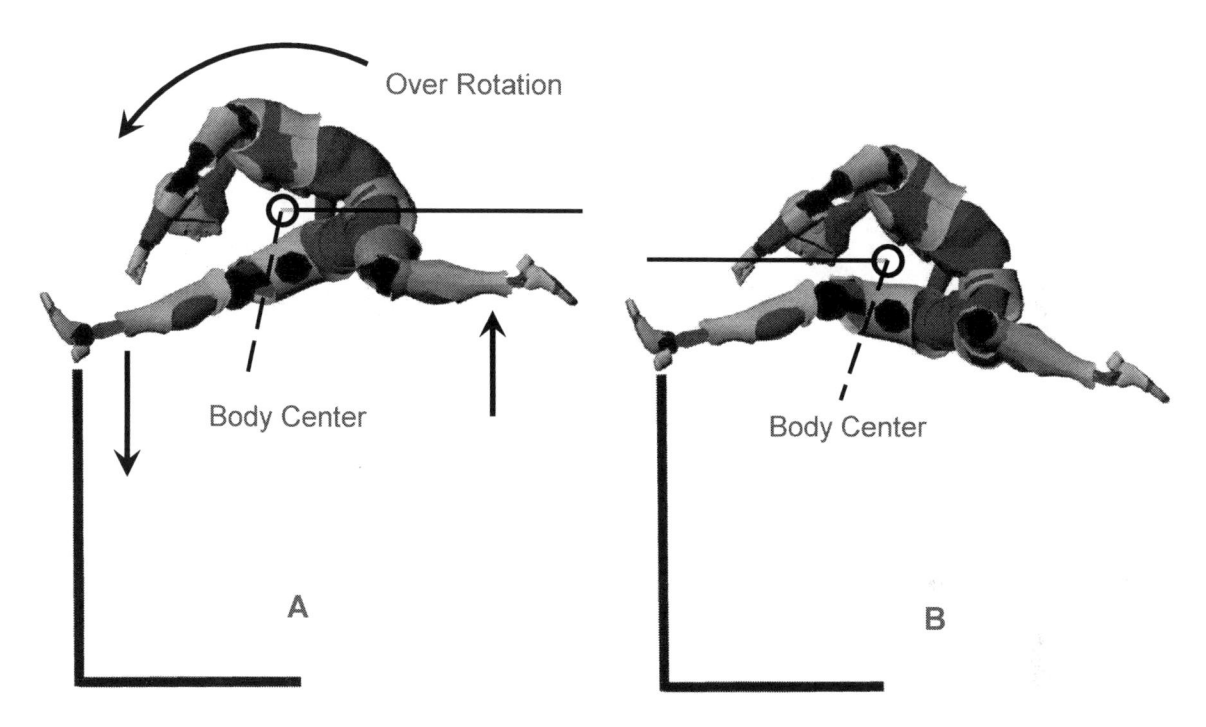

Figure 13-4: Problems Due To Excessive Forward Body Rotation Going Over the Hurdle

Thus, as the athlete moves into the barrier, the rotation problem continues to hamper hurdle clearance. The over rotated hurdler (A in the Figure), despite achieving a tight body position **and** fully extending the Lead lower leg to clear the Lead foot, still has to raise the Body COG higher than the hurdler that controlled their body rotation (B in the Figure). In addition, the upward momentum of the Trail leg has thrown the Trail heel higher than the Trail knee, which will soon create yet another problem.

As the Trail knee reaches the hurdle (Figure 13-5), the Trail heel of the over rotated athlete (B) continues to move upward, driving the Trail knee down. In contrast, the athlete that controlled the body rotation (A) has the ability to place the Trail knee and foot at the same height as the hips, allowing minimal clearance. This heel-up-knee-down action is common in hurdlers that over rotate and, once again, forces the athlete to jump higher in the air to clear the knee.

The over rotation problem continues to disrupt the hurdle clearance as the athlete comes down, off the hurdle. As seen in the Figure, as both athletes begin their descent the following sequence occurs:

1. Since Athlete A falls from a greater height ground impact is greater, forcing the hurdler to use more energy (and time) to stop the fall.

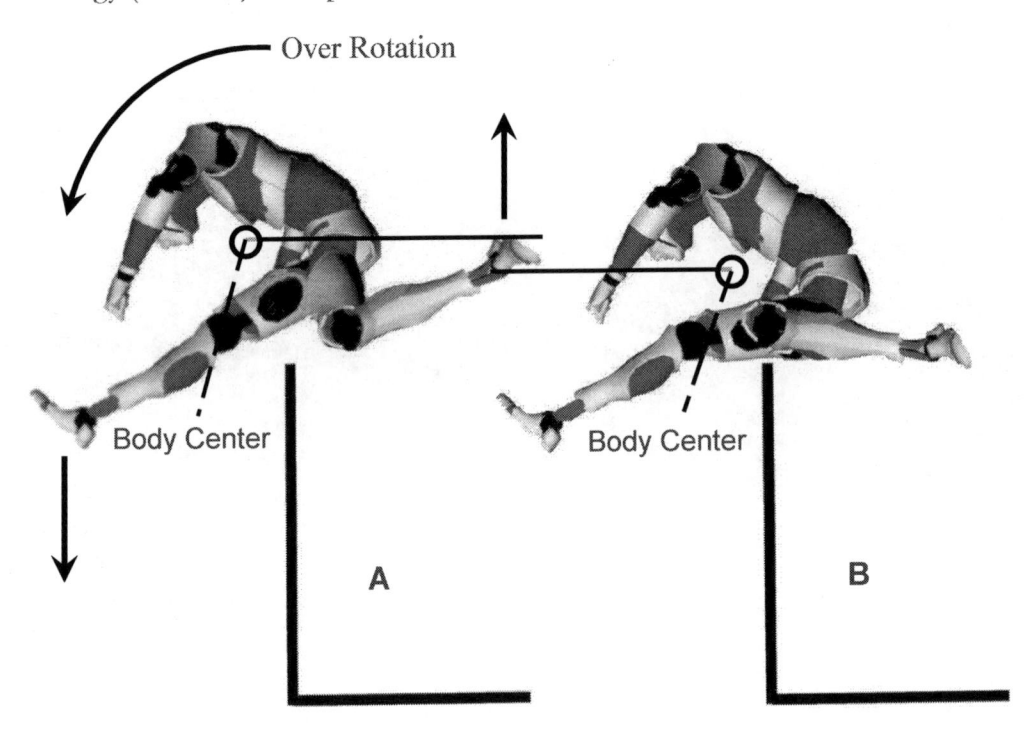

Figure 13-5: Problems Created Due To Excessive Forward Body Rotation Coming Off the Hurdle

2. At the peak, the Lead Leg of Athlete A has already begun its move toward the ground. Athlete B, on the other hand, has the ability to delay leg extension, which allows a much faster "leg snap" coming off the barrier.
3. Since the unwanted body rotation continues to move the hips and Trail Leg up and away from the ground, the athlete finds it difficult to recover the leg and move the hips under the Touchdown point. This further delays the recovery during the Ground Phase coming off the barrier, as well as increasing the Horizontal braking forces.

In conclusion, there is absolutely no support (except tradition) to teach a hurdler to "dive" into a hurdle. This is one of the most detrimental actions an athlete can develop in their Hurdle technique, and one of the most difficult to resolve once it has been ingrained. Athletes that have this problem in their hurdle technique have to live with, at best, average hurdle clearance times.

(2) The Race Management Issue

In the past, it was assumed that the primary reason why the Short Hurdle race was almost twenty percent slower than the same distance Sprint race, and the Long Hurdle race was almost ten percent slower than the 400 meter Sprint race, was due to the demands of negotiating the ten barriers. With a more comprehensive analysis of both Events, it is evident that this long-held conclusion is not entirely correct.

In fact, the difficulties presented in properly managing the steps between the hurdles are at least as important a performance factor as hurdle clearance. Perhaps more importantly, **poor hurdle race management between the barriers can be far more devastating to the final result than poor hurdle clearance**.

1. **The Short Hurdles**: As was presented in Chapter 1 (see Table 1-2), the rules that define the steps between the Short Hurdles dictate that the athlete make significant Stride Length alterations to successfully negotiate the barriers. New research indicates that each of the three Steps between the hurdles is unique, each has its own set of goals and, as a group, dictates the success potential of clearing the next obstacle.

   In addition, each of the three Steps makes significant alterations in the basic Sprint Mechanics. In fact, these alterations are so dramatic that Speed training for Short race hurdlers should not focus on the standard Sprint Model. Instead, new approaches must be developed to train the 3 Step Sprint Model used between the hurdles. This increased emphasis is further underlined by the realization that, due to these issues, the US has lost several Olympic and World Championship medals in the Short Hurdles.

2. **The Long Hurdles**: Compared to the Short race, the 400 Hurdles presents an entirely different, and even more complex Race Management challenge. The first problem, presented in Chapter 1 (see Table 1-2), is that the typical step pattern for the first part of the race (13 for Men and 15 for Women) forces the athletes to over stride to reach the barriers. To produce this pattern, the hurdler needs to alter the tempo of the stride to such a degree that Speed training for Long race hurdlers should not focus on the standard Sprint Model. Instead, new approaches are needed to insure that the athletes have a chance to ingrain the required Long Hurdles Over Stride Model.

   The second problem arises when fatigue sets in, forcing the athlete to alter the step pattern by adding one or two additional step(s) sometime during the second part of the race. The additional step produces the ancillary problem of having to hurdle with the opposite leg, but the real issue is that the athlete must suddenly switch from the 13/15 tempo pattern to the 14/16 pattern. Add the fatigue factor to this and it becomes evident that this race is one of the most technically and physically demanding events on the Track.

   Due to these issues, the US has lost several Olympic and World Championship medals in the closing stages of the Long Hurdles. Since these problems have been present for a long time, and have not been resolved or even minimized, new approaches must be developed to train the 13/15 and 14/16 Tempo Model used between the hurdles.

(3) Tempo Training Issue

One focus that has been lacking in Hurdle training has been Maximum Speed tempo training, with the focus on properly developing Stride Rate as well as Stride Length.

Stride Rate: The Stride Rate in the Short Hurdle race fluctuates wildly from very low to very high as the hurdlers moves through the nine sets of barriers. Since this tempo can only be produced by running over hurdles at race pace, training methods need to be developed to allow athletes to develop this tempo, not only at the athlete's race pace, but a superior pace as well.

For the Long Hurdle race, although the Stride Rate is consistent between the barriers, the tempo is much slower than the Long Sprint due to the demands that the required step pattern places on the performance. As is true in the Short race, since this tempo can only be produced by running over hurdles at race pace, training methods need to be developed to allow athletes to develop this tempo, not only at the athlete's race pace, but a superior pace as well.

Stride Length: In the Short race, Stride Length varies as wildly as Stride Rate. In addition, the length of the stride over the barrier is significantly longer, while all of the Steps between the hurdles are shorter, than the Sprint stride. This, and the fact that reaching the correct Touchdown distance going into each barrier is critical to a successful performance, makes it imperative that training methods be developed to allow athletes to produce the proper Stride Lengths both over and between the hurdles.

Although the Stride Lengths between the Long Hurdles are consistent, they are significantly longer than a Sprint stride at the same speed. Thus, Hurdle training runs need to be developed that drive athletes to match their Model Stride Length (if unavailable, use the results presented in Table 1-1) while at maximum effort, with immediate feedback on the success of the effort.

(4) Practice Mechanics Verses Competition Mechanics Issue

With an enormous base of data on elite Hurdlers, both in practice and competition, it has become evident that what most hurdlers do in practice does not match the demands of their race in competition. Whether it is the Short or Long Hurdles, the Stride Rate, Stride Length, and tempo demands are so far from the Sprint event that developing the event by primarily using Sprint based training is inefficient at best and detrimental at worst.

If the purpose of Sprint based practice is to develop the Maximum Sprint Speed of the hurdler, which **is** related to performance, then this effort is worthwhile. However, if this not the case, then allowing the athlete to perform training runs that do not demand the Stride Rate, Stride Length, and tempo of the Hurdle race is very short sighted. In addition, practice sessions using primarily

Sprint training ingrains the consistent Sprint Stride Rate, Stride Length, and tempo, which is contrary to what is really needed for success in the Hurdle race.

This conclusion provides insight into why so many young hurdlers do well in the collegiate system, but fail to improve or even match these performance levels once they complete their eligibility. While in college, they compete in meets almost every week for six months a year, sometimes running several Hurdle races a day, sometimes multiple days in succession. This gives them up to seventy high intensity race intervals a year that no practice session can come close to matching. In addition, with the number of multiple races (including any sprint or relay races) that the collegiate hurdler typically is expected to do, the hurdle endurance component is also trained at the same intense levels. This type of quality training is so impactful that athletes with little or no between-meet training, or even poor coaching, can produce quality performance simply due to this training effect.

Once out of the collegiate system, an elite athlete may run in eight competitions a year, if they are lucky. In addition, only the Short race will involve more than one race per meet. Thus, with an 80 percent drop in these high intensity workouts, and virtually no hurdle endurance component, the athlete is at a distinct disadvantage. Unless they are lucky enough to find (or retain) a good coach, their performances will decline.

Good coaches must recognize the major training effect that competitions provide, and adjust their practice sessions accordingly. Too often, competitions are treated as "breaks between training", when they should be recognized as the pinnacle of this process. Finally, training strategies must be developed an attempt to achieve the same type of maximal training effect that is found in competition.

(5) The Weight Issue

How much weight an athlete must accelerate down the track and over the barriers is a much greater issue than most coaches and athletes realize. There are two situations where this issue becomes a major problem:

1. **The Overweight Athlete**: If a male hurdler is more than seven percent body fat, or a female hurdler is more than eleven percent body fat, than they are dragging too much weight down the track. In fact, the problem is much worse than was typically believed.

   Returning to the example of the Vertical Force demands of a typical 73 Kilogram (160 Pound) male hurdler, if the athlete becomes lazy and puts on ten percent more fat (7.3 Kilograms (16 Pounds)), then the amount of force needed to maintain the same Air Time would be:

   $$\text{Vertical Force} = 80.3*(2.23)/.124 = 1444 \text{ Newtons (324 Pounds)}$$

and when you add the increased body weight (787 Newtons (177 Pounds)) into the equation, the Total Vertical Force becomes:

Total Vertical Force = 1444+787 Newtons = 2231 Newtons (501 Pounds)

This points to the fact that, for this same athlete with their added fat levels to hurdle at the same elite level they achieved before they packed on the weight, they would need to generate **10 percent more Vertical Force during each ground contact** (2231 Newtons to 2024 Newtons). Now, since this additional weight was added as fat, and not muscle, there is no logical way that the athlete would be able to increase their force production. In fact, if you assume that the athlete can still produce their "pre-feasting" force levels at their new weight, than their Ground Time would go from .124 to .139 seconds. This would drop the performance from world record level to that of a Poor quality elite athlete, simply due to the fact that **the hurdler added body weight that did not contribute to their ability to generate force**.

2. **The Bulked Up Athlete**: If an athlete adds body weight by adding muscle mass, it must be remembered that **for every one pound of muscle added to the body, two pounds of additional ground force is needed to offset the weight gain** for performance to improve. Thus, the goal of any strength improvement program must be to maximize the power of the lower body while minimizing the weight gain from adding additional muscle mass.

   The biggest strength program mistake that athletes make is by bulking up the upper body. Adding ten pounds to the chest and arms by increasing their bench press levels may be aesthetically pleasing, but since this added weight is almost as worthless as putting on body fat, the resulting performance decrement is just a devastating. Physics doesn't care if the additional weight comes from muscle or fat, if the gain is not offset by additional force gains exerted on the ground, then the performance will suffer.

Chapter Summary:

In summary, the maximal Horizontal Velocity that a hurdler can produce is dependent upon the amount of effective Vertical force that the athlete can apply during ground contact. If this force can be increased through either strength gain or efficiency improvement, the overall performance will improve.

There are, however, three Hurdle Issues, all related to the effective application of Effective Force, that are unavoidable, and must be confronted by all performers

Prelude To The Remaining Hurdle Sections

Since the focus of this presentation is on Hurdle Mechanics, the development of the athlete's Strength potential will not be focused upon. It is assumed that the athlete and coach understand how to elicit the required improvements in this area, as well as the critical nature of this endeavor.

Instead, those mechanical factors that have been determined to be critical in the production of an elite Hurdle performance will be scrutinized. These results will be presented for both Men and Women elite athletes. For each of the significant mechanical performance variables that are discussed, values for poor, average, and good elite performers will be presented. In using this terminology, it must be realized that a poor performance for an elite hurdler would constitute an excellent performance for even a collegiate quality hurdler. However, since this is the level with which the elite performer must contend, even this level of performance must be improved upon.

In addition, the values presented are those results produced by an athlete of a typical elite hurdler body build. Thus, those athletes that are either taller or shorter than this typical build will require a slight revision in many of the results. For instance, if the athlete is extremely long legged, the performer has an advantage in producing length results like Stride Length and, thus, these results will appear to be higher than an average size hurdler. On the other hand, long legs will hinder speed results like leg Velocity and, thus, these results will appear to be lower than the average size hurdler. In comparison, if the hurdler is short legged, this will provide an advantage in producing speed results like leg Velocity and, thus, these results will appear to be higher than an average size hurdler. Similarly, short legs will hinder length results like Stride Length and, thus, these results will appear to be lower than an average size hurdler.

To properly compare results between all hurdlers, leg lengths must be taken into consideration. Although the High Performance Reports that have been generated in the past do take leg length into consideration, the actual process is sufficiently complex to make it impossible to be either described or performed easily. Thus, the numerical results that are presented herein are done **only as a descriptive tool**.

Finally, since the Short Hurdles and the Long Hurdles are distinctively different events, the results will be separately presented. Initially the Short Hurdles will be examined, followed by a brief description on how the Long Hurdle race results deviate from the shorter races.

PART SEVEN: HURDLE MECHANICS

INTRODUCTION

THE HURDLE GOLDEN POSITION

After analyzing thousands of athletes over many years, coupled with actual interactive, on-track teaching sessions with elite athletes, a single "Golden Position" has been identified as the benchmark to judge overall Full Speed Hurdle Mechanics. If an athlete can arrive at this position in the proper body position, at the right distance, and at the required Velocity, then the Hurdle action will be successful.

The Figure below identifies this Position as the point of Lead Leg ankle cross going into the hurdle. If the athlete can reach this position, at the correct distance from the hurdle, while producing a Velocity of 9.0 meters per second, all criteria have been met.

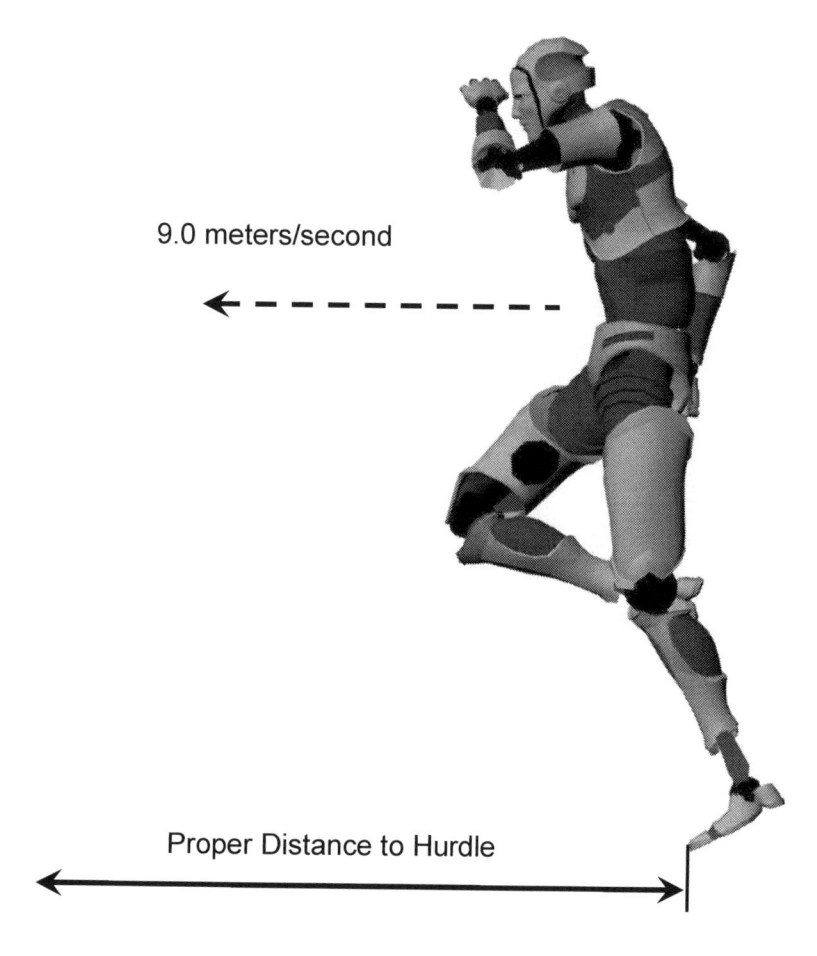

Lead Leg Ankle Cross Going Into the Hurdle: The Hurdle Golden Position

This single Position has been termed "Golden" since, to achieve it, the athlete must perform all subsequent Mechanics properly, and possess the explosive strength to make the most of the actions. In addition, since the Hurdle action sets up the steps between the barriers, then is repeated over and over, matching this position is the only way to allow the athlete to successfully continue to produce the proper Mechanics during subsequent strides and hurdles.

If there are any mechanical flaws, or strength deficiencies, this Position simply cannot be produced, as well as insuring a decrement in the overall Hurdle result.

The information contained in Part Seven describes how elite hurdlers achieve this goal.

CHAPTER 14

CRITICAL GENERAL PERFORMANCE DESCRIPTORS FOR THE SHORT HURDLES

In the Hurdle performance, **General Performance Descriptors** identify the result of the athlete's effort. These descriptors identify how well the athlete is doing, however, they do not identify how the performer is mechanically producing the results. Those general descriptors that are directly related to performance include:

1. **Horizontal Velocity**
2. **Air Time**
3. **Stride Length**
4. **Ground Contact Time**
5. **Stride Rate**

Although these descriptors do not identify specifically how the elite athlete produces a successful Hurdle performance, they will indicate the general areas that must be emphasized to accomplish this task.

With the exception of Horizontal Velocity, these results will be divided into those related to the elite performance over the hurdle and between the hurdles.

Horizontal Velocity

The most obvious General Performance Descriptor in the Hurdle race is Horizontal Velocity. Ignoring the importance of the Start, the athlete that can produce the greatest amount of Horizontal Velocity, and maintain it over and between the barriers, will be the most successful.

As simple as this seems, this result also points out the weakness in looking at these general descriptors for assistance in effectively evaluating the performance. Although the Velocity result will indicate how fast the athlete is moving, it gives no information regarding how the hurdler is producing the result. Thus, except for categorizing a hurdler, this result is of little use to a coach.

For the elite hurdlers, the range of Horizontal Velocity values is presented in Figure 14-1. As with all results presented herein, the results are in terms of good, average, and poor values. These are based upon the results of all elite 110/100 Hurdlers analyzed to date.

These Velocity results are interesting in that the best Velocity result for the elite Men hurdlers is virtually the same as the result of the best woman hurdlers. This is a result of the differences in the rules concerning Hurdle height and spacing of the two events that were discussed in Chapter 1. Since the Men must project their body center much higher over the barrier, and the distance between the barriers are much closer (in relation to their leg length), generating Horizontal Velocity is a much more difficult task.

Horizontal Velocity

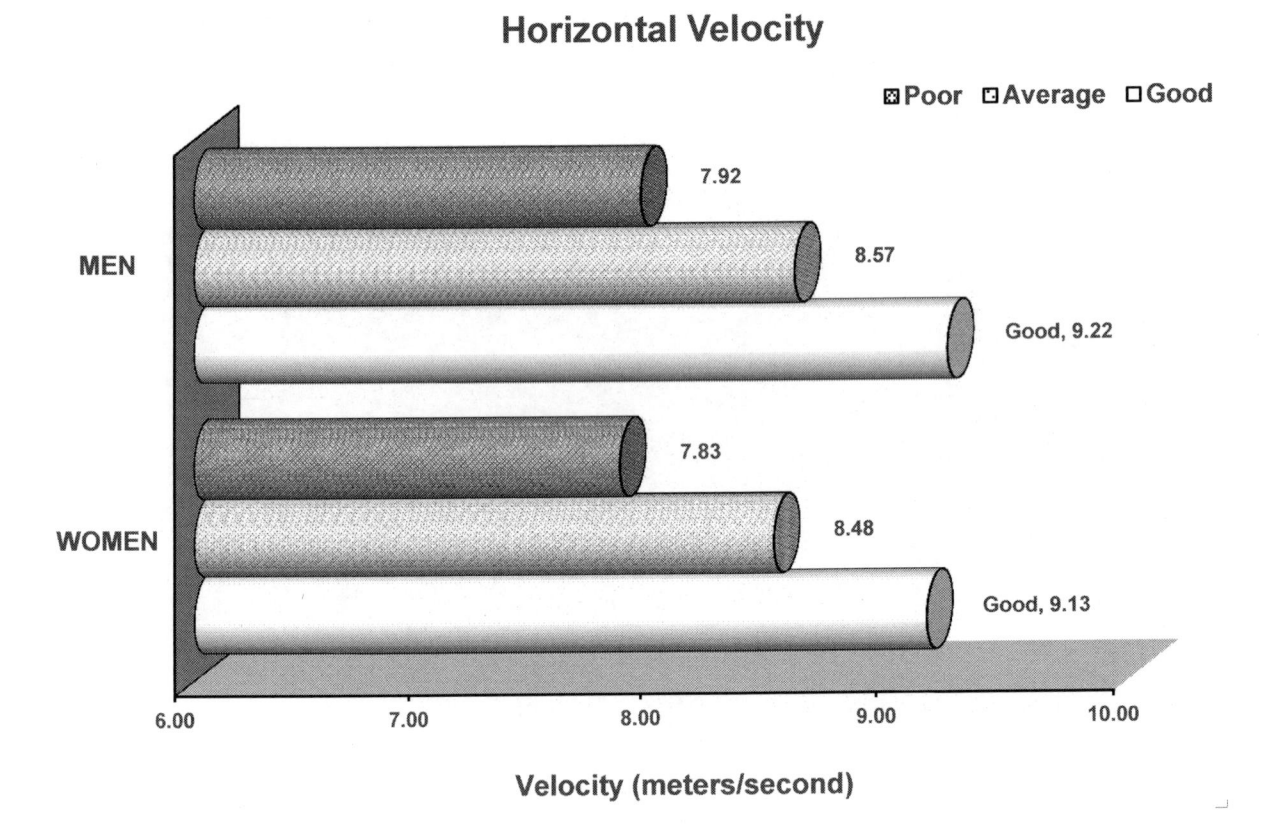

■ Poor ▨ Average □ Good

MEN
- 7.92
- 8.57
- Good, 9.22

WOMEN
- 7.83
- 8.48
- Good, 9.13

Velocity (meters/second)

Figure 14-1: Horizontal Velocity Results

Air Time

If the research on the Sprint has made anything clear it is the fact that, while in the air, since nothing can be done to increase the Velocity of the athlete in any direction, it should be minimized to as great an extent as possible. Thus, unless Air Time is required to prepare the body for the next ground contact, or produce a required Stride Length, it should be minimized as much as possible.

Over the Hurdle

Since a barrier must be cleared, the height of the hurdle will dictate the minimum amount of time the hurdler must spend in the air. Likewise, the Air Time will dictate the minimum length of the Hurdle stride.

Since the hurdle forces the athlete to deviate from the normal Sprint Mechanics in a detrimental fashion, the amount of deviation should be minimized as much as possible. Thus, the better hurdlers minimize the Air Time over the barrier. This is accomplished through superior Mechanics, which allow the athlete to minimize the amount the body must be elevated to clear the barrier.

Figure 14-2 shows the Air Time over the hurdle for all elite hurdlers analyzed to date.

Air Time

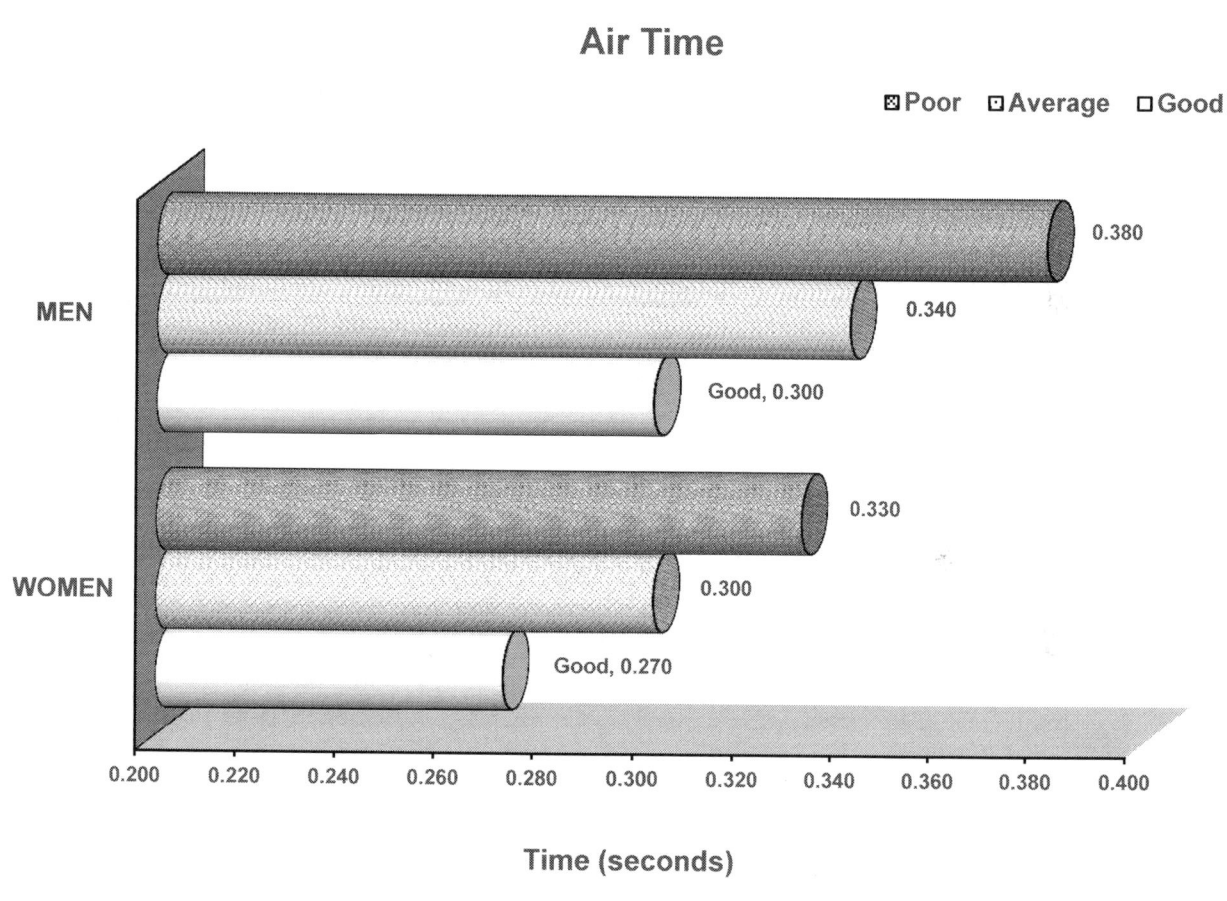

Poor | **Average** | **Good**

MEN
- Poor: 0.380
- Average: 0.340
- Good: 0.300

WOMEN
- Poor: 0.330
- Average: 0.300
- Good: 0.270

Time (seconds)

Figure 14-2: Air Time Over the Hurdle

It is evident that, due to the need to clear the barriers, Hurdle Air Time far exceeds that of a Sprint performance (see Figure 8-5). In fact, even the best hurdlers are in the air about two (Women) or three (Men) times longer than their Sprint performance.

It should come as no surprise that this Air Time is directly related to how much the hurdler must raise their body center to clear the barrier. This distance is determined by three factors; the quality of the Hurdle technique (Mechanics), the athlete's Anthropometrics, and the Flexibility of the athlete.

Critical General Performance Descriptors For the Short Hurdles

As shown in Figure 14-3, if the hurdler has excellent Hurdle technique, they are able to tightly compress their body around their body center, allowing them to clear the barrier with a much lower body center as compared to a hurdler with poor technique. Since the Vertical clearance margin is very small, especially in the Men's race, every millimeter saved means a significant difference in Air Time.

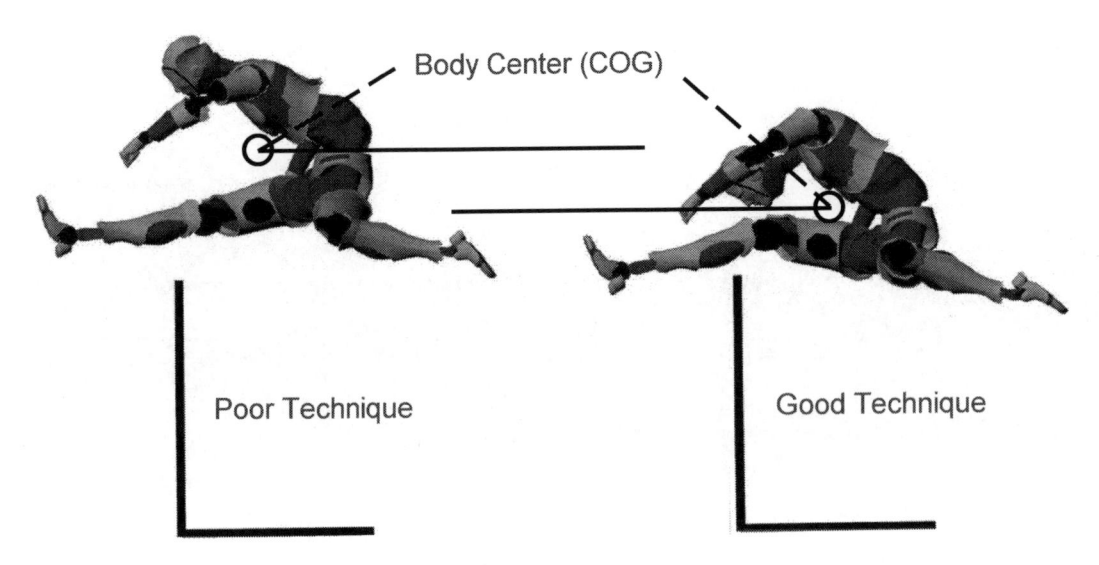

Figure 14-3: Body Center Position Over the Hurdle

Regardless of the quality of the Hurdle technique, the anthropometrics of the athlete is a major factor in dictating how much the body center must be raised to clear the barrier. As seen in Figure 14-4, Physics dictates that the performer who is short, with short legs, will be forced to raise their body center much higher as compared to a hurdler who is tall, with long legs (assuming that both are running at the same Speed).

Figure 14-4: The Anthropometric Height Factor

This height handicap is evident coming off of the barrier as well. Compared to the tall hurdler, the body center of the short performer will fall farther as it returns to the ground.

The importance of minimizing Air Time cannot be underestimated since it affects the following:

1. **Effective Force**: Since the athlete cannot exert ground forces while in the air, the Hurdle Air Time should be minimized.
2. **Expended Force**: Since the height the body center is raised is directly related to the amount of Vertical force required (more height needs more effort), the Hurdle Air Time should be minimized.
3. **Impact Force**: Since the Vertical force required to stop the downward fall of the performer is directly related to the height the body center is raised (more height produces faster fall), the Hurdle Air Time should be minimized.
4. **Stride Length**: As will be seen, the height the body center is raised is directly related to the Hurdle Stride Length results (more height produces longer Stride Length). Since all elite athletes competing in the Short Hurdles have difficulties squeezing three steps between the barriers (see Table 1-2), the Hurdle Air Time should be minimized.

Steps Between the Hurdles

The Air Time results of the three Steps between the Short Hurdle barriers, as visually shown in Figure 14-5, are the best indicators of the goal of each of these three Steps.

It is evident, from the distance covered, that the Air Times for the three Steps are not the same. In addition, it is also apparent that the body positions at Touchdown and Takeoff for each Step are different, indicating that there are different goals for each Step.

Figure 14-5: Air Times for the Steps Between the Hurdles

Critical General Performance Descriptors For the Short Hurdles

These differences become more apparent when they are compared to the Air Times of the Sprint Stride (Figure 14-6). Whereas the Sprint Stride produces a strong, dynamic, and repeatable Air Time and body position, the Hurdle Stride appears short, tentative, and highly variable.

Figure 14-6: Air Times for the Sprint Stride

For a more detailed comparison of the three Steps, the numerical Air Time results for elite hurdlers are shown in Figure 14-7.

As was true in the Sprint stride, Air Times that are too short or too long have a negative effect on performance. Air times are even more critical in the Short Hurdles because the overall Stride Lengths of the three Steps must be precise enough to produce the exact Takeoff distance into the next barrier. If one Air Time is off, then the remaining efforts must compensate to get the Steps back in synch, thus disrupting these Steps as well. With this in mind, the question becomes one of how best to divide the three Steps to produce the best performance.

Due to the unique nature of the Hurdle event, there are certain demands that determine how best to distribute the Step effort:

1. **The Hurdle**: Since the athlete must negotiate the barrier, this effort produces several results that must be dealt with:
    a. **Hurdle Stride Length**: The overall Hurdle Stride Length dictates the total length of the three Steps between the hurdles. The shorter the Hurdle Stride, the more distance that must be covered by the Steps between the barriers.
    b. **Vertical Demands**: Since the athlete must raise the body much higher than the normal Sprint stride to clear the barrier, the body is falling Vertically downward much faster at Touchdown coming off the hurdle. This demands the expenditure of a great deal of effort to stop this fall, as well as trying to increase the forward momentum and preparing to deal with the next hurdle.

2. **The Step Distance**: For the most part, Step distance is determined by the Air Time. Thus, the total Air Time (about 0.3 seconds) needs to be distributed between the three Steps in the most efficient way possible. **The most important thing to realize about the Steps between the hurdles is that, in both the Men's and Women's elite level race, the distance available (about 6.0 meters for Men, 5.8 meters for Women) is much shorter than what the athlete would generate in a normal Sprint stride** (see Chapter 1, Tables 1-1 and 1-2).

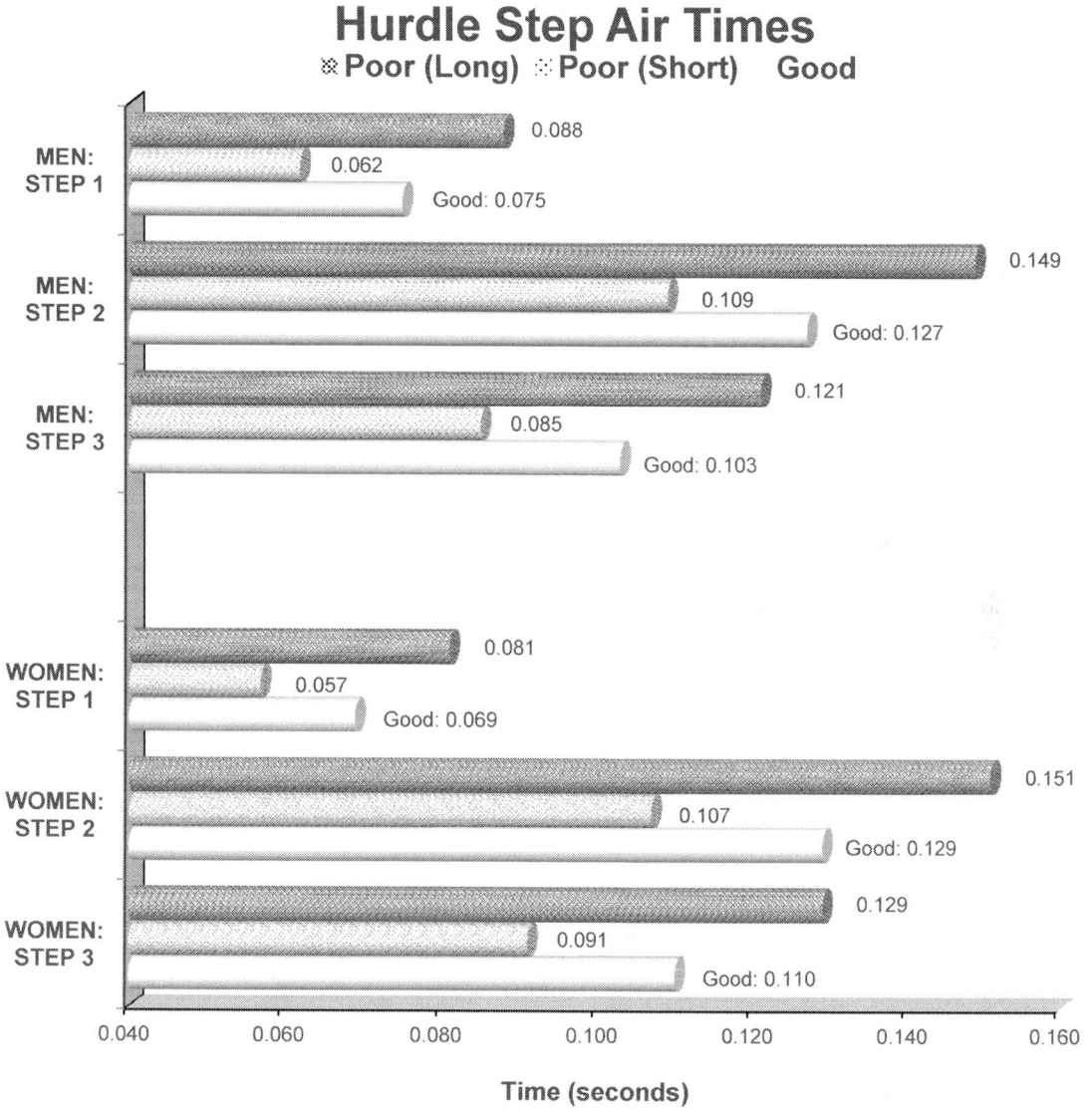

Hurdle Step Air Times
Poor (Long)　Poor (Short)　Good

Category	Poor (Long)	Poor (Short)	Good
MEN: STEP 1	0.088	0.062	0.075
MEN: STEP 2	0.149	0.109	0.127
MEN: STEP 3	0.121	0.085	0.103
WOMEN: STEP 1	0.081	0.057	0.069
WOMEN: STEP 2	0.151	0.107	0.129
WOMEN: STEP 3	0.129	0.091	0.110

Time (seconds)

Figure 14-7: Air Times for the Steps Between The Short Hurdles

For both Men and Women, the first Step has, by far, the shortest Air Time (24% of the total). Since the hurdler is coming down off the barrier, the object is to control the body descent while actually producing Horizontal Velocity as well. This Step is termed the **Fall Step** and, if performed properly, allows the rapid transition from a Vertically oriented hurdle action to a Horizontally directed action toward the next barrier.

As will be seen, the Fall Step is the most technical non-hurdle step in the race. Success in this action is primarily related to how well the body is positioned coming off the hurdle. Regardless of how strong an athlete may be, if their position at Touchdown coming off the barrier is not perfect, it is impossible to properly control the transition from Vertical to Horizontal emphasis.

Step Two, termed the **Shuffle Step**, is the longest in the air (42%) and is used to drive the hurdler Horizontally toward the next barrier. The extended Air Time is critical in producing a long enough Stride Length so that the final Step can be shortened in preparation for the next Hurdle action.

Easily the longest of the Steps, this is the only one that lasts as long as a typical Sprint stride. As will be seen, however, due to the demands of the Steps on either side of this middle Step, the Mechanics of the Shuffle Step is far removed from the recommended Sprint action. For these same reasons, this Step is the only one that can effectively be used to recover from problems created during Hurdle Clearance and/or Step One.

Finally, Step Three is termed the Preparatory or **Prep Step** since its only goal is to properly prepare the athlete to land in the proper position to attack the barrier in the most effective manner possible. With an Air Time lasting between the other Steps (34%), it is considerably shorter than a Sprint stride, and typical of how all good athletes shorten the last Air Time going into a jump.

The key to producing a solid third Step lies in properly negotiating the previous Hurdle, then successfully producing the correct results for Steps One and Two. If this happens, then the athlete can produce a controlled short step, hit the proper Takeoff position, and have the opportunity to get the most out of the Hurdle action.

On the other hand, if Step Three begins either too far or too close, then the Prep Step must be altered since the proper Touchdown distance into the Hurdle must be achieved. If the hurdler finds themselves too far away at the end of Step Two, then the Pre Step Air Time must be increased to reach the proper Hurdle Touchdown position. This eliminates the ability to keep the body low going into the Hurdle action, forcing the athlete to spend more time and energy to clear the barrier.

If poor Hurdle and Step management places the athlete too close when Step three begins, it forces the hurdler to shorten the Prep Step even more than normal. If the athlete is quick enough to accomplish this, then nothing is lost. However, if the athlete cannot recover quickly enough (usually due to fatigue late in the race), then the hurdler will find themselves too close to the barrier at Touchdown. At best, this will force the performer to brake, generate enough Vertical Velocity to jump the barrier, and deal with all the bad after effects from that point forward. At worst, the barrier will be so close that some part of the hurdle will be impacted, severely disrupting the race.

It should be evident that producing the proper Air Times between the barriers is the key to a successful race. It should also be noted that, to accomplish this, proper Hurdle clearance is critical, along with handling the demands of the Ground Phases of the Steps between the hurdles.

Stride Length

Since the performer must manage ten barriers; as well as the Steps before, between, and after the hurdles, the manner in which they maximize the Effective Force while minimizing the Expended Force, Impact Force will determine, to a large degree, the outcome of the race. One of the best measures of the success of this force application can be found in the resulting Stride Length that it produces.

Over the Hurdle

Figure 14-8 indicates the Stride Length consequences of the extended Hurdle Air Time. In comparison to their Sprint results (see Figure 8-3), the hurdlers are covering up to twice the distance during Hurdle clearance.

Stride Length

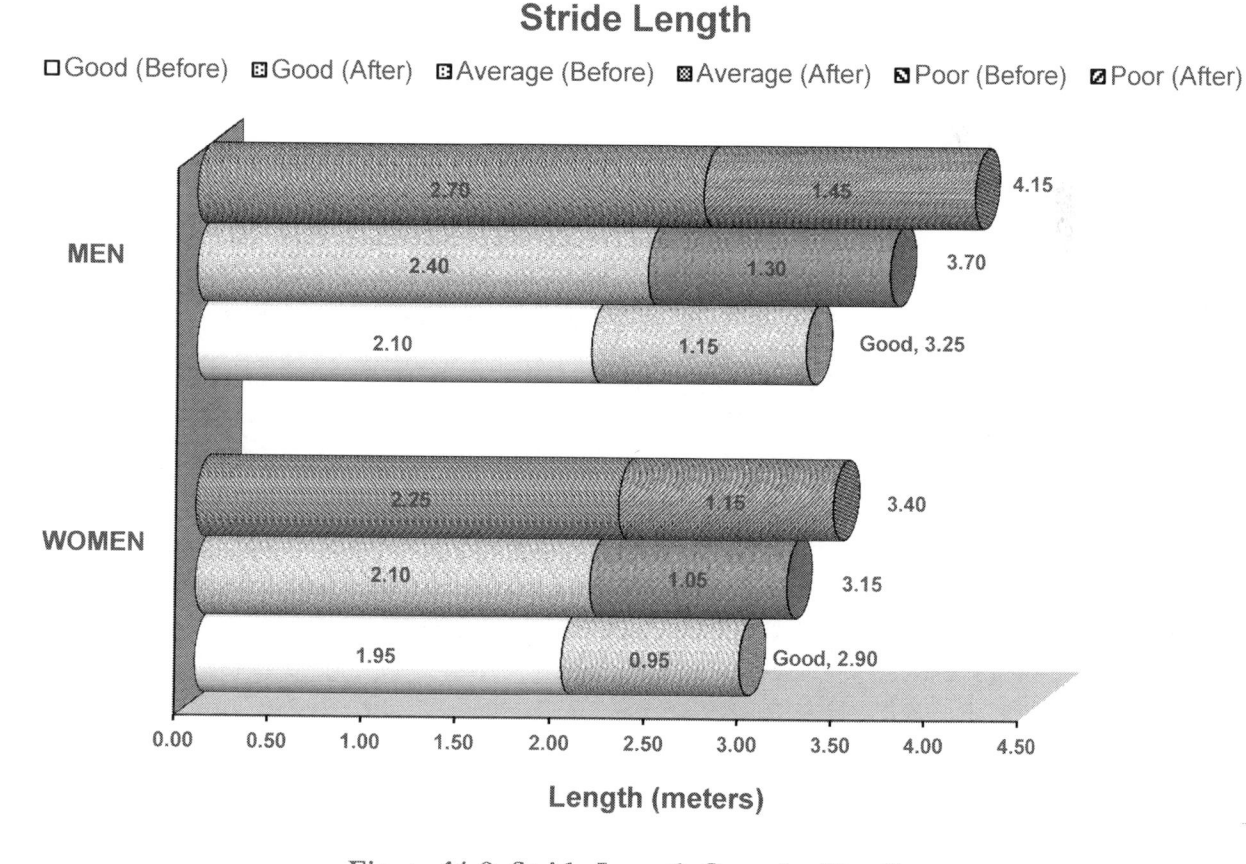

☐ Good (Before) ▣ Good (After) ▣ Average (Before) ▣ Average (After) ▣ Poor (Before) ▣ Poor (After)

MEN
- 2.70 | 1.45 | 4.15
- 2.40 | 1.30 | 3.70
- 2.10 | 1.15 | Good, 3.25

WOMEN
- 2.25 | 1.15 | 3.40
- 2.10 | 1.05 | 3.15
- 1.95 | 0.95 | Good, 2.90

Length (meters)

Figure 14-8: Stride Length Over the Hurdle

There are three interesting trends that are inherent in these length results. First, note that the lengths of the before and after results are not equal. If a performer wishes to clear a barrier as efficiently as possible, mathematics indicates that they should project their body center so that it reaches its peak directly over the hurdle.

Although this would be the preferred body center path, hurdlers are prevented from doing this due to the need to clear the extended Lead Leg as it is rotated up and over the barrier. As shown in Figure 14-9, this forces the athlete to shift the peak of the body center well before the barrier. Moreover, the height of the body center must be increased so that it will clear the hurdle on the way down. Thus, the unbalanced before/after Stride Lengths are an unavoidable, and detrimental consequence of the demands of the event. The better hurdlers, however, will reduce this consequence by minimizing the Lead Leg clearance.

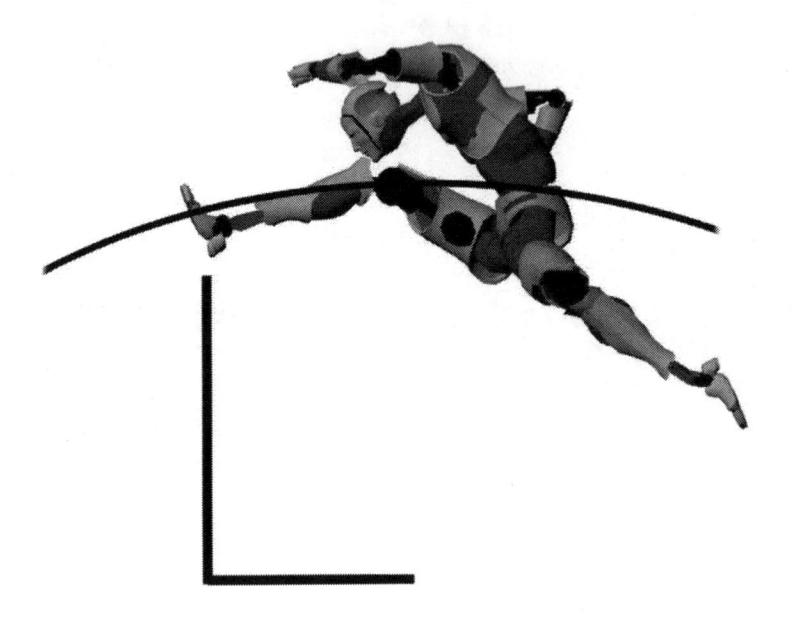

Figure 14-9: Actual Body Center Path Over the Hurdle

The second trend is that, as with Horizontal Velocity, the Women 100 Hurdlers outperform the Men in minimizing stride distance (as well as Air Time). Once again, this situation is produced by the differences in the rules governing the two events, specifically the large difference in the heights of the barriers (Table 1-1). Since the Women have much less challenge to clear the barrier, their Stride Length can be greatly reduced. It should be noted, however, that Figure 14-8 shows that only the better Women hurdlers take major advantage of this shortened Stride Length opportunity.

Finally, and most notably, **the length into the barrier is the most important result since, if a hurdler does not land within 8 centimeters (3 inches) of the proper Touchdown distance, producing the proper Hurdle Mechanics is simply not possible**. If the landing is too far, the athlete must jump higher to ensure Hurdle clearance. If too close, then the hurdler must jump higher to avoid hitting the barrier. Either situation results in having to slam on the brakes, and emphasize Vertical instead of Horizontal projection into the hurdle. And the greater the distance from the proper Touchdown point, the worse the disruption becomes.

Steps Between the Hurdles

Air Time and Ground Time produce the Stride Length and Stride Rate for the Steps between the hurdles. Figure 14-10 visually presents the Length results. As with the Air Time results, the Short-Long-Short pattern can be seen in the Stride Lengths for the Fall, Shuffle, and Prep Steps.

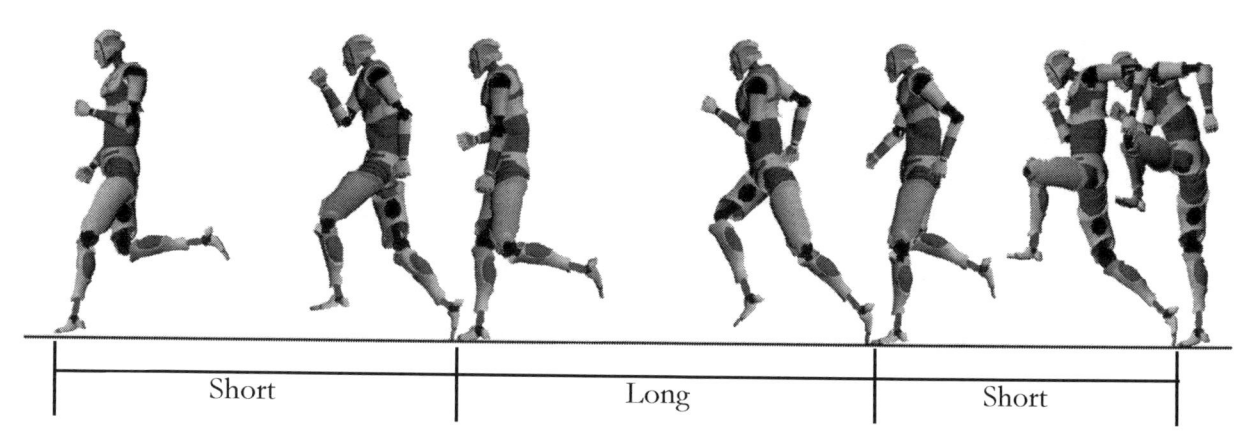

Figure 14-10: Stride Lengths for the Steps Between the Hurdles

The Step One goal of slowing the downward fall of the body coming off the hurdle, while also managing to increase Horizontal Velocity can be seen in the resultant short Stride Length of the first Step.

The Step Two Length, critical in completing the movement shift from Vertical to Horizontal emphasis, can be seen. Likewise, the additional demands of producing sufficient Stride Length to allow the athlete to properly attack the next hurdle requires the longest Stride Length for the Second Step.

Finally, if the hurdle is properly negotiated, and then followed by successful Steps One and Two, it allows the athlete to produce the classic short, penultimate step seen in all efficient human powered jump events.

A more exact comparison of the three Step Lengths for elite hurdlers is presented in Figure 14-11. As can be seen, the extremely short length of Step One indicates just how difficult it is to stop the downward fall coming off the barrier and, at the same time, not only avoid slowing down but actually increasing the Horizontal Velocity.

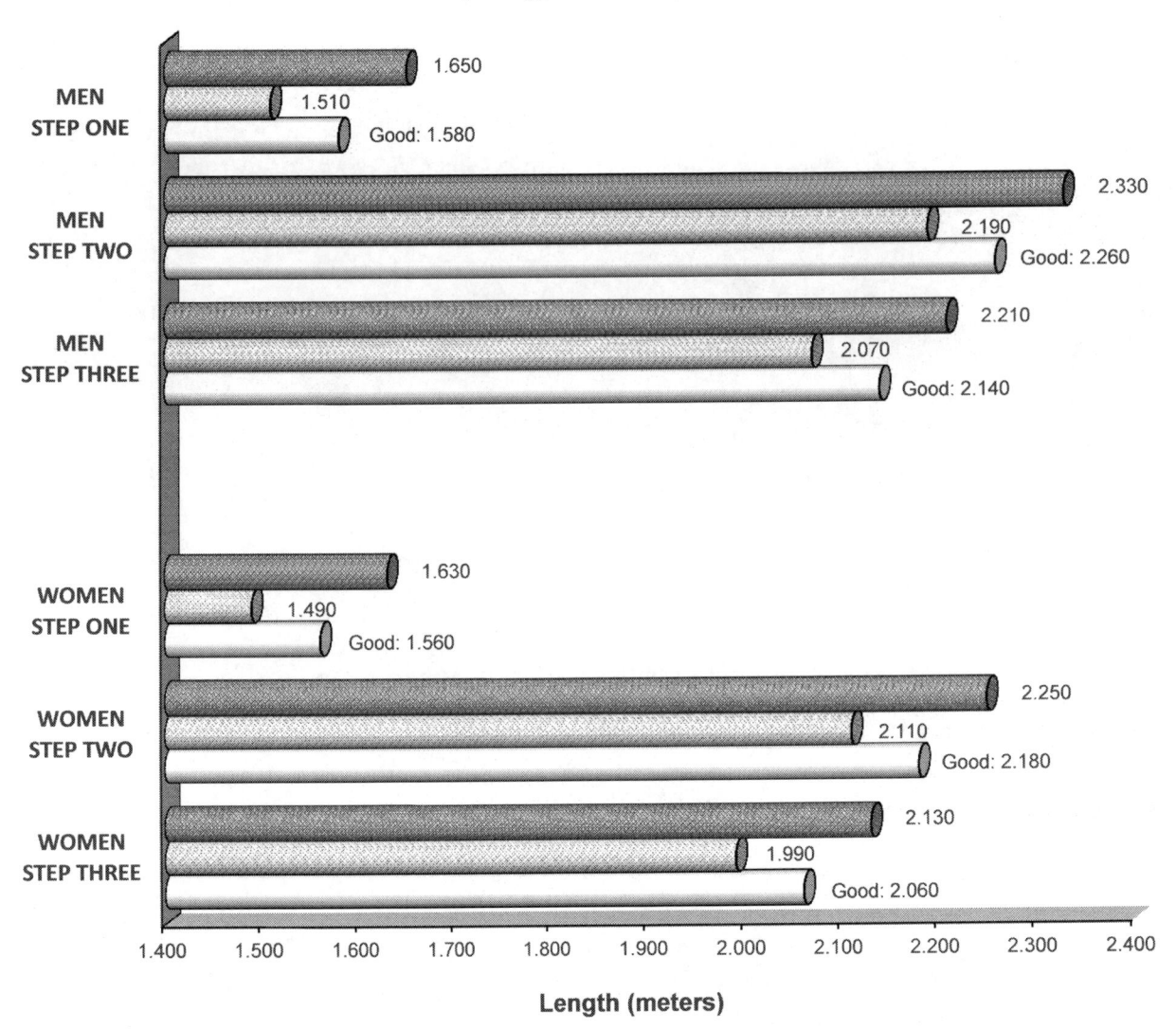

Hurdle Step Stride Length
▩ Poor (Long)   ▨ Poor (Short)   ☐ Good

MEN STEP ONE
- Poor (Long): 1.650
- Poor (Short): 1.510
- Good: 1.580

MEN STEP TWO
- Poor (Long): 2.330
- Poor (Short): 2.190
- Good: 2.260

MEN STEP THREE
- Poor (Long): 2.210
- Poor (Short): 2.070
- Good: 2.140

WOMEN STEP ONE
- Poor (Long): 1.630
- Poor (Short): 1.490
- Good: 1.560

WOMEN STEP TWO
- Poor (Long): 2.250
- Poor (Short): 2.110
- Good: 2.180

WOMEN STEP THREE
- Poor (Long): 2.130
- Poor (Short): 1.990
- Good: 2.060

Length (meters)

Figure 14-11: Stride Lengths for the Steps Between the Hurdles

As expected, Step Two is the longest, and is used to set up the all-important body position into the next hurdle. Finally, if properly prepared, the Prep Step can be shortened, placing the body the correct distance From the Hurdle and ready to attack the barrier.

Ground Time

Of all of the General Performance Descriptors, Ground Time throughout the race provides the greatest insights into how the elite Hurdle performance is accomplished. Since the Ground Phase is the only time when the athlete can apply force to alter the body's Velocity, it is not surprising that this is where great hurdle results are produced.

Into the Hurdle

Figure 14-12 shows the Ground Time results involved in hurdle clearance for all elite hurdlers analyzed to date.

Ground Time

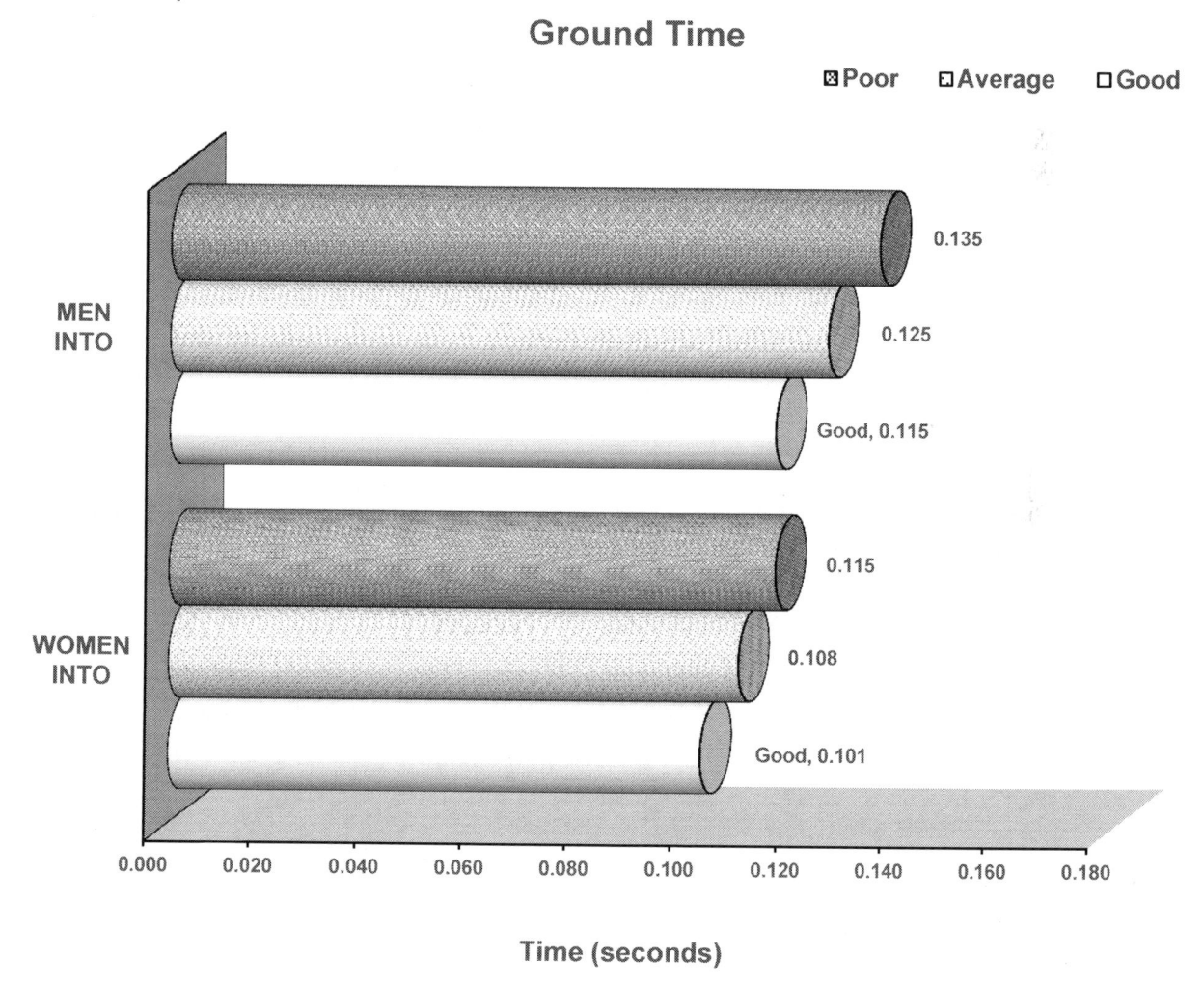

Poor — Average — Good

MEN INTO:
- Poor: 0.135
- Average: 0.125
- Good: 0.115

WOMEN INTO:
- Poor: 0.115
- Average: 0.108
- Good: 0.101

Time (seconds)

Figure 14-12: Ground Time Into the Hurdle

Ground Time is dependent upon how quickly the hurdler can produce the ground forces required to successfully project the body into the barrier. As the Figure indicates, the better hurdlers minimize this variable, resulting in an increase in Stride Rate and, therefore, an increase in Horizontal

Velocity (assuming no other results are affected by this change). The reason that the Men's results are higher that the Women's, despite the Men's strength advantage, is due to the significant hurdle height difference between the two races.

Steps Between the Hurdles

Whereas Hurdle Race Management allows the best performance to occur, and Air Time both over and between the barriers allows the hurdler to achieve the goal of each Step, it is the Forces exerted during ground contact that actually produce these results. For the Steps between the barriers, Figure 14-13 visually demonstrates the Ground Time results for elite hurdlers.

Figure 14-13: Ground Times for the Steps Between the Hurdles

As with Air Time, it is visually evident that, from the distance covered, the Ground Times for the three Steps are not the same. Moreover, these differences become even more apparent when they are compared to the Ground Times of the Sprint Stride (Figure 14-14). The visually obvious pattern of Short-Long-Short seen in the movement between the barriers is in sharp contrast to the repetitive Ground Phase of the Sprints.

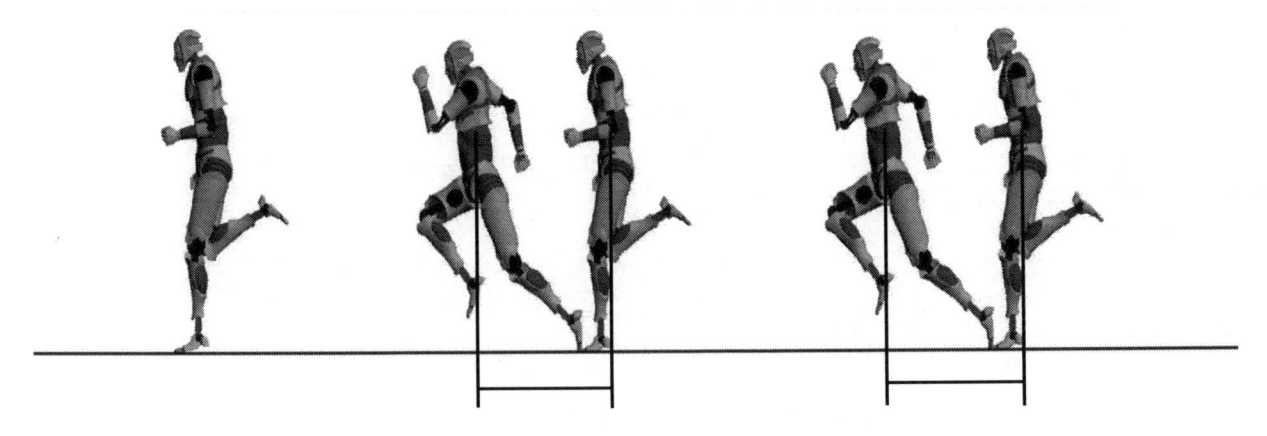

Figure 14-14: Ground Times for the Sprint Stride

A more exact comparison of the three Steps, the numeric Ground Time results for elite hurdlers are shown in Figure 14-15

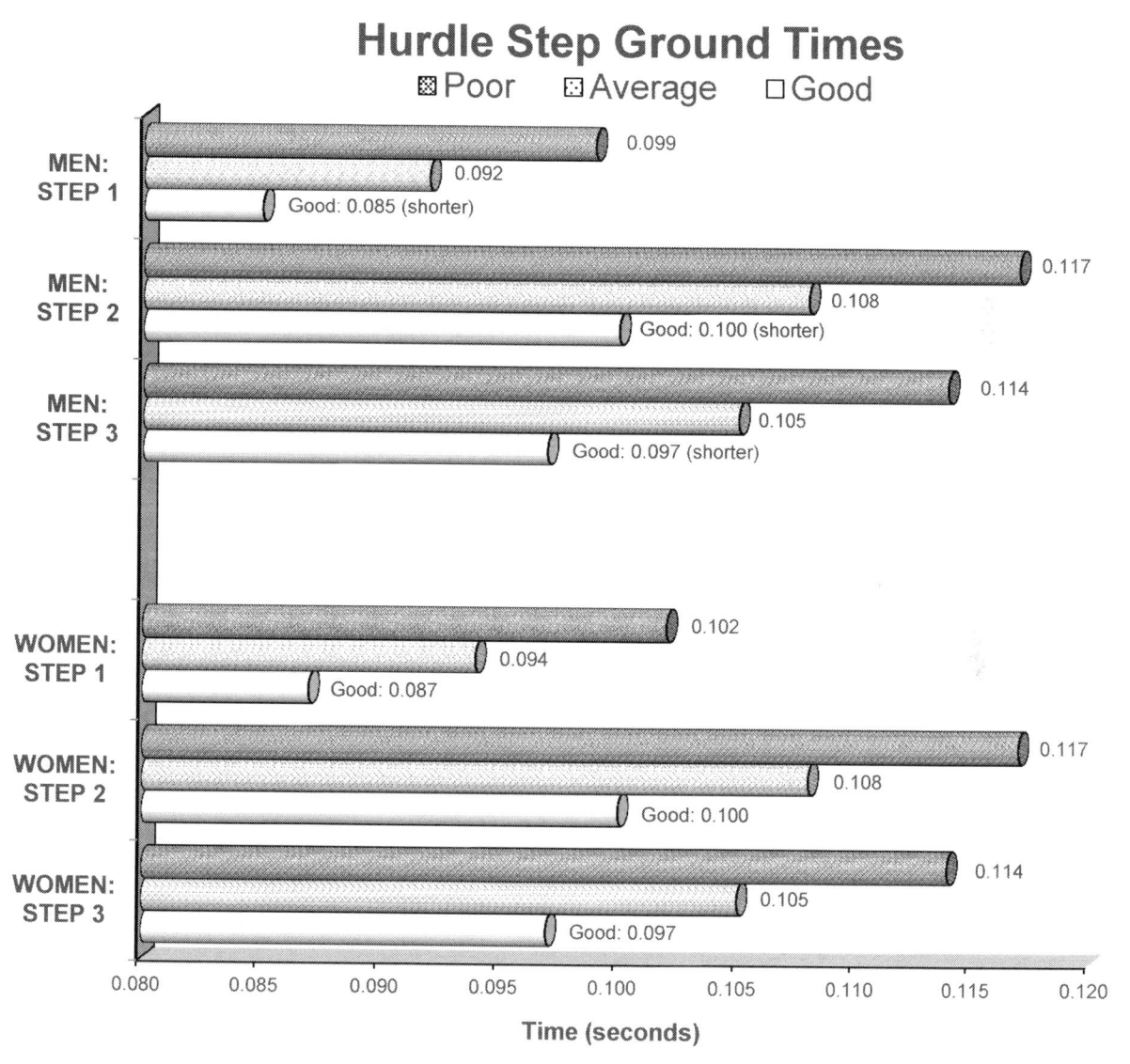

Hurdle Step Ground Times

Poor / Average / Good

MEN: STEP 1
- Poor: 0.099
- Average: 0.092
- Good: 0.085 (shorter)

MEN: STEP 2
- Poor: 0.117
- Average: 0.108
- Good: 0.100 (shorter)

MEN: STEP 3
- Poor: 0.114
- Average: 0.105
- Good: 0.097 (shorter)

WOMEN: STEP 1
- Poor: 0.102
- Average: 0.094
- Good: 0.087

WOMEN: STEP 2
- Poor: 0.117
- Average: 0.108
- Good: 0.100

WOMEN: STEP 3
- Poor: 0.114
- Average: 0.105
- Good: 0.097

Time (seconds)

Figure 14-15: Ground Times for the Steps Between the Hurdles

As in the Sprint race, the key to performance in the Hurdles lies in the athlete's ability to minimize the time spent on the ground, while still achieving the mechanical goals of the event. For the Steps between the barriers, these goals are:

1. **Step One**: Stop the fall of the body as it comes off the hurdle, while gaining back some of the Horizontal Velocity lost while clearing the barrier.
2. **Step Two**: Finish the task of halting the downward Velocity of the body still remaining from Step One, generate additional Horizontal Velocity and, finally, produce sufficient Vertical effort to create the Stride Length needed to set up Step Three.
3. **Step Three**: Generate additional Horizontal Velocity, as well as prepare the body position for the next Hurdle Stride.

If the hurdle is negotiated correctly, Step One is relatively simple. Likewise, if Step Two is executed properly, Step Three can be can be used to allow the athlete to powerfully move into the next barrier.

It has become apparent that, as long as the hurdle is negotiated properly, the critical Step between the barriers is Step Two. This is due primarily to the fact that this Step must produce the greatest number of goals, as well as having the longest Air Time and Ground Time of the three Steps. This, coupled with the fact that Step Two is the best place to recover from problems created from less than perfect technique elsewhere, makes this Step the true keystone of the event.

Stride Rate

The Stride Rate, or leg turnover, is the best indicator of the tempo of the activity. In the Sprint, the Tempo was a constant from the first Step out of the Blocks to the Finish. In the Short Hurdles, due to the presence of the barriers and the restrictive distance between the hurdles, the Stride Rate is constantly changing.

Going Into and Over the Hurdle

Although Stride Rate is not normally discussed in reference to hurdle clearance, if the typical definition is applied, the Rate for the best elite hurdlers would be 2.4 steps per second for Men and 2.7 steps per second for Women.

Steps Between the Hurdles

Figure 14-16 presents the Hurdle Steps Stride Rate results. The high turnover rate of the Fall Step, more than 30 percent faster than an elite Sprint Rate, demonstrates the dynamic move off the barrier. The Rate drop of 50 percent as the athlete moves into the Shuffle Step shows how the emphasis shifts to moving toward the next hurdle. Finally, the Rate increases, once again, as the athlete executes the Prep Step.

The large shift in Stride Rate, from a low of well under three steps per second for the Hurdle stride to a high of well over six steps per second for the Fall Step, indicates just how difficult the challenge is to successfully complete this race with a constantly changing tempo.

Critical General Performance Descriptors For the Short Hurdles

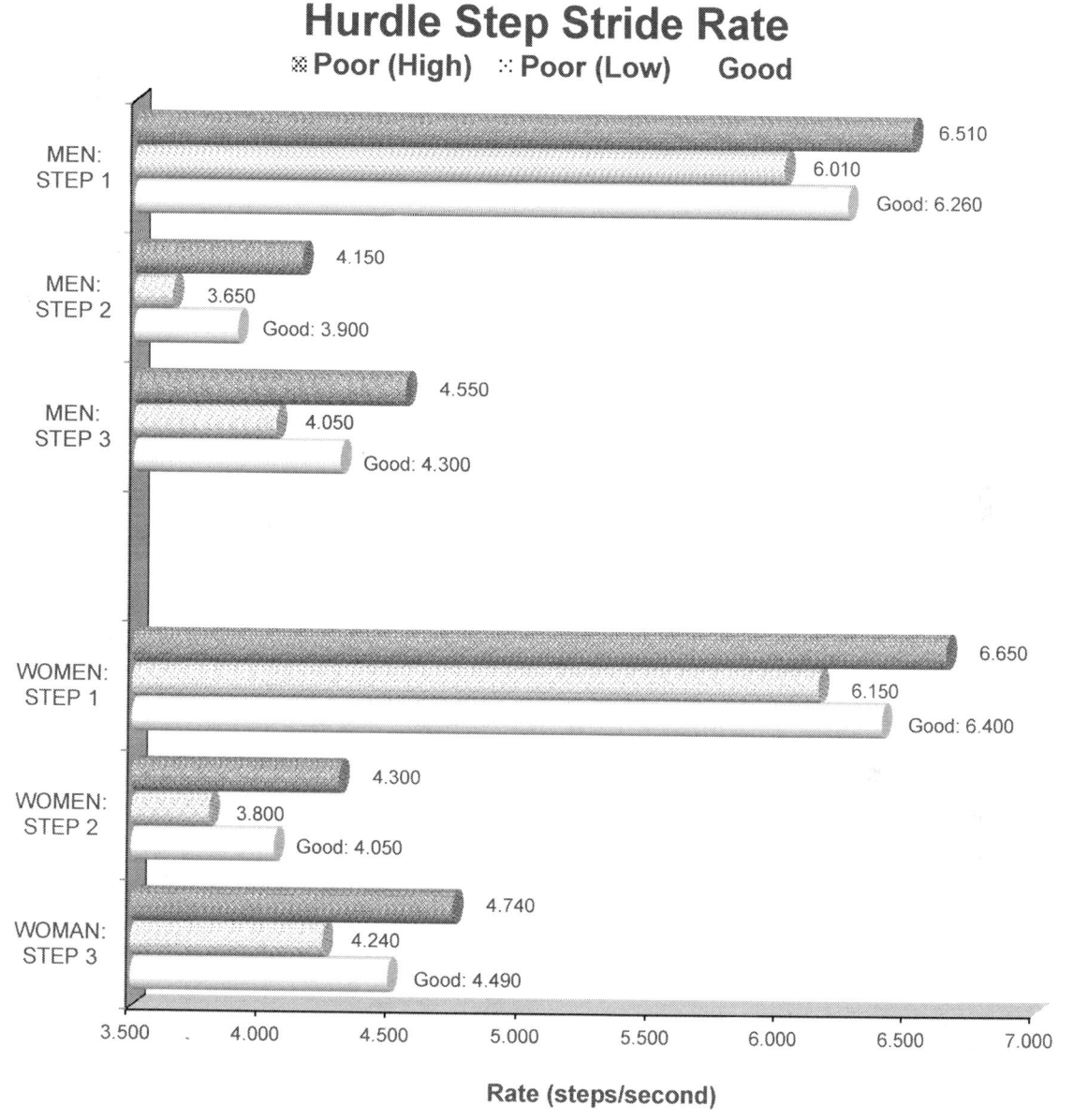

Hurdle Step Stride Rate
▩ Poor (High) ⋯ Poor (Low) Good

Category	Poor (High)	Poor (Low)	Good
MEN: STEP 1	6.510	6.010	6.260
MEN: STEP 2	4.150	3.650	3.900
MEN: STEP 3	4.550	4.050	4.300
WOMEN: STEP 1	6.650	6.150	6.400
WOMEN: STEP 2	4.300	3.800	4.050
WOMAN: STEP 3	4.740	4.240	4.490

Rate (steps/second)

Figure 14-16: Stride Rates for the Steps Between the Hurdles

Chapter Summary:

In summary, elite Hurdle performance is achieved through improving hurdle time by decreasing both Air Time over the barrier and Ground Contact Time into and off the hurdle. The key to this action begins with landing in the proper Touchdown position going into the hurdle, controlling the body rotation while minimizing the time over the barrier, then landing with the body center over the foot at Touchdown.

> To properly set up each of the next barriers, the three Steps between the hurdles must be properly managed, each with their own specific goals for success.

Realizing what it takes to produce an elite Hurdle performance is one thing, understanding how the elite hurdler actually accomplish this task is another problem altogether. To resolve these questions, more specific performance variables must be investigated.

CHAPTER 15

CRITICAL SPECIFIC PERFORMANCE DESCRIPTORS FOR THE SHORT HURDLES

In the Hurdle performance, **Specific Performance Descriptors** identify how the performer is mechanically producing the critical General Performance Descriptors previously identified. Those specific descriptors that are directly related to performance include:

1. **Lateral Segment Action**
2. **Trunk Angle**
3. **Horizontal Foot Speed at Touchdown**
4. **Horizontal Foot Distance at Touchdown**
5. **Knee Separation at Touchdown**
6. **Upper Leg Motion**
7. **Upper Leg Rotational Speed**
8. **Lower Leg Motion**
9. **Lower Leg Rotational Speed**

A complete understanding of these variables will provide a base around which to develop a mechanically sound hurdler, as well as focusing the talents of the athlete in the most productive manner possible. All results will be divided into those related to the elite performance over the hurdle and between the hurdles.

Lateral Segment Action

The goal in hurdling is to move straight ahead, either by sprinting or hurdling, as quickly as possible. To accomplish this, all efforts should be made in either the forward or upward directions. Any excessive Lateral (sideways) movements of the body segments therefore, are unwanted.

Into and Over the Hurdle

In the hurdle stride, Lateral motion should be eliminated whenever possible. Although many times these actions cannot be avoided due to the body movements required to clear the barrier, they should be recognized and minimized as much as possible. The biggest problem in producing efficient Lateral motion rests in the movement of the Lead and Trail Legs. If the Lead Leg is not brought directly at the hurdle, not only will the action slow the hurdle stride by forcing the leg to travel farther (a curved instead of a straight path), but the arms will be forced to swing out to offset the leg motion and maintain balance.

The movement of the Trail Leg is a special case since it must be moved Laterally (swung out) to properly clear the barrier. Since the trunk and arms must also be moved Laterally to offset this leg movement, efforts should be made to minimize the amount of offset that must be produced. To accomplish this, the lower leg segment of the Trail Leg should be flexed as much as possible when it is brought over the hurdle. This action will reduce the amount of offsetting counter motion the trunk and arms will have to produce to balance the Trail Leg action.

In the Short Hurdle races, the trunk must be lowered a significant amount to clear the higher barrier, allowing the trunk to provide most of the motion required to counter the Lateral leg action. In fact, the better Men's hurdlers create very little arm action over the barrier. It should be emphasized, however, that this minimal arm action is a result of properly balancing the Lateral leg actions with the trunk. If this balancing is not done properly, however, simply restricting the arm action (as emphasized by many coaches) will only cause unwanted balance problems.

Regardless of the race, if the athlete produces excessive Lateral motion with the legs, or fails to use the trunk and arms to properly counter the leg action, the hurdler will fall sideways coming off the hurdle, and waste time between the barriers in recovering Lateral balance. If Lateral upper body motion is to be improved, it is typically done by improving the Trail Leg recovery motion since the upper body motion is primarily produced to offset this action. Thus, if the Trail Leg action is improved, the upper body motion will improve automatically.

Steps Between the Hurdles

If the Hurdle Stride is performed correctly, the three Steps between the hurdles can be performed with virtually no Lateral body movements. Step One includes the completion of the Trail Leg recovery, however, if hurdle clearance is done properly then most of the Lateral action is completed prior to ground contact. Good Hurdle Mechanics allows the athlete to focus on the Vertical and Horizontal demands of the Steps between.

However, if the Lateral movements over the barrier have not been precisely balanced, then the hurdler must spend precious time and energy bringing the body back into balance as it moves between the barriers. To add another task to an already complex movement is extremely detrimental to performance and must be avoided if an elite level is to be attained.

Trunk Angle

The basis for the proper philosophy on how to teach the Short Hurdles can be found in the trunk angles during the ground contact portion of the race. In summary, the key to success lies in **leading with the hips and lower body** throughout the entire race. This is in direct contrast with the traditional coaching belief that the emphasis should be on leading with the upper body. As will be seen, this errant belief has hindered the performance over the barriers for too long and must be abandoned.

Into and Over the Hurdle

Trunk angles going into and over the barrier are shown in Figure 15-1. The two most striking conclusions are:

1. **The Small Amount of Trunk Flexion at Touchdown and Takeoff**: Traditional instruction emphasizes maximally increasing trunk flexion (forward body lean) going into the hurdle. In fact, this action is simply not found in proficient hurdlers. At Touchdown, the trunk is upright, with the hips leading the way into the barrier. At Takeoff, the trunk has flexed only enough to help balance the recovery of the Lead Leg. Finally, once airborne, additional flexion is used to continue to lift the Lead Leg. In contrast, the poorer athletes flex (dive) to a greater degree going into the hurdle and, as will be seen, make hurdle clearance a much more difficult task.
2. **The Small Amount of Trunk Flexion Over the Hurdle**: After Takeoff, the amount of additional trunk flexion is relatively limited. That is not to say that the better athletes do not, as is traditionally taught, tightly compact the body to allow a lower hurdle clearance. They do, but, as seen in the Figure, this position is achieved more by bringing the lower body up to the trunk than the trunk down to the lower body.

Figure 15-1: Trunk Angles at Touchdown, Takeoff, and Maximum Flexion Going Into and Over the Hurdle

The actual angular values for the trunk angles are shown in Figure 15-2 (results for Men and Women are close enough to be shown as one). Note that the trunk angles for the better hurdlers are always **more upright** than the less proficient performers.

Trunk Touchdown, Takeoff and Max Flexion Angles

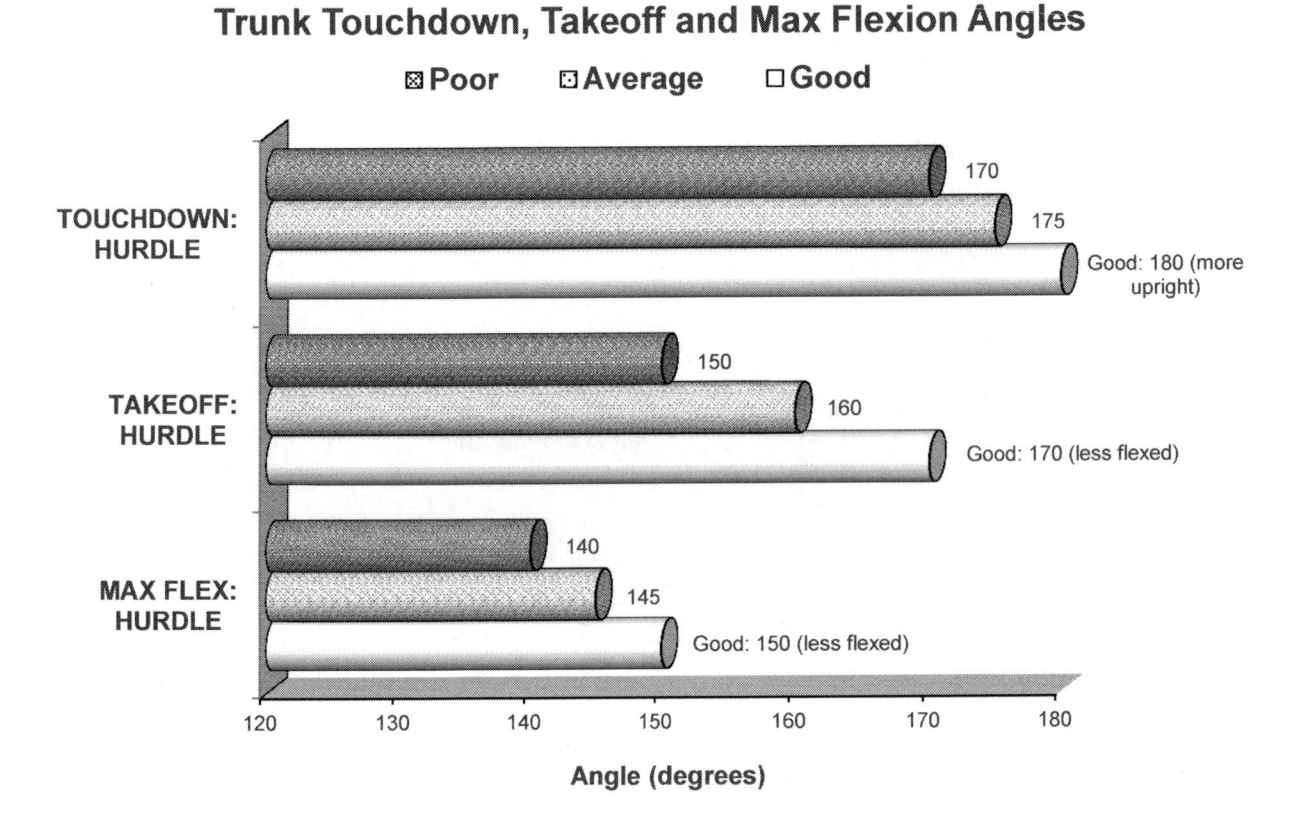

TOUCHDOWN: HURDLE
- Poor: 170
- Average: 175
- Good: 180 (more upright)

TAKEOFF: HURDLE
- Poor: 150
- Average: 160
- Good: 170 (less flexed)

MAX FLEX: HURDLE
- Poor: 140
- Average: 145
- Good: 150 (less flexed)

Angle (degrees)

Figure 15-2: Trunk Angles at Touchdown, Takeoff and Maximum Flexion Going Into and Over the Hurdle

It is interesting to note that, although the total trunk range of motion (Touchdown to Max Flexion) is the same for all of the elite hurdlers (30 degrees), as indicated previously, how it is achieved is very different. The better hurdlers balance the Ground-Air trunk flexion evenly, producing 33 percent of the flexion going into the barrier and 67 percent during the Air phase. The less proficient athletes land with more flexion to begin with, then produce 76 percent of the flexion during the Ground phase, leaving only a small part (33%) to be completed while going over the barrier

As will be seen later in the Chapter, this variation makes a large difference in Hurdle performance.

Steps Between the Hurdles

To produce the three Horizontally directed, Front Side dominated Steps between the barriers, the hips and lower body must lead the way. This begins with the Step One body action coming off the hurdle (Figure 15-3). During the Ground Phase, the action of the hurdler forcefully extending the upper body while, at the same time using the Ground Leg to drive the lower body forward, results in a virtually upright position at Takeoff.

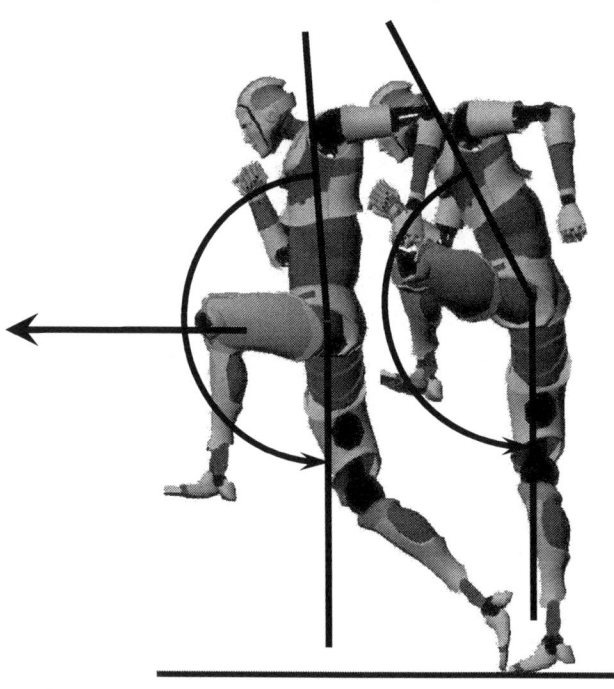

Critical Specific Performance Descriptors For the Short Hurdles

Figure 15-3: Trunk Angles at Touchdown and Takeoff Coming Off the Hurdle (Step One)

The upright trunk angles maintained during both Step Two and Step Three are demonstrated in Figures 15-4 and 15-5.

Figure 15-4: Step Two Trunk Angles at Touchdown and Takeoff

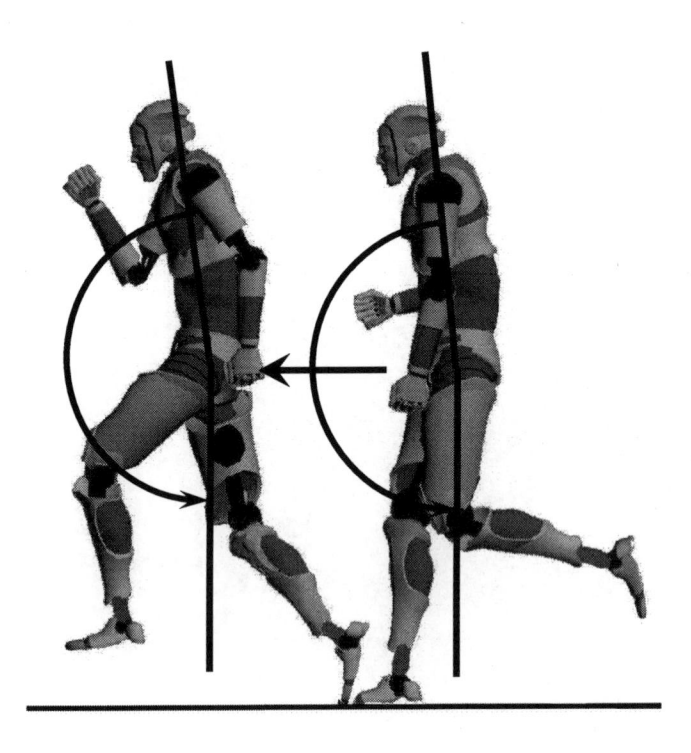

Critical Specific Performance Descriptors For the Short Hurdles

Figure 15-5: Step Three Trunk Angles at Touchdown and Takeoff

    The upright trunk angles maintained during both Step Two (Figure 15-4) and Step Three (Figure 15-5) indicate the continued emphasis of leading the Steps between the Hurdles with the hips and lower body.

    The actual angular values for the trunk angles are shown in Figure 15-6 (results for Men and Women are close enough to be shown as one). Note that, in every case, the trunk angles for the better hurdlers are always **more upright, both at Touchdown and Takeoff** than the less proficient performers.

    The results indicate that, coming off the barrier, the athlete extends the trunk about 12 degrees, bringing the upper body to an almost upright position at Takeoff (177 degrees). This extension provides the leverage needed to complete the recovery of the Trail Leg, as well as bring the hips and lower body forward at Takeoff.

    For the remaining Steps between the hurdles, the trunk angle averages more than 177 degrees, much more upright than the elite Sprint Stride. This serves to maintain the hips forward position, allowing the lower body to lead the drive toward the next barrier.

    As will be seen, the purpose of the upright trunk alignment is to place the body in the proper position at Touchdown going into the hurdle.

Trunk Touchdown and Takeoff Angles

▧ Poor　⋯ Average　　Good

TOUCHDOWN: STEP 1
- 155
- 160
- Good: 165 (upright)

TOUCHDOWN: STEP 2
- 169
- 174
- Good: 179 (upright)

TOUCHDOWN: STEP 3
- 166
- 171
- Good: 176 (upright)

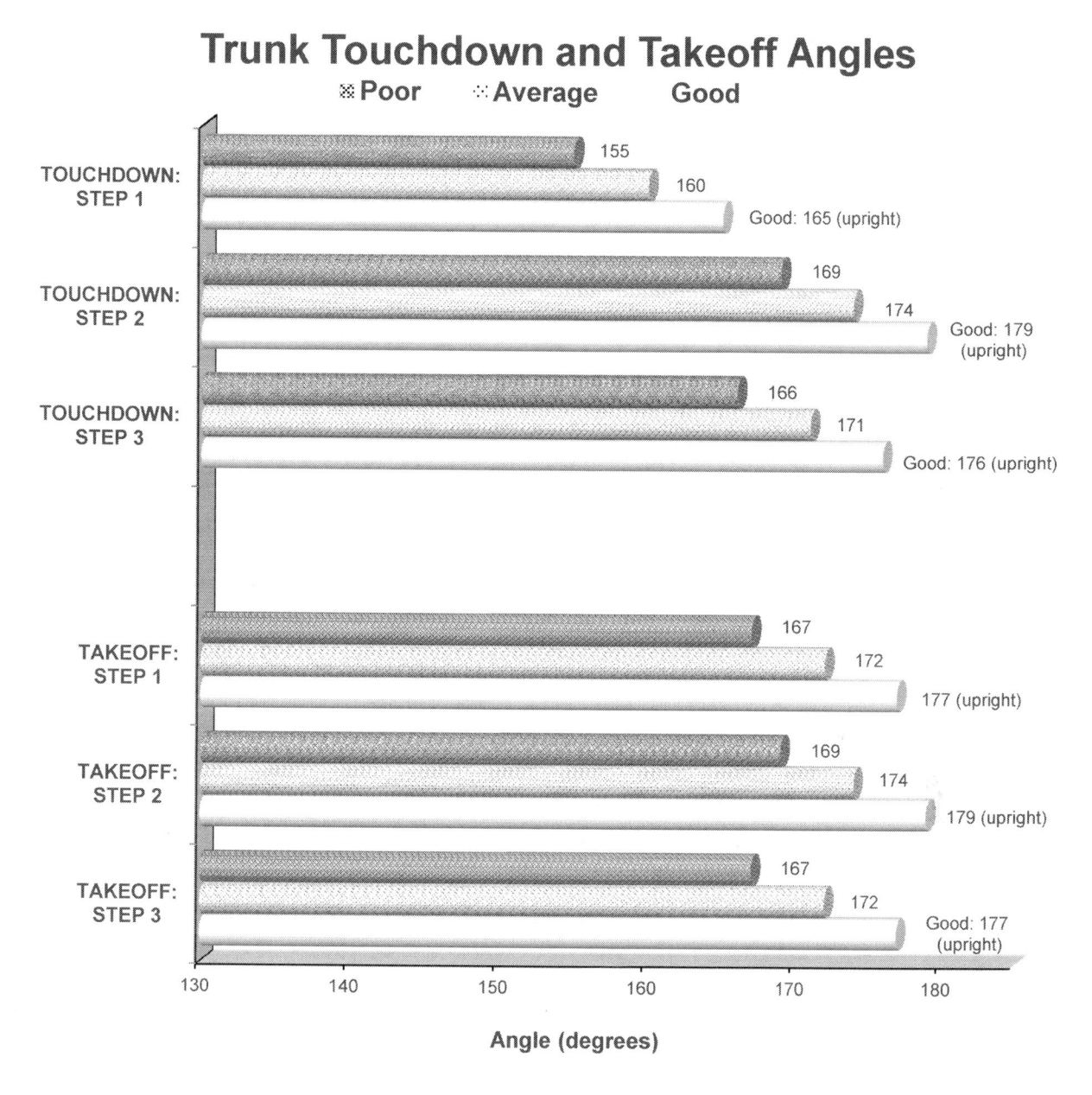

TAKEOFF: STEP 1
- 167
- 172
- 177 (upright)

TAKEOFF: STEP 2
- 169
- 174
- 179 (upright)

TAKEOFF: STEP 3
- 167
- 172
- Good: 177 (upright)

Angle (degrees)

Figure 15-6: Trunk Touchdown and Takeoff Angles for the Steps Between the Hurdles

Horizontal Foot Speed at Touchdown

As was true in the Sprints, the Horizontal Speed at which the foot hits the ground can, when necessary, be used to help generate the Vertical forces required to drive the body into the air. It is a critical performance factor, for very different reasons, in negotiating the hurdles and moving between the barriers.

Into the Hurdle

The Hurdle stride demands some unique adaptations to the normal Sprint stride in order to clear the barrier. Since the body must be projected higher into the air than normal, a large amount of Vertical Velocity must be created during ground contact going into the hurdle.

One of the ways Vertical Velocity can be produced is to have the Touchdown foot moving forward, with respect to the ground, when ground contact occurs. As seen in Figure 15-7, when the ground stops the forward foot motion, it rotates the hurdler up and over the Ground Leg (similar to a pole vaulter using a steel pole).

Since the hurdler is moving at a high forward Speed, it is easy to produce a large forward foot speed at Touchdown by simply **not** attempting to recover the foot backward (with respect to the performer) as Touchdown approaches. In fact, if the hurdler makes no effort to recover the foot, it will hit the ground at the same forward speed as the hurdler.

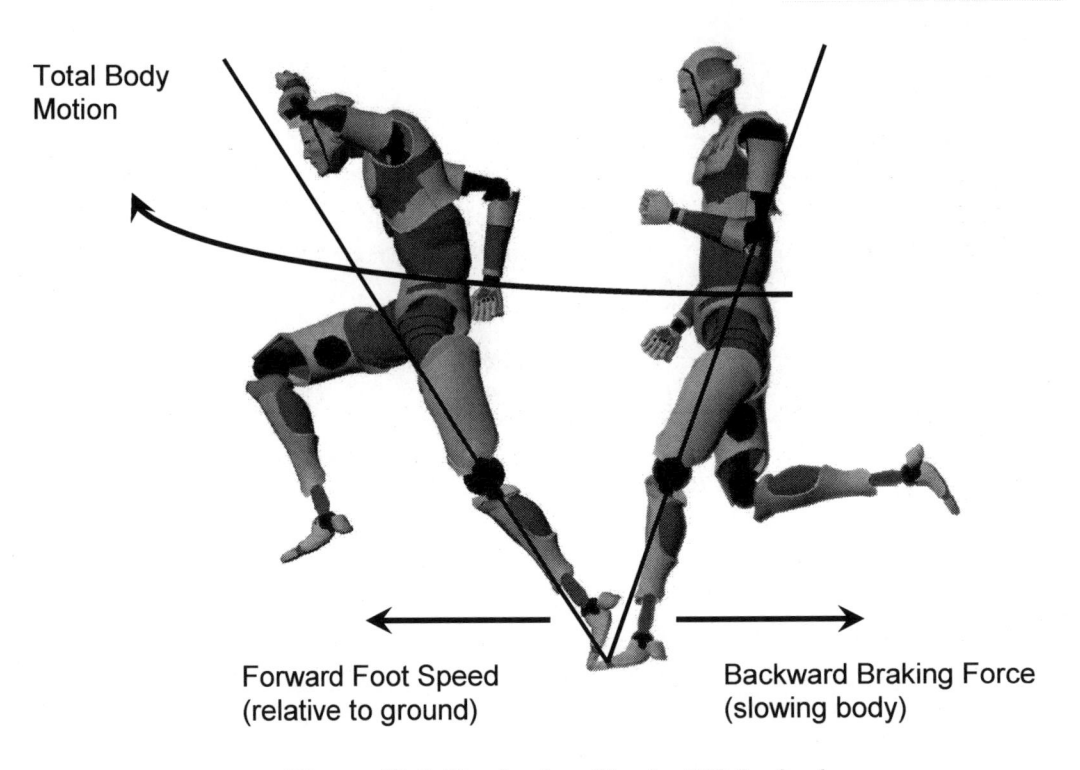

Figure 15-7: Producing Vertical Velocity by Vaulting Over the Ground Leg

Unfortunately, there is one major drawback to using the Ground Leg to vault the body over the hurdle: the ground force that stops the foot (and produces the Vertical Speed) also slows the forward Speed of the hurdler. To minimize this unwanted loss of forward Speed, the better hurdlers produce much of the needed lift in a different manner. This approach consists of using the upper leg extensors (hamstrings and gluteals) to forcefully extend the upper leg as Touchdown occurs, effectively pulling the upper body up and over the Touchdown leg. This results in the same production of body lift, but without the unwanted forward braking force since the performer, not the ground, is producing the effort to move the body upward.

Due to the difficulty of producing sufficient upper leg extensor power, no hurdler can eliminate all forward braking going into the hurdle. It can, however, be minimized by attempting to pull the foot backward, in relation to the performer, as fast as possible at Touchdown. Although no performer can actually have the foot moving backward fast enough to hit the ground with the foot moving backward with respect to the ground, the better hurdlers come closer to actually producing this result.

This concept may be difficult to follow, but assume you are in a car, traveling 30 miles per hour. As you approach a telephone pole you stick your hand out. Although the pole is not moving, your hand strikes the pole at 30 miles per hour since that is how fast the car is moving. Now, if you are foolish enough to move your hand forward an additional 10 miles per hour (in relation to the car) just before you reach the telephone pole, your hand will now be traveling 40 miles per hour as it strikes the pole (30+10=40).

If, instead of moving your hand forward, you move it backward at 10 miles per hour (in relation to the car), your hand will strike the pole at only 20 miles per hour (30-10=20). Better yet, if you could move your hand backward at 30 miles per hour (in relation to the car), the car's forward speed and the hand's backward speed would offset each other and the hand would touch the pole at 0 miles per hour (30-30=0), causing no damage.

This, in essence, is the problem facing the hurdler. Moving forward at 9 meters per second means that, to avoid hitting the ground with the foot moving forward, the leg motion must be such that the foot is moving backward (in relation to the hurdler) at a Speed of at least 9 meters per second (Figure 15-8). If not, as in the case of the hand hitting the pole, the foot will receive a backward push or braking force, slowing the hurdler.

In fact, regardless of the quality of the hurdler, it is impossible to avoid producing this braking force. To date, there has been no hurdler strong enough to produce the Vertical Velocity required to raise the body high enough to clear the barrier without producing some braking force. The better performers, however, minimize the problem by producing foot speeds that are closer to their hurdling Speed.

Figure 15-9 shows the Horizontal foot speed at Touchdown, in relation to the performer, going into the hurdle for all elite athletes analyzed to date. Referring back to the Horizontal Velocity results presented in Figure 14-1, note that, even for the good performer, there is significant compromise in the foot speed going into the hurdle. For example, the foot Velocity for the average male elite hurdler is more than 3 meters per second slower than the body Velocity. Thus, significantly more braking will occur at Touchdown, in comparison to the typical Sprint stride.

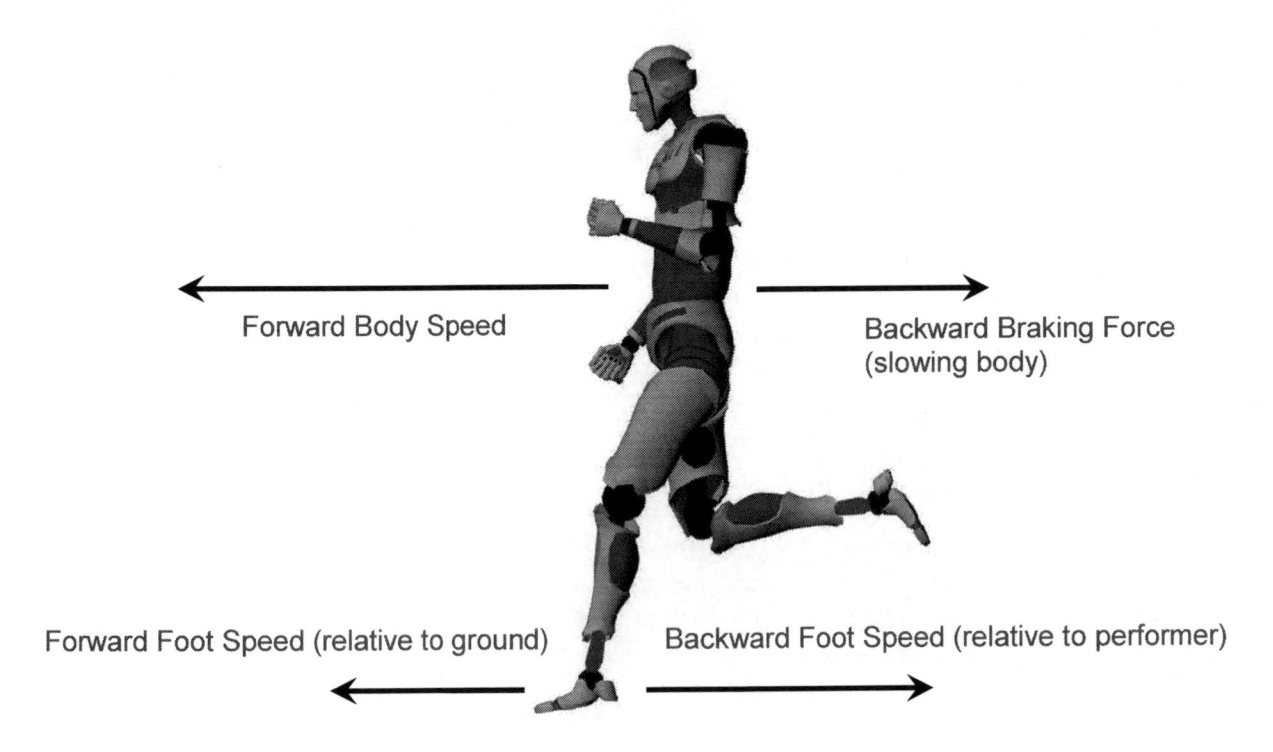

Critical Specific Performance Descriptors For the Short Hurdles

Figure 15-8: Horizontal Foot Speed at Touchdown Into the Hurdle

Horizontal Foot Speed at Touchdown

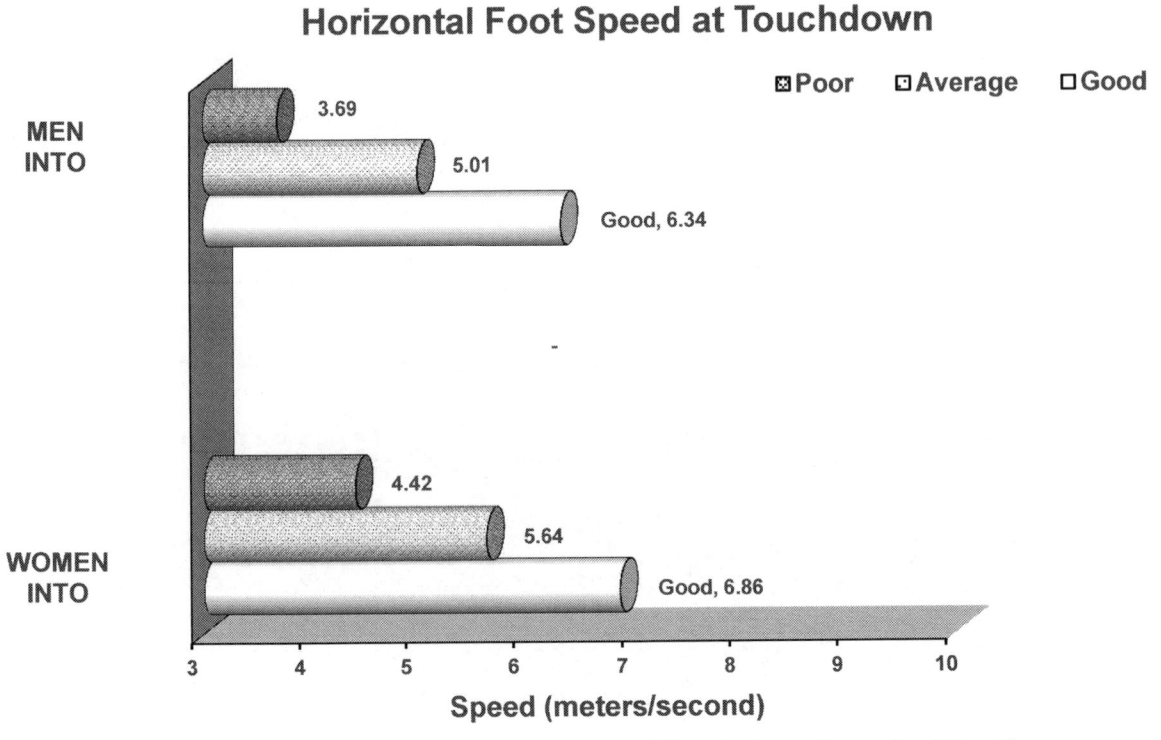

MEN INTO
- Poor: 3.69
- Average: 5.01
- Good: 6.34

WOMEN INTO
- Poor: 4.42
- Average: 5.64
- Good: 6.86

Speed (meters/second)

Figure 15-9: Horizontal Foot Speed at Touchdown Into the Hurdle

With this much braking, significant Horizontal Velocity is lost over each hurdle. Thus, one of the major goals of the three Steps between the barriers will be to regain (and possibly increase) this Velocity.

Steps Between the Hurdles

The action of Step One (Fall Step), coming off the hurdle, is an entirely different foot speed story. The purpose of this ground contact is to stop the fall of the body and direct the movement forward, toward the next barrier (Figure 15-10).

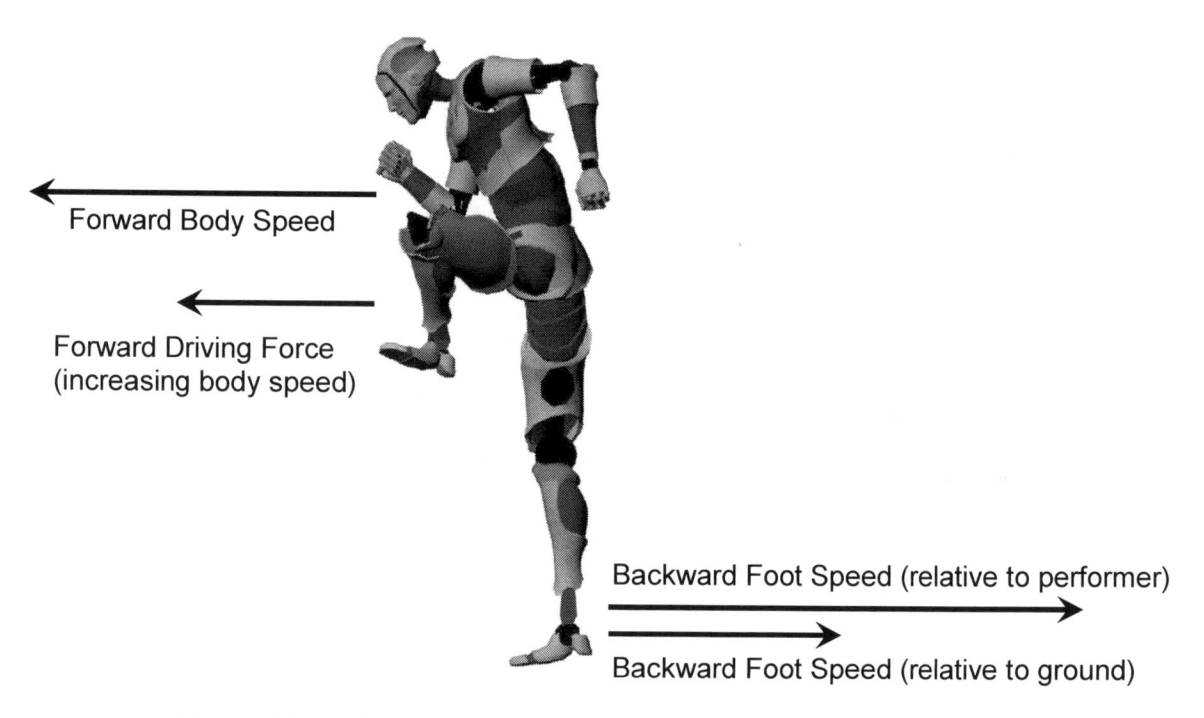

Figure 15-10: Step One Horizontal Foot Speed at Touchdown

Since a large amount of Vertical Velocity is not required until the next hurdle, the need for minimizing the braking force is critical if the Horizontal Velocity lost during hurdle clearance is to be regained. Thus, the foot speed with respect to the performer should be as high as possible, in the backwards direction, to reduce the forward braking at ground impact

In fact, coming off the barrier, good hurdlers can actually have the foot moving backward fast enough to produce a backward speed with respect to the ground. This eliminates virtually all forward braking and quickly moves the performer toward the next hurdle.

Critical Specific Performance Descriptors For the Short Hurdles

Chapter 14 identified Step Two (Shuffle Step) as the primary Step used to generate Horizontal Velocity during the Hurdle race. The image in Figure 15-11 shows the Horizontal foot speed at Touchdown, in relation to the performer and the ground, for Step Two. This Step is similar to Step One in its ability to generate Horizontal Velocity, however, since it starts in a more stable position, and the Ground Time is longer, it is much more effective.

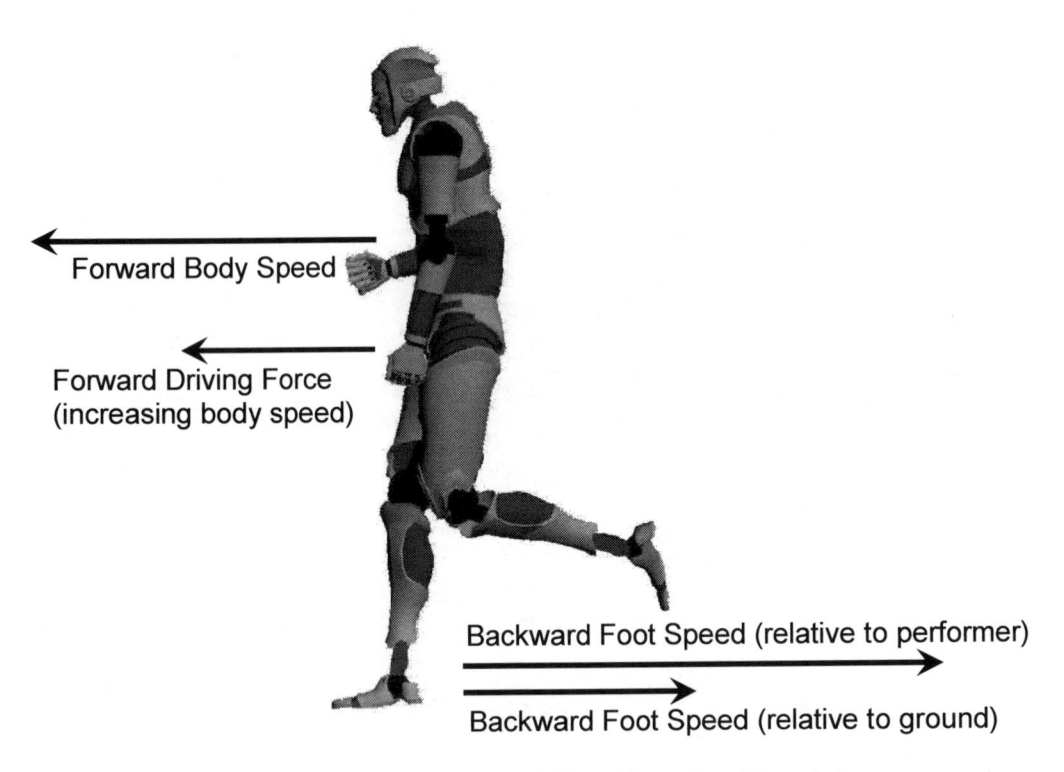

Figure 15-11: Step Two Horizontal Foot Speed at Touchdown

Figure 15-12 shows the Horizontal foot speed at Touchdown for each of the three Steps, in relation to the performer, going into and coming off the hurdle for all elite athletes analyzed to date. Since the results of the Men and Women are similar, they are presented as one.

The ability for Steps One and Two to produce Horizontal Velocity throughout the entire Ground Phase can be seen in the fact that, for the best hurdlers, the foot speed at Touchdown is greater than their forward Velocity (see Figure 14-1). Step Three does not allow the same positive contribution, but since its goal is to prepare for the next hurdle clearance, it is unable to continue this trend.

The importance of good Mechanics is underlined by the realization that, if the maximum improvement in Horizontal Velocity production is to be obtained in Steps One and Two, then the athlete must reach the highest level of performance for the foot speed results. If an athlete is only in the Average or Poor range, they will still be able to generate Velocity in the two Steps, but not as efficiently.

Horizontal Foot Speed at Touchdown

STEP ONE
- Poor: 7.5
- Average: 8.4
- Good: 9.3

STEP TWO
- Poor: 7.8
- Average: 8.6
- Good: 9.4

STEP THREE
- Poor: 5.2
- Average: 6.0
- Good: 6.8

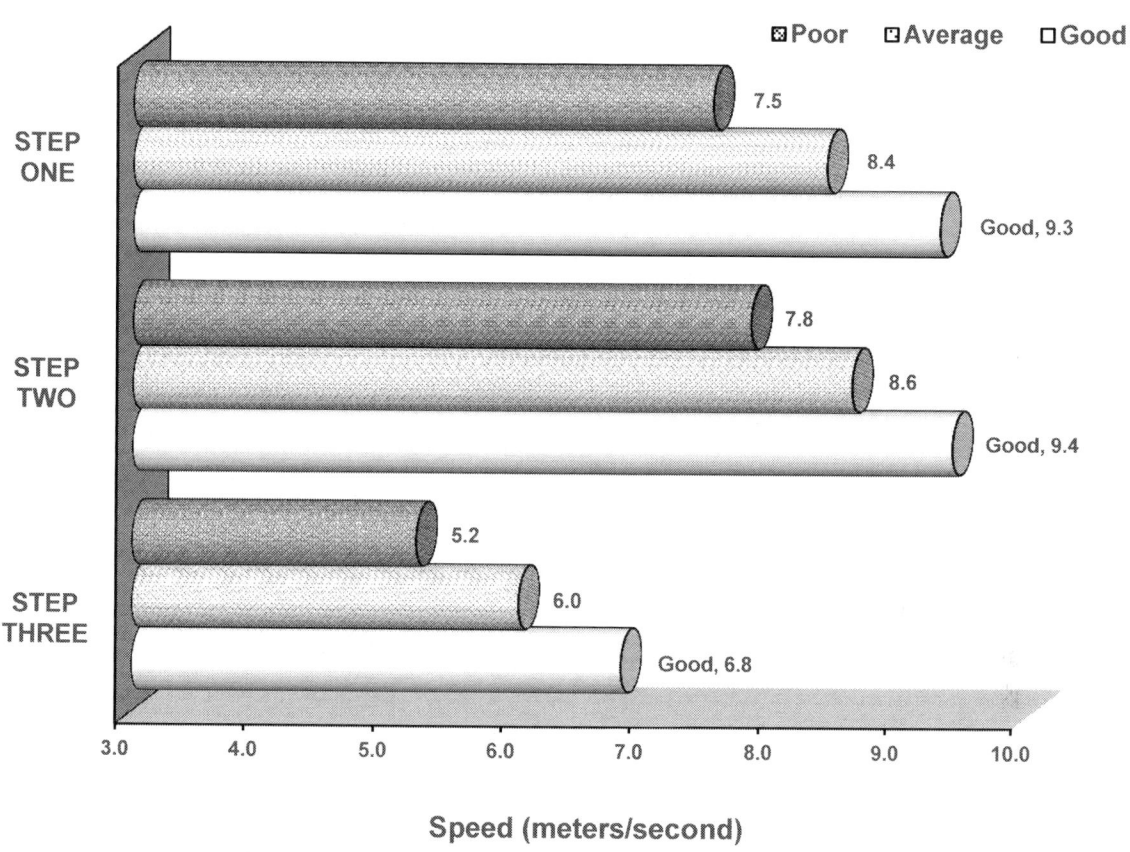

Speed (meters/second)

Figure 15-12: Horizontal Foot Speed at Touchdown Between the Hurdles

Horizontal Foot Distance at Touchdown

To take advantage of the foot speed at Touchdown, the hurdler must place the foot at the correct position when ground contact occurs.

Into the Hurdle

As discussed in the previous section, to produce Vertical Speed to clear the hurdle, while avoiding large amounts of forward braking, large amounts of leg speed and strength are needed. To give the upper and lower legs greater range of motion in order to project the body into the air, hurdlers land with the foot in front of the body as the hurdle stride is begun (Figure 15-13).

Although all hurdlers are forced to reach out and use the ground to help generate the required Vertical Velocity to clear the barrier, better athletes are able to minimize the foot distance by utilizing the strength of the upper leg extensors and lower leg flexors. Thus, with the ability to apply more muscular force to the ground, they can generate the necessary Vertical Speed to clear the barrier while minimizing ground contact time and forward braking.

As previously indicated, the research on hurdling indicates that the better elite athlete hurdlers are favoring a decrease in Ground Time, which rules out any increase in leg range of motion. Thus, they are actually minimizing the Horizontal Touchdown distance in an effort to minimize the Ground Time into the hurdle.

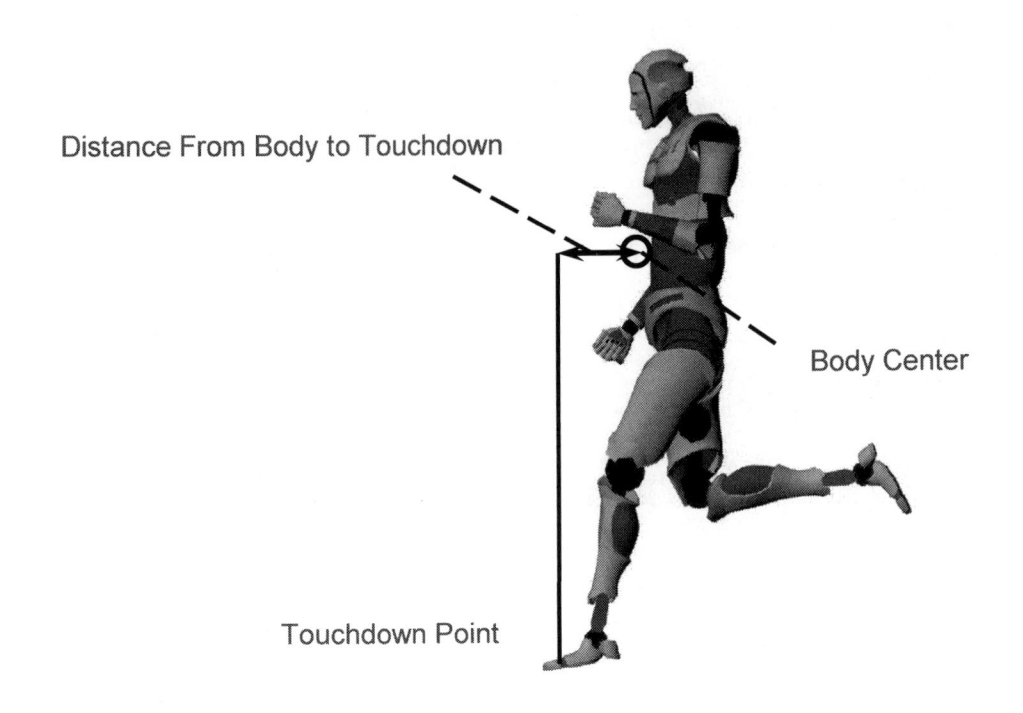

Figure 15-13: Horizontal Distance From the Foot to the Body Center at Touchdown Into the Hurdle

This result raises a number of questions concerning how the better hurdlers are minimizing this Touchdown distance going into the barrier. From the available data, it is evident that the performers are accomplishing this in three ways:

1. **Properly Preparing the Ground Leg for Touchdown**: This will be further discussed in the leg motion and speed results.

2. **Producing Better Hurdle Clearance Mechanics**: Since the reason the hurdler must increase the foot distance is to produce the Vertical lift needed to clear the hurdle, if this lift requirement can be minimized, then the foot distance can be reduced.

   The example previously presented indicated that, going into the hurdle, the elite athlete was able to generate an average Vertical force of 2024 Newtons (454 Pounds) during ground contact, which was sufficient to produce the required 2.23 meters per second change of Vertical Velocity during the elite Ground Time of .124 seconds. However, if the hurdler could improve the Hurdle technique to the point where they could squeeze over the barrier by only needing a 1.92 meters per second change of Vertical Velocity, the required Vertical force would be greatly reduced. Remembering that Newton's second law states:

   $$\text{Vertical Force} = \text{Mass} * (\text{Change in Vertical Velocity}) / \text{Ground Time}$$

   it is evident that a reduction in the required Velocity would decrease the force. In fact, the force savings of the example (from 2.23 to 1.92) would be 180 Newtons (40 Pounds). Thus, the hurdler could reduce the Body COG to foot distance since less force would be required.

3. **Developing Sufficient Leg Strength to Generate the Necessary Velocity During a Shorter Ground Time**: As previously discussed, the biggest problem in hurdling is to stop the downward fall of the body and produce upward projection into the Hurdle. To accomplish this, large Vertical forces must be produced during ground contact. The example previously presented indicated that, going into the hurdle, the elite athlete was able to generate an average Vertical force of 2024 Newtons (454 Pounds) during ground contact, which was sufficient to produce the required 2.23 meters per second change of Vertical Velocity during the elite Ground Time of .124 seconds.

   If, however, the athlete is unable to produce this large amount of ground force, the performance will not be elite in caliber. This can best be explained by assuming that the same 714 Newton (160 pound) hurdler used in the previous example was only able to generate 1670 Newtons (375 Pounds) of Vertical ground force. After subtracting the amount of force required to simply support the athlete's weight, the force remaining to alter the Vertical Velocity would be:

   $$\text{Vertical Force} = 1670 - 714 = 956 \text{ Newtons (215 Pounds)}$$

Now, with less than elite level of Vertical force, some compromises in performance must be made. Remembering that Newton's second law states:

Vertical Force = Mass*(Change in Vertical Velocity)/Ground Time

then, as Vertical Force decreases, the possible compromises must come from either Mass, Change in Vertical Velocity, or Ground Time. Since the mass of the athlete cannot be changed, this factor is not a possibility. Likewise, unless the hurdler is willing to severely decrease the Hurdle Stride Length (and hit every hurdle), the change in Vertical Velocity cannot be altered. This leaves only Ground Time as the variable that can be altered. In fact, if the Ground Time is increased from .124 to .170 seconds, then the athlete can produce the required Vertical Velocity with the decreased force potential.

The penalty for this increase in Ground Time is an increase in hurdle clearance time that is sufficient to take the performance out of the elite level. In fact, the force and Ground Time values presented in this example are typical for a collegiate level hurdler.

Thus, by developing the ability to produce greater ground forces, the elite hurdlers have the ability to decrease Ground Time (which decreases hurdle time) without affecting the other performance results (like Stride Length and hurdle clearance).

As can be seen, to minimize the Touchdown distance and get the most out of this action, the hurdler must be technically competent and very strong in those muscle groups that are active during this phase of the race. These groups include the hamstring and gluteal muscles since these are needed to pull the body over the Touchdown point during the initial portion of ground contact. More than any other factor, the strength of these muscles dictate the ability of a hurdler to produce an elite level of hurdle clearance.

Figure 15-14 shows the results for the Horizontal distance the foot is in front of the body at Touchdown into the hurdle, for all elite athletes analyzed to date.

It is surprising to realize that such a small difference in distance at Touchdown (7-8 centimeters) can shift an athlete from the best and the worst of the elite hurdlers. However, a with a ground force averaging over 2000 Newtons, with an initial spike of over 4000 (900 Pounds) at Touchdown (see Figure 13-1), it is easy to see how important it is to take the effort to control this result.

Horizontal Foot Distance at Touchdown

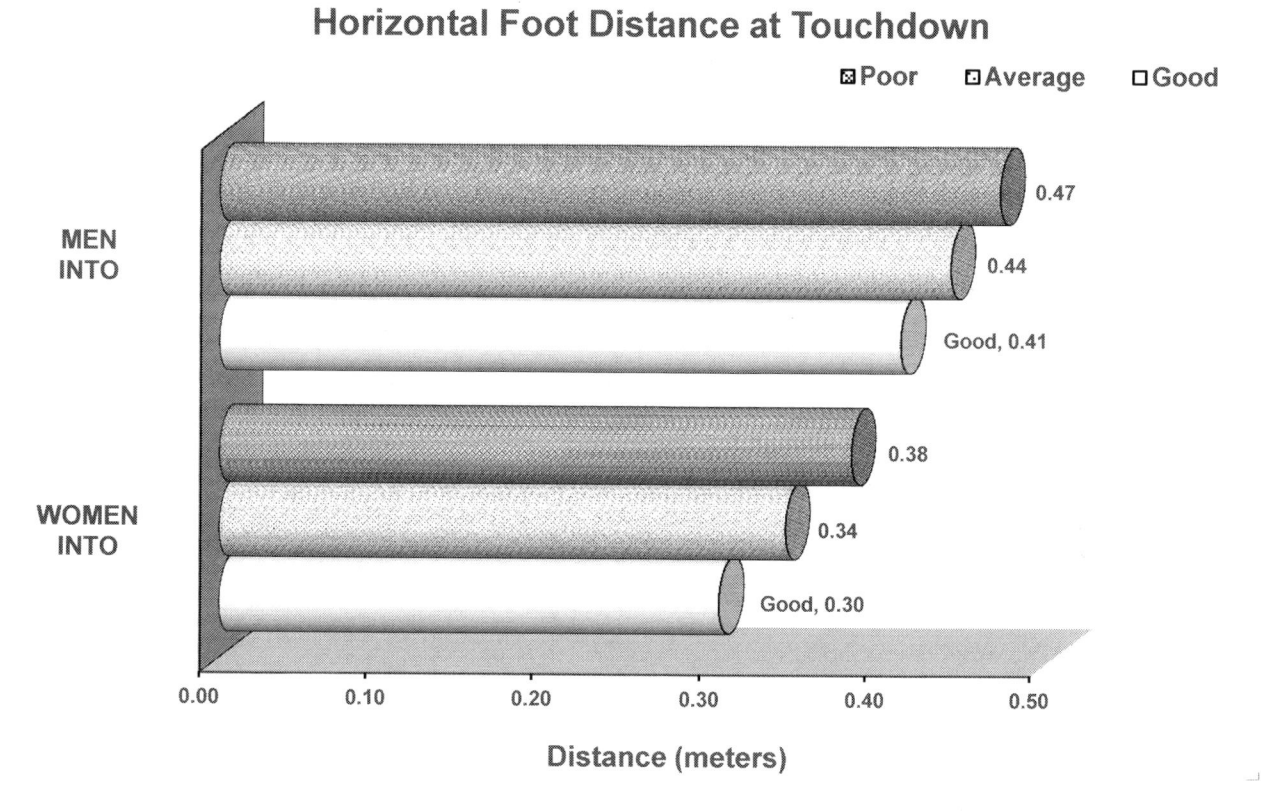

	Poor	Average	Good
MEN INTO	0.47	0.44	0.41
WOMEN INTO	0.38	0.34	0.30

Distance (meters)

Figure 15-14: Horizontal Foot Distance at Touchdown Into the Hurdle

Steps Between the Hurdles

In contrast to the problems encountered going into the barrier, the Mechanics of coming off and moving between the hurdles is far different. Since Vertical Velocity is not of importance (there is no barrier), and the premium is in generating Horizontal Velocity, Touchdown should occur with the foot as close to the body as possible. The best example of this occurs in Step One, as the hurdler comes off the barrier (Figure 15-15).

This position serves to virtually eliminate the forward braking at impact, and allows the hurdler to direct the stride off of the hurdle forward, toward the next hurdle. Better performers, in fact, have actually landed with the body ahead of the Touchdown point.

The landing position for Step Two (Figure 15-16) is considerably larger than Step One, however, since the athlete needs the time to accomplish all of the goals of this most critical Step (see Chapter 14), this increased distance is required. Fortunately, the high Horizontal foot speed at Touchdown for this Step (Figure 15-12) minimizes the detrimental effects of this position.

Finally, in preparation for the hurdle stride, the Touchdown distance for Step Three is similar to a typical Sprint Stride, which places it between those of Steps One and Two..

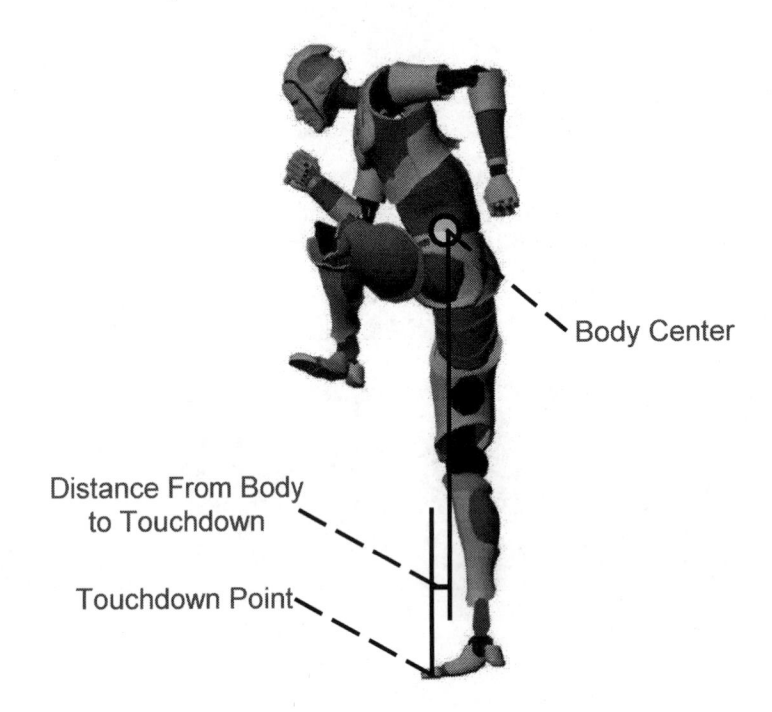

Critical Specific Performance Descriptors For the Short Hurdles

Figure 15-15: Horizontal Distance From the Foot to the Body Center at Touchdown Off the Hurdle (Step One)

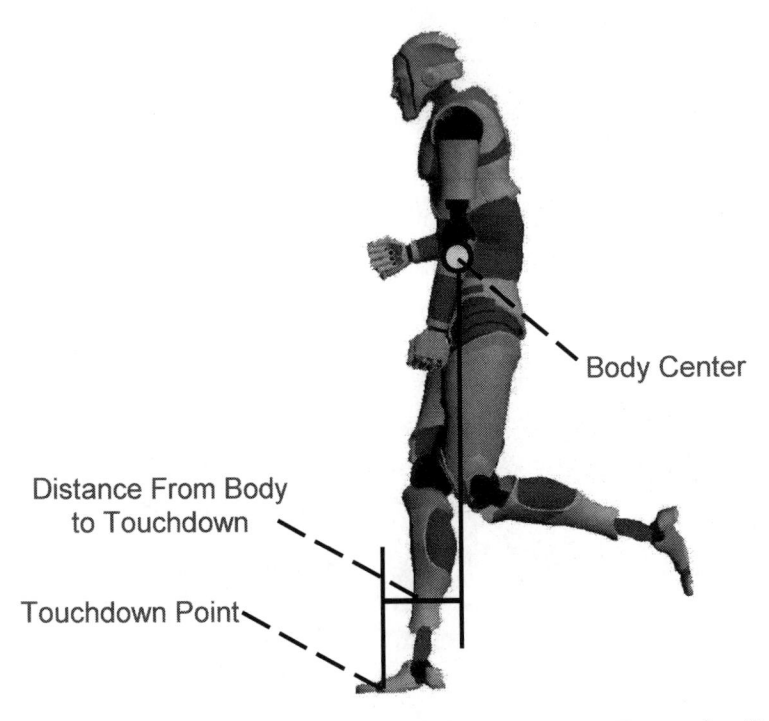

Figure 15-16: Horizontal Distance From the Foot to the Body Center at Touchdown for Step Two

For comparison purposes, Figure 15-17 shows all of the Touchdown distances created during hurdle interaction. As previously indicated, Step One (off the hurdle) has the smallest distance (1) and is focused on moving off the barrier. Step Two (2) is the most dynamic of the Steps between and is used to create the most Horizontal Velocity. Step Three (3) is used to set the body up for hurdle clearance, and is most like a Sprint landing. Finally, the Touchdown distance going into the barrier (4) demonstrates how much more "blocking" action must be done to generate the Vertical Velocity needed to clear the hurdle.

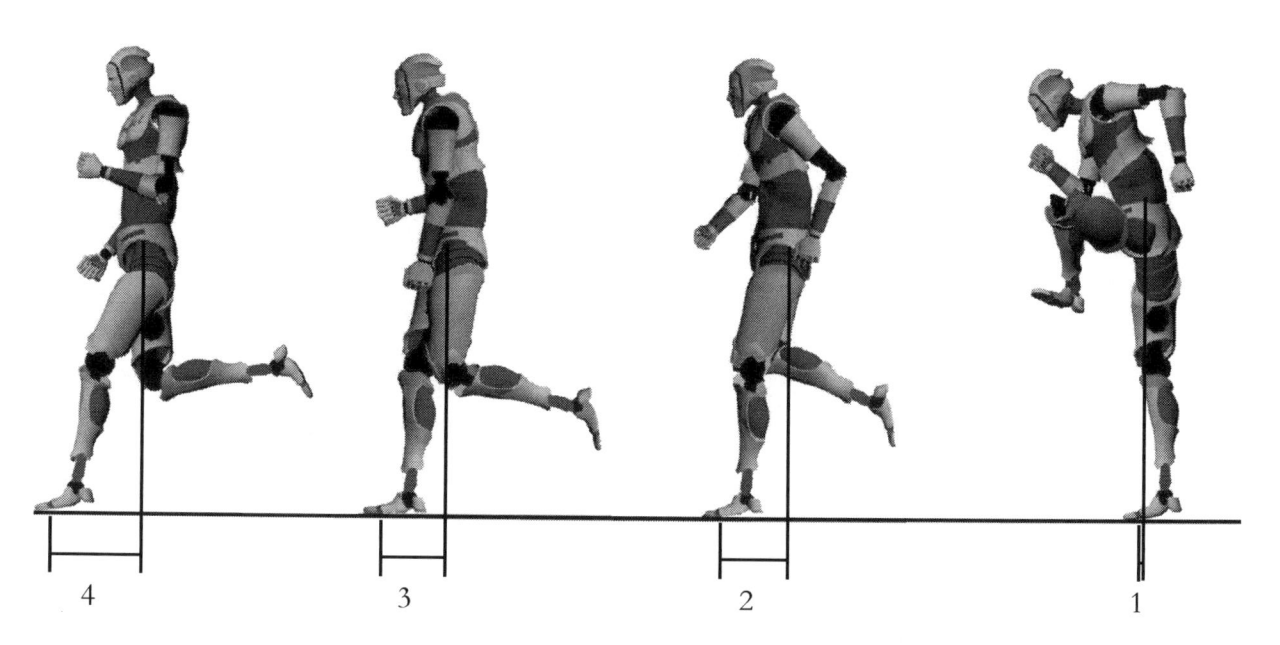

Figure 15-17: Horizontal Touchdown Distances Into and Between the Hurdles

Figure 15-18 shows the results for the Horizontal distance the foot is in front of the body at Touchdown for all three Steps between the hurdles for all elite athletes analyzed to date. For comparison purposes, the results from the Hurdle Stride (Figure 15-14) are also included. These numbers point to three important observations:

1. **The Best Minimize the Distance**: The best hurdlers produce smaller Touchdown distances for all three Steps. As in the Sprint (Figures 9-5 and 9-6), this serves to minimize the amount of Horizontal braking, but requires not only excellent Step Mechanics but also superior levels of leg strength.
2. **There are Gender Differences**: Due to the considerable difference in hurdle height between the two Events, even with their strength advantage the Men must use a greater body Touchdown distance going into the hurdle to help them generate sufficient Vertical Velocity to clear the barrier. Interestingly, the increased technical demands and the additional time

required to clear the hurdle allow the Men to land in a better position at the beginning of Step One.

Horizontal Foot Distance at Touchdown
Poor · Average · Good

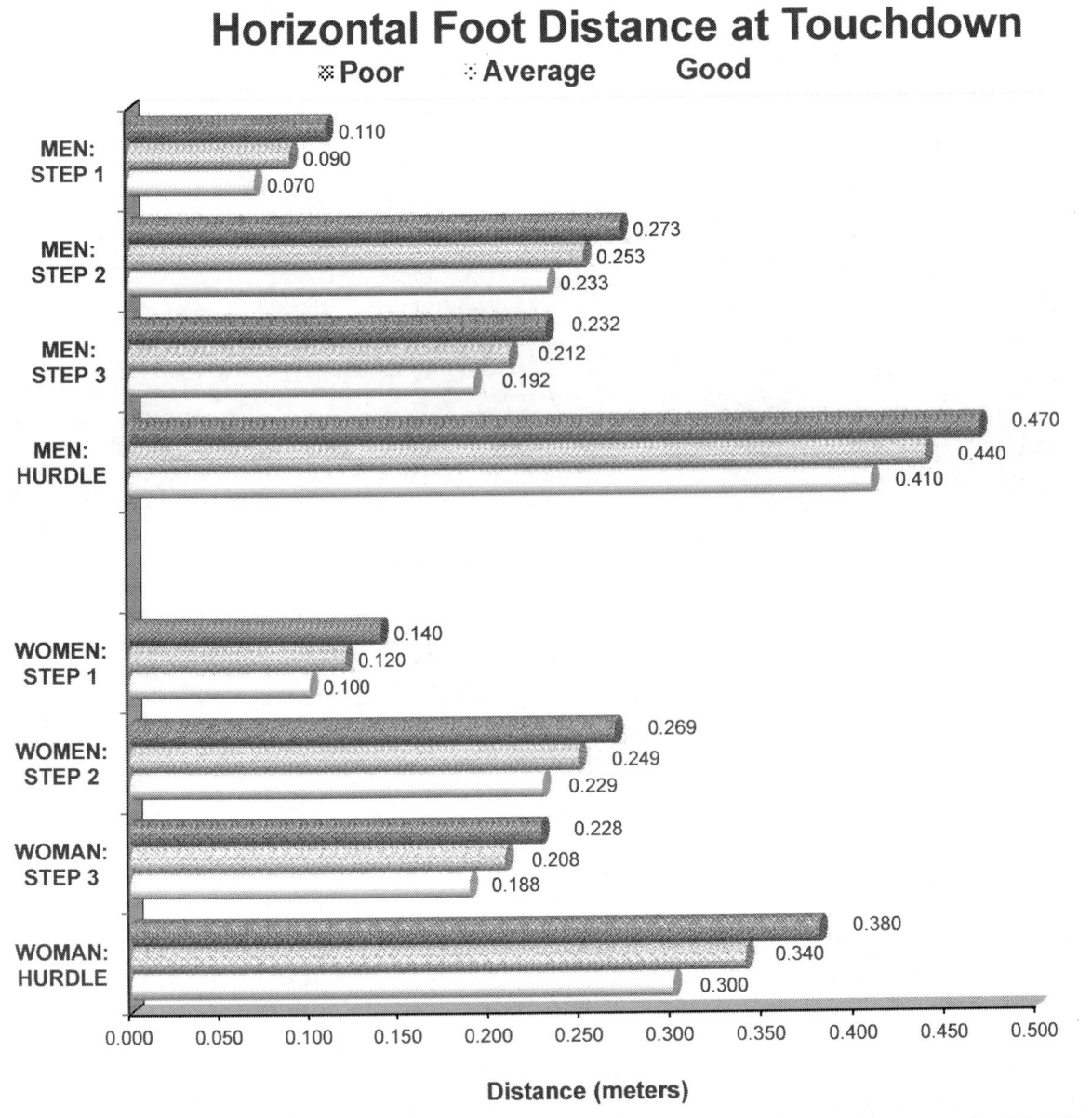

Category	Poor	Average	Good
MEN: STEP 1	0.110	0.090	0.070
MEN: STEP 2	0.273	0.253	0.233
MEN: STEP 3	0.232	0.212	0.192
MEN: HURDLE	0.470	0.440	0.410
WOMEN: STEP 1	0.140	0.120	0.100
WOMEN: STEP 2	0.269	0.249	0.229
WOMAN: STEP 3	0.228	0.208	0.188
WOMAN: HURDLE	0.380	0.340	0.300

Distance (meters)

Figure 15-18: Horizontal Foot Distance at Touchdown for the Steps Between the Hurdles

3. **There are Gender Similarities**: As can be seen in the Figure (15-18), the body Touchdown distances for Steps Two and Three are virtually the same for both Men and Women. However, due to the height (and leg length) differences, this indicates that Women have to work harder to achieve the goals of these two Steps.

Knee Separation Distances at Touchdown

As is true in Sprint Mechanics (Chapter 9), the amount of knee separation at Touchdown throughout the Hurdle race can be used as a visual benchmark indicating how well an athlete is shifting their movements toward the front of the body as ground contact is initiated.

Into the Hurdle

The better the preparation going into the barrier, the closer the knees are at Touchdown (Figure 15-19). However, even the best hurdlers must allow a relatively large separation due to the Vertical demands of the hurdle stride.

There are many reasons why this knee separation result may have to be increased:

1. If the athlete poorly manages the Steps between the hurdle and must reach with the Touchdown leg to achieve the proper distance to the hurdle.
2. If the hurdler does not have sufficient strength to generate the additional forces needed to clear the barrier.
3. If the performer has poor Hurdle Mechanics, and requires additional force to jump even higher than necessary.

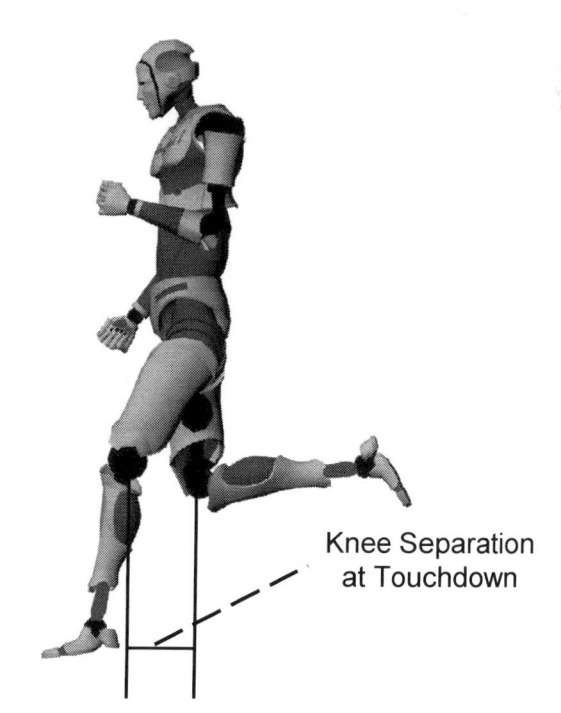

Figure 15-19: Knee Separation at Touchdown Into the Hurdle

All of these situations will result in a poor landing position at Touchdown going into the hurdle, which will, in turn, demand a greater range of motion for the recovery (Lead) leg, increased Ground Time, and increased force (and Energy) expenditure. For all of these reasons, when multiplied by the ten hurdles that will make the same excessive demands, this situation can have a devastating effect on performance.

The actual values for knee separation at Touchdown going into the hurdle are shown in Figure 15-20. Note that, even with their advantage in strength levels, the extreme difference in Hurdle heights between the two Short races force the Men to allow a greater separation distance to give them time to generate the additional effort to clear the barrier.

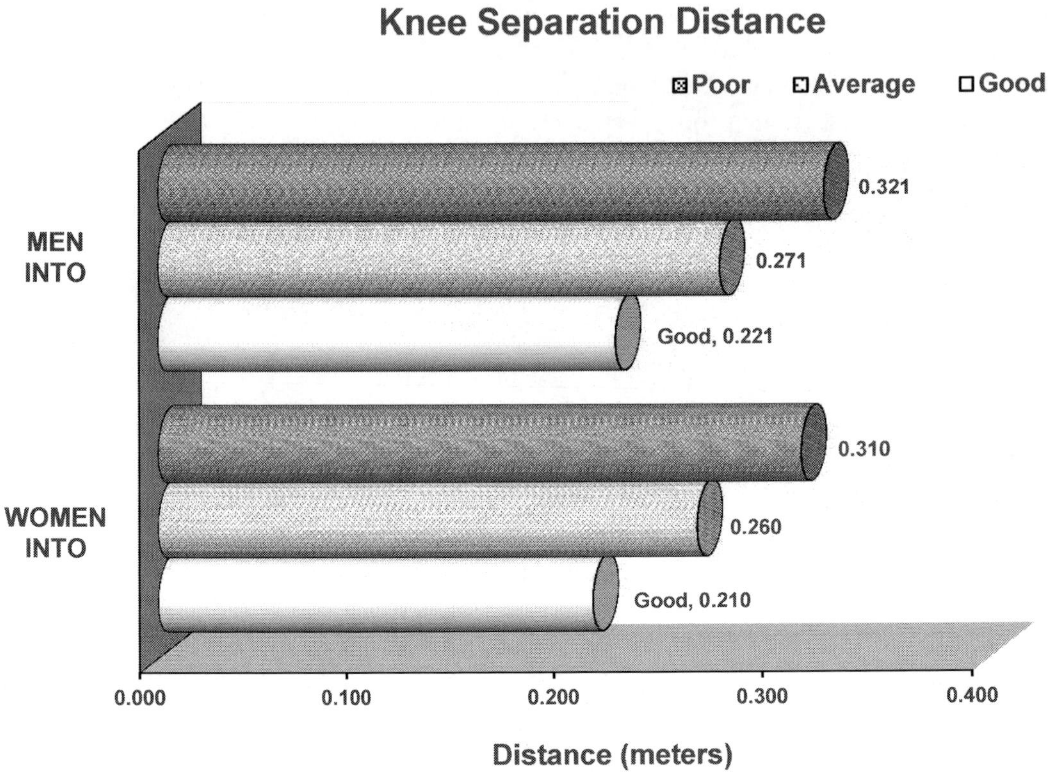

Knee Separation Distance

	Poor	Average	Good
MEN INTO	0.321	0.271	0.221
WOMEN INTO	0.310	0.260	0.210

Distance (meters)

Figure 15-20: Knee Separation Distances Into the Hurdles

Between the Hurdles

The first major indicator of just how Front Side dominant the Steps between the hurdles are can be visually seen in Figure 15-21. Coming off the hurdle (A), Step One is initiated with the Trail Leg being placed well in front of the Ground Leg at Touchdown. This extreme Front Side position, found in no other Track event, demonstrates the athlete's effort to drive off the barrier and regain as much Horizontal Velocity as possible.

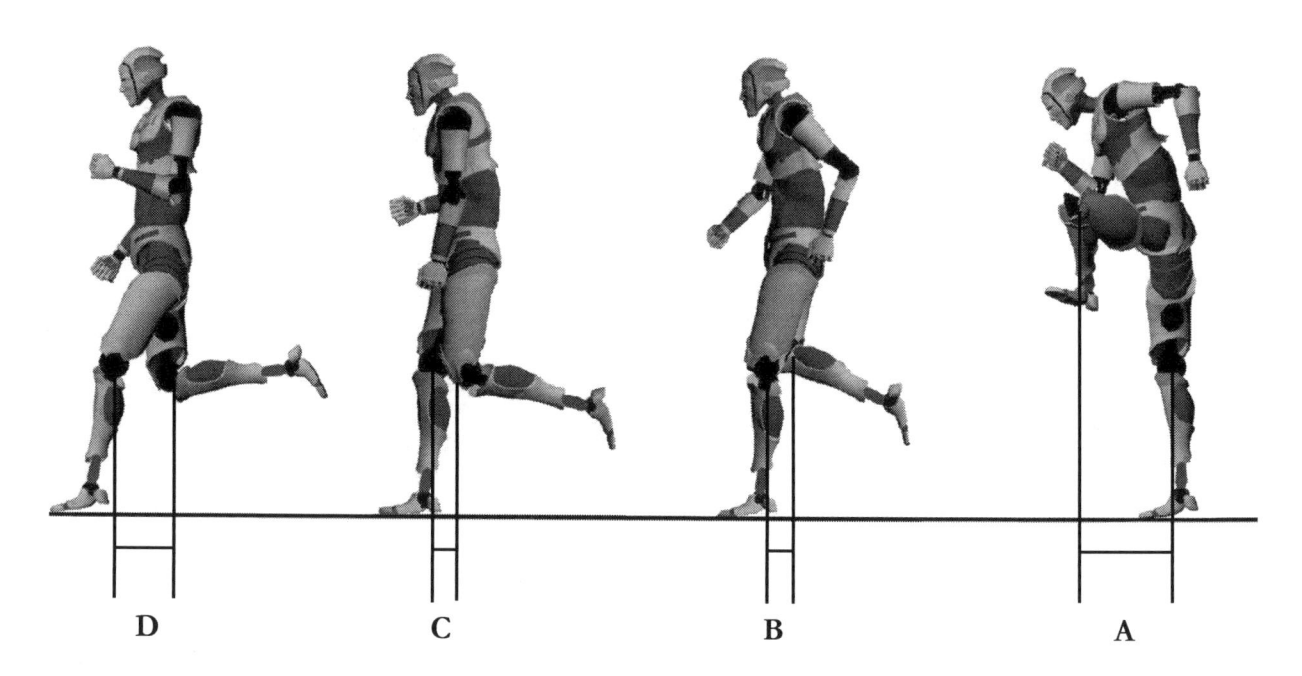

Figure 15-21: Knee Touchdown Separation Distances Between the Hurdles

Even though Step Two must produce the largest Stride Length, the better hurdlers continue the Front Side emphasis by landing with the knees almost together (B). Achieving this position is the key to producing the goals of Step Two, and a major contributor to the success of the Steps between the hurdles.

If Steps One and Two are executed properly, the Front Side action can continue into Step 3 (C). This successful preparation allows the athlete to shorten the Prep Step and move into the Hurdle Stride.

For comparison purposes, the relatively large knee separation at Touchdown going into the hurdle (D) is shown. As mentioned previously, the large Vertical demands of clearing the hurdle forces even the most powerful athletes to utilize greater knee separation to help generate the necessary Vertical Velocity.

The actual values for the knee separation at Touchdown are shown in Figure 15-22. For comparison purposes, the results from the Hurdle Stride (Figure 15-20) are also included. Note that, throughout the race, the better elite performers maximize the knee separation coming off the Hurdle (in front of the body), while minimizing the separation between the barriers.

Knee Separation Distance

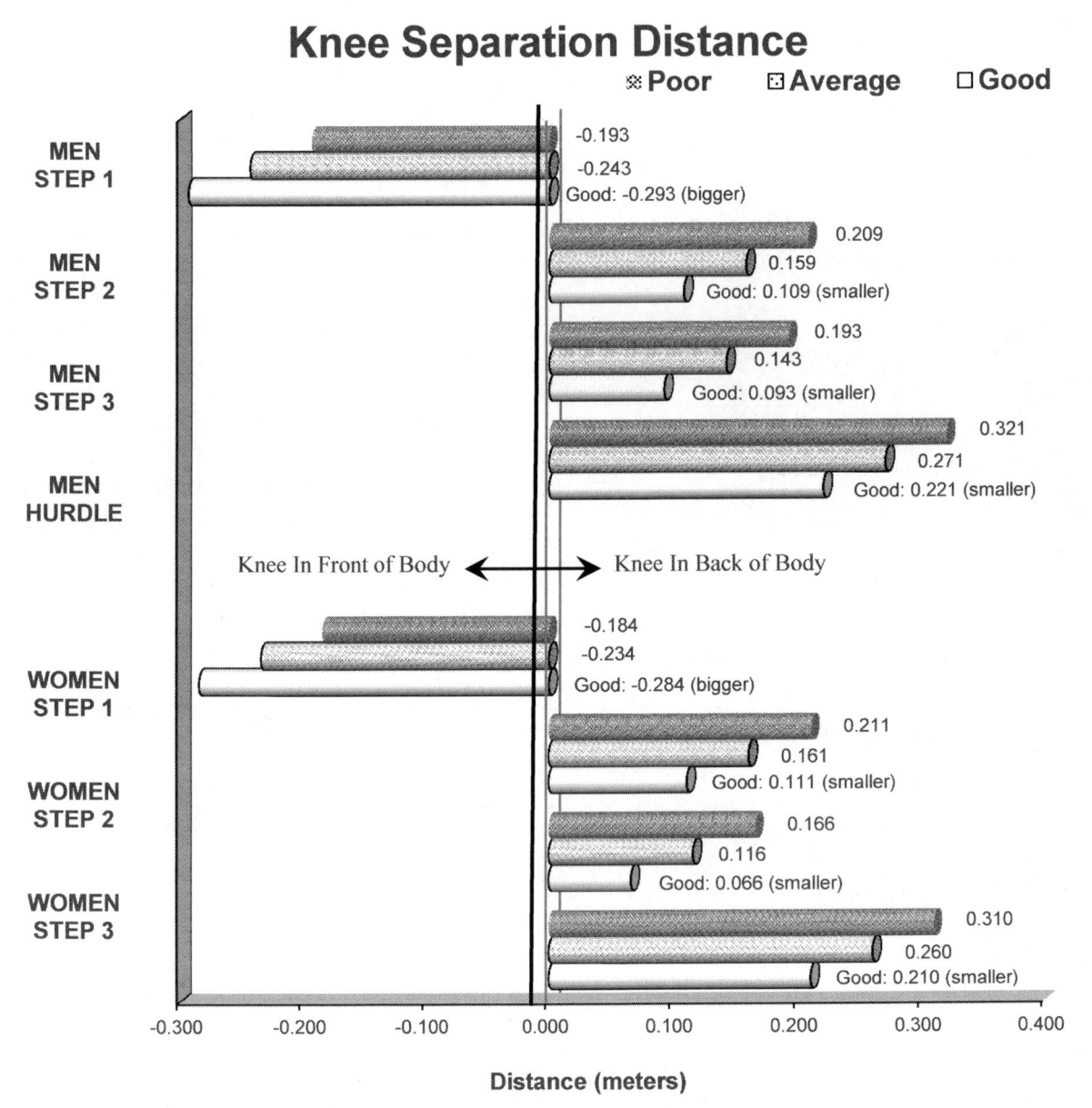

MEN STEP 1
- Poor: -0.193
- Average: -0.243
- Good: -0.293 (bigger)

MEN STEP 2
- Poor: 0.209
- Average: 0.159
- Good: 0.109 (smaller)

MEN STEP 3
- Poor: 0.193
- Average: 0.143
- Good: 0.093 (smaller)

MEN HURDLE
- Poor: 0.321
- Average: 0.271
- Good: 0.221 (smaller)

← Knee In Front of Body   Knee In Back of Body →

WOMEN STEP 1
- Poor: -0.184
- Average: -0.234
- Good: -0.284 (bigger)

WOMEN STEP 2
- Poor: 0.211
- Average: 0.161
- Good: 0.111 (smaller)

WOMEN STEP 3
- Poor: 0.166
- Average: 0.116
- Good: 0.066 (smaller)

WOMEN STEP 3
- Poor: 0.310
- Average: 0.260
- Good: 0.210 (smaller)

Distance (meters)

Figure 15-22: Knee Separation Distances for the Steps Between the Hurdles

Upper Leg Motion

Whenever results of the legs are being presented, the critical performance producers are finally being addressed. As long as the core trunk strength is sufficient to allow the legs to exert their maximum force potential, they will always the key to the success of the event.

Into and Over the Hurdle

There are three critical positions for the upper leg during ground contact of hurdle clearance; the positions at Touchdown and Takeoff going into, and maximum flexion going over the barrier (Figure 15-23).

As was the case in Sprinting, the better hurdlers tend to maximize upper leg extension at Touchdown (on the runner shown, this would produce a smaller angle) and minimize extension at Takeoff (a larger angle). The large extension at Touchdown is produced to minimize body to foot Touchdown distance and, thus, decrease braking forces. The large extension at Takeoff is needed to provide the Vertical lift needed to clear the hurdle.

These leg motions going into the hurdle are produced to minimize Ground Time and make leg recovery as efficient as possible. It must be emphasized, however, that a very good angle at one position is only beneficial if the other result is acceptable. Poor results here commonly indicate a lack of leg strength (indicated by insufficient extension at Touchdown or excessive extension at Takeoff).

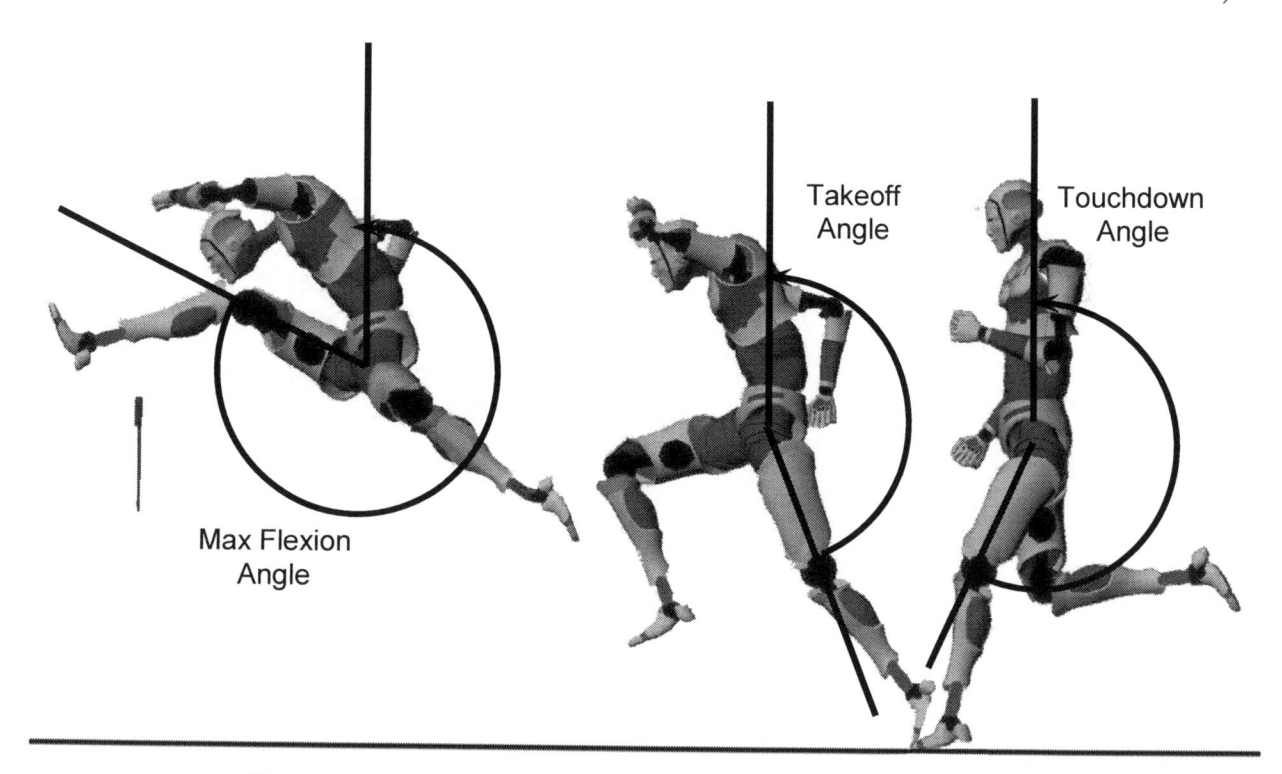

Figure 15-23: Upper Leg Positions Into and Over the Hurdle

Figure 15-24 shows the results for the upper leg motion into and over the hurdle for all elite athletes analyzed to date. Note that, although the Touchdown position for the Men and Women are virtually the same, the Women extend the upper leg significantly more in an effort to produce Vertical Velocity at Takeoff. Likewise, due to the difference in hurdle height, the Men must produce more upper leg flexion going over the barrier.

Upper Leg Motion: Into and Over the Hurdle

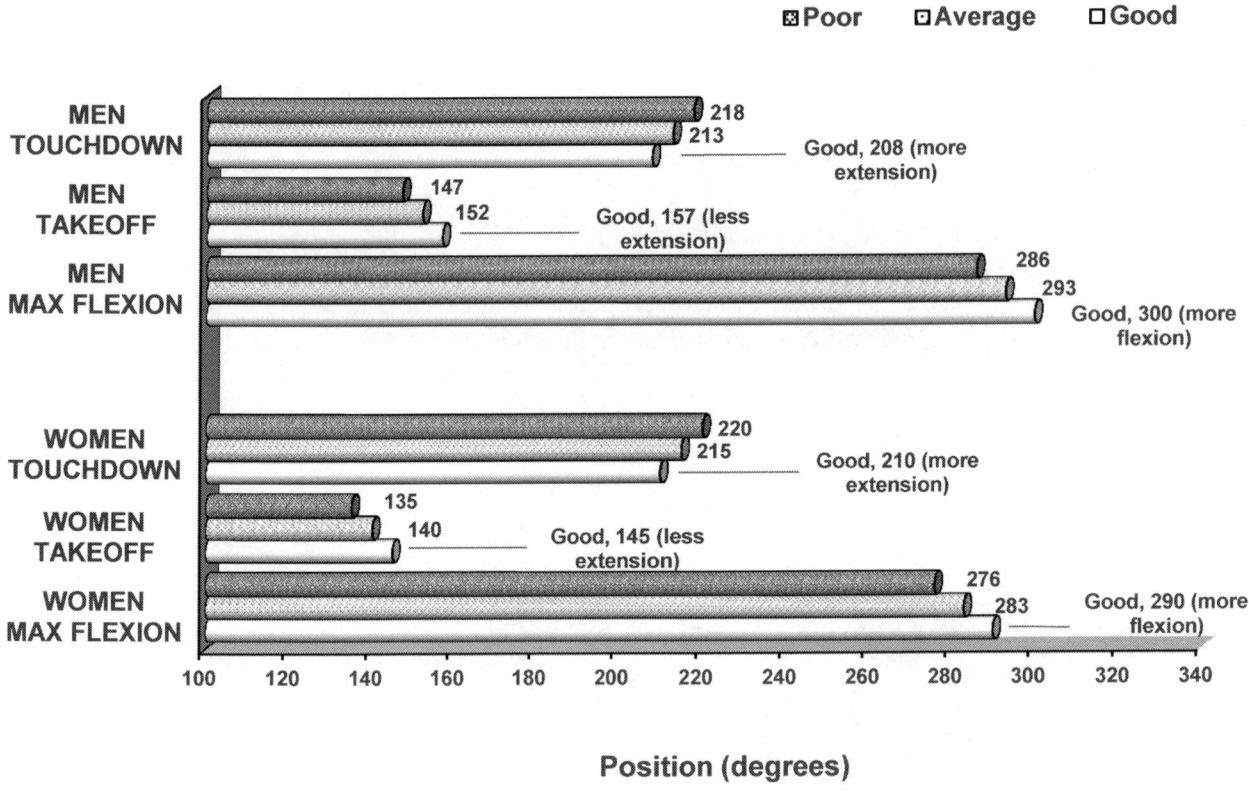

■ Poor   ▨ Average   □ Good

Category	Poor	Average	Good
MEN TOUCHDOWN	218	213	208 (more extension)
MEN TAKEOFF	147	152	157 (less extension)
MEN MAX FLEXION	286	293	300 (more flexion)
WOMEN TOUCHDOWN	220	215	210 (more extension)
WOMEN TAKEOFF	135	140	145 (less extension)
WOMEN MAX FLEXION	276	283	290 (more flexion)

Position (degrees)

Figure 15-24: Upper Leg Motion Into and Over the Hurdle

Between the Hurdles

Step One, coming off the barrier, has three performance related positions for the upper leg. The first is the position of the Trail Leg at Touchdown (Figure 15-25). The best hurdlers recover the leg both high and forward, producing a large maximum flexion position. This position allows the athlete to produce a greater downward and backward action at Touchdown at the end of Step One. This allows Step Two to halt the downward fall of the hurdle and, most importantly, generate Horizontal Velocity down the track.

Trail Leg Flexion Angle

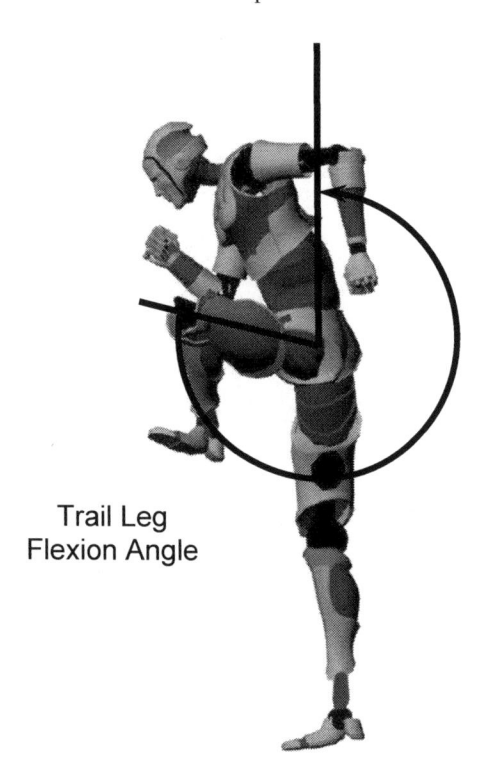

Figure 15-25: Trail Leg Upper Leg Motion at Touchdown Coming Off the Hurdle (Step One)

The final Step One upper leg positions are produced by the Lead Leg. Coming off of the hurdle (Figure 15-26), the better hurdlers tend to maximize upper leg extension at Touchdown (on the runner shown, this would produce a smaller angle), while minimizing upper leg extension at Takeoff (in this case, a larger angle).

The large extension at Touchdown is again produced to minimize body to foot Touchdown distance and, thus, decrease braking forces. Since Vertical emphasis is not needed coming off of the hurdle, upper leg extension is minimized at Takeoff to decrease Ground Time.

As in the upper leg motion into the hurdle, these leg motions coming off of the hurdle are produced to minimize Ground Time and make leg recovery as efficient as possible. It must be emphasized, however, that a very good angle at one position is only beneficial if the other result is acceptable.

Poor results here commonly indicate poor Mechanics, or a lack of leg strength (indicated by excessive extension at Takeoff).

Poor Hurdle Mechanics results in the athlete producing insufficient extension at Touchdown, which places the foot well in front of the body at Touchdown. This is one of the most detrimental outcomes in the Event since it hinders the fall of the body off of the barrier, as well as producing unwanted Horizontal braking during Step One. This, in turn, forces the performer to over-extend the upper leg at Takeoff in an attempt to recover the lost momentum, further detracting from the goals of Step One.

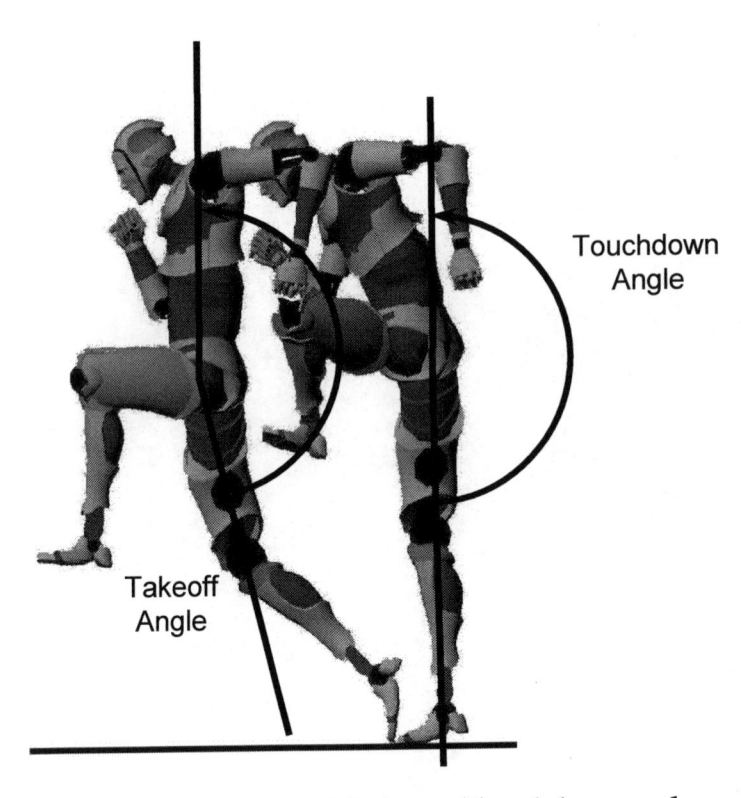

Figure 15-26: Lead Leg Upper Leg Motion at Touchdown and Takeoff Coming Off the Hurdle (Step One)

Figure 15-27 shows the actual results for the upper leg motion off the hurdle for all elite athletes analyzed to date (results for Men and Women are close enough to be shown as one).

The degree that Trail Leg flexion is emphasized can be seen in the fact that it exceeds what is generated in the Sprint Stride by 30 degrees. This extreme position places the foot three times higher from the track, providing a powerful position from which to attack the next Ground Phase.

The goal of Step One to Fall off the barrier is achieved by minimizing the range of motion of the upper leg during ground Contact. As seen in the Figure, the total range of motion, from Touchdown to Takeoff is a mere 25 degrees (185-160). The realization that this is **70 degrees less than the range of motion found in the Sprint** underscores just how compact this action off the barrier is executed by the top elite hurdlers.

Critical Specific Performance Descriptors For the Short Hurdles

Upper Leg Angles Off the Hurdle

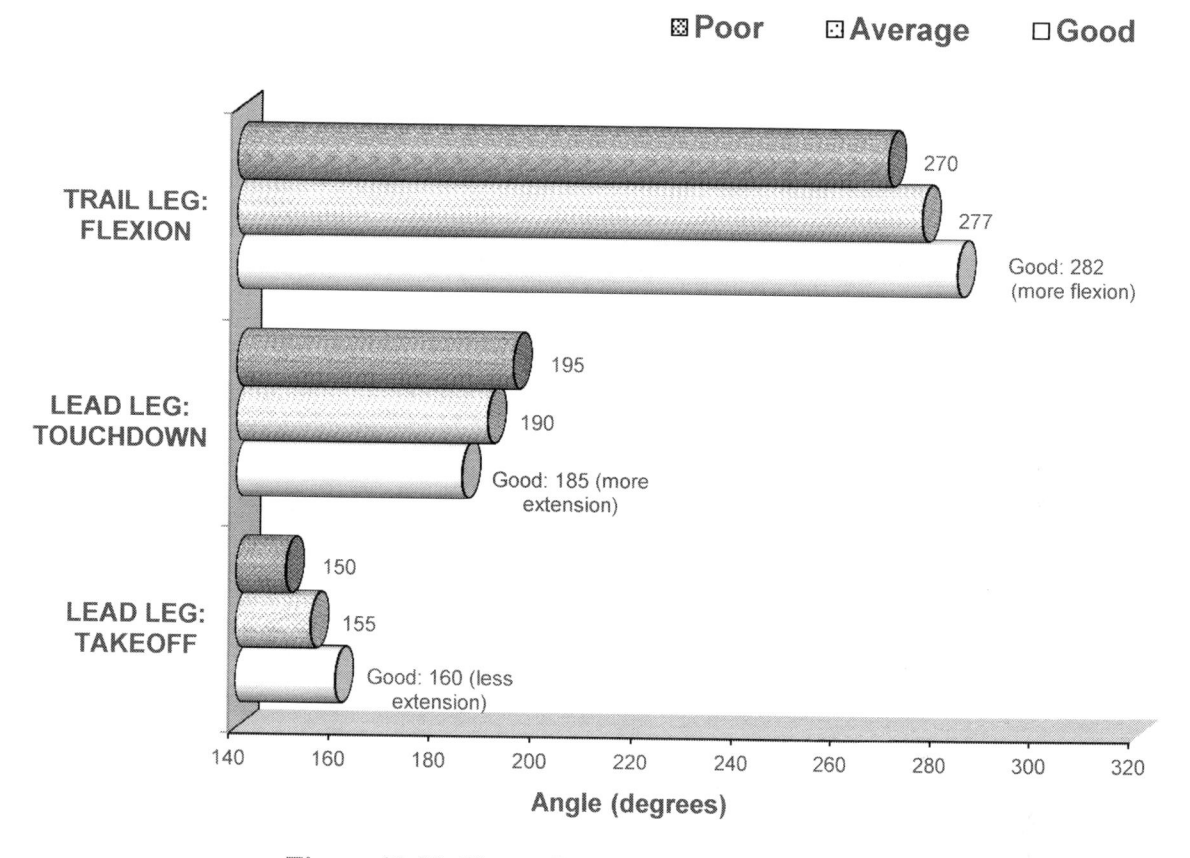

■ Poor ▦ Average □ Good

TRAIL LEG: FLEXION
- 270
- 277
- Good: 282 (more flexion)

LEAD LEG: TOUCHDOWN
- 195
- 190
- Good: 185 (more extension)

LEAD LEG: TAKEOFF
- 150
- 155
- Good: 160 (less extension)

Angle (degrees)

Figure 15-27: Upper Leg Motion Off the Hurdle

Technically speaking, Step One is the most difficult portion of the entire race. If not executed exactly right, it leads to the greatest decrement in performance. If properly executed, however, Step One sets up the next two Steps to generate Horizontal Velocity and prepare the athlete to attack the next hurdle.

For both Steps Two and Three (Figure 15-28), the goal of leading with the hips and maintaining the Front Side emphasis can be seen in the continued truncated upper leg extension at Takeoff (A).

In contrast to Step One, the full flexion position (B) is minimized in both Steps to allow the hips to lead the drive toward the next hurdle, emphasize the Horizontal projection, as well as controlling the Stride Lengths.

For comparison, the full extension (A) and full flexion (B) positions of the Sprint Stride are shown in Figure 15-29. Note the decrease in upper leg range of motion due to both the decrease in extension (Front Side emphasis) and flexion (Horizontal projection and Stride Length control).

Critical Specific Performance Descriptors For the Short Hurdles

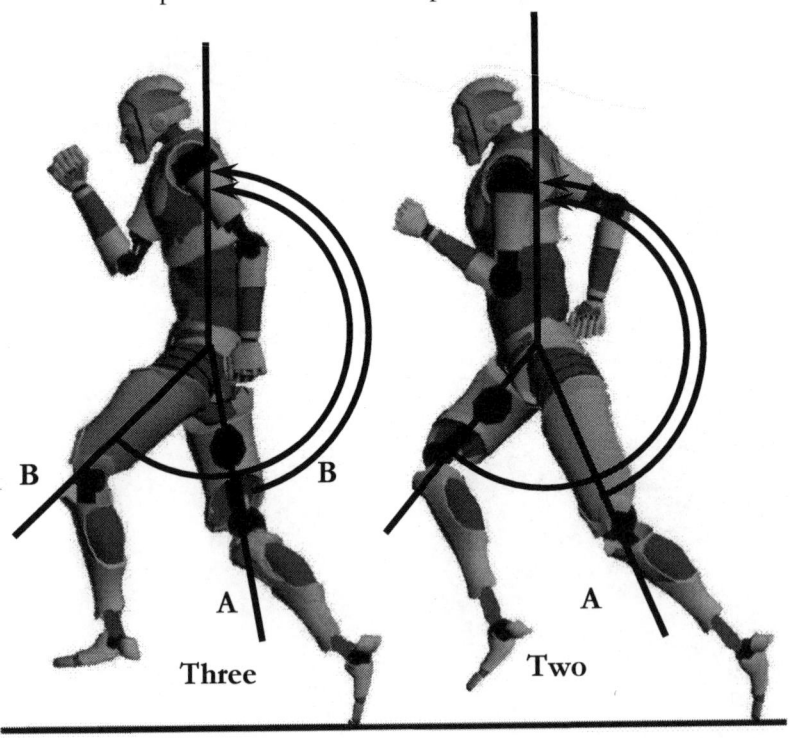

Figure 14-28: Step Two and Three Upper Leg Full Extension (A) and Full Flexion (B) Between the Hurdles

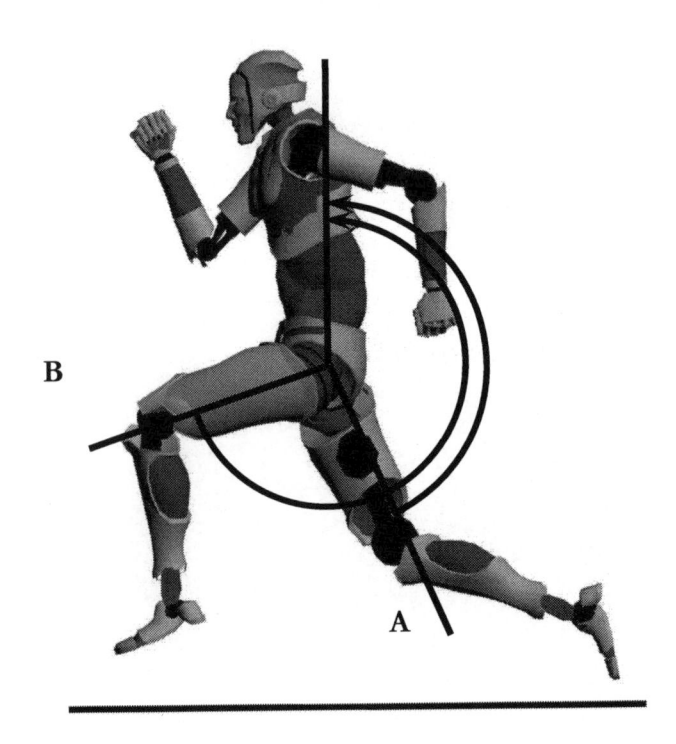

Figure 15-29: Upper Leg Full Extension (A) and Full Flexion (B) for the Sprint Stride

The actual angular values for the upper leg full extension and flexion angles for Steps Two and Three are shown in Figure 15-30.

The magnitude of the upper leg Velocity at Touchdown coming off of the hurdle indicates just how hard the best performers are moving toward the next barrier. The mechanical precision required to land with an extended leg, directly under the body, at these rotational speeds is extremely demanding.

Upper Leg Angles

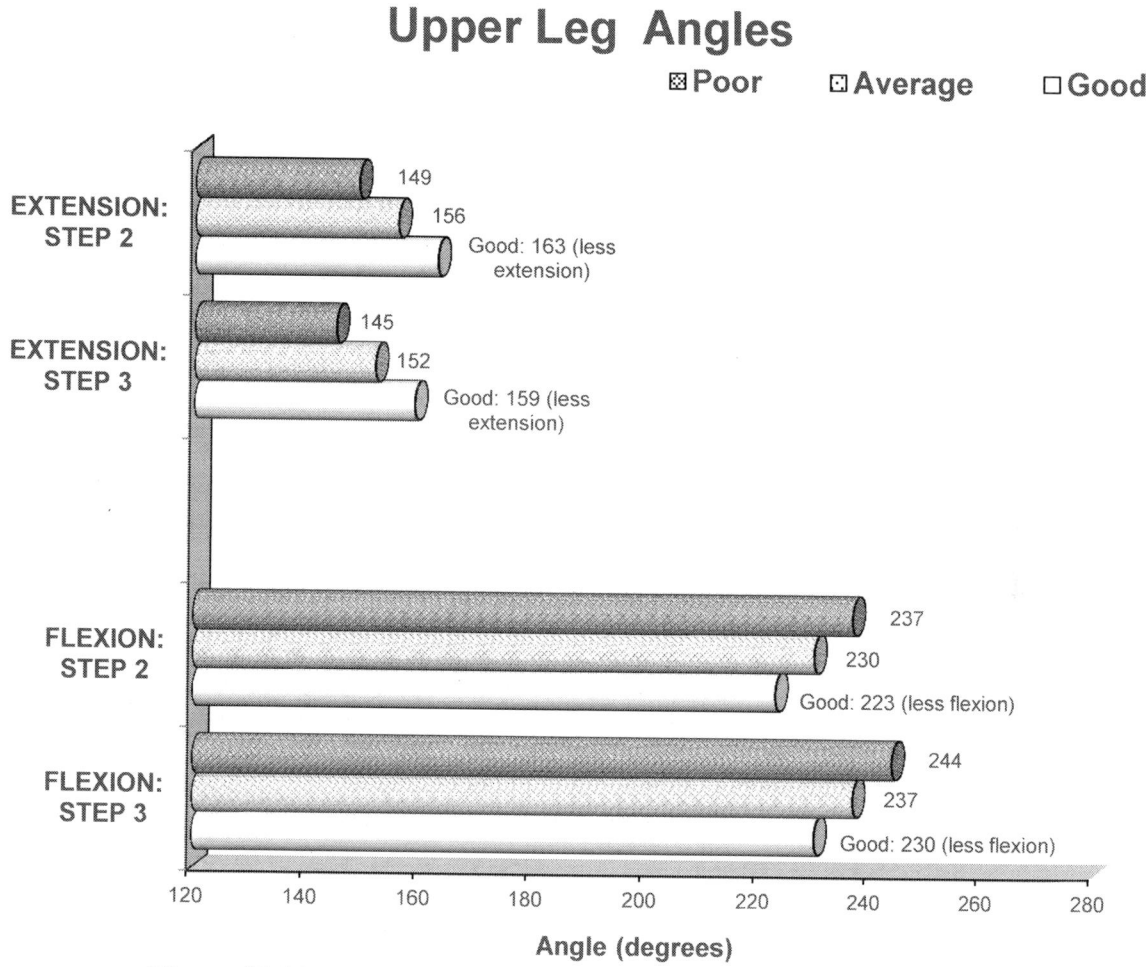

■ Poor   ▨ Average   ☐ Good

EXTENSION: STEP 2
- Poor: 149
- Average: 156
- Good: 163 (less extension)

EXTENSION: STEP 3
- Poor: 145
- Average: 152
- Good: 159 (less extension)

FLEXION: STEP 2
- Poor: 237
- Average: 230
- Good: 223 (less flexion)

FLEXION: STEP 3
- Poor: 244
- Average: 237
- Good: 230 (less flexion)

Angle (degrees)

Figure 15-30: Upper Leg Angles at Full Extension and Full Flexion for Steps 2 and 3 Between the Hurdles

Note that, at Touchdown, the extension angles for the better hurdlers are always **larger** than the less proficient performers. Likewise, at Takeoff, the extension angles for the better hurdlers are always **smaller**. This supports the conclusion that, during the entire Hurdle race, the better athletes are leading with the hips, shortening the Ground Time, and using Front Side Mechanics to a greater extent.

As is true in Sprint Mechanics, the ability to produce superior upper leg Mechanics in Hurdling depends not only in understanding (and executing) the proper Mechanics, but also having the strength and power to take advantage of the superior movement patterns. Suffice it to say, without great levels of strength and power, the proper Hurdle Mechanics cannot be produced.

Upper Leg Rotational Speed

To get the most out of the legs during ground contact over and between the hurdles, the upper legs must possess great speed and strength. Of all of the specific performance variables, **upper leg rotational speed is the most critical Specific Performance Descriptor in the production of an elite Hurdle performance**.

Into the Hurdle

At Touchdown going into the hurdle, the upper leg should be rapidly extending. As seen in Figure 15-31, by extending, the backward foot speed with respect to the performer is increased, which decreases the forward braking going into the hurdle. Then, during ground contact, the speed of extension should increase to a maximum, projecting the hurdler over the Ground Leg and toward the barrier.

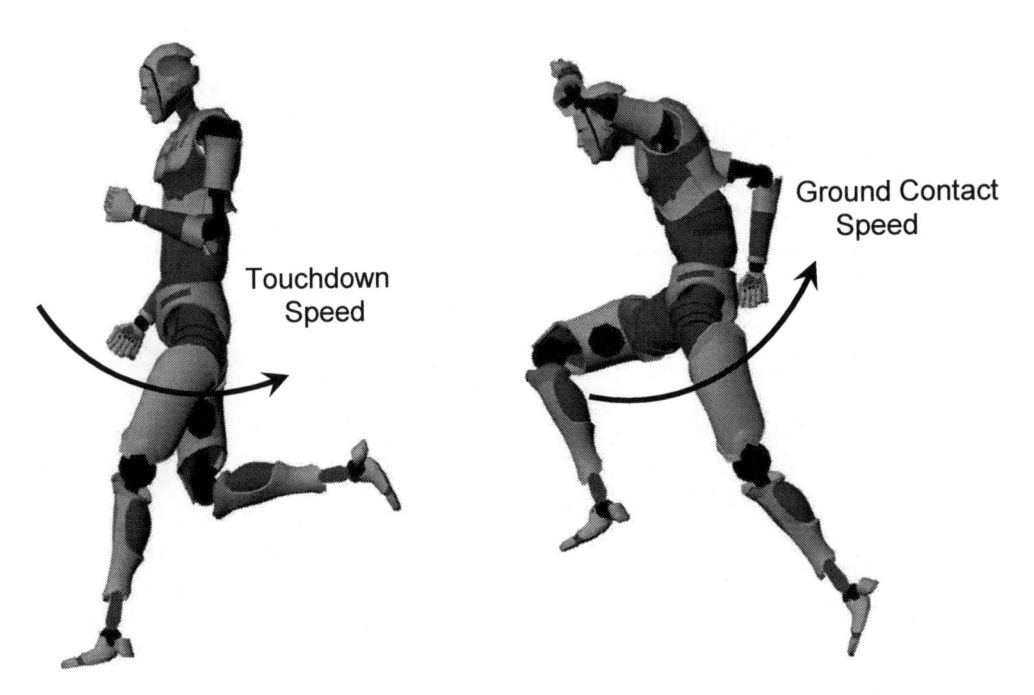

Figure 15-31: Upper Leg Rotational Speed at Touchdown and Ground Contact Going Into the Hurdle

The athlete that can generate high upper leg speeds will improve virtually every one of the Specific Performance Descriptors, which translates into a higher level of success. The problem is that much of this speed must be generated using concentric contraction of the upper leg extensors, which makes the task very difficult.

Figures 15-32 shows the average rotational speed of the upper leg going into the hurdle for all elite athletes analyzed to date.

Upper Leg Speed Into the Hurdle

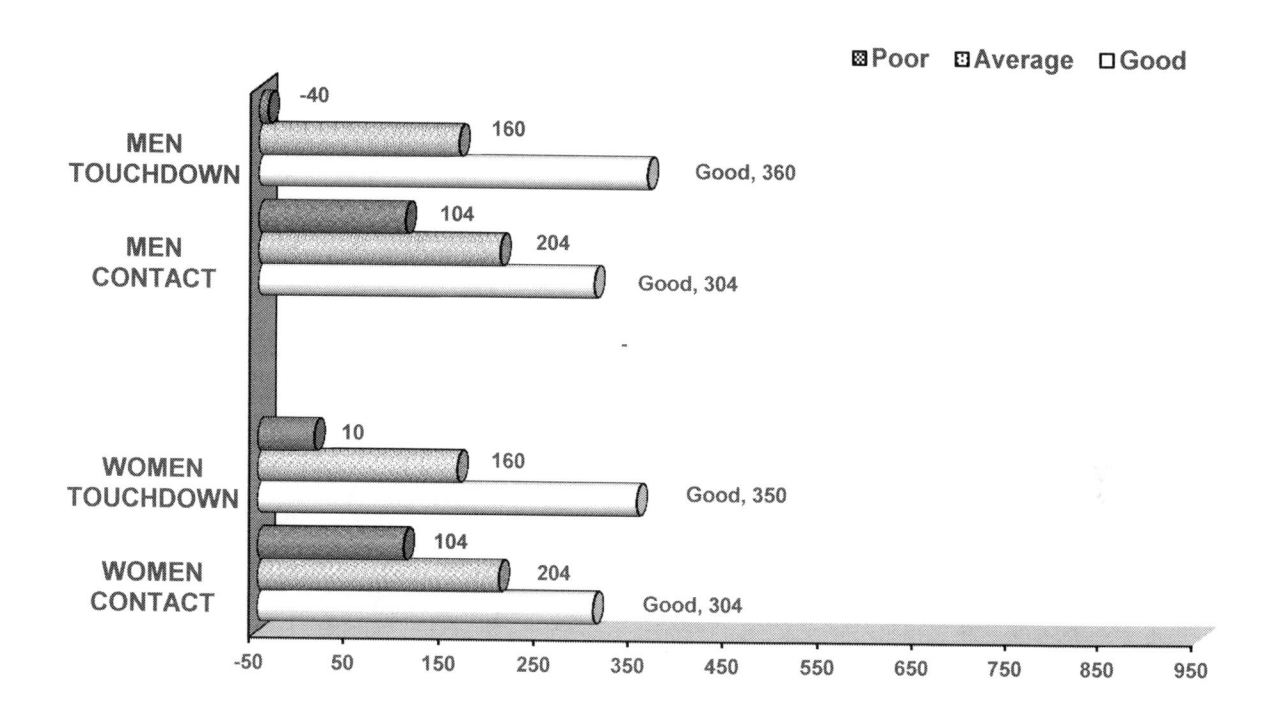

■ Poor ▨ Average ☐ Good

MEN TOUCHDOWN: -40, 160, Good 360
MEN CONTACT: 104, 204, Good 304
WOMEN TOUCHDOWN: 10, 160, Good 350
WOMEN CONTACT: 104, 204, Good 304

RotationalSpeed (degrees/second)

Figure 15-32: Upper Leg Rotational Speed at Touchdown and Ground Contact Going Into the Hurdle

Of all the upper leg results, **the upper leg Speed at Touchdown is the most critical since it affects both the amount of forward braking and the amount of ground contact time.** Since decreasing Ground Time is the primary way elite hurdlers maximize hurdle clearance, properly preparing the leg for Touchdown is a critical movement.

Once ground contact has occurred, the upper leg extensors must be powerful enough to maintain the extension action through Takeoff. As shown in Figure 15-32, only the best performers can come close to accomplishing this task.

Between the Hurdles

The magnitude of the Lead upper leg Velocity at Touchdown coming off the hurdle (Step One) indicates just how powerfully the best performers are moving toward the next barrier (Figure 15-33). The mechanical precision required to land with an extended leg, directly under the body, at these rotational speeds is extremely demanding.

As in the stride going into the hurdle, the upper leg speed at Touchdown and during ground contact coming off the hurdle is of critical importance. Since this stride should be directed forward (not upward), there is no need to slow the body down by producing Vertical Velocity. Thus, the upper leg should land with high extension speed, with every attempt made to try to maintain the speed during ground contact. Since the Lead Leg is extended, and moving through a large range of motion, the hurdler is in good position to maximize this value. In fact, the upper leg rotational speeds produced at Touchdown are some of the highest leg speeds produced in any athletic event.

Since the upper leg is already extending at a high rotational rate coming off the hurdle, and large Touchdown forces are encountered, even the top elite hurdlers will have difficulty maintaining this rotational speed.

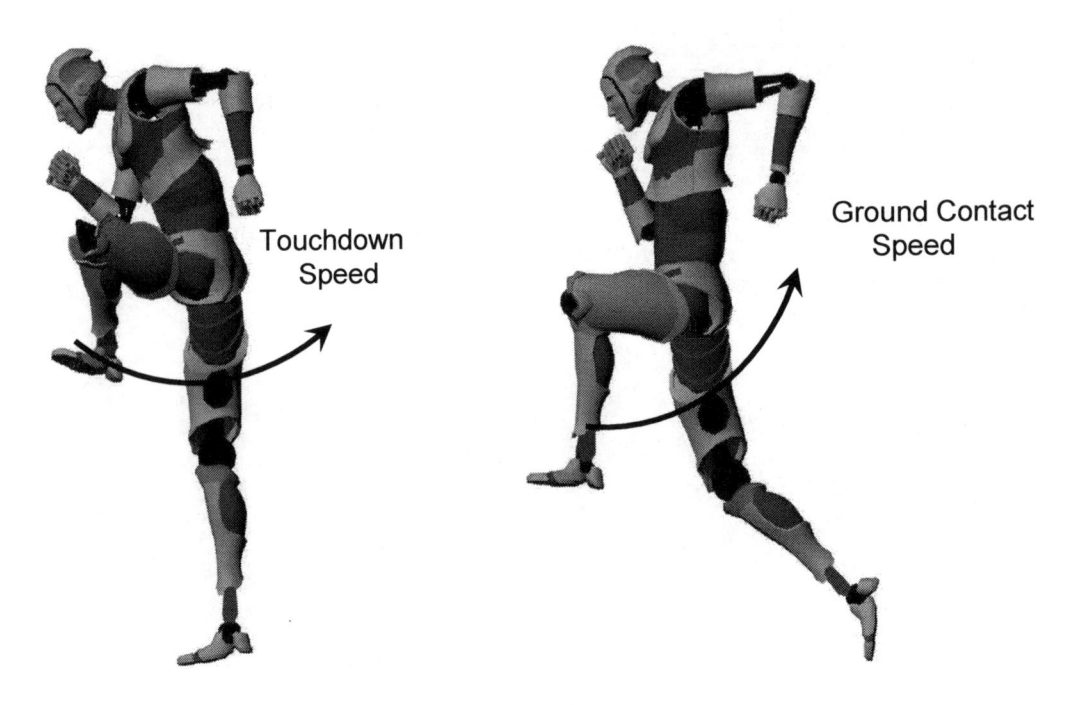

Figure 15-33: Upper Leg Rotational Speed Touchdown and Ground Contact Off the Hurdle

The Horizontal emphasis demanded of Steps Two and Three require large upper leg Speeds during ground contact (Figure 15-34). Since Step Two is the stride that demands the greatest Stride Length and Horizontal Velocity production, success hinges on generating large leg Speeds. Fortunately, the high leg recovery produced coming off the hurdle (Step One), allows the mechanically proficient athlete the ability to produce this level of upper leg Speed at Touchdown. The hurdler must then attempt to maintain this Speed during the Ground Phase if the goals of Step Two are to be reached.

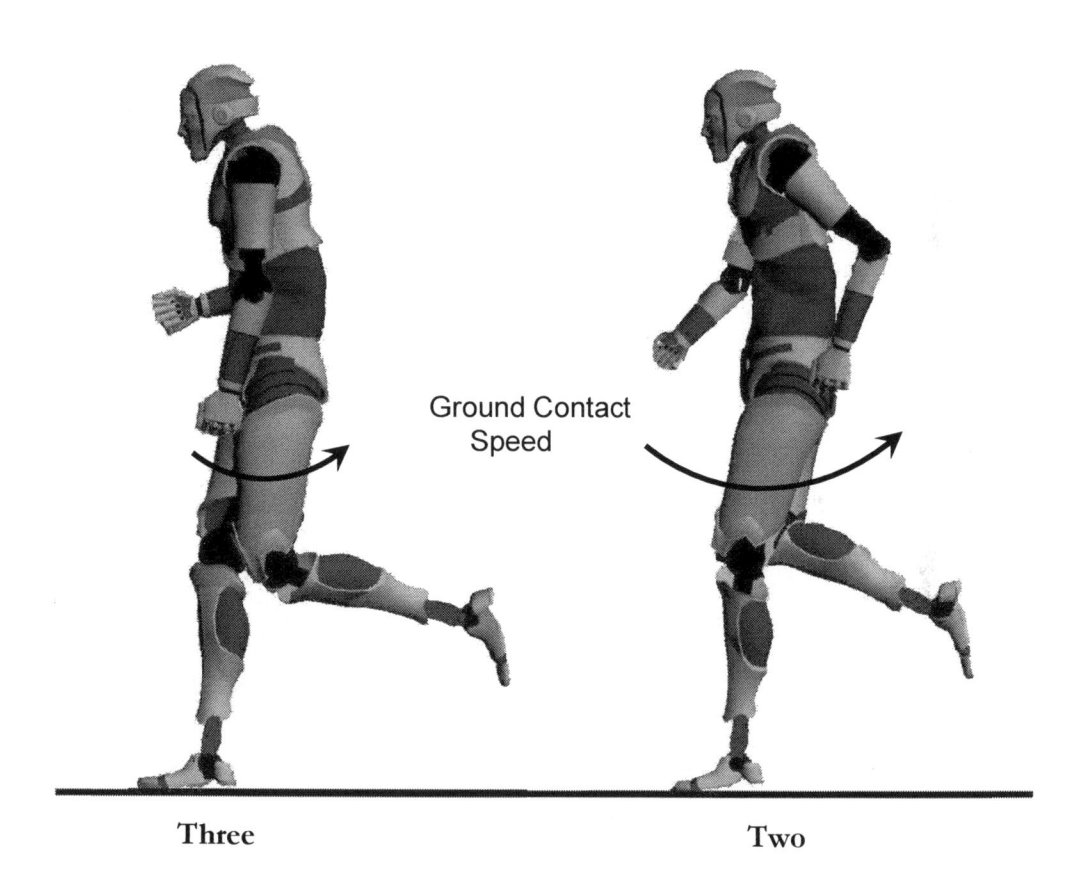

Figure 15-34: Step Two and Three Upper Leg Rotational Speed During Ground Contact

If Step Two is successful, then Step Three can be used to prepare the body for the hurdle stride. This Preparatory Step requires only sufficient upper leg Speed to move the hips forward (not up) into the Hurdle Stride.

Figure 15-35 shows the rotational Speeds of the upper leg for the Steps between the hurdles for all elite athletes analyzed to date (results for Men and Women are close enough to be shown as one).

Critical Specific Performance Descriptors For the Short Hurdles

From these results, it is evident that Steps One and Two are "attack steps", where the athlete is hitting the ground with an aggressive upper leg Speed, then trying to maintain it during ground contact. The results are an increase in the Horizontal Velocity down the track.

Upper Leg Speed Between the Hurdles

■ Poor ☒ Average ☐ Good

Step	Poor	Average	Good
STEP ONE TOUCHDOWN	560	700	840
STEP ONE CONTACT	277	477	677
STEP TWO TOUCHDOWN	500	640	780
STEP TWO CONTACT	270	470	670
STEP THREE TOUCHDOWN	150	200	250
STEP THREE CONTACT	300	400	500

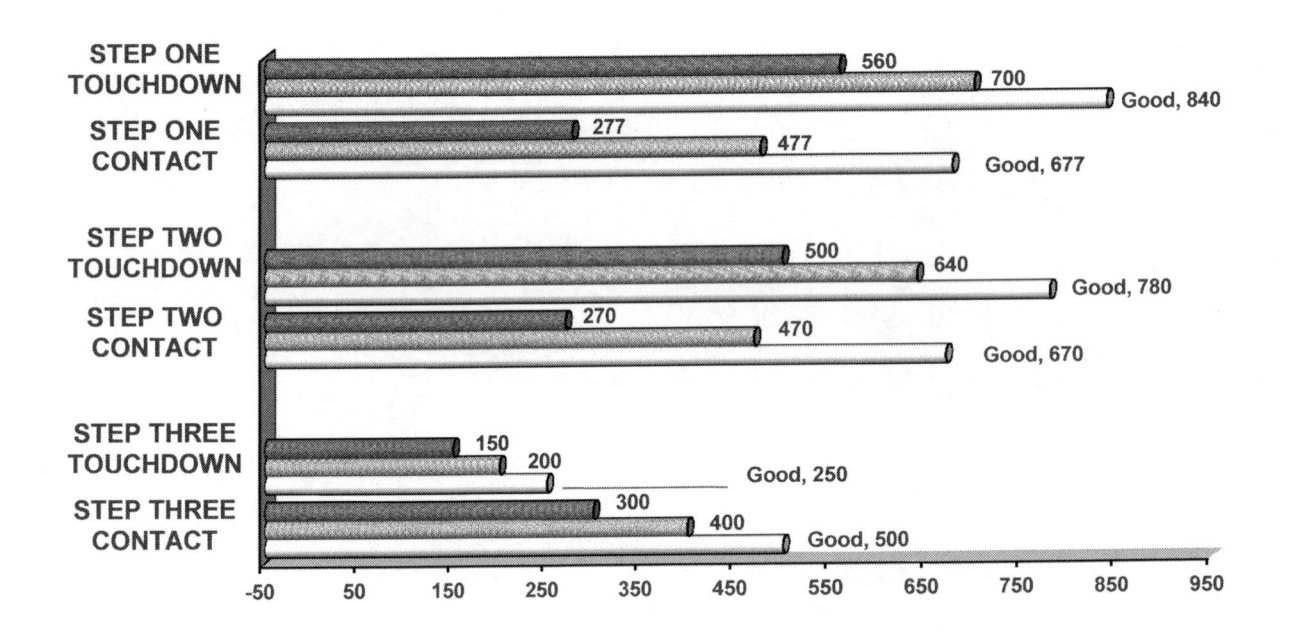

Rotational Speed (degrees/second)

Figure 15-35: Upper Leg Speed Off the Hurdle

The results of Step Three indicate the classic Preparatory Step into a jump. At Touchdown, the upper leg is extending slowly. During ground contact the leg just "rides over" the Touchdown point, projecting the body Horizontally toward the Hurdle Stride with virtually no Vertical projection.

Lower Leg Motion

The motion of the lower leg is one of the most important, and misunderstood actions in the Hurdle Event. If controlled properly, it allows the proper Mechanics to occur. If misused, it effectively eliminates the athlete's ability to produce world class Mechanics.

Into the Hurdle

There are two possible ways to best use the Lead Leg as it is rotated into the hurdle stride. The first belief is that, to make the movement into the hurdle as quick as possible, the Lead Leg must be rapidly rotated forward, into the hurdle stride. Since this leg leads the body into the hurdle, it not only sets the tempo, but also the direction of the stride. To maximize the tempo (quickness), and produce the proper direction emphasis (forward), the lower leg must be rapidly flexed to a small angle (heel next to the buttocks) as soon as possible after the Lead Leg leaves the ground going into the hurdle. This position should then be maintained, to as great a degree as possible, until the heel of the Lead Leg crosses the Ground Leg.

The second line of belief states that, to help the hurdler produce upward lift, the lower leg should remain more extended (as in the high jump). In addition, this greater angle gives the athlete more control of the Lead Leg since the speed of lower leg extension is much lower going into the hurdle.

The most recent research on Hurdle Mechanics indicates that the better elite hurdlers are following the second method: increasing the lower leg angle going into the hurdle (Figure 15-36). Although this is the least favored belief among coaches, it does explain how the elite hurdler is controlling the Lead Leg position while helping in the production of the necessary Vertical lift.

Figure 15-36: Lower Leg Recovery Motion Into the Hurdle

Figure 15-37 shows the maximum lower leg flexion angle and flexion at the point when the ankle crosses the opposite knee of the trail leg as the performer moves into the hurdle for all elite athlete hurdlers investigated to date.

Lower Leg Recovery Into the Hurdle

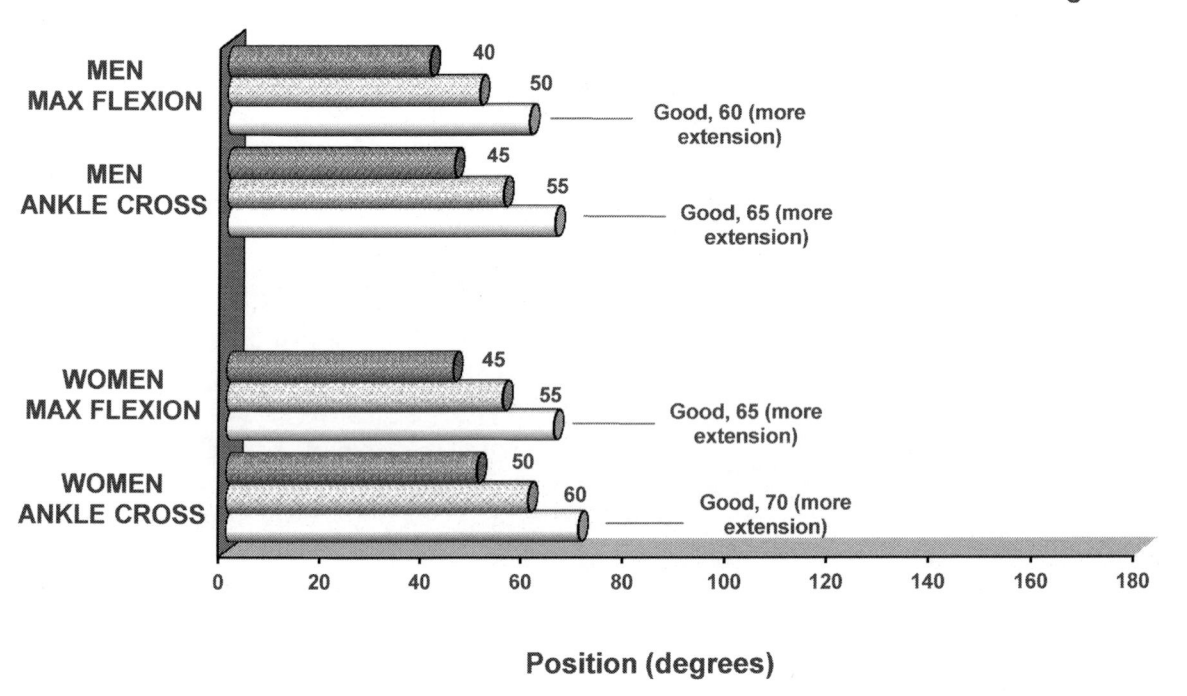

☒ Poor ☐ Average ☐ Good

MEN MAX FLEXION: 40 / 50 / Good, 60 (more extension)
MEN ANKLE CROSS: 45 / 55 / Good, 65 (more extension)
WOMEN MAX FLEXION: 45 / 55 / Good, 65 (more extension)
WOMEN ANKLE CROSS: 50 / 60 / Good, 70 (more extension)

Position (degrees)

Figure 15-37: Lower Leg Motion Into the Hurdle

From the data, it is apparent that the amount of lower leg flexion is controlled going into the barrier. This gives the hurdler much better control of the Lead Leg going over the hurdle, allowing it to come as close to the barrier as possible without making contact. In fact, those athletes who use the traditional method of flexing the lower leg, then extending it toward the barrier, are more likely to strike the hurdles with their Lead Leg.

Between the Hurdle

Although the lower leg is not a critical contributor to Hurdle Mechanics during ground contact going into the hurdle, there are two critical positions for the lower leg during ground contact coming off the hurdle (Step One): Touchdown and Takeoff (Figure 15-38).

Coming off of the hurdle, the better hurdlers tend to maximize lower leg extension at Touchdown (on the runner shown, this would produce a larger angle) while maximizing leg flexion at Takeoff (in this case, a smaller angle). The large extension at Touchdown is produced to regain ground contact and begin pulling the body toward the next hurdle. The large flexion at Takeoff indicates that, instead of extending the lower leg to drive the body upward, the emphasis is in pulling the body forward toward the next hurdle.

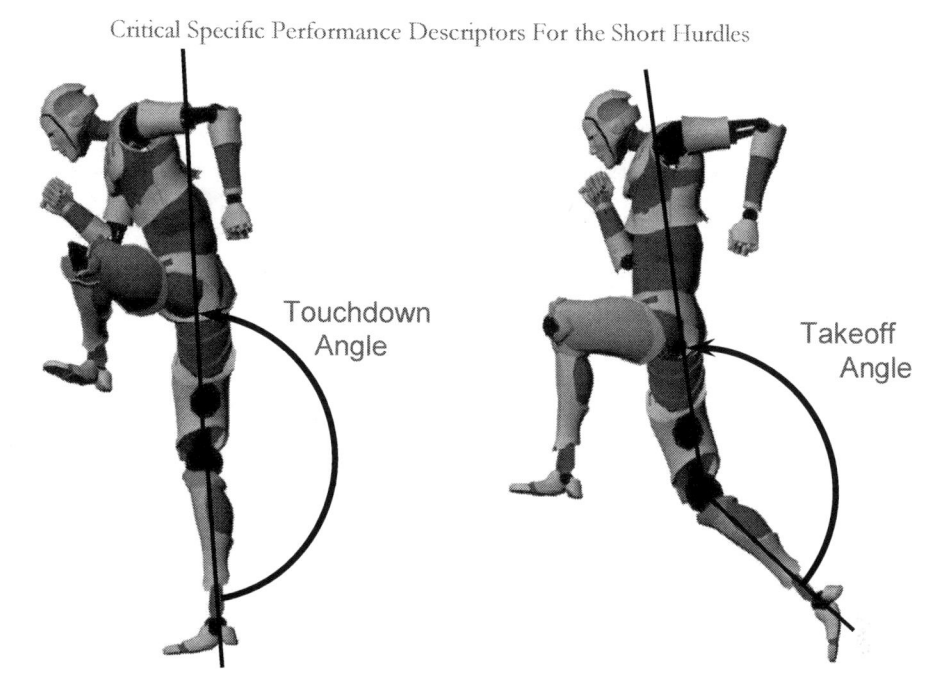

Critical Specific Performance Descriptors For the Short Hurdles

Figure 15-38: Lower Leg Motion Off the Hurdle for Step One

Figure 15-39 shows the lower leg recovery motion at Touchdown and Takeoff, as the performer comes off of the hurdle, for all elite athlete hurdlers investigated to date.

Lower Leg Motion Off the Hurdle

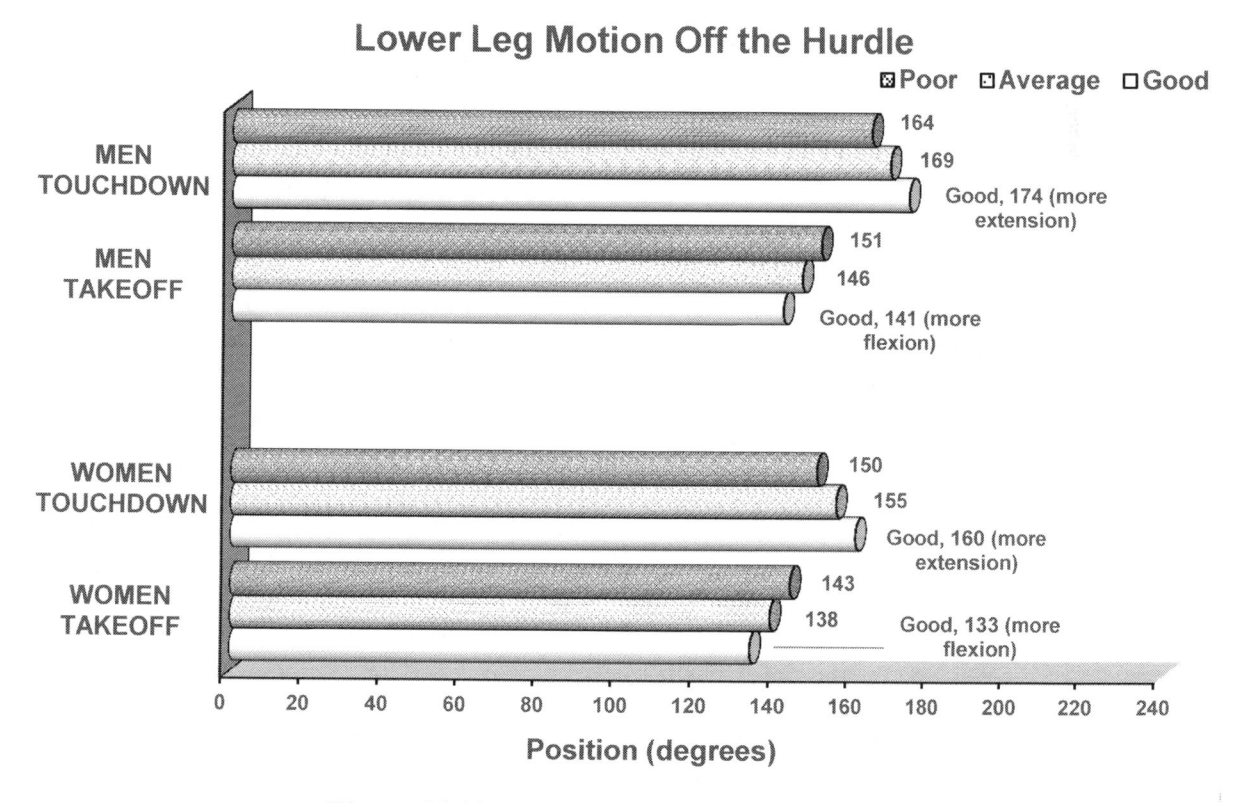

Category	Poor	Average	Good
MEN TOUCHDOWN	164	169	174 (more extension)
MEN TAKEOFF	151	146	141 (more flexion)
WOMEN TOUCHDOWN	150	155	160 (more extension)
WOMEN TAKEOFF	143	138	133 (more flexion)

Position (degrees)

Figure 15-39: Lower Leg Motion Off the Hurdle

Critical Specific Performance Descriptors For the Short Hurdles

The lower leg flexion at Takeoff during Step One is an extreme example of how an athlete can drive the body down the track. In fact, for Front Side Mechanics to occur, the lower leg angle at Takeoff must be minimized.

As shown in Figure 15-40, the angle at Takeoff for both the Sprint and the remaining two Steps between the hurdles (Two and Three) is far from being fully extended as the athlete leaves the ground. In fact, it can be seen that the lower leg angle produced in these Hurdle Steps is about the same as in the Sprint Stride.

Despite the complex demands of the Hurdle race, it is visibly evident that the action of the lower leg in Hurdle Mechanics is virtually identical to that of the Sprint stride.

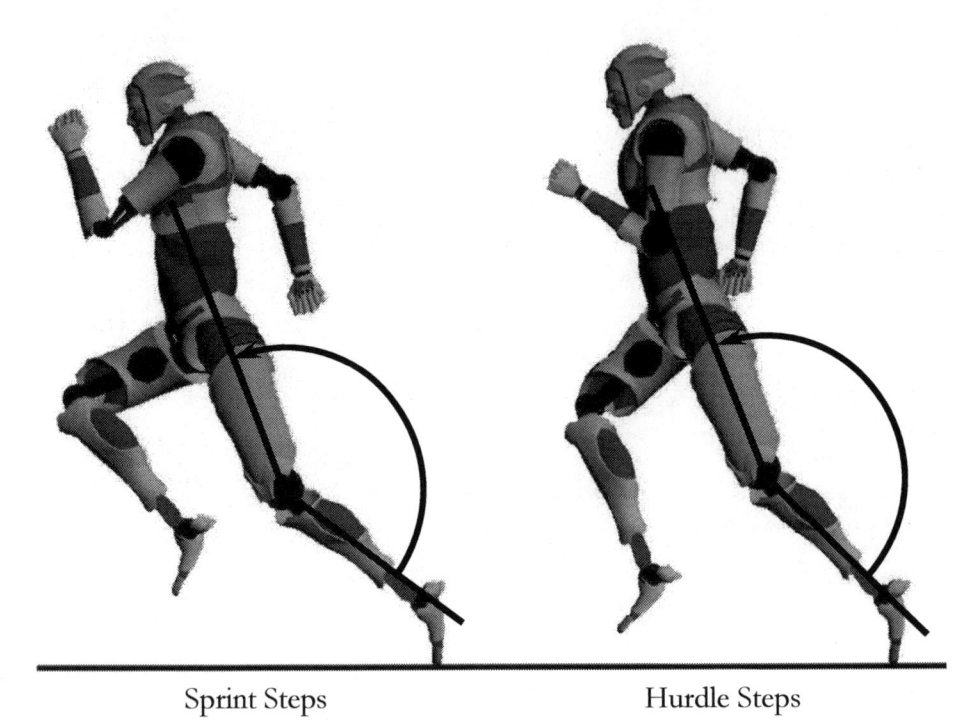

Sprint Steps   Hurdle Steps

Figure 15-40: Lower Leg Angles at Takeoff for Sprints and the Steps Between the Hurdles

Figure 15-41 shows the actual results at Takeoff of the lower leg for Steps Two and Three for all elite athletes analyzed to date (results for Men and Women are close enough to be shown as one).

As can be seen, for both Steps, lower leg extension is halted at around 160 degrees, a full 20 degrees short of full extension. As in the Sprint Mechanics, this action trades the potential small gain in ground force for a much shorter Ground Time. In addition, it keeps the hips and legs from moving behind the body, into the unwanted Back Side Mechanics region.

Lower Leg Angles

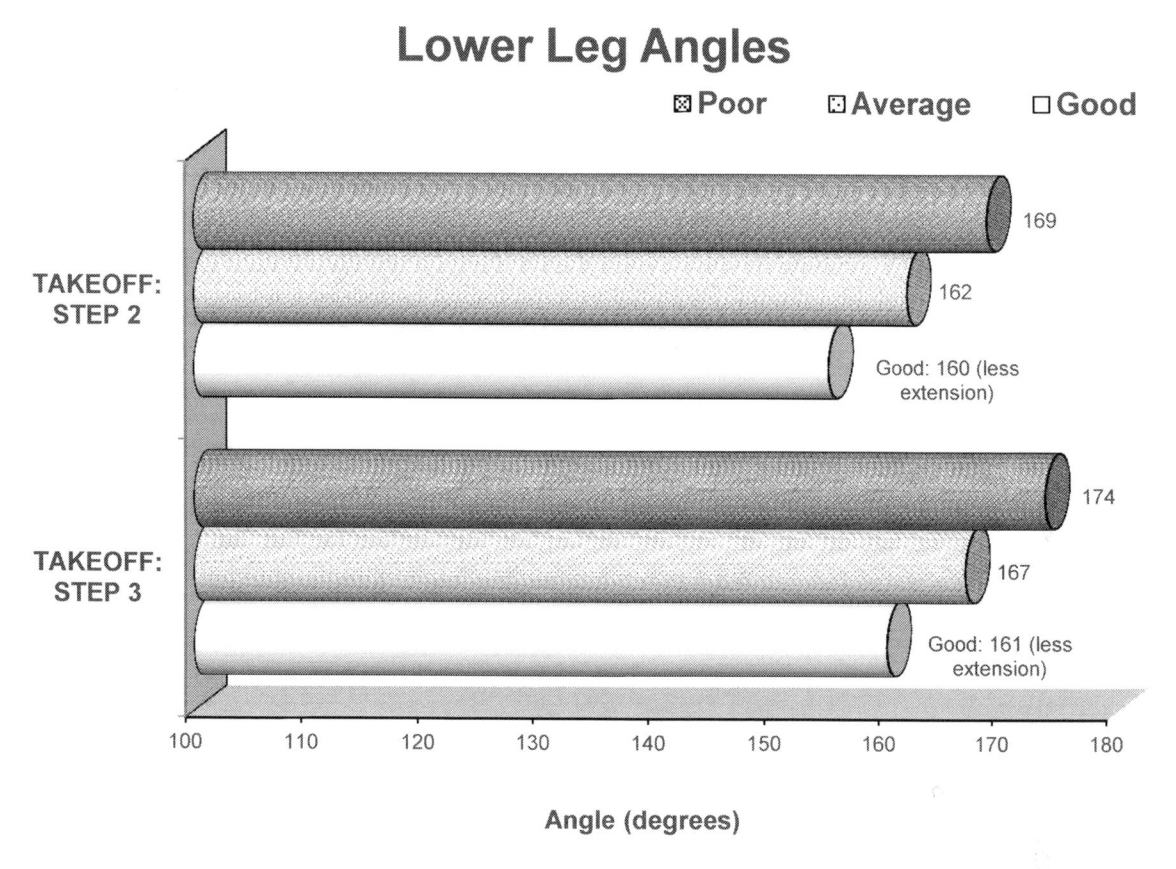

TAKEOFF: STEP 2
- Poor: 169
- Average: 162
- Good: 160 (less extension)

TAKEOFF: STEP 3
- Poor: 174
- Average: 167
- Good: 161 (less extension)

Angle (degrees)

Figure 14-41: Lower Leg Angles at Takeoff for Steps Two and Three Between the Hurdles

After Takeoff, how the lower leg swings through during its recovery further emphasizes the Horizontal nature of the Steps between the Hurdles. As seen in Figure 15-42, when compared with the Sprint Stride, the maximum flexion angle of the lower leg in these Hurdle Steps is much more extended. This position, similar to the last strides of a Long Jump approach, allows the athlete to drive the lower body forward, toward the next barrier.

Figure 15-43 shows the actual maximum flexion results of the lower leg for Steps Two and Three for all elite athletes analyzed to date (results for Men and Women are close enough to be shown as one).

When compared to the Sprint maximum flexion angles (see Figure 9-16), the Hurdle results for Steps Two and Three are much larger (more extension), supporting the conclusion that the leg is contributing to the Horizontal drive toward the next barrier. In fact, this position is so extended that, during the leg recovery action, the toe is brought through very low to the ground. This position is similar to Triple Jump Step Mechanics, which also emphasizes Horizontal projection.

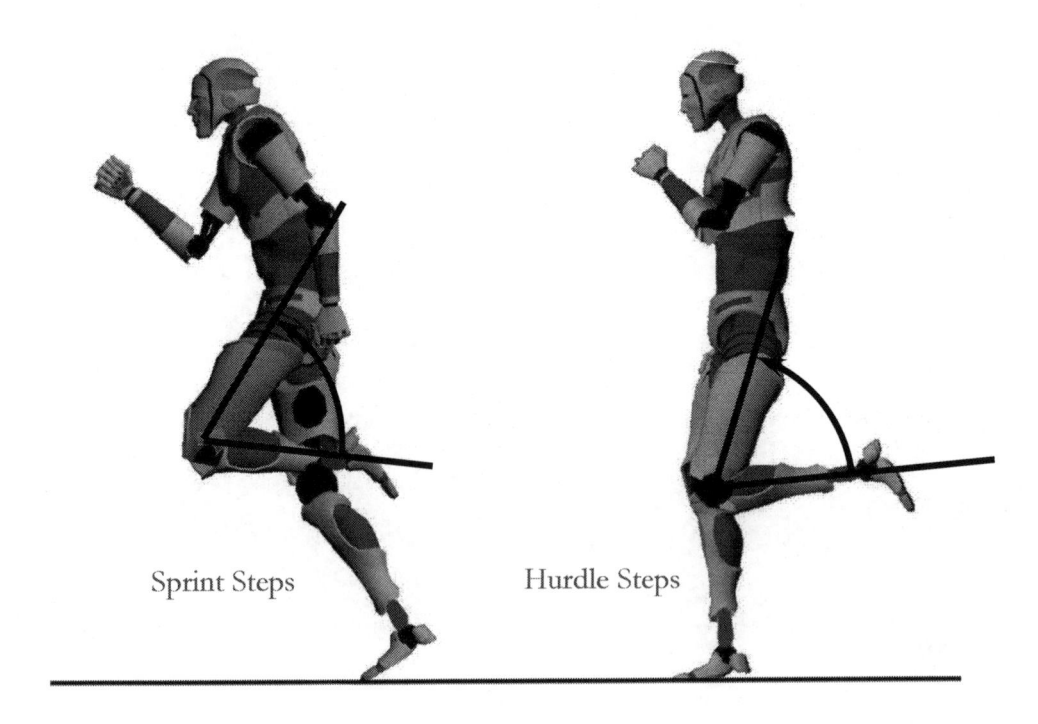

Critical Specific Performance Descriptors For the Short Hurdles

Sprint Steps   Hurdle Steps

Figure 15-42: Lower Leg Angles at Maximum Flexion for the Steps Between the Hurdles

Lower Leg Angles

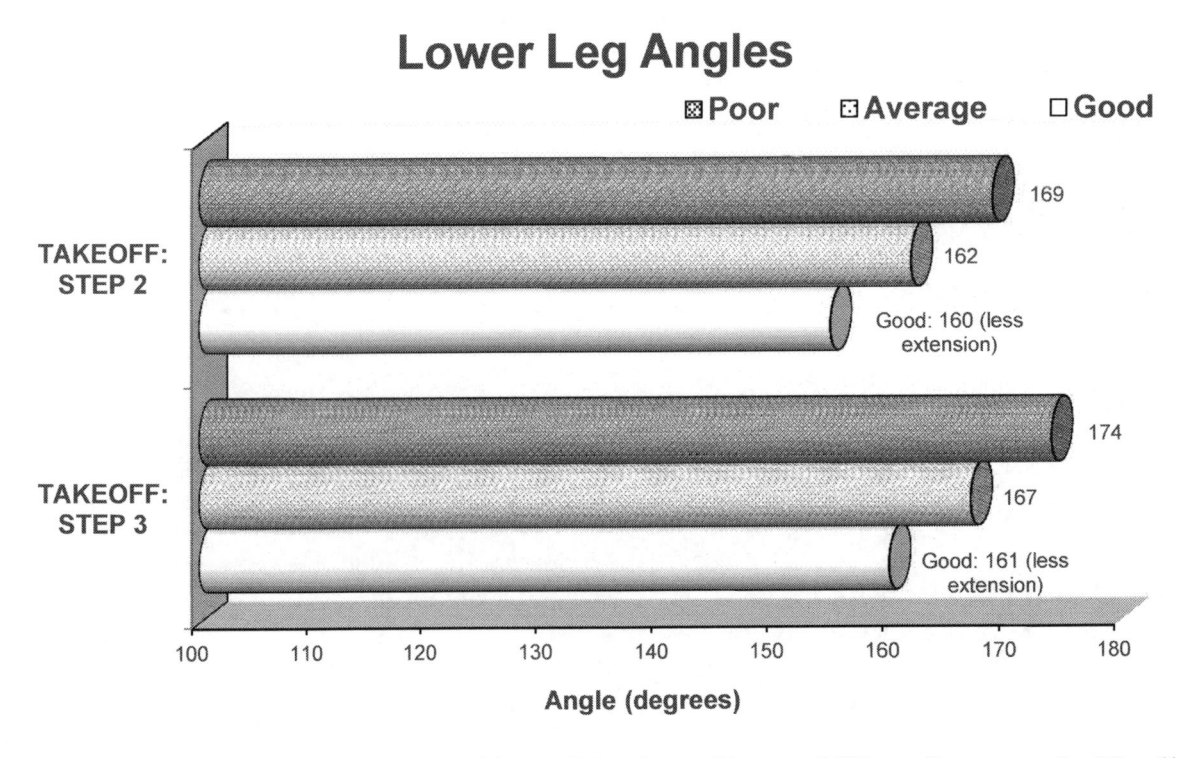

▩ Poor   ▨ Average   ☐ Good

TAKEOFF: STEP 2
- Poor: 169
- Average: 162
- Good: 160 (less extension)

TAKEOFF: STEP 3
- Poor: 174
- Average: 167
- Good: 161 (less extension)

Angle (degrees)

Figure 15-43: Lower Leg Angles at Takeoff for Steps Two and Three Between the Hurdles

Lower Leg Rotational Speed

As mentioned previously, the role of the Lead lower leg during the stride going into the hurdle is one of maintaining a controlled, relatively extended position (about 65 degrees). This goal precludes the need for developing any level of lower leg rotational speed, so it is not a factor in Hurdle Mechanics.

In contrast, lower leg speed is a major factor as the performer moves between the barriers.

Steps Between the Hurdles

Since the Step One stride should be directed forward (not upward), there is no need to slow the body down by producing Vertical Speed. Thus, at Touchdown, the lower leg should be flexing to avoid Horizontal braking (Figure 15-44).

To continue this effort during ground contact, the lower leg should greatly increase in flexion speed (instead of attempting to extend the lower leg). Since Vertical Speed is not needed during this stride, lower leg extension is neither needed nor wanted. Thus, the lower leg is attempting to pull the body forward (not upward), into the next stride.

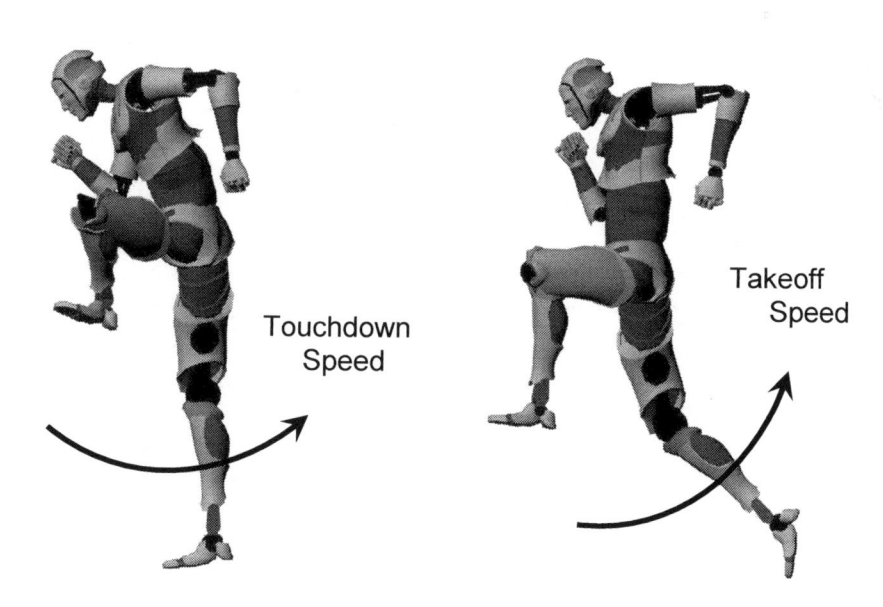

Figure 15-44: Lower Leg Rotational Speed Off the Hurdle (Step One)

Figure 15-45 shows the Touchdown and ground contact rotational Speeds, coming off the hurdle, for all of the elite athletes analyzed to date.

Critical Specific Performance Descriptors For the Short Hurdles

Lower Leg Speed Off the Hurdle

■ Poor ▨ Average ▫ Good

MEN TOUCHDOWN: 0 / 30 / Good, 60
MEN CONTACT: 30 / 190 / Good, 350
WOMEN TOUCHDOWN: 0 / 20 / Good, 40
WOMEN CONTACT: 3 / 120 / Good, 238

Rotational Speed (degrees/second)

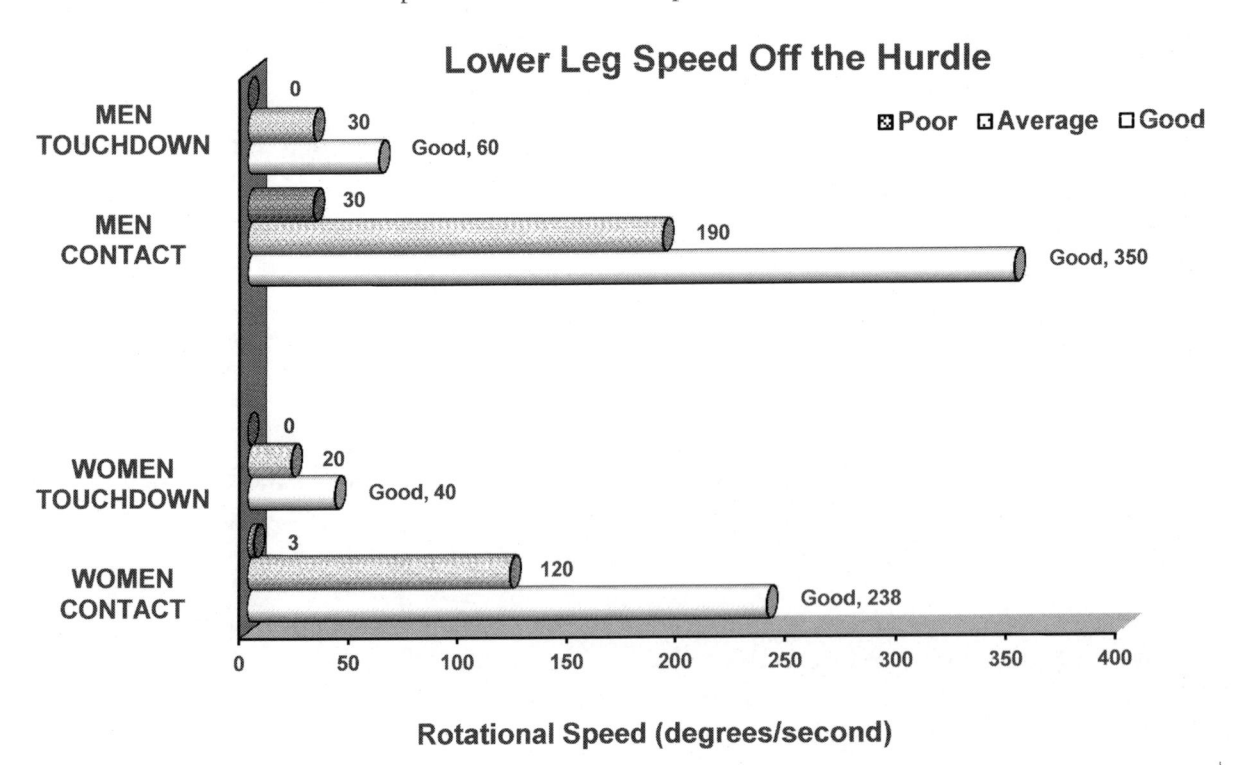

Figure 15-45: Lower Leg Speed Off the Hurdle (Step One)

It is evident that the better hurdlers land with an active lower leg flexion rotation, pulling the body forward toward the next barrier with an abbreviated recovery stride. In contrast, the poorer athletes land with a stationary lower leg then rotate over a stationary limb, creating an action that launches the athlete into an extended recovery stride.

For Steps Two and Three, the role of the lower leg is to remain as stationary as possible, allowing the upper leg to dominate the movement. Thus, lower leg Speed is not a positive contributor in the success of these Steps.

Chapter Summary:

The Specific Performance Descriptors point to the fact that success in the Short Hurdles is determined by the ability of the athlete to generate great amounts of explosive strength at the proper time. Generally, the proper mechanical application of this strength results in an elite performance that is characterized by a brief hurdle clearance, small Hurdle Stride Length, and superior body position coming off the hurdle.

Since success in hurdle clearance is greatly determined by where the athlete lands going into the hurdle, and how they prepare the body prior to Takeoff, it is critical for the performer to control the body so that the proper body actions can be executed while airborne.

Critical Specific Performance Descriptors For the Short Hurdles

> The three Steps between the Hurdles, if properly executed, stop the fall off the barrier, increase (regain) Horizontal Velocity, and prepare the body for the next Hurdle Stride.

CHAPTER 16

CRITICAL GENERAL PERFORMANCE DESCRIPTORS FOR THE LONG HURDLES

Although all of the hurdle clearance trends that were found in the Short Hurdles are also evident in the Long Hurdles, due to the length of the race, some compromises are made to account for the fatigue factor. In addition, the nature of the Steps between the hurdles is radically different. These differences will be presented in Chapters 16 and 17.

With the exception of Horizontal Velocity, these results will be divided into those related to the elite performance over the hurdle and between the hurdles.

Horizontal Velocity

Since the Long Hurdle race covers more than 300 meters, the body cannot complete the event solely on the anaerobic systems. This forces even the elite athlete to compromise in the areas of speed and energy expenditure. As the elite hurdle results of Figure 16-1 indicate, this causes a decrease in Velocity, in the non-fatigue state, of approximately 11 percent in the Women's race as compared to the Short Hurdle results.

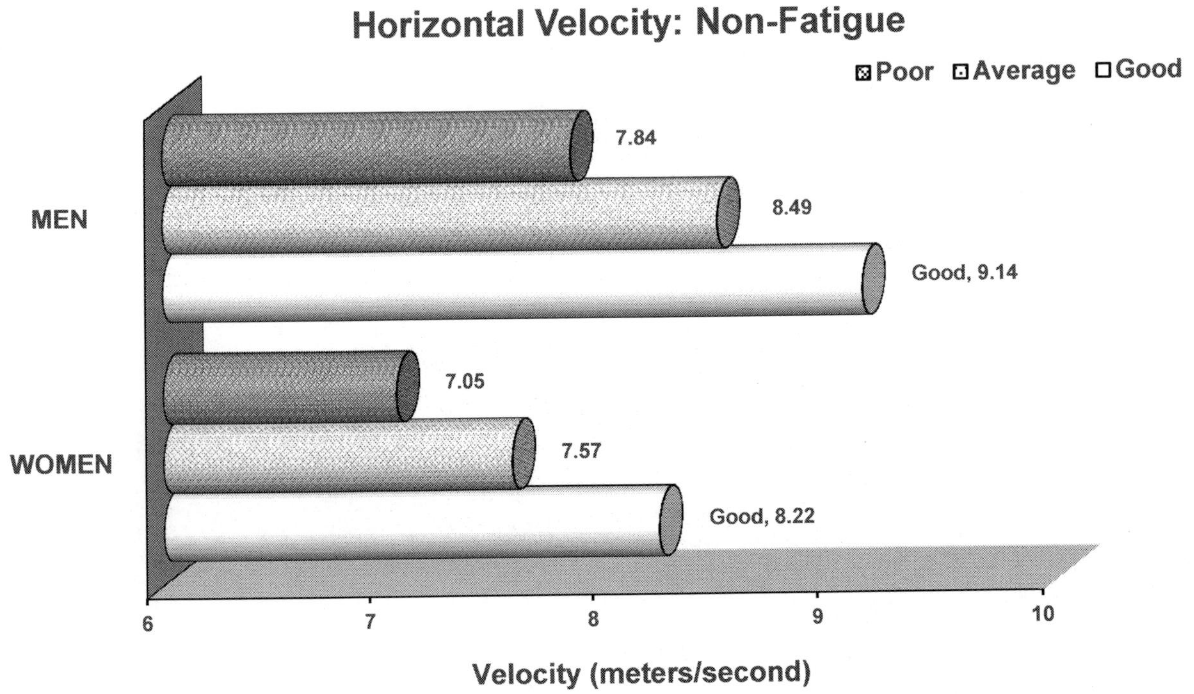

Horizontal Velocity: Non-Fatigue

Poor   Average   Good

MEN
- Poor: 7.84
- Average: 8.49
- Good: 9.14

WOMEN
- Poor: 7.05
- Average: 7.57
- Good: 8.22

Velocity (meters/second)

Figure 16-1: Non-Fatigue Horizontal Velocity Results

The same Velocity decrement is not evident in the comparison between the Short and Long Men's race. This is due to the fact that the Short race is run over hurdles that are much higher. Thus, the additional time required to negotiate the higher hurdle is about the same as the additional time required to handle the fatigue situation in the longer race. Thus, the velocities of the two races are approximately equal.

Regardless of the quality of the elite hurler, some decrement in Velocity occurs as fatigue sets in. As shown in Figure 16-2, the decrement in Velocity is approximately 17 percent as compared to the non-fatigue state.

Horizontal Velocity: Fatigue

Category	Poor	Average	Good
MEN	6.63	7.28	7.93
WOMEN	5.88	6.39	6.86

Velocity (meters/second)

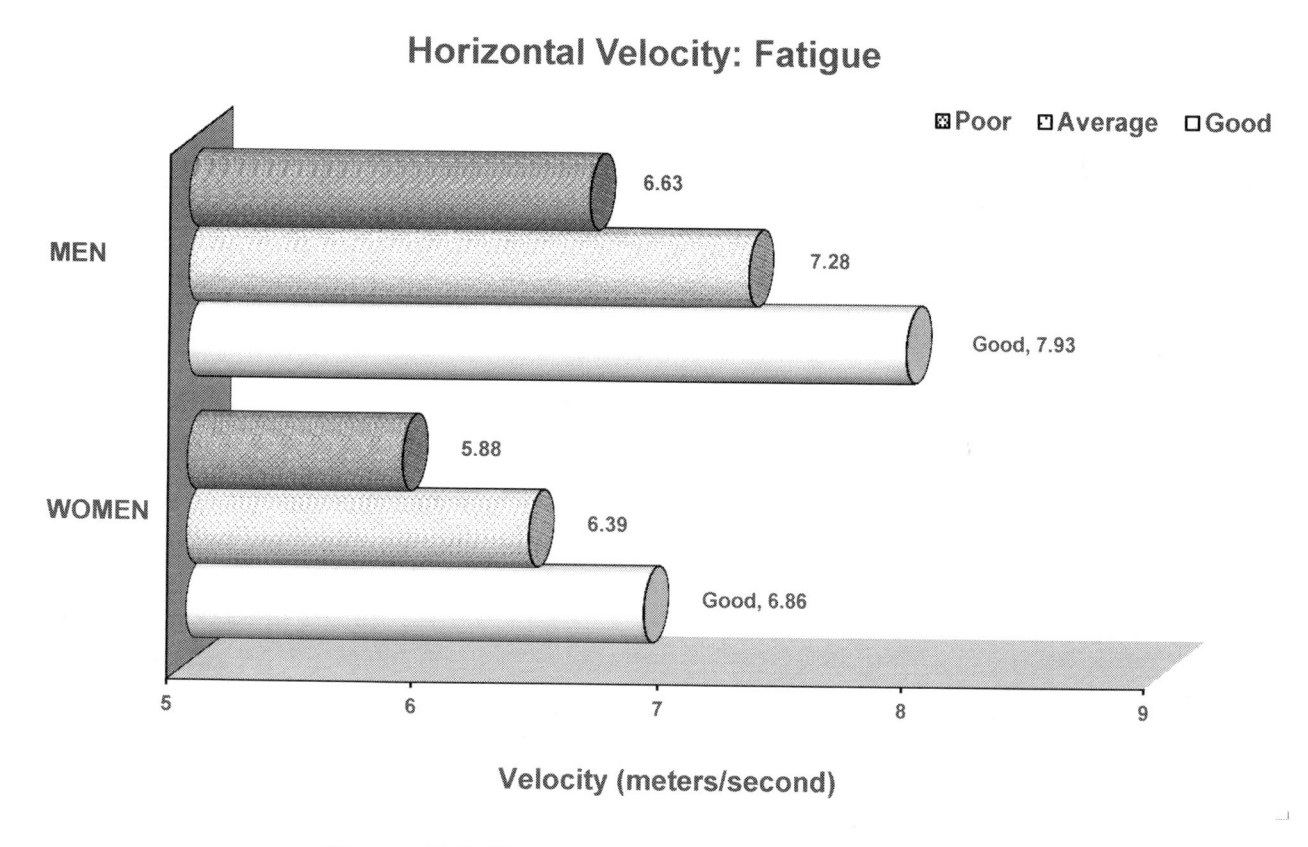

Figure 16-2: Fatigue Horizontal Velocity Results

As in all fatigue related races, the better hurdlers maximize their non-fatigue Velocity, while limiting their loss of Velocity in the fatigue state.

Air Time

As was true in the Short Hurdles, unless Air Time is required to prepare the body for the next ground contact, or produce a required Stride Length, it should be minimized as much as possible.

Over the Hurdle

Since the height of the Long Hurdles is less than the Short race, the expectation would be for the Long race Hurdlers to produce a shorter Air Time over the hurdle. Instead, as shown in Figures 16-3, this is not the case.

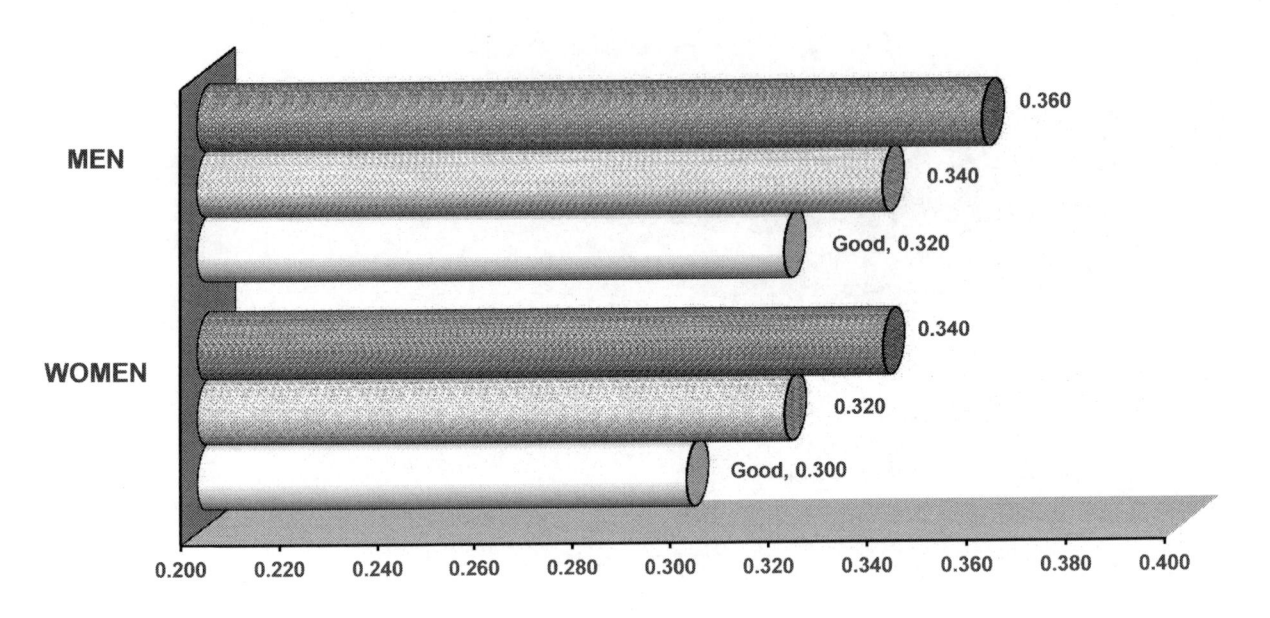

Air Time: Non-Fatigue

■ Poor ▫ Average ▫ Good

MEN
- 0.360 (Poor)
- 0.340 (Average)
- Good, 0.320

WOMEN
- 0.340 (Poor)
- 0.320 (Average)
- Good, 0.300

Time (seconds)

Figure 16-3: Non-Fatigue Air Time Over the Hurdle

As can be seen, Air Time results are approximately the same, if not slightly higher, than the Short Hurdles (see Figure 14-2). This is due to the fact that since, in the Long Hurdles, the athlete must lengthen their Stride Length to produce the non-fatigue 13 (Men) or 15 (Women) step pattern used by the typical elite hurdler, this additional Air Time is used to produce a slightly longer Hurdle Stride Length to contribute to this effort.

Therefore, in the Long Hurdles, this step pattern criterion makes the need for minimal hurdle clearance less of a critical factor. Thus, the Air Time should still be minimized, but not to the extent that it makes reaching the required step pattern difficult to attain.

In the fatigue state, as shown in Figure 16-4, Air Time remains virtually the same for the best performers. For the less proficient athletes, however, fatigue and the inability to manage the race (not being able to reach the correct Touchdown position going into the Hurdle) produce increased Air Times that severely detract from performance.

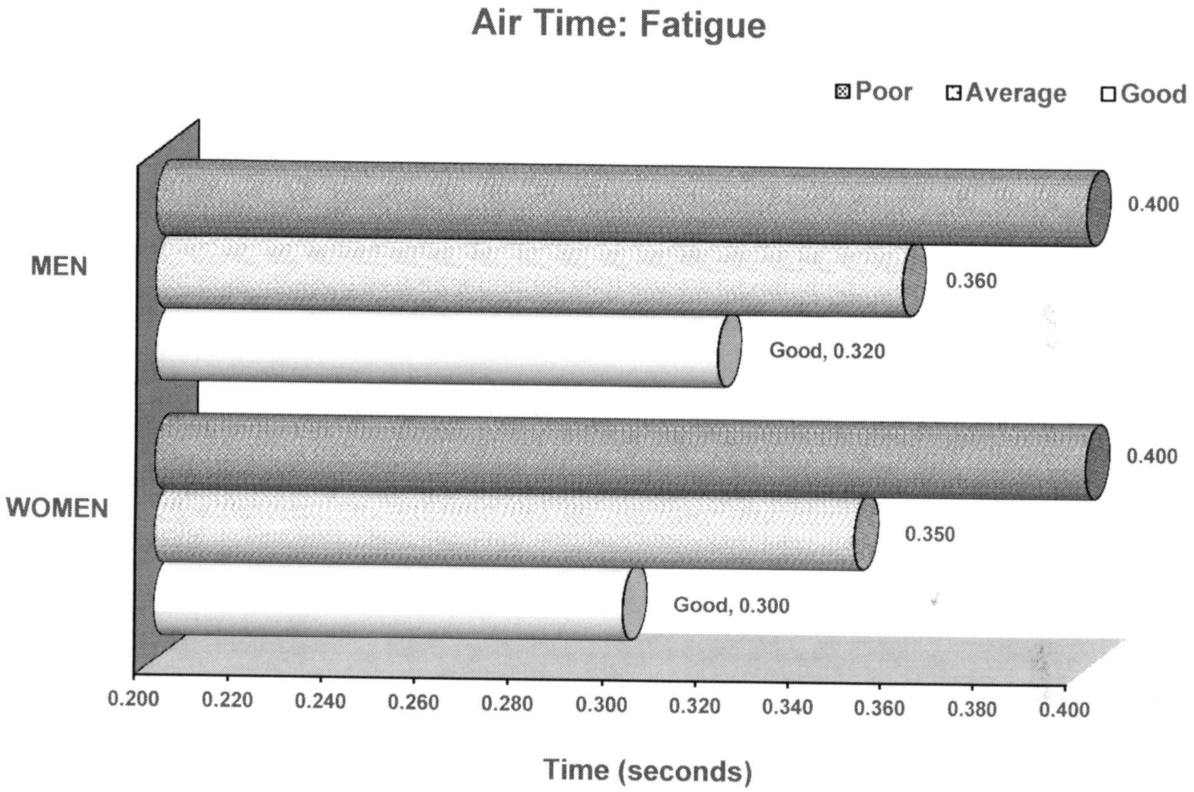

Air Time: Fatigue

MEN
- Poor: 0.400
- Average: 0.360
- Good: 0.320

WOMEN
- Poor: 0.400
- Average: 0.350
- Good: 0.300

Time (seconds)

Figure 16-4: Fatigue Air Time Over the Hurdle

The fact that Air Time does not change in fatigue for the proficient performer, while those unable to maintain proper Mechanics see a large performance decrement, has been seen in other running events.

Steps Between Hurdles

In the Short Hurdle race, the issue with the Steps between the hurdles is trying to fit three Steps into a situation where the barriers are too close together. In the Long Hurdle race, the problem is reversed.

In the Long race, since the Steps have to be longer than the standard Sprint stride, and there are a large number (13-16), the Mechanics for the Steps between the barriers are virtually the same as the Sprint. The challenge in this race is to generate sufficient Air Time to cover the additional distance required to produce the selected stride pattern. Chapter 1 (Table 1-2) indicated that the Men's race demanded a nine percent greater Stride Length, while the Women's race required an even larger twelve percent increase. Since the only way to produce this increased length at a given Speed is to increase Air Time, every Long Hurdler must expend additional energy to produce these results.

The actual between the hurdles Air Time results for the best elite hurdlers, throughout the race, are presented in Figure 16-5. The standard 400 meter Sprint Air Time is identified for comparison purposes.

Long Hurdle Air Times

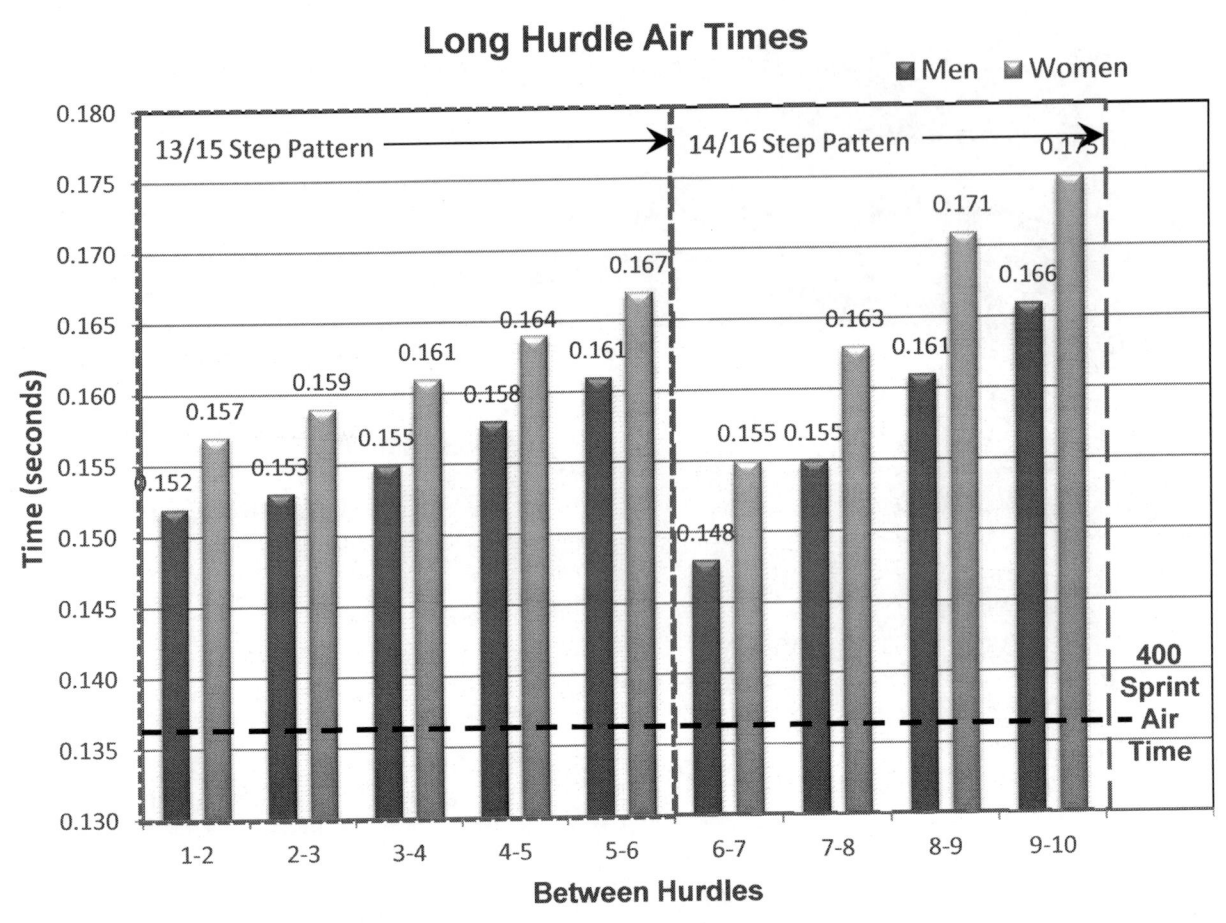

Figure 16-5: Air Times for the Steps Between The Long Hurdles

For most Long race Hurdlers, a pattern of 13 Steps is used by Men and 15 for Women. Sometime in the later part of the race, when fatigue sets in, the pattern shifts to 14 for Men and 16 for Women. In the example above, the change occurs between the sixth and seventh hurdles.

It is evident that the increased Air Time demands throughout the race require much more energy than the standard Sprint, especially for the Women. In addition, there are four additional factors that make this situation even more demanding:

1. **The Velocity Issue – Part One**: The results in the Figure are for the top elites, running at World Record pace. For those athletes running slower, they will need even more Air Time to cover the same amount of distance. The problem with the Long Hurdles is than everyone, regardless of the Speed down the track, must all cover the same amount of distance. Thus, the unfortunate truth is that the slower, less proficient athletes have to actually expend greater effort to produce the same step pattern as do the faster performers.
2. **The Velocity Issue – Part Two**: Regardless of the quality of the hurdler, as fatigue sets in and Velocity decreases, the Air Times must increase if the athlete is to maintain their step pattern. As Figure 16-5 indicates, the actual early race (13/15 pattern) Air Times are slightly shorter at the beginning of the race, then begin to get longer as the athlete starts to fatigue and begins to struggle to maintain the pattern. When the 13/15 pattern cannot be maintained, then the athlete must switch to the late race pattern (14/16), which brings the Air Time back to an achievable value. As fatigue continues to increase (slowing the hurdler), the Air Time begins to climb once again. If the demands increase to a point where the athlete cannot maintain the pattern, another Step will have to be added to allow the race to be completed.
3. **The Tempo Issue – Part One**: Since the between the hurdle Air Time is always greater than the typical Sprint Air Time, the Race Tempo that a Long Hurdler must become accustomed to is much different (slower) as well. This difference indicates that **Long Hurdle athletes should do most of their short speed work at tempos that match their Hurdle Tempo, not their Sprint Tempo**.
4. **The Tempo Issue – Part Two**: As Figure 16-5 demonstrates, since the Air Time changes between every hurdle, with a major shift when the step pattern changes, the tempo changes constantly, throughout the race. This tempo shift indicates that **Long Hurdle athletes should do most of their long speed work at tempos that match their Hurdle Tempo, not their Sprint Tempo**. In addition, most fatigue based training should be done over some combination of barriers, which should always include the shift from the 13/15 to the 14/16 pattern.

For a long period of time, the Short Hurdle race has been deemed the most difficult technical even on the track. With this information, the Long Hurdles can, for an entirely different set of reasons, lay claim to this title.

Stride Length

As with the Short race, since the Long Hurdler must manage ten barriers; as well as the Steps before, between, and after the hurdles, the manner in which they maximize the Effective Force while minimizing the Expended Force, Impact Force will determine, to a large degree, the outcome of the race. One of the best measures of the success of this force application can be found in the resulting Stride Length that it produces.

Over the Hurdle

Figure 16-6 indicates the non-fatigue Stride Length consequences of the extended Hurdle Air Time. In comparison to their Sprint results, the hurdlers are covering up to twice the distance during hurdle clearance.

These length results are slightly higher than the Short Hurdles (Figure 14-8), even though the hurdle height is significantly lower. As discussed in the Air Time results, this is due to the over stride requirement imposed by the step pattern used by the elite hurdlers.

Stride Length: Non-Fatigue

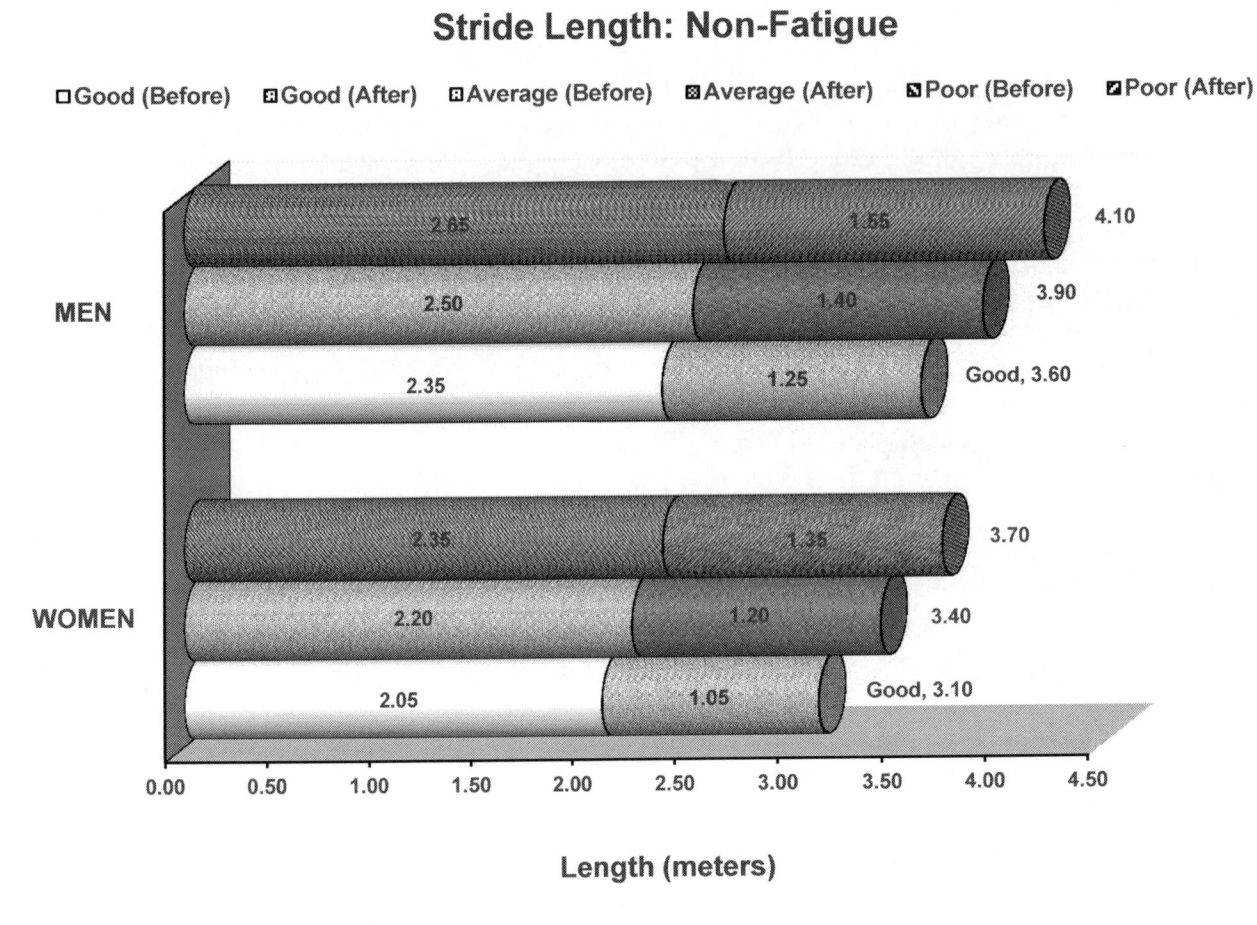

□ Good (Before)   ▩ Good (After)   ▥ Average (Before)   ▨ Average (After)   ▧ Poor (Before)   ▤ Poor (After)

MEN
- 2.65 / 1.55 / 4.10
- 2.50 / 1.40 / 3.90
- 2.35 / 1.25 / Good, 3.60

WOMEN
- 2.35 / 1.35 / 3.70
- 2.20 / 1.20 / 3.40
- 2.05 / 1.05 / Good, 3.10

Length (meters)

Figure 16-6: Non-Fatigue Stride Length Over the Hurdle

In the fatigue state, as shown in Figure 16-7, Stride Length suffers approximately a 10 percent decrement. Since the hurdler is in the air the same amount of time (see Figures 16-3 and 16-4), the decrease in Stride Length is solely due to the decrease in Horizontal Velocity. Thus, the critical importance of striving to minimize ground contact Time, both in non-fatigue and fatigue, is further emphasized. Additional data on this conclusion will be presented in the discussion on Ground Times.

Stride Length: Fatigue

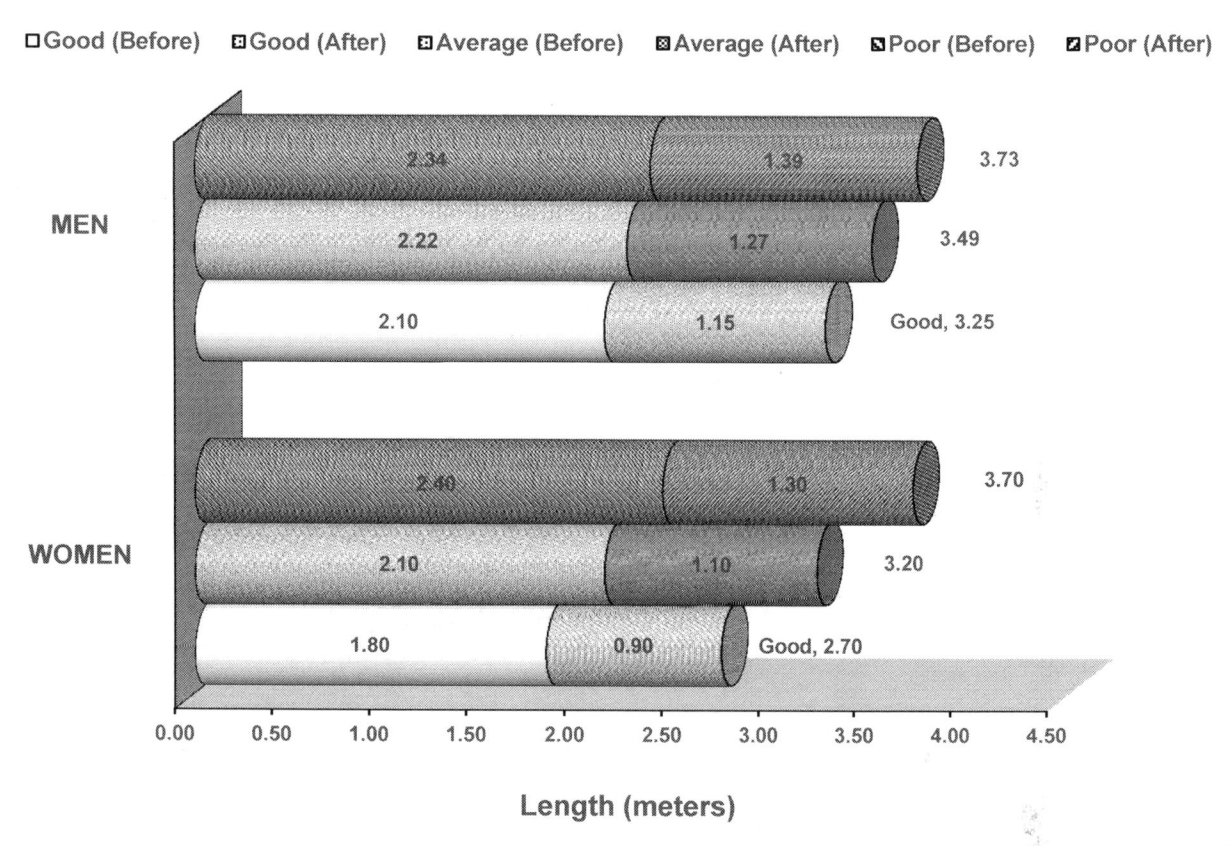

□ Good (Before)　■ Good (After)　■ Average (Before)　■ Average (After)　■ Poor (Before)　■ Poor (After)

MEN
- 2.34 | 1.39 | 3.73
- 2.22 | 1.27 | 3.49
- 2.10 | 1.15 | Good, 3.25

WOMEN
- 2.40 | 1.30 | 3.70
- 2.10 | 1.10 | 3.20
- 1.80 | 0.90 | Good, 2.70

Length (meters)

Figure 16-7: Fatigue Stride Length Results Over the Hurdle

Steps Between the Hurdles

Since the Steps between the hurdles must all be extended to produce the required step pattern, there are no unusual changes in the Sprint Mechanics utilized in the Long Sprint race. The obvious challenge for the hurdler lies in the task of generating the longer Air Times and Stride Lengths using the same Sprint movement patterns.

For the Men, the early race 13 step pattern demands a Stride Length of 2.5 meters, while the 15 step pattern for the Women requires 2.2 meters (see Table 1-1). These length are almost exactly the Stride Lengths of the best Long Sprinters (see Figure 10-4) but, since the hurdlers are running 1.5 meters per second slower, the Men have to over stride by nine percent and the Women by 12 percent.

Ground Time

Since the Ground Phase is the only time when the athlete can apply force to alter the body's Velocity, it is not surprising that this is where great hurdle results are produced.

Into the Hurdle

Due to the same between the hurdles Stride Length demands that required high Air Time and Hurdle Stride Length results, the Ground Time going into the hurdle is also higher than expected in the Long Hurdles. Figure 16-8 shows the non-fatigue Ground Time results involved in hurdle clearance for all elite hurdlers analyzed to date.

Ground Time: Non-Fatigue

■ Poor ▫ Average ▫ Good

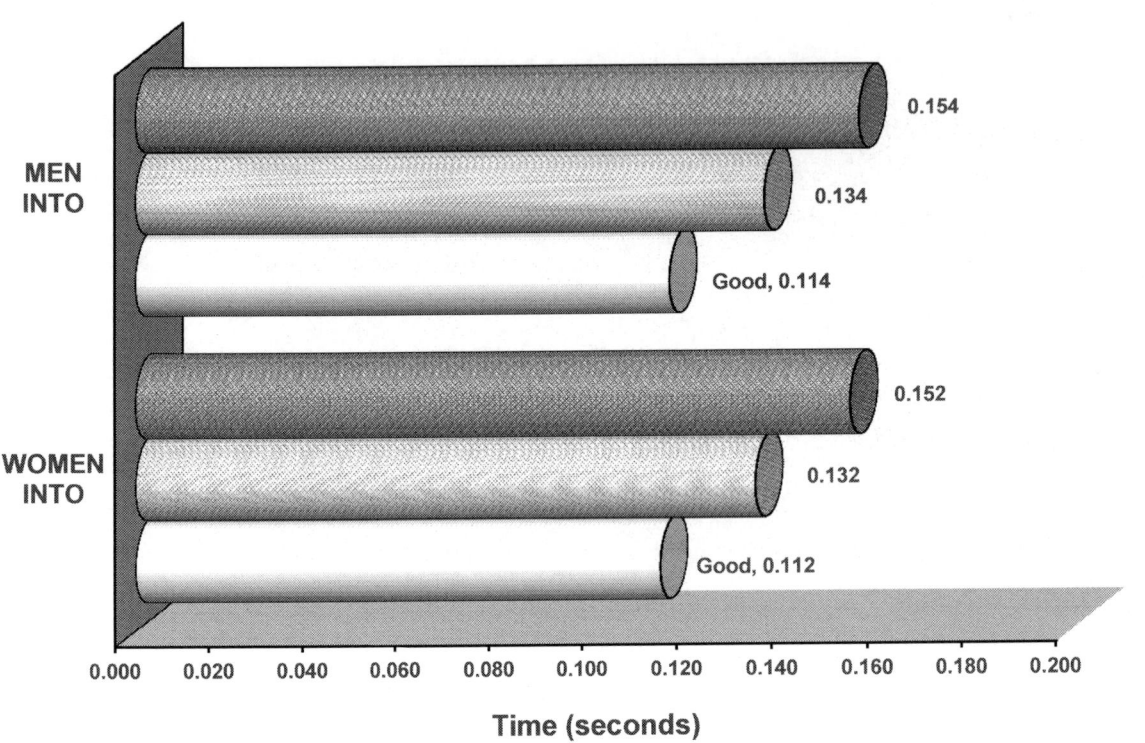

MEN INTO:
- Poor: 0.154
- Average: 0.134
- Good: 0.114

WOMEN INTO:
- Poor: 0.152
- Average: 0.132
- Good: 0.112

Time (seconds)

Figure 16-8: Non-Fatigue Ground Time Into the Hurdle

As in the Short Hurdles, minimizing the Ground Time is the key to producing faster hurdle times and, therefore, greater Horizontal Velocity. Unfortunately, this reduction of time requires the expenditure of large amounts of strength and, therefore, energy. Thus, the compromise in the Long Hurdles is balancing the Speed of the race with the available Speed endurance.

In comparison, Figure 16-9 shows the fatigue Ground Times for all elite athletes investigated to date. Note that all of the trends found in both the Short Hurdles and non-fatigue portion of the

Long Hurdles are also found in these results. For both going into and coming off the barrier, minimizing the Ground Time result continues to be the key to performance.

Ground Time: Fatigue

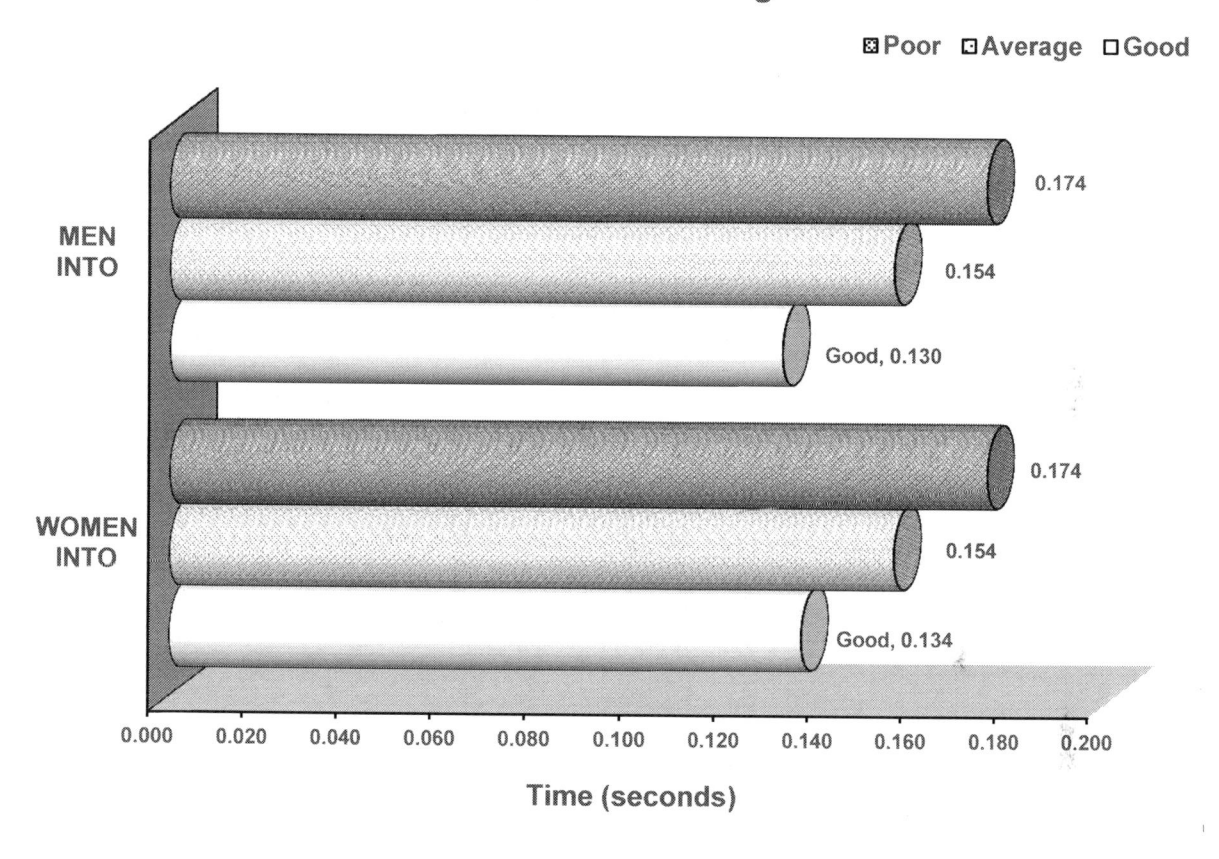

	Poor	Average	Good
MEN INTO	0.174	0.154	0.130
WOMEN INTO	0.174	0.154	0.134

Figure 16-9: Fatigue Hurdle Ground Time Into the Hurdle

Steps Between the Hurdles

The burden of the unique demand for increased Air Time and Stride Length for the Steps between the hurdles falls on the Ground Time results. Since these increased air and length performance results can only be generated when the athlete is in contact with the ground, the true demands of the race are evident in these values.

The actual Ground Time results for the best elite hurdlers, throughout the race, are presented in Figure 16-10. The standard 400 meter Sprint Ground Time is identified for comparison purposes.

The level of difficulty in the Long Hurdle race has become apparent with previously discussed data, however, the Ground Time results are even more dramatic. As can be seen, for the great majority of the race, **the Ground Time demands for the Steps between the hurdles are equal to** those of the typical Long Sprint Stride (see Figure 10-7). In fact, the Women's results are actually lower than their Sprint results. The realization that these athletes must generate the additional Air and Length results, during the same (or lesser) time on the ground, is the best indicator of the enormous challenge this race presents.

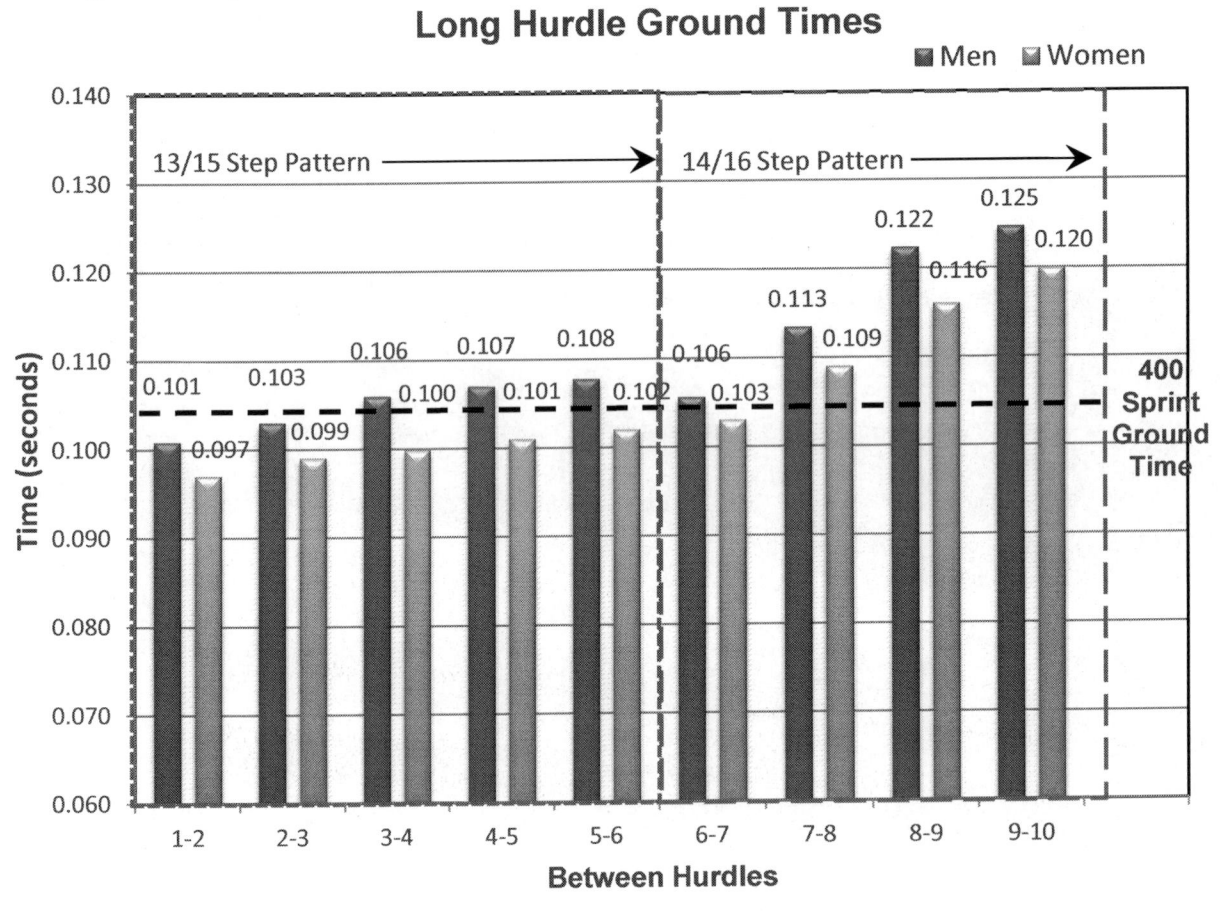

Figure 16-10: Ground Times for the Steps Between the Long Hurdles

Stride Rate

The Stride Rate, or leg turnover, is the best indicator of the tempo of the activity. In the Short Hurdles, due to the presence of the barriers and the restrictive distance between the hurdles, the Stride Rate was constantly changing from Step to Step. In the Long Hurdles, the Rate also fluctuates, but for different reasons.

Going Into and Over the Hurdle

Although Stride Rate is not normally discussed in reference to hurdle clearance, if the typical definition is applied, the Rate for the best elite hurdlers would be 2.3 steps per second for Men and 2.4

steps per second for Women in non-fatigue, and 2.2 steps per second for Men and 2.3 steps per second for Women in fatigue.

Steps Between the Hurdles

The actual Stride Rate results for the best elite hurdlers, throughout the race, are presented in Figure 16-11. The standard 400 meter Sprint Stride Rate is identified for comparison purposes.

Long Hurdle Stride Rate

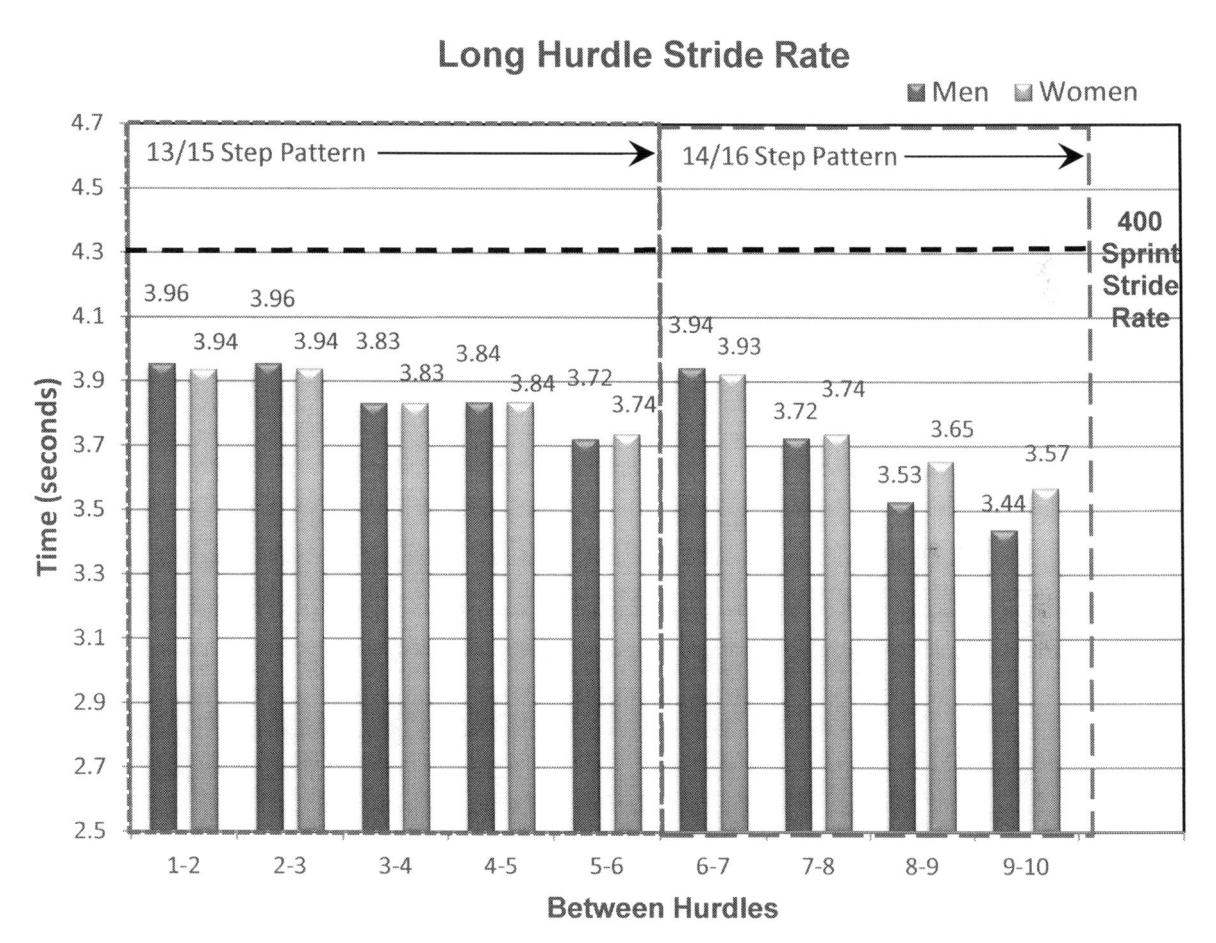

Between Hurdles	Men	Women
1-2	3.96	3.94
2-3	3.96	3.94
3-4	3.83	3.83
4-5	3.84	3.84
5-6	3.72	3.74
6-7	3.94	3.93
7-8	3.72	3.74
8-9	3.53	3.65
9-10	3.44	3.57

1-2 through 5-6: 13/15 Step Pattern
6-7 through 9-10: 14/16 Step Pattern
400 Sprint Stride Rate: 4.3

Figure 16-11: Stride Rates for the Steps Between the Long Hurdles

These results underline the difficulty of the Long Hurdle race. First, throughout the race, the hurdlers are forced to over stride to achieve their stride pattern, which drives the Stride Rate down. Second, as fatigue sets in and Horizontal Velocity decreases, to maintain the early race stride pattern (13/15) the athletes must over stride even more. As shown in Figure 16-11, the hurdlers switch to their late race stride pattern (14/16) when the Rate drops to just above 3.7 steps per second.

Finally, if the athlete maintains this pattern to the finish (most do), then the Stride Rate over the last two hurdles drop so low that just reaching the barrier becomes a major effort. This is why the vast majority of the race management problems occur between hurdles eight, nine, and ten.

> **Chapter Summary:**
>
> With several compromises due to the fatigue factor, one of the keys to the Long Hurdle performance is, like the Short Hurdles, achieved through decreasing hurdle clearance time by decreasing ground contact time as well as the time required to negotiate the barrier. This result must be tempered due to the increased Stride Length demands of the race, but should be minimized as much as possible.
>
> In the Long Hurdles, the step pattern issue involves increasing Air Time and Stride Length to achieve the necessary distance required to successfully reach the next barrier. The effort required by the athlete to produce these results makes this one of the most difficult Events in Track.

The next section investigates how the elite Long race Hurdlers actually accomplish this task.

CHAPTER 17

CRITICAL SPECIFIC PERFORMANCE DESCRIPTORS FOR THE LONG HURDLES

In presenting the Specific Performance Descriptors for the Long Hurdles, comparisons will be made with the Short Hurdle results. Since the only difference between the non-fatigue and fatigue results is in the magnitude, only the non-fatigue values are presented.

It is important to realize that every Descriptor that was significant in the Short Hurdle performance is also significant in the Long Hurdles. Thus, to review the specifics of each of the Descriptors, refer to the corresponding results in Chapter 15.

Lateral Segment Action

In the Long Hurdles, as in the Short race, certain Lateral segment motions are required to properly negotiate the barrier. Although attaining the Lateral positions is easier due to the lower height of the hurdle, the same concepts apply in both the Short and Long races.

In the Long Hurdles, the barriers do not require a large trunk action, so the arms must be used to a significant extent during hurdle clearance. It should be emphasized that, in the Long race, both the arms and trunk should be allowed to move laterally to balance the leg motion. Restricting the arm action (as emphasized by many coaches) will only cause unwanted balance problems.

Trunk Angle

The concepts of the Mechanics of the trunk angle movement in the Long Hurdle race is similar to the Short race, with some specific modifications due to the different Rules constraints between the two Events.

Into and Over the Hurdle

For hurdle clearance, as in the Short race, the key to success lies in **leading with the hips** going into the barrier.

The actual angular values for the trunk angles are shown in Figure 17-1 (results for Men and Women are close enough to be shown as one). Note that the trunk angles for the better hurdlers are always **more upright** than the less proficient performers (see Figure 15-1 for measurement information).

Whereas the Short Hurdle athletes did most of the trunk flexion while in the air, the best Long hurdlers do **all** flexion during the Air Phase.

Trunk Touchdown, Takeoff, and Max Flexion Angles

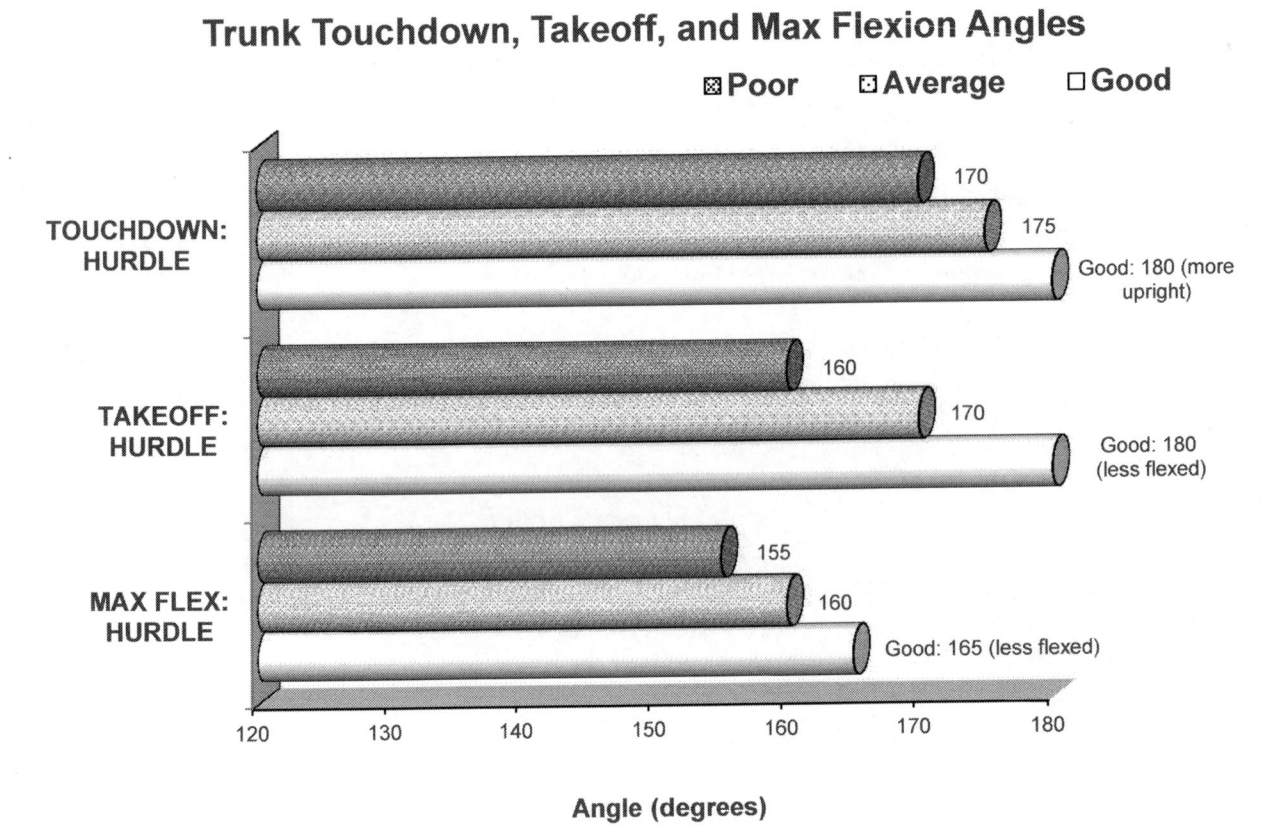

TOUCHDOWN: HURDLE
- Poor: 170
- Average: 175
- Good: 180 (more upright)

TAKEOFF: HURDLE
- Poor: 160
- Average: 170
- Good: 180 (less flexed)

MAX FLEX: HURDLE
- Poor: 155
- Average: 160
- Good: 165 (less flexed)

Angle (degrees)

Figure 17-1: Trunk Angles at Touchdown, Takeoff and Maximum Flexion Going Over the Hurdle

The real surprise is the relatively small amount of trunk flexion that occurs. For the best Long race Hurdlers, **the total amount of flexion, from Touchdown into to maximum flexion over the hurdle is only fifteen degrees.** It is apparent that the majority of the hurdling action occurs in the lower, not the upper body.

Steps Between the Hurdles

Due to the extended length stride pattern demands of the Long race (as opposed to the shortened length pattern of the Short race), the Mechanics of the Steps between the hurdles should be patterned after the Sprint Stride Model (see Chapter 9).

Horizontal Foot Speed at Touchdown

As was true in the Sprints and the Short Hurdles, the Horizontal speed at which the foot hits the ground can, when necessary, be used to help generate the Vertical forces required to drive the body into the air. It is a critical performance factor, for very different reasons, in negotiating the hurdles and moving between the barriers.

Into the Hurdle

The foot speed at Touchdown for the Long Hurdler is just as critical, if not more, as for the Short Hurdler. In the Short race, a superior result equates to greater Speed. For the Long Hurdler, the same result means not only better Speed, but better economy. This results not only in better non-fatigue results, but the delay of the onset of fatigue.

Figure 17-2 shows the Horizontal foot speed at Touchdown, in relation to the performer, going into the hurdle for all elite athletes analyzed to date (see Figure 15-8 for measurement information). These results are similar to the Short Hurdle results.

Horizontal Foot Speed at Touchdown

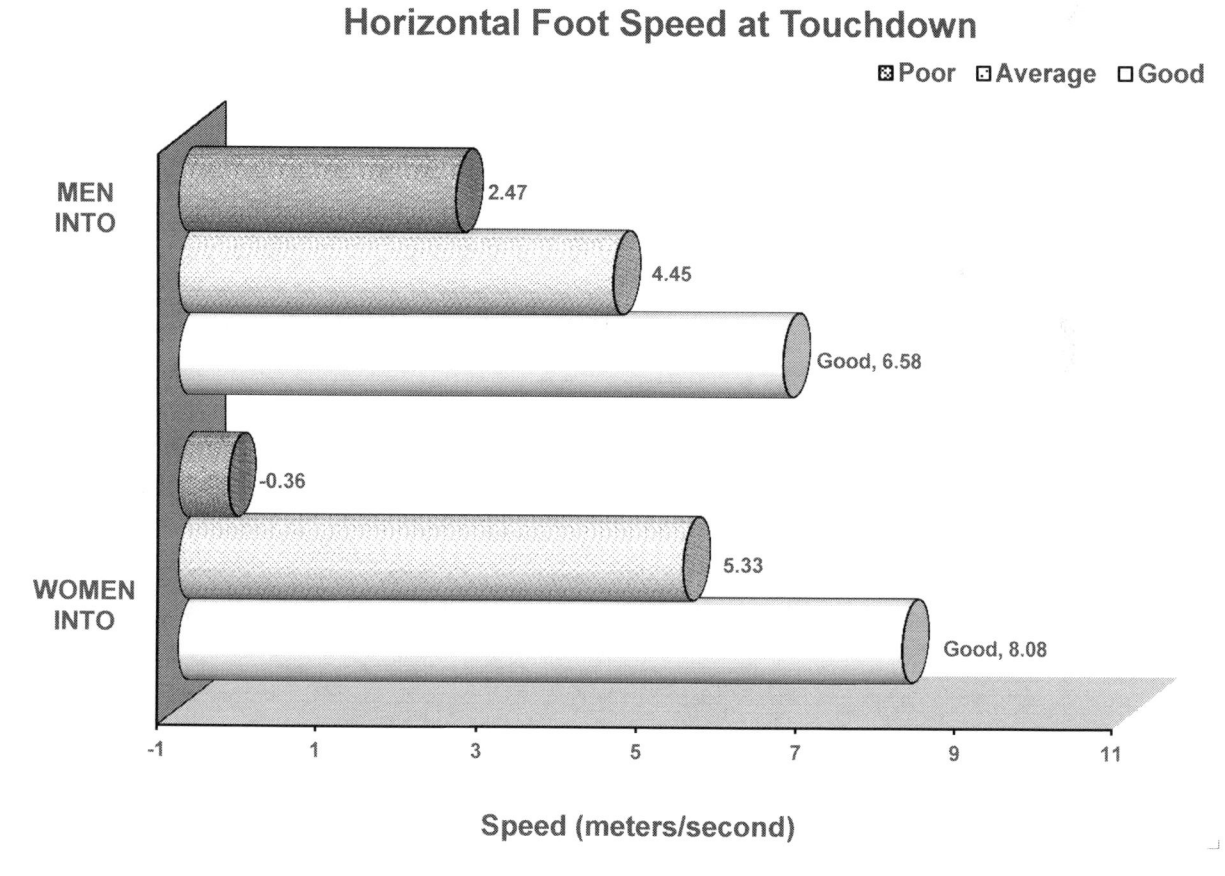

☒ Poor ☐ Average ☐ Good

MEN INTO:
- 2.47
- 4.45
- Good, 6.58

WOMEN INTO:
- -0.36
- 5.33
- Good, 8.08

Speed (meters/second)

Figure 17-2: Horizontal Foot Speed at Touchdown Into The Hurdle

Note that the values for the Women hurdlers vary greatly (note that the negative value indicates that the foot is actually moving forward with respect to the performer at ground contact).

This variability trend is found in all of the Long Hurdle results since the Women's hurdle height is so low that it has allowed athletes with very poor Hurdle technique to be competitive in the race.

Referring to the fatigue Horizontal Velocity of the hurdlers (Figure 16-2), the better athletes generate foot speeds close to their actual Speed down the track.

Steps Between the Hurdles

As with the Short Hurdles, the action of Step One (Fall Step), coming off the hurdle, is an entirely different foot speed story. The purpose of this ground contact is to stop the fall of the body and direct the movement forward, toward the next barrier (Figure 17-3: see Figure 15-10 for measurement information).

Horizontal Foot Speed at Touchdown

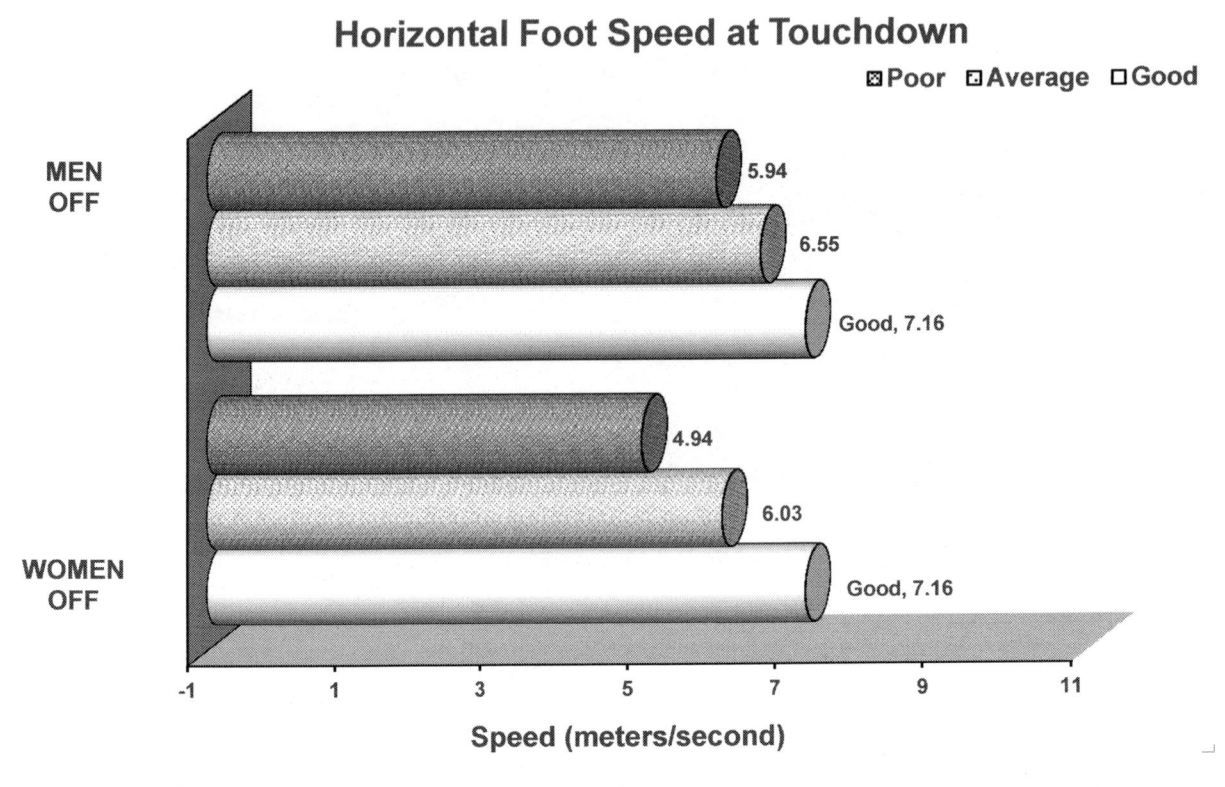

	Poor	Average	Good
MEN OFF	5.94	6.55	7.16
WOMEN OFF	4.94	6.03	7.16

Figure 17-3: Horizontal Foot Speed at Touchdown Off the Hurdle (Step One)

Since a large amount of Vertical Velocity is not required until the next hurdle, the need for minimizing the braking force is critical if the Horizontal Velocity lost during hurdle clearance is to be regained. Thus, the foot speed with respect to the performer should be as high as possible, in the backwards direction, to reduce the forward braking at ground impact.

Although good Short race hurdlers can actually have the foot moving backward fast enough to produce a backward speed with respect to the ground, due to the extended Stride Length demands of the Long race, this isn't possible (see Figure 16-1). However, the better hurdlers do produce higher foot speed values, which minimizes braking and quickly moves the performer toward the next hurdle.

After coming off the barrier, until the next hurdle is encountered, the foot speed results revert to those found in the Long Sprint (see Chapter 11).

Horizontal Foot Distance at Touchdown

As in the Short Hurdles, to take advantage of the foot speed at Touchdown, the hurdler must place the foot at the correct position when ground contact occurs.

Into the Hurdle

Figure 17-4 shows the Horizontal foot distance at Touchdown, in relation to the hurdler, for all elite athletes analyzed to date (see Figure 15-13 for measurement information).

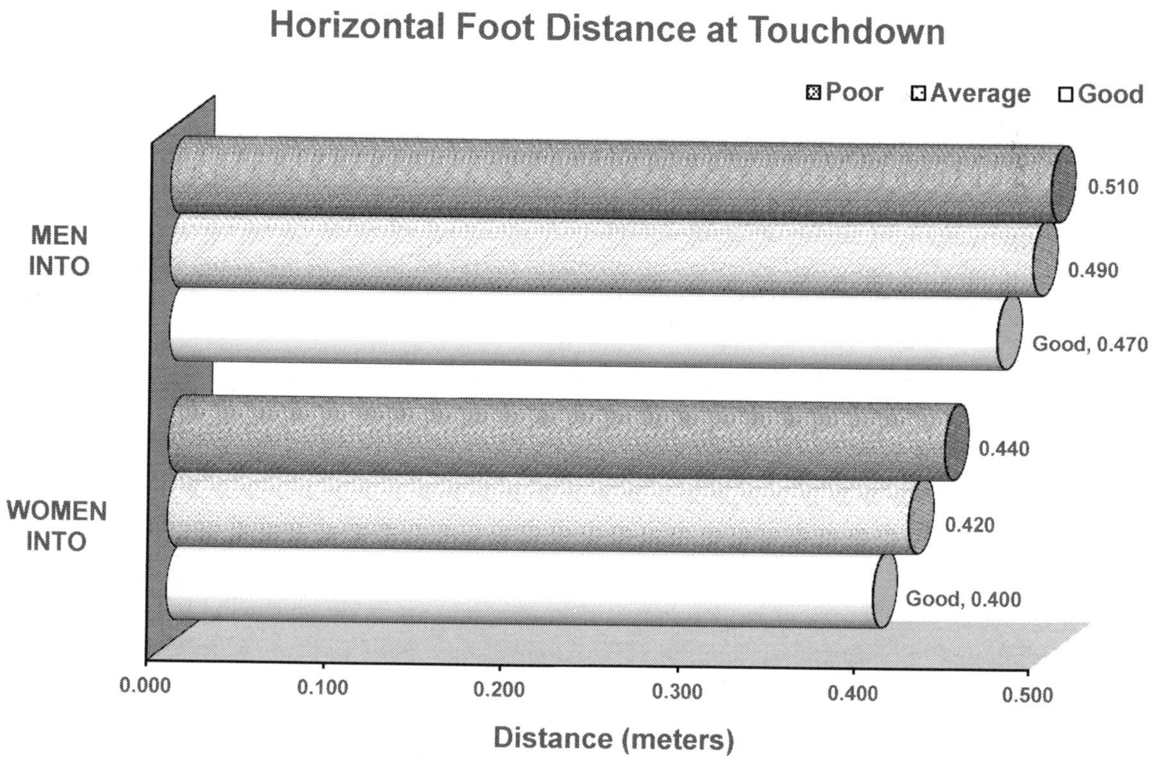

Horizontal Foot Distance at Touchdown

MEN INTO:
- Poor: 0.510
- Average: 0.490
- Good: 0.470

WOMEN INTO:
- Poor: 0.440
- Average: 0.420
- Good: 0.400

Distance (meters)

Figure 17-4: Horizontal Foot Distance at Touchdown Into the Hurdle

Horizontal foot distance results are an area where compromises must be made due to the fatigue factor. Long race Hurdlers land approximately 20 percent farther in front of the body center as compared to the Short race Hurdlers. Although this action produces Horizontal braking, it serves to help produce the critical Vertical Velocity by vaulting the hurdler over the extended leg. This compromise, to a point, is more energy efficient and must be used, to some extent, by all Long race Hurdlers. The better hurdlers, however, have the strength endurance to minimize this reliance.

As was evident in the Short Hurdles, the excessive height difference between the Men's and Women's hurdles allows the Women the opportunity to avoid significantly altering the Sprint stride to clear the barrier. The superior results shown by the Women in both foot speed and distance are a direct result of this situation.

Steps Between the Hurdles

Figure 17-5 shows the Horizontal foot distance at Touchdown, in relation to the hurdler, for all elite athletes analyzed to date (see Figure 15-15 for measurement information).

Horizontal Foot Distance at Touchdown

☒ Poor   ☐ Average   ☐ Good

MEN OFF
- 0.260
- 0.240
- Good, 0.220

WOMEN OFF
- 0.240
- 0.220
- Good, 0.200

Distance (meters)

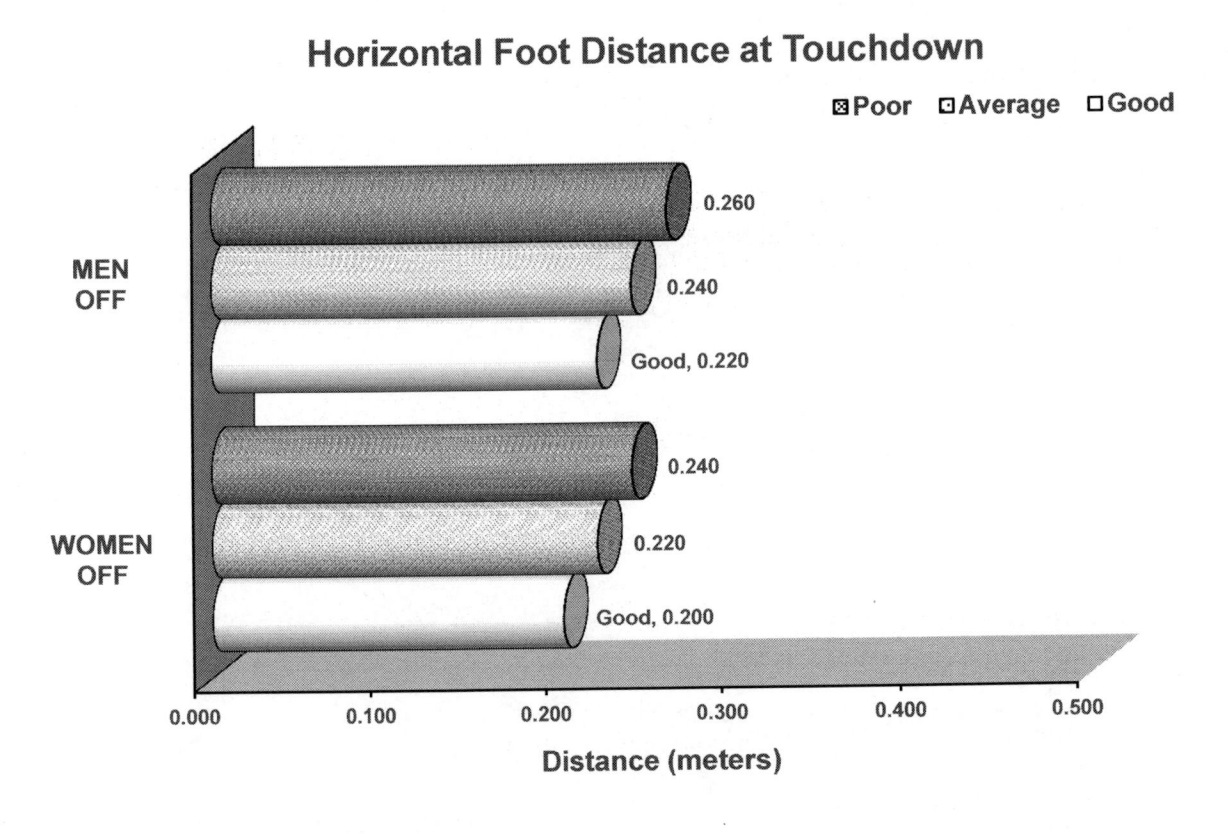

Figure 17-5: Horizontal Foot Distance at Touchdown Off the Hurdle (Step One)

After coming off the barrier, until the next hurdle is encountered, the foot distance results revert to those found in the Long Sprint (see Chapter 11).

Knee Separation Distances at Touchdown

As is true in both the Sprint and Short Hurdles, the amount of knee separation at Touchdown throughout the Hurdle race can be used as a visual benchmark indicating how well an athlete is shifting their movements toward the front of the body as ground contact is initiated.

Into the Hurdle

The better the preparation going into the barrier, the closer the knees are at Touchdown (Figure 17-6: see Figure 15-19 for measurement information). However, even the best hurdlers must allow a relatively large separation due to the Vertical demands of the hurdle stride.

Knee Separation Distance

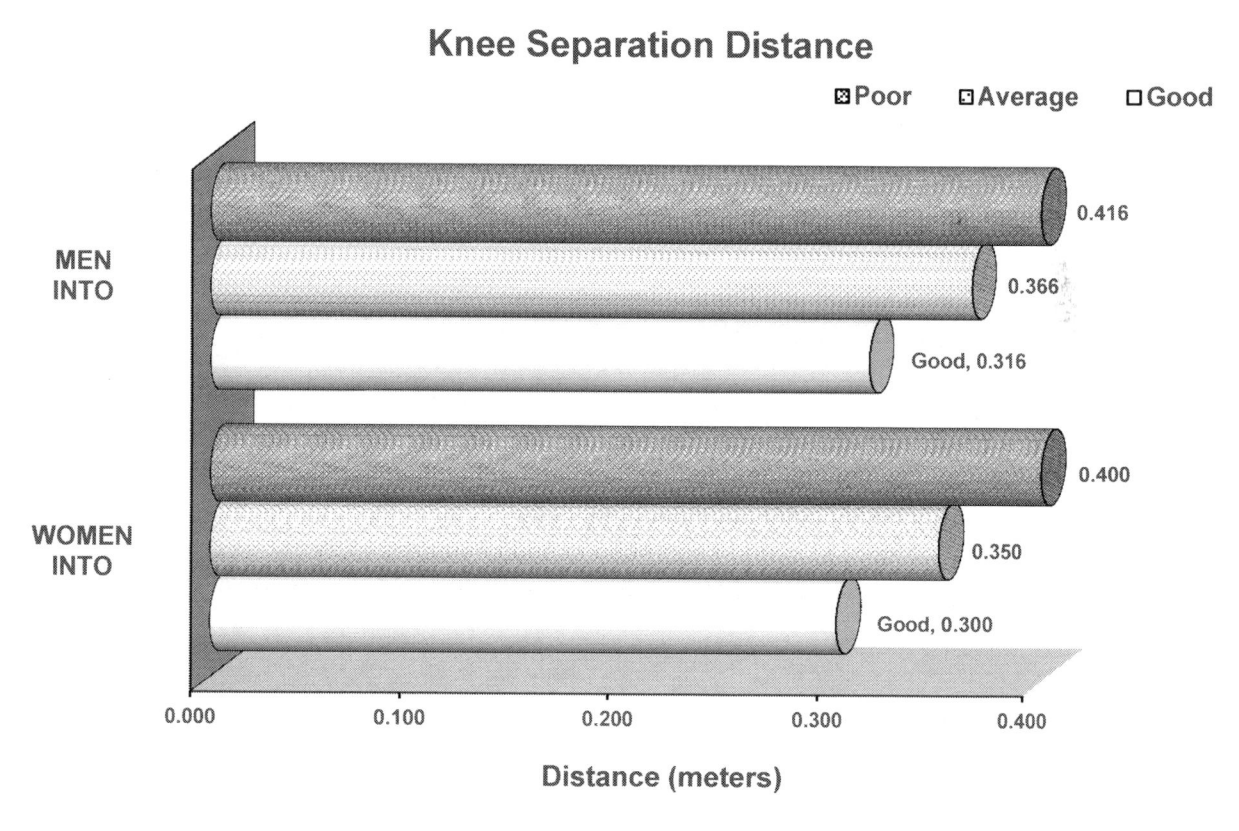

☒ Poor   ▨ Average   ☐ Good

MEN INTO:
- Poor: 0.416
- Average: 0.366
- Good: 0.316

WOMEN INTO:
- Poor: 0.400
- Average: 0.350
- Good: 0.300

Distance (meters)

Figure 17-6: Knee Separation Distances Into the Hurdles

As in the Short Hurdles (see Figure 15-20), with their advantage of a much lower hurdle height the Women can produce a smaller separation distance. However, in spite of the decreased hurdle height of the Long race, both the Men and Women Long hurdlers use a greater knee separation than the Short race. Once again, this is due to the need to cover additional distance to achieve the required step pattern.

Between the Hurdles

Coming off the hurdle, the Trail Leg is placed well in front of the Ground Leg at Touchdown (Figure 17-7: see Figure 15-21A for measurement information) For comparison purposes, the results from the Hurdle Stride are also included. Similar to the Short race, this extreme Front Side position demonstrates the athlete's effort to drive off the barrier and regain as much Horizontal Velocity as possible.

Knee Separation Distance

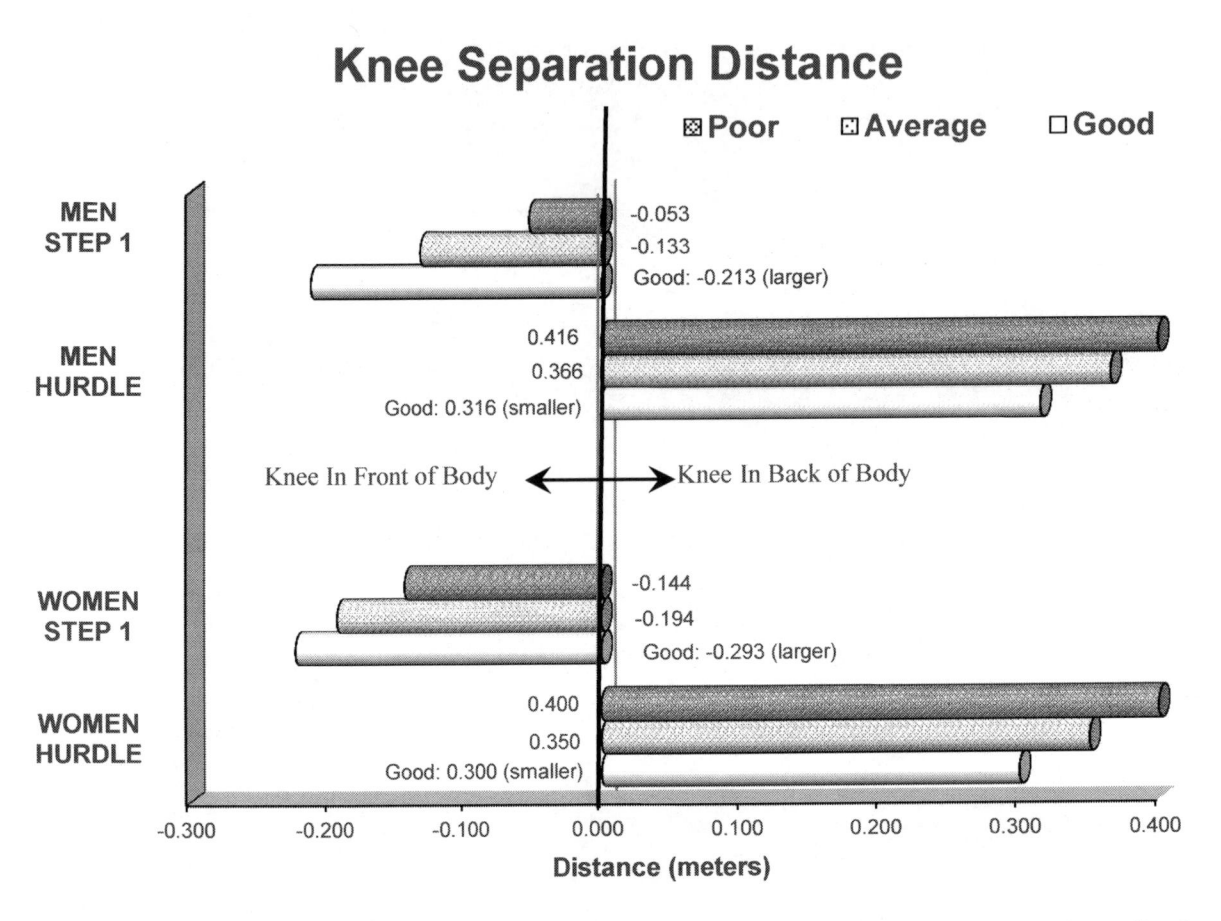

☒ Poor ☒ Average ☐ Good

MEN STEP 1
- Poor: -0.053
- Average: -0.133
- Good: -0.213 (larger)

MEN HURDLE
- Poor: 0.416
- Average: 0.366
- Good: 0.316 (smaller)

← Knee In Front of Body | Knee In Back of Body →

WOMEN STEP 1
- Poor: -0.144
- Average: -0.194
- Good: -0.293 (larger)

WOMEN HURDLE
- Poor: 0.400
- Average: 0.350
- Good: 0.300 (smaller)

Distance (meters)

Figure 17-7: Knee Separation Distances for the Step Coming Off the Hurdle (Step One)

After coming off the barrier, until the next hurdle is encountered, the knee separation results revert to those found in the Long Sprint (see Chapter 11).

Upper Leg Motion

As in the Short Hurdle race, whenever results of the legs are being presented, the critical performance producers are finally being addressed.

Into and Over the Hurdle

Figures 17-8 shows the results for the upper leg motion into the hurdle for all elite athletes analyzed to date (see Figure 15-23 for measurement information). In comparing these values to the Short race (see Figure 15-24), note that the benefit of having a lower hurdle to clear allows the Long race Hurdlers to produce a smaller range of motion both on the ground (50 verses 70 degrees) and in the air (85 verses 140 degrees), even though they must moderate their technique to generate the increased Stride Length demand that is present in the Long race.

Upper Leg Motion: Into and Over the Hurdle

- MEN TOUCHDOWN: Poor 231, Average 226, Good 221 (more extension)
- MEN TAKEOFF: Poor 162, Average 167, Good 172 (less extension)
- MEN MAX FLEXION: Poor 247, Average 252, Good 257 (more flexion)
- WOMEN TOUCHDOWN: Poor 228, Average 223, Good 218 (more extension)
- WOMEN TAKEOFF: Poor 160, Average 165, Good 170 (less extension)
- WOMEN MAX FLEXION: Poor 245, Average 250, Good 255 (more flexion)

Position (degrees)

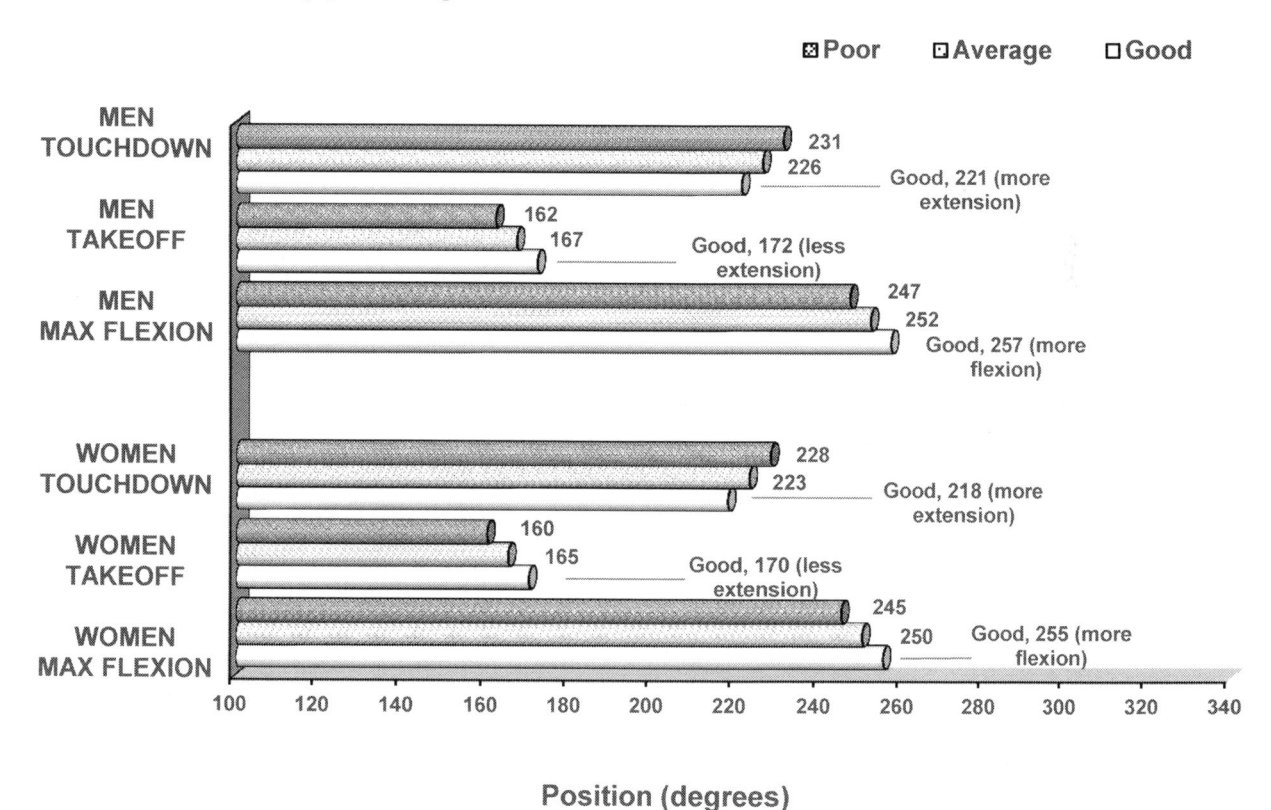

Figure 17-8: Upper Leg Motion Into and Over The Hurdle

This moderation includes more extension at Touchdown, less extension at Takeoff, and less flexion at maximum flexion – all of the alterations that would be expected when clearing a hurdle that is considerably lower, while still striving to create a longer Stride Length.

Between the Hurdles

As in the Short Hurdle, the Long Hurdle Step coming off the barrier has three performance related positions for the upper leg. The first is the position of the Trail Leg at Touchdown (see Figure 15-25 for measurement information). The best hurdlers recover the leg both high and forward, producing a large maximum flexion position. This position allows the athlete to produce a greater downward and backward action at Touchdown at the end of this recovery step. This allows the next step to halt the downward fall of the hurdle and, most importantly, generate Horizontal Velocity down the track.

The final upper leg positions are produced by the Lead Leg. Coming off of the Hurdle (see Figure 15-26 for measurement information), the better hurdlers tend to maximize upper leg extension at Touchdown, while minimizing upper leg extension at Takeoff. As in the Short Hurdle race, the goals of this segment are to:

1. **Minimize Body to Foot Touchdown Distance**: This action will insure a decrease in braking forces. Since Vertical emphasis is not needed coming off of the Hurdle, upper leg extension is minimized at Takeoff to decrease Ground Time.
2. **Minimize Ground Time and Make Leg Recovery as Efficient as Possible**: It must be emphasized, however, that a very good angle at one position is only beneficial if the other result is acceptable. Poor results here commonly indicate poor Mechanics, or a lack of leg strength (indicated by excessive extension at Takeoff).

Figure 17-9 shows the actual results for the upper leg motion off the hurdle for all elite athletes analyzed to date (results for Men and Women are close enough to be shown as one).

Similar to the Short race, the degree that Trail Leg flexion is emphasized can be seen in the fact that it exceeds what is generated in the Sprint Stride by over 20 degrees. This extreme position places the foot almost three times higher from the track, providing a powerful position from which to attack the next Ground Phase. The fact that the leg is recovered just as high as in the Short Hurdle race (see Figure 15-27), even though the hurdles are much lower, indicates the importance of this action.

The goal of the Step off the barrier is achieved by minimizing the range of motion of the upper leg during ground Contact. As seen in the Figure, the total range of motion, from Touchdown to Takeoff is a mere 48 degrees (200-152). Although not as dramatic as the Short Hurdle race, the realization that this is **47 degrees less than the range of motion found in the Sprint** underscores just how compact this action off the barrier is executed by the top elite hurdlers.

Upper Leg Angles Off the Hurdle

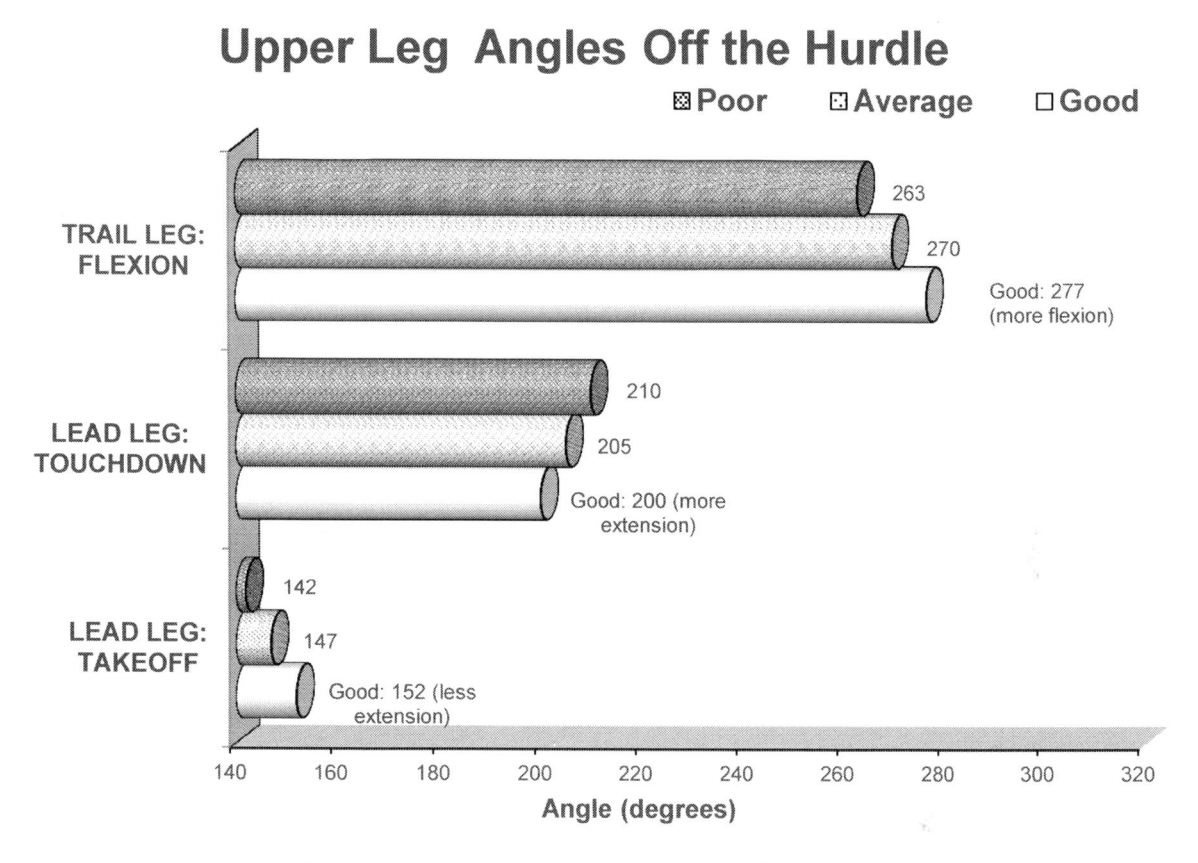

■ Poor　▧ Average　□ Good

TRAIL LEG: FLEXION
- 263
- 270
- Good: 277 (more flexion)

LEAD LEG: TOUCHDOWN
- 210
- 205
- Good: 200 (more extension)

LEAD LEG: TAKEOFF
- 142
- 147
- Good: 152 (less extension)

Angle (degrees)

Figure 17-9: Upper Leg Motion Off The Hurdle

For all Hurdle races, Short or Long, the Step off the hurdle is the most difficult portion of the entire race. If executed properly, it allows the athlete to move powerfully into the next barrier. If not, it can be the causes of the greatest decrement in performance.

After coming off the barrier, until the next hurdle is encountered, the upper leg motion results revert to those found in the Long Sprint (see Chapter 11).

Upper Leg Rotational Speed

As in the Short Hurdle, to get the most out of the legs during ground contact over and between the hurdles, the upper legs must possess great speed and strength. Of all of the specific performance variables, **upper leg rotational speed is the most critical Specific Performance Descriptor in the production of an elite Hurdle performance.**

Into the Hurdle

Due to the importance of this action, it's not surprising that the upper leg rotational speed results are similar to the Short Hurdles. Thus, at Touchdown going into the hurdle, the upper leg should be rapidly extending (see Figure 15-31 for measurement information). By extending, the backward foot speed with respect to the performer is increased, which decreases the forward braking going into the hurdle. Then, during ground contact, the speed of extension should increase to a maximum, projecting the hurdler over the Ground Leg and toward the barrier.

Figure 17-10 shows the average rotational speed of the upper leg going into the hurdle for all elite athletes analyzed to date. In comparison to the Short race (see Figure 15-32), the Speed results of the Long race are equal or greater.

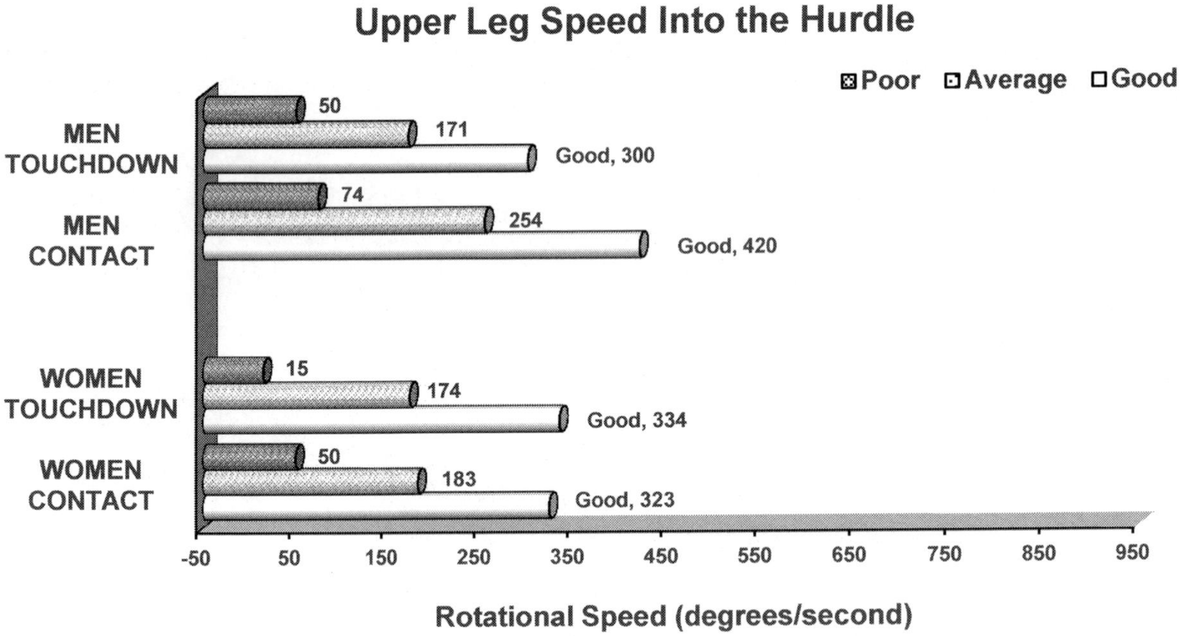

Upper Leg Speed Into the Hurdle

☒ Poor ▨ Average ☐ Good

Category	Poor	Average	Good
MEN TOUCHDOWN	50	171	300
MEN CONTACT	74	254	420
WOMEN TOUCHDOWN	15	174	334
WOMEN CONTACT	50	183	323

Rotational Speed (degrees/second)

Figure 17-10: Upper Leg Rotational Speed at Touchdown and Ground Contact Going Into the Hurdle

As in the Short race, **the upper leg Speed at Touchdown is the most critical since it affects both the amount of forward braking and the amount of ground contact time.** Since decreasing Ground Time is the primary way elite hurdlers maximize hurdle clearance, properly preparing the leg for Touchdown is a critical movement.

Once ground contact has occurred, the upper leg extensors must be powerful enough to maintain the extension action through Takeoff. As shown in the Figure, only the best performers can come close to accomplishing this task.

Between the Hurdles

The magnitude of the upper leg Velocity at Touchdown coming off the hurdle indicates just how powerfully the best performers are moving toward the next barrier (see Figure 15-31 for measurement information). The mechanical precision required to land with an extended leg, directly under the body, at these rotational speeds is extremely demanding.

As in the Short Hurdle race, the goals of this segment are to:

1. **Land with the Lead Upper Leg at High Extension Speed**: This will allow the hurdler to avoid braking and begin to move toward the next barrier.
2. **Make Every Effort to Maintain the Rotational Speed**: The amount of Horizontal Velocity that can be generated is related to how powerfully this can be accomplished.

Figure 17-11 shows the rotational Speeds of the upper leg for the Step coming off the hurdle for all elite athletes analyzed to date (results for Men and Women are close enough to be shown as one).

As with the Short race (see Figure 15-35), it is evident that this Step is an "attack step", with the athlete hitting the ground with an aggressive upper leg Speed, then trying to maintain it during ground contact. The results are an increase in the Horizontal Velocity down the track.

Upper Leg Speed Off the Hurdle

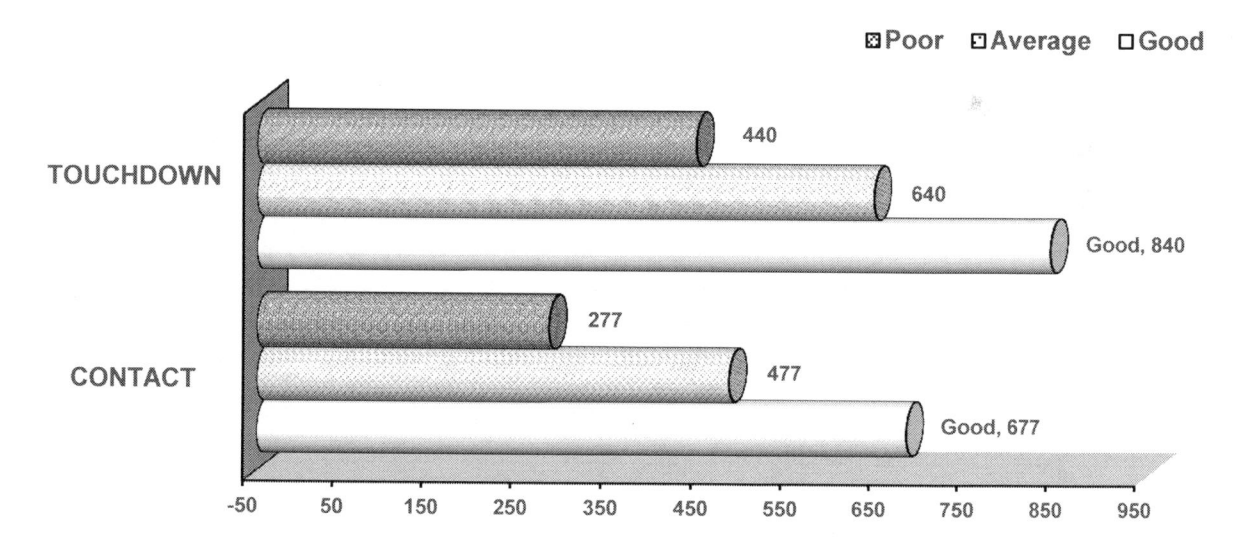

☒ Poor ☐ Average ☐ Good

TOUCHDOWN
- 440
- 640
- Good, 840

CONTACT
- 277
- 477
- Good, 677

Rotational Speed (degrees/second)

Figure 17-11: Upper Leg Rotational Speed at Touchdown and Ground Contact Coming Off the Hurdle

After coming off the barrier, until the next hurdle is encountered, the upper leg Speed results revert to those found in the Long Sprint (see Chapter 11).

Lower Leg Motion

As in the Short Hurdles, the motion of the lower leg is one of the most important, and misunderstood actions in the Hurdle Event. If controlled properly, it allows the proper Mechanics to occur. If misused, it effectively eliminates the athlete's ability to produce world class Mechanics.

Into the Hurdle

As presented in Chapter, the most recent research on Hurdle Mechanics indicates that the better elite hurdlers are increasing the lower leg angle going into the hurdle (see Figure 15-36 for measurement information). Although this is the least favored belief among coaches, it does explain how the elite hurdler is controlling the Lead Leg position while helping in the production of the necessary Vertical lift.

Figure 17-12 shows the maximum lower leg flexion angle and flexion at the point when the ankle crosses the opposite knee of the trail leg as the performer moves into the hurdle for all elite athlete hurdlers investigated to date.

Lower Leg Recovery Into the Hurdle

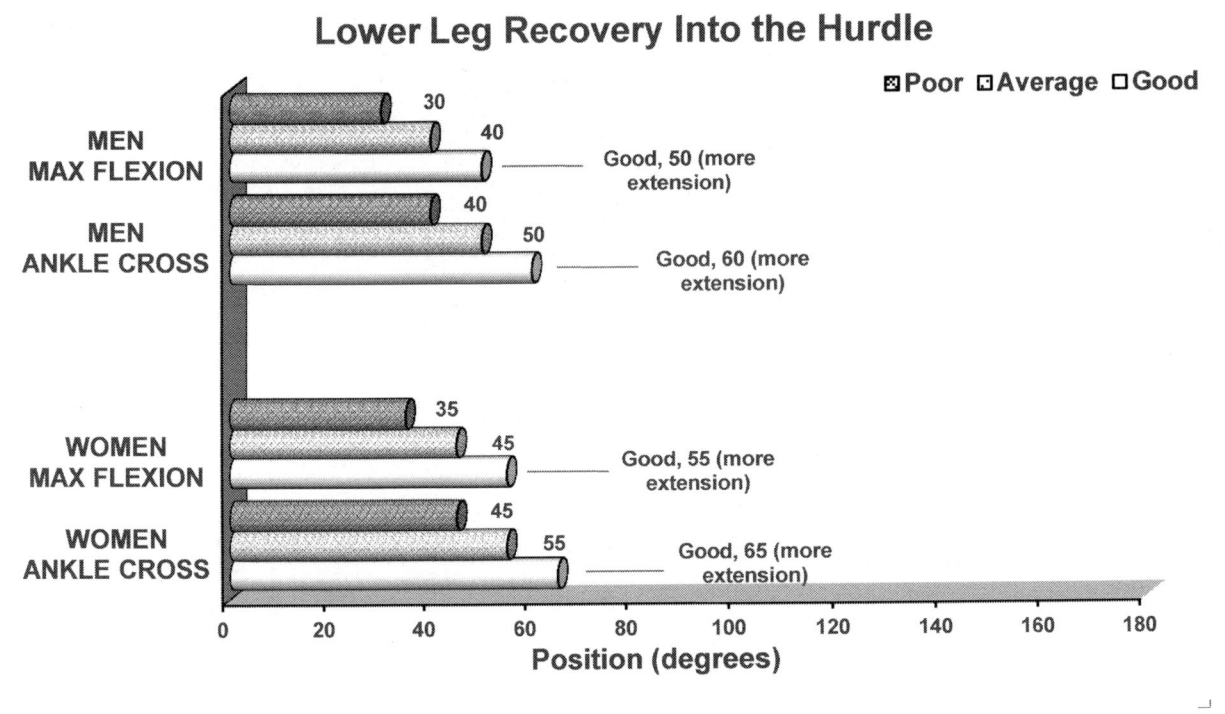

Category	Poor	Average	Good
MEN MAX FLEXION	30	40	50 (more extension)
MEN ANKLE CROSS	40	50	60 (more extension)
WOMEN MAX FLEXION	35	45	55 (more extension)
WOMEN ANKLE CROSS	45	55	65 (more extension)

Position (degrees)

Figure 17-12: Lower Leg Motion Into The Hurdle

Although flexion is not as limited as in the Short Hurdles, it is apparent that the amount of lower leg flexion is managed going into the barrier. This gives the hurdler much better control of the Lead Leg going over the hurdle, allowing it to come as close to the barrier as possible without making contact.

Between the Hurdle

Although the lower leg is not a critical contributor to Hurdle Mechanics during ground contact going into the hurdle, there are two critical positions for the lower leg during ground contact coming off the hurdle; Touchdown and Takeoff (see Figure 15-38 for measurement information).

As in the Short Hurdle race, the goals of this segment are to:

1. **Maximize Lower Leg Extension at Touchdown**: This will serve to position the lower leg to minimize braking and drive toward the next barrier.
2. **Generate Large flexion at Takeoff**: This action will allow the upper and lower leg, in unison, to pull the body forward toward the next hurdle.

Figure 17-13 shows the lower leg recovery motion at Touchdown and Takeoff, as the performer comes off of the hurdle, for all elite athlete hurdlers investigated to date.

Lower Leg Motion Off the Hurdle

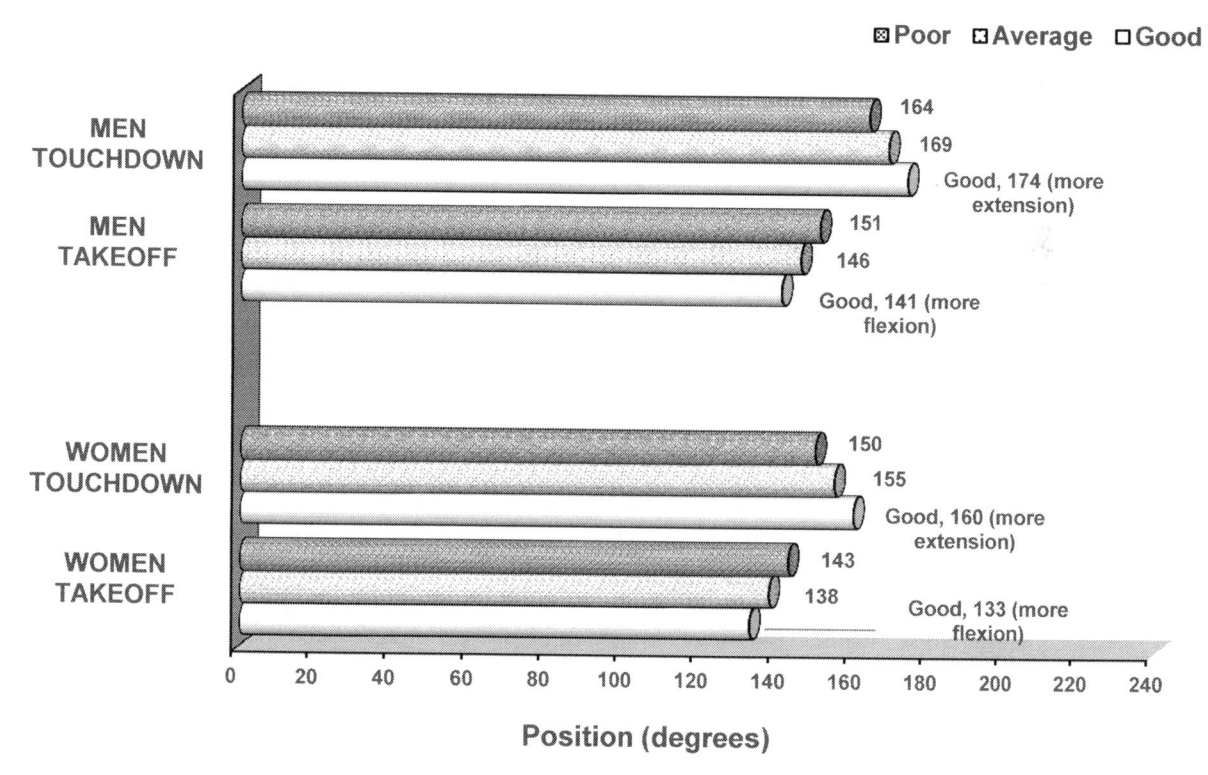

Category	Poor	Average	Good
MEN TOUCHDOWN	164	169	174 (more extension)
MEN TAKEOFF	151	146	141 (more flexion)
WOMEN TOUCHDOWN	150	155	160 (more extension)
WOMEN TAKEOFF	143	138	133 (more flexion)

Position (degrees)

Figure 17-13: Lower Leg Motion Off The Hurdle

The lower leg flexion at Takeoff during the step off the hurdle is an extreme example of how an athlete can drive the body down the track. In fact, for Front Side Mechanics to occur, the lower leg Angle at Takeoff must be minimized.

Critical Specific Performance Descriptors For the Long Hurdles

After coming off the barrier, until the next hurdle is encountered, the lower leg motion results revert to those found in the Long Sprint (see Chapter 11).

Lower Leg Rotational Speed

As mentioned in the Short Hurdles Chapter (15), the role of the Lead lower leg during the stride going into the hurdle is one of maintaining a controlled, relatively extended position. This goal precludes the need for developing any level of lower leg rotational speed, so it is not a factor in Hurdle Mechanics.

In contrast, lower leg Speed is a factor as the performer moves between the barriers.

Steps Between the Hurdles

Since the Step coming off the hurdle should be directed forward (not upward), there is no need to slow the body down by producing Vertical Speed. Thus, at Touchdown, the lower leg should be flexing to avoid Horizontal braking (see Figure 15-44 for measurement information). Figure 17-14 shows the Touchdown and ground contact speeds, coming off of the hurdle, for all of the elite athletes analyzed to date.

Lower Leg Speed: Off

Poor / Average / Good

MEN TOUCHDOWN: 0, 20, Good 40
MEN CONTACT: -110, 90, Good 290
WOMEN TOUCHDOWN: 0, 10, Good 20
WOMEN CONTACT: -220, 31, Good 210

RotationalSpeed (degrees/second)

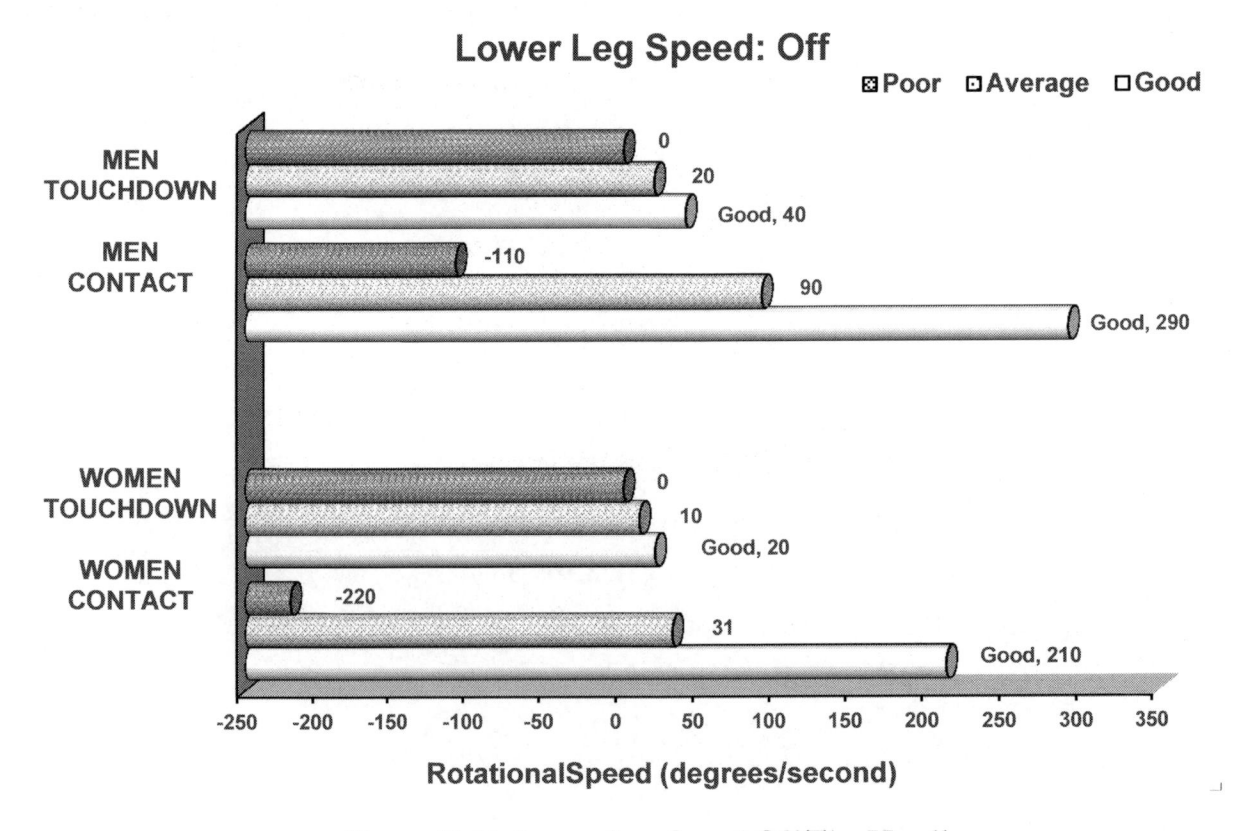

Figure 17-14: Lower Leg Speed Off The Hurdle

As was the case in the Short race, the better hurdlers land with an active lower leg flexion rotation, pulling the body forward toward the next barrier with an abbreviated recovery stride.

After coming off the barrier, until the next hurdle is encountered, the lower leg Speed results revert to those found in the Long Sprint (see Chapter 11).

Chapter Summary:

As in the Short Hurdles, it is evident that both the General and Specific Performance Descriptors point to the fact that success in the Long Hurdle race is determined by the ability of the athlete to generate great amounts of explosive strength at the proper time. It is also apparent that, due to the fatigue factor and the step pattern demands, the Long Hurdler must compromise many of the variables in an effort to economize the Hurdle effort. The most successful Long Hurdler is the one who is able to produce the most economical performance, while having the training level to minimize the compromises to the greatest extent possible.

Generally, the proper mechanical application of this strength results in an elite performance that is characterized by a brief hurdle clearance, relatively small hurdle Stride Length, and superior body position coming off the hurdle.

Since success in hurdle clearance is greatly determined by where the athlete lands going into the hurdle, and how they prepare the body prior to Takeoff, it is critical for the performer to control the body so that the proper body actions can be executed while airborne.

Coming off the hurdle, if properly executed, stops the fall off the barrier, increases (regains) Horizontal Velocity, and drives the body toward the next hurdle stride. The steps between the hurdles are mechanically similar to the Sprint Stride, with increased Air Time required to generate the Stride Length necessary to achieve the selected step pattern.

PART EIGHT: FRONT SIDE AND BACK SIDE HURDLE MECHANICS

CHAPTER 18

FRONT SIDE AND BACK SIDE HURDLE MECHANICS

Early in the research effort in the elite Hurdle events, it became apparent that the successful athletes were focusing their efforts on the leg action that took place in front of the body. The results presented in Chapters 13-17, as well as research done by many others, support this conclusion. In fact, the more the hurdler can shift the critical ground contact efforts to the front of the body both going into and coming off the barrier, the more successful the Hurdle performance (Figure 18-1).

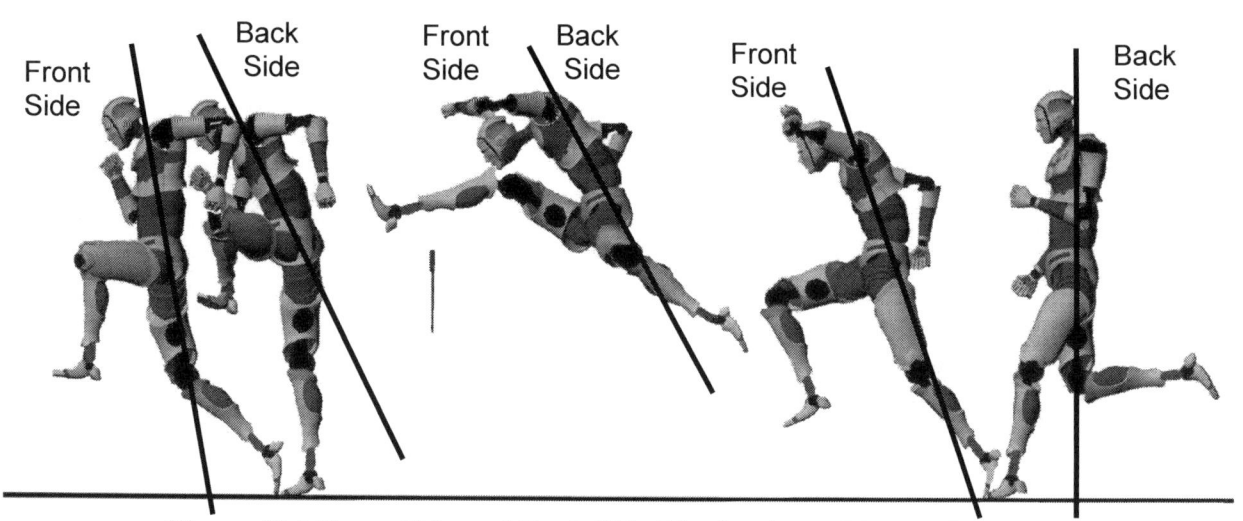

Figure 18-1 Front Side and Back Side Mechanics at Hurdle Clearance

As can be seen, in the hurdle action, this Front Side emphasis is even more critical due to the increased demands required to project the body over the barrier, as well as the need to lead the drive into the hurdle with the hips and lower body.

Since the majority of the Hurdle race involves sprinting without hurdles, and the hurdle strides demand an exaggerated emphasis on Front Side Mechanics in the effort to lead with the hips, this concept is just as critical in the non-hurdle Steps. As shown in Figure 18-2, the Steps between the barriers, especially in the Short Hurdles, are even more Front Side dominant than the Sprint Strides.

As pointed out in Chapter 12, the key to producing elite Sprint performance lies in emphasizing Front Side Mechanics, while minimizing Back Side Mechanics. To accomplish this, the athlete must understand the proper concept, including an active Touchdown and an active Takeoff. To be successful, both over and between the hurdles, the action must be dominated by Front Side Mechanics.

Front Side and Back Side Hurdle Mechanics

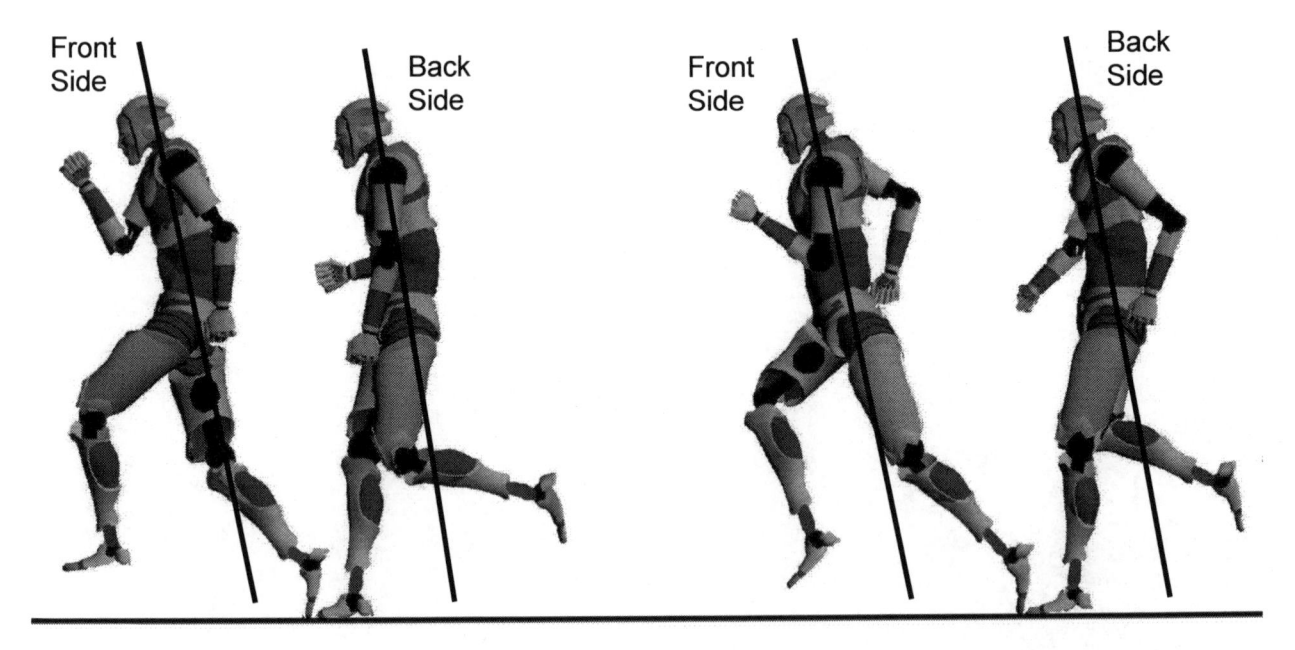

Figure 18-2 Front Side and Back Side Mechanics in the Steps Between the Hurdle

In the Hurdle race, if the athlete fails to emphasize Front Side action, or loses the emphasis due to fatigue, the body is placed in a poor position going over and between the barriers. This results in hurdle strikes, as well as difficulty in maintaining the proper stride pattern.

Chapter Summary:

As with the Sprints, the key to producing elite Hurdle performance is emphasizing Front Side Mechanics, while minimizing Back Side Mechanics.

APPENDIX A

INDIVIDUAL SPRINT ANALYSIS

For Elite Sprint Athletes and their Coaches, Individual Sprint analyses can be found online at www.compusport.com

APPENDIX B

INDIVIDUAL HURDLE ANALYSIS

For Elite Hurdle Athletes and their Coaches, Individual Hurdle analyses can be found online at www.compusport.com

Made in the USA
Lexington, KY
20 December 2015